Foreign Operation Methods

Foreign Operation Methods

Theory, Analysis, Strategy

Lawrence S. Welch

Melbourne Business School, Australia

Gabriel R.G. Benito

BI Norwegian School of Management, Norway

Bent Petersen

Copenhagen Business School, Denmark

Edward Elgar
Cheltenham, UK • Northampton, MA, USA

Published by
Edward Elgar Publishing Limited
The Lypiatts
15 Lansdown Road
Cheltenham
Glos GL50 2JA
UK

Edward Elgar Publishing, Inc.
William Pratt House
9 Dewey Court
Northampton
Massachusetts 01060
USA

Paperback edition 2008
Paperback edition reprinted 2014, 2016

A catalogue record for this book is available from the British Library

Library of Congress Cataloguing in Publication Data
Welch, Lawrence S., 1945–
    Foreign operation methods : theory, analysis, strategy / Lawrence S.
    Welch, Gabriel R.G. Benito, Bent Petersen.
        p. cm.
    Includes bibliographical references and index.
    1. International business enterprises—Management. 2. Foreign trade
    regulation. 3. International trade. I. Benito, Gabriel R.G., 1960– II.
    Petersen, Bent. III. Title.

    HD62.4.W433 2007
    658'.049–dc22   2007000728

ISBN   978 1 84542 044 4 (cased)
        978 1 84720 926 9 (paperback)

Printed and bound by CMP (UK) Limited, Poole, Dorset, BH12 4NU.

Contents

Preface

Over the last three decades there has been an explosion of teaching and research in international business. The subject of this book, foreign operation methods (or modes), has been an important component of this growth. Whether separately, or as a part of courses such as international business, international business strategy, international management, international marketing or internationalization, foreign operation methods receive disparate treatment. However, it could be said that the field of international business has reached the point where the subject of foreign operation methods deserves specialist treatment, and there have been courses focused on this area emerging in various countries. This book has been devised with such a specialist subject in mind. Nevertheless, it is recognized that for many lecturers the value of the book will be not necessarily as a text for a specialist course but as a contributory text for a broader course, with the operation mode component as an important part of the content. In courses such as international strategy or international management it is difficult to deal with many of the issues disconnected from operation mode questions. To some extent mode questions can be said to define international strategy and management issues. Foreign operation methods have been covered under various banners in existing treatments – foreign market servicing methods and foreign entry modes are common equivalent terms.

Given the considerable theoretical development relating to foreign operation methods it is opportune for a treatment which sets out the 'state of the art' of research in the field. In Part 1 of the book various theoretical perspectives pertaining to mode choice are covered, providing a setting for the examination of the different modes in detail. An overview is provided of the growing theoretical focus on the attempt to better understand the why, what and how of mode decisions. Part 2 of the book is concerned with description and analysis of the various operation mode forms that are available to companies to employ in international operations, individually or in combination – the basic toolkit. A particular feature of the book is its emphasis on contractual modes. Such modes have often been treated as second-best or 'hybrid' solutions, and hence have been somewhat neglected in the past. The third part of the book deals with the important area of mode strategy, covering a range of topics that take mode issues into new territory and, it could be said, provide a challenge to existing perspectives and research, including concepts such as mode stretching, mode switching, mode addition and mode combination. The fourth part concludes the book.

All three authors have been involved in teaching and research in the field for long periods, in a range of countries, and their research has been published in a wide range of international journals and edited books. The spread of cultures and country locations of the authors gives the book a strong cross-cultural flavour, as well as many company examples from diverse countries, including small and large, multinational firm perspectives. In this connection, we would like to acknowledge the valuable input by numerous managers and MBA students to the company cases in the book.

Furthermore, we acknowledge the support of our respective business schools in this endeavour: Melbourne Business School, BI Norwegian School of Management and Copenhagen Business School. We have received assistance in various forms from our colleagues over many years in the development of our ideas incorporated in the book. We would like to acknowledge the contributions of Torben Pedersen and Christian Geisler Asmussen (both Copenhagen Business School); Kim Vasant Nielsen (PA Consulting, Copenhagen); Birgitte Grøgaard, Geir Gripsrud, Carl Arthur Solberg and Sverre Tomassen (BI Norwegian School of Management); Rajneesh Narula (University of Reading); Rebecca Piekkari and Reijo Luostarinen (Helsinki School of Economics); Peter Liesch (University of Queensland); Catherine Welch (University of New South Wales); and Denice Welch (Melbourne Business School).

Lawrence S. Welch
Gabriel R. G. Benito
Bent Petersen

PART I

Introduction and theory

1. Introduction

Foreign operation methods – their choice, use, management and change – represent a critical component of international business activity. Once described as a 'frontier issue' in international business, the issue of foreign operation methods (sometimes referred to as foreign market servicing methods or modes) is now recognized by researchers, lecturers and practitioners alike as basic to any discussions about companies' international business strategies and performance. For example, Reid and Rosson (1987, 7) concluded that the 'coupling between entry mode and foreign market operations . . . is a particularly tight one. In fact, we would argue that the choice of entry mode almost *determines* how foreign market operations will be conducted'. Of course, practical concerns with the use of different operation modes, and associated managerial training programmes, have long been an integral part of international business development by companies. A variety of other organizations servicing and providing assistance to these firms, such as government-supported trade assistance agencies, have been similarly involved in training, and the provision of information and network services focused on foreign operation methods, such as exporting to specific foreign markets or how to go about international licensing.

METHOD (MODE) OPTIONS

We shall elaborate more fully on the nature of foreign operation methods or modes (terms used interchangeably) later, but in a broad or general sense they refer to the way of operating in foreign markets used by internationalizing organizations. Overall they might be classified as contractual, exporting or investment modes (see Figure 1.1), although some methods straddle such a broad classification: for example, contractual joint ventures. Within these broad categories there are many different variations, and one of the themes of this book is the multiplicity of mode options for companies which allow for quite fine-grained variations from one foreign market situation to another. Contractual modes, for instance, include franchising, licensing, management contracts, international subcontracting and project operations, with a wide range of forms within each of these categories. Other approaches to mode categorization are feasible,

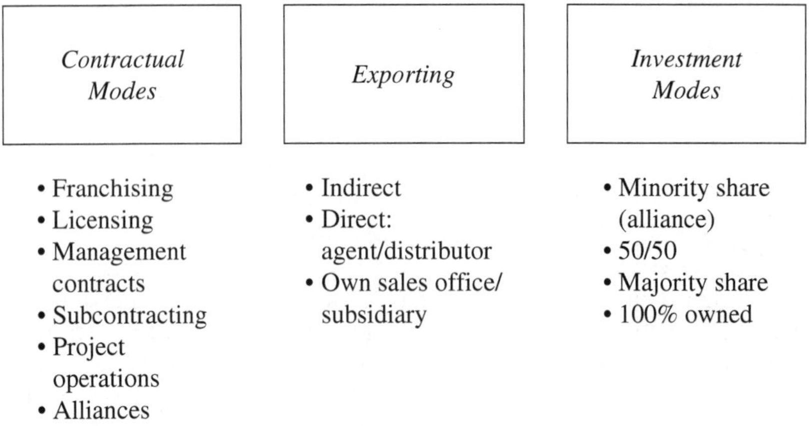

Contractual Modes	Exporting	Investment Modes

- Franchising
- Licensing
- Management contracts
- Subcontracting
- Project operations
- Alliances

- Indirect
- Direct: agent/distributor
- Own sales office/ subsidiary

- Minority share (alliance)
- 50/50
- Majority share
- 100% owned

Figure 1.1   Major foreign operation method options

of course, and we shall consider alternatives later that are aligned to different theoretical perspectives. As well, we shall be stressing the possibilities of mode combinations in any foreign market. Commonly used by companies, although relatively neglected in academic research, they dramatically increase the options and potential flexibility for companies in dealing with diverse foreign market situations. It is not feasible in any book to cover all aspects of the complexity and detail of individual mode groups, let alone the multiplicity of mode combination possibilities, but there is sufficient coverage in this book to give the reader a good feel for the nature and range of mode options that are available to companies as they seek to internationalize.

GROWING INTEREST IN MODE ISSUES

International business is now an important area in many business programmes within higher education institutions throughout the world. As part of the growth of the area there has been an expanding interest in operation mode issues in both teaching and research. This interest is not just in terms of the characteristics of individual modes, for example international franchising, but also in terms of their use in relation to each other and to broader concerns such as international management or marketing. The importance of the subject of foreign operation modes is reflected in their treatment in the wide range of textbooks on international business – of a general nature, as well as those covering areas like international marketing,

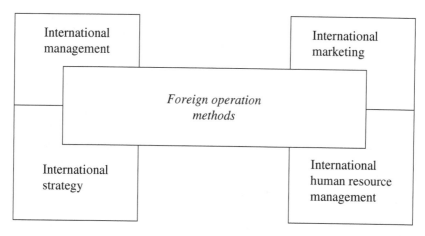

Figure 1.2   Foreign operation methods embedded in many subject areas

international management and global business strategy, as illustrated in Figure 1.2. The treatment of the topic is somewhat scattered and varied in breadth and depth in these textbooks. Typically, it involves a brief consideration of the characteristics of the different modes, often in one or two chapters. Related aspects might be treated within the context of other diverse topics: for example, managing subsidiaries or headquarter–subsidiary relations. Overall, then, in textbooks in international business, foreign operation methods receive varied treatment, but there is a general recognition of the importance of the topic.

INTERNATIONAL MANAGEMENT

As illustrated in Figure 1.2, operation modes occupy a key place in different subject areas of international business. When considering international management issues, so much depends on mode choice: the nature and character of the management process, including aspects like control, coordination and staffing, are driven by the type of foreign operation. If we compare licensing and a wholly owned subsidiary, there are substantial differences in management demands. With a wholly owned subsidiary, a company is in a powerful position to be able to integrate and control what happens in the subsidiary. This capacity is significantly diminished in the case of a licensing arrangement, with the extent of formal control over the activities of the licensee dependent on the exact nature of the terms of the licensing agreement. Staffing moves between parent and wholly owned subsidiary – as a way of supporting control of, and coordination with, the subsidiary – may be out of the question with respect to a foreign licensee. Informal methods of control, in fact, may be more effective. In contrast, a management contract arrangement means that the contractor will have its own staff within the foreign contractee – managing its operations, in whole or in part. Despite the reference to the various types of operation modes in international management textbooks, it is often the case that treatment of management issues does not include the important differences that type of mode can have on the array of management questions and solution options.

INTERNATIONAL MARKETING

For international marketers, choice of mode drives the nature of the marketing process and the options available in terms of marketing strategy. For example, the choice by an exporter between using an agent or distributor in a foreign market may have a large impact on the ability to determine pricing policy. It can be extremely difficult to control the final price charged by the distributor in the foreign market. Likewise, a company might find that it has little or no influence over the pricing policy of its foreign licensee under the terms of the licensing agreement. In contrast, a parent company is in a position to be able to direct pricing within its wholly owned subsidiary.

GLOBAL BUSINESS STRATEGY

Foreign operation methods are often seen as a core issue in the way companies develop and implement their internationalization strategies. From a corporate strategy perspective, such decisions essentially deal with the boundaries of the firm (or the scope of the corporation) along spatial, activity and governance dimensions. Pertinent questions include 'in what countries does the company operate?', 'what does the company do there?' and 'how are its operations organized there?' Such questions are key corporate strategy decisions, alongside those dealing with issues such as the degree of diversification, acquisition versus other forms of expansion, and the overall organization of the corporation.

More narrowly, foreign operation methods can also be treated as an element of the specific internationalization strategies followed by given companies. According to current thinking in international business, there is no single internationalization strategy that is universally appropriate. A strategy makes sense if it provides a good match between a firm's resources and capabilities and the market conditions it faces. According to Bartlett and Ghoshal (1989), who popularized the so-called 'integration–responsiveness typology' of international strategies, there are four distinct strategy types: international, multi-domestic, global and transnational. One key factor is the extent to which there are significant competitive advantages to be gained by integrating activities on a world-wide basis, especially economies of scale and scope, which favours a global strategy. Another important factor is the extent to which market and resource conditions in specific locations demand local adaptation and responsiveness, which favours a multi-domestic strategy. The presence of strong integration as well as responsiveness factors would call for a transnational strategy.

Finally, international strategies, perhaps entailing a simple adaptation of domestic practices to selected export markets, could be appropriate if integration as well as responsiveness factors are relatively negligible. Hill et al. (1990) argue that the choice of foreign operation method should take into consideration the overall strategy used by a company in its attempt at competing beyond the domestic context.

COURSES ON FOREIGN OPERATION METHODS

This book provides a treatment in breadth and depth of the subject of foreign operation methods so that it could be used as the prescribed textbook in courses, especially at the Masters level, specializing in the subject. As well, though, this book should act as an ideal accompaniment to courses in different international business subjects where lecturers are seeking to include a stronger focus on foreign operation methods within their particular subject orientation, be it international marketing, management or international business strategy.

Similarly, this book should be relevant for a wide range of management training programmes in international business, and more specifically on various aspects of foreign operation methods. While the theoretical aspects of the book may not be of strong interest, the analysis and strategy sections should be particularly relevant, covering as they do many of the practical aspects of different modes, when and how they might be appropriate in international business development, and how they can be formed into coherent strategies. An important contribution of this book is to provide a strong strategic focus on foreign operation methods, going beyond much of the earlier treatment which has tended to concentrate pre-eminently on the practical aspects of using individual modes – to the detriment of strategic issues such as mode combinations, mode flexibility and mode development over time.

RESEARCH INTEREST

Alongside the growing interest in international business as a broad area of study at many educational and training institutions there has been an increasing research focus on international business issues. This has been reflected in the development of a multitude of broad and specialized international business journals where research results are published. In 2006, the oldest, *Management International Review*, was in its 46th year, the *Journal of International Business Studies* in its 37th year, but many are of more recent origin: for example, *International Business Review* (1992), *Journal of International Marketing* (1993) and *Journal of International Entrepreneurship* (2003). Inevitably, research on foreign operation methods has been an important component of the expanding research on international business. Both internationalization (or process) and economics perspectives – two of the more important approaches to developing a theoretical and research base for the understanding of international business activities – have focused heavily on patterns and choice of foreign operation methods by internationalizing companies in seeking to develop underlying explanations of international business development. Very early empirical research by Nordic scholars (Johanson and Wiedersheim-Paul, 1975; Luostarinen, 1979), which traced the pattern of internationalization by companies over time, led to a search for explanations of the revealed pattern, and in the process an evolving theory of internationalization. Since then, there has been a growing body of research dealing with foreign operation modes. In some cases this has treated broad operation mode issues; in others, there has been a narrower focus on particular modes and issues connected with them, or in relation to other concerns such as management or mode use in particular foreign markets.

As existing areas of international business evolve, or new areas emerge, the process tends to spill over into questions that pertain to the use of foreign operation modes. For example, in a study of start-up companies in high technology, where it was concluded that the operation mode decision was of critical importance, Burgel and Murray (2000, 15) added: 'within the research stream of international entrepreneurship, curiously little attention has been devoted to the empirical analysis of foreign market entry forms'. Undoubtedly, this situation will change as research (and teaching) on international entrepreneurship continues to grow, providing further insights into the entrepreneurial use of foreign operation modes at different stages of internationalization. The first part of this book will feature an overview of the various strands of research on foreign operation methods, providing an account of, or 'state of play' in, thinking about foreign operation methods within the field of international business.

MANAGERIAL CONCERNS

Interest in operation mode aspects of internationalization at a practical level also appears to have been increasing as globalization and its impacts become an ever-present reality for companies in all countries, putting pressure on them to consider more creative ways of operating as they seek to enter and expand in an increasing number of more diverse foreign markets. As it is, research has shown that it is difficult for companies to develop widespread international sales without spreading the range of operation modes used over time. Early research on patterns of internationalization, not surprisingly, indicated that there tended to be a deepening in the form of operation used by companies in individual foreign markets over time, representing increased resource commitment, as sales developed: for manufacturing firms this would often mean a shift from exporting via an agent, to the use of a sales subsidiary in the foreign market, and then perhaps to the establishment of a manufacturing facility. At the same time, research also indicated that there tended to be a broadening in the types of modes used as international activities increased for individual companies, seemingly contrary to a preference to stick with a known mode or modes that had served companies in their international development. As the diversity of foreign market situations increases, creating varied opportunities and threats that often demand a shift in operation mode compared to those used in the past, firms find it more and more difficult to continue with a given mode set.

Some companies have been able to achieve extensive internationalization over an extended period (for example, Pilkington glass), and there is an undeniable logic in utilizing a mode or modes that a company has become skilled and adept at using in different foreign markets, thereby reducing overall risk and uncertainty as new market situations are confronted (Welch and Welch, 2004). However, research has shown also that mode choices are frequently driven by the approach of interested foreign parties, often unsolicited, for example seeking a licensing deal, or wanting to act as an agent for an exported product, or wanting to become the master franchisee for a particular market. For a firm that has only used licensing as its way of operating internationally, it could well be approached by a potential licensee that wants to set this within a joint venture arrangement. Such an approach may be difficult to refuse when equity is paid for by the technology transfer, perhaps along with used machinery and other equipment transfers. In general, therefore, whatever the mode preferences of companies, it is difficult to internationalize and avoid the demands to use a wider range of operation modes over time. As a result, there is a need to understand and develop skills in using different modes, to broaden the mode competence set – beyond the most obvious and including modes that might seem, at the time and on the surface, uninteresting or inappropriate. This book serves such a purpose, introducing readers to the diversity of mode forms and providing some practical guidelines as to their use and their place in international strategy. The experience of internationalizing companies would seem to show that companies can never be certain when such knowledge might be called upon, whatever their plans. Just as importantly, there needs to be a minimal level of mode knowledge if the array of mode options are to be included for consideration as mode choice situations arise, often when there is perceived pressure for rapid decision making (Calof, 1993).

BEYOND ENTRY MODES

In much of the academic literature on foreign operation modes the topic is dealt with under the heading of 'entry modes', becoming for many a generic term covering foreign operation mode use in all situations – even when modes are being switched and the entry context no longer applies. This terminology is unfortunate as well because it has tended to focus mode thinking and analysis on the entry situation, rather than the longitudinal context in which mode use is applicable. The research shows that mode change in individual foreign markets is common in internationalizing companies, and mode development, sometimes to a substantial degree, occurs with a given mode as its use proceeds – what might be called 'within-mode' expansion (Petersen et al., 2001). In addition, change could be brought about by the addition of a new mode to the use of an existing mode, rather than replacement: for example, licensing being added to a joint venture some years after its establishment. Likewise, a mode might be deleted from an initial mode package after some time. Limited research indicates that mode additions to the initial mode arrangement are far from uncommon (Clark et al., 1997), but there has been so little research on this phenomenon that it is hard to generalize on the circumstances, patterns of use and explanations of mode additions and deletions.

LONGITUDINAL CONTEXT: HISTORY MATTERS

What is clear from research into mode use and change is that the historical context is important in understanding mode choice in mode change situations. At times, some companies find it difficult to extract themselves from past mode commitments – of resources and to relationships – however strong the rationale for change might be. Also, there may be concern about

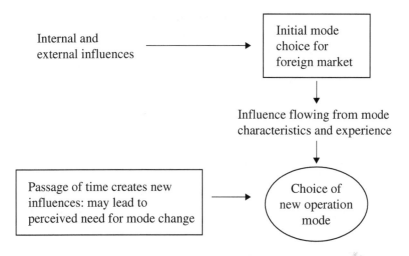

Source: Adapted from Luostarinen and Welch (1990, 13).

Figure 1.3 Mode change decisions – history matters

competitive action by a replaced licensee or other former foreign partner firm. Inevitably, too, the evaluation of new mode and market prospects and challenges will be coloured by previous mode experiences in individual markets. This is illustrated in Figure 1.3: whatever the reasons for the choice of a particular mode (or mode package) at the outset, circumstances are bound to change, which may lead to a perception that the initial mode should be altered in a certain way. However, this has to be balanced against the impact flowing from the experience and constraints associated with the type of initial mode and its use over a period of time. In a licensing study by one of the authors (Welch, 1999), an Australian company had entered the UK market via a licensing deal. Initially without experience in licensing, it had signed a 15-year licensing agreement without a minimum performance clause. As it turned out, the licensee used the arrangement to kill the technology. Not surprisingly, the company's representative in an interview declared that they would never use licensing again ('a bad mode!'). It was involved in joint venture negotiations with a German company at the time.

MODE FLEXIBILITY

In general, as companies internationalize they tend to make a range of mode adjustments in individual markets as well as from an overall perspective, typically driven by a mix of internal and external opportunities and pressures. Consequently, mode flexibility becomes an important element of the ability of companies to respond to the need to change, despite the tendency to stick with already used and learned methods. This tendency was shown to be particularly important in a study of the mode choices of a sample of UK high-technology companies on entry to the foreign markets in which they were operating. Burgel and Murray (2000, 54) found that the 'strongest predictor of the chosen foreign entry mode was the existing, domestic sales mode' and that this was 'arguably due to the presence of embedded routines and experiences with the domestic sales mode'. Also, past foreign mode decisions inevitably create a set of commitments that sometimes can be difficult to discard. As a result, we argue that companies need to design and use modes in ways that contribute to flexibility, putting them in a position to make required changes more readily. Effectively, we place a stress on the 'what next' question at the same time as the 'what mode' question is raised at the outset. While a difficult task for companies, flexibility is one of the themes we shall be emphasizing throughout the book, particularly in the strategy section, reflecting a focus on the dynamics of mode choice, use and change.

MODE COMBINATIONS

It was noted earlier that mode combinations (or packages) rather than singular modes are commonly used by companies in their foreign operations. The focus on singular modes has been convenient from a number of perspectives. For internationalization researchers this provided a concrete basis for tracing the international development of companies as companies usually can point to the mode commitments they have made in the past. Given the variation in characteristics of different modes, it has been possible to examine the array of factors driving international decision-making. As part of this analysis, the delineation of individual characteristics, and the comparison between singular modes, has provided useful information for practitioners deciding on what mode to use in foreign markets. It should be stressed that it is important to have an understanding of what individual modes are like and what they can deliver for companies, but this is often only the first step in mode utilization. The reality is that companies frequently are having to go much further than this in the process of trying to develop a workable and profitable mode arrangement for different and changing foreign market conditions and relationships, and in the light of their own changing circumstances. The next step in mode utilization is to consider how individual modes might be combined in order to achieve more effective foreign market penetration. For many companies this is a

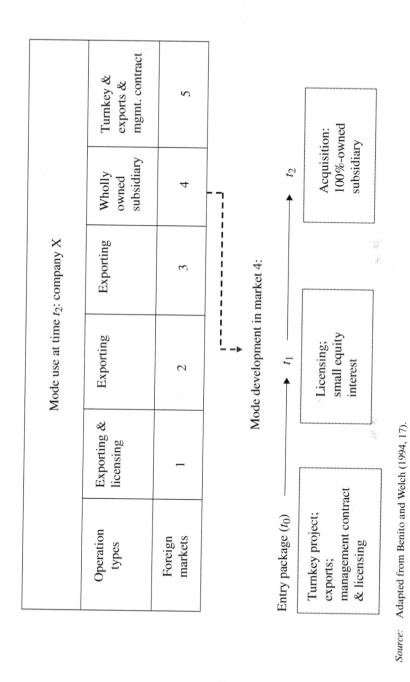

Mode use at time t_2: company X

Operation types	Exporting & licensing	Exporting	Exporting	Wholly owned subsidiary	Turnkey & exports & mgmt. contract
Foreign markets	1	2	3	4	5

Mode development in market 4:

Entry package (t_0) ⟶ t_1 ⟶ t_2

| Turnkey project; exports; management contract & licensing | Licensing; small equity interest | Acquisition: 100%-owned subsidiary |

Source: Adapted from Benito and Welch (1994, 17).

Figure 1.4 Mode packages and change

natural step, often dictated by particular market circumstances: for example, rather than full acquisition as the preferred form of operations, a firm may have a joint venture as the only acceptable option, and therefore seeks ways to achieve a greater measure of control, perhaps via the addition of a management contract arrangement, thereby creating a mode package, with different parts of the package performing different roles, but contributing to overall objectives. Figure 1.4 illustrates the diversity of approaches to mode use which a company might employ in different foreign markets. In some markets company X is using a single mode (for example, exporting in market 3), in others it is using mode combinations. In market 4, it is using a wholly-owned subsidiary, but this evolved from initial entry via a mode package (at t_0: a turnkey plus operation), later altered to a licensing plus package (at t_1).

A mode package could evolve with growing activities in a given market, without mode switching. An example is the way in which the operations of the Finnish multinational Kone (elevators and escalators) in Japan expanded (see Chapter 12, Box 12.5). Clearly, mode combinations may be very important to companies, and have major implications for mode theories and company strategies, so we will have this aspect as an important consideration throughout the book. We consider this to be a major contribution of the book as mode combinations have been largely neglected in the treatment of mode issues in the international business literature.

STRUCTURE OF THE BOOK

The overall structure of the book is shown in Figure 1.5. The first main section of the book (Chapter 2) presents an overview of the development of ideas, concepts and theories, and related empirical research, pertaining to foreign operation modes in international business. This includes the more established behavioural, networks and economics perspectives, as well as coverage of a range of newer approaches, such as the resource-based view of the firm and the connections between inward-oriented and outward-oriented internationalization activities of companies. The coverage deals with both empirical and theoretical aspects. 'In-box' presentations of some of the key mode studies are provided at different points in order to provide some insight into how the body of knowledge in this area has developed.

The next section of the book covers the description and analysis of the various operation methods. In a sense this is the toolbox of international operations. Details and characteristics of each mode are provided within the broad categories of contractual, exporting and investment modes. How they

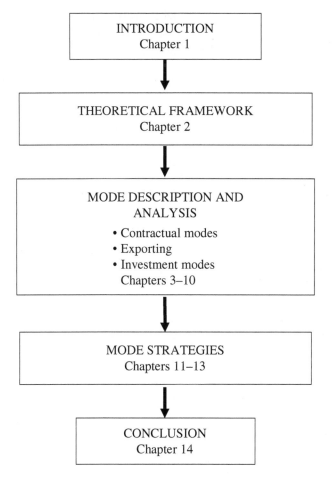

Figure 1.5   Book structure

might be used, ways they might make a positive contribution to foreign
market penetration, their drawbacks and an evaluation of their effectiveness
are analysed. Many examples of company experiences in various aspects of
using each mode, both individually and in combination, are provided. We
have attempted to throw a wide net over the various mode options, and the
broad categorization should not be seen as definitive (other approaches are
feasible and will be considered later). Some modes do not fit easily into one
particular category; for example, a contractual joint venture could be
included in the investment or contractual mode category. Also the boundaries
are frequently straddled in mode combination situations. For companies, the

concern is to find a mode solution to a need they face in a foreign market, working from problem to solution. In this context definitions can seem highly irrelevant: the issue is not what a mode is called, or how it is defined, but whether it will do a particular job.

The third main section of the book is concerned with the strategic implications of foreign operation methods. The separate and substantial emphasis on strategy is an important, distinguishing feature of the book. A major focus of this section is not just the mode choice in a given situation, and what it might deliver to the company at that point in time in a particular foreign market, but also mode use within a company's overall international business development through time. We analyse both mode stretching and switching strategies, the former involving ways of extending or expanding the use of an existing mode, without making a wholesale switch, perhaps including the addition of another mode to enhance the utility and value of the initial mode. Combination strategies, whether applied at the outset or as international operations develop, are an important component of overall mode strategy – potentially contributing to flexibility, profitability, control and risk reduction – and their treatment is a significant innovation in analysis and practical use of modes by companies.

The concluding section draws together the three main sections of the book, providing an overview of the treatment of foreign operation methods, with a focus on mode choice. Issues connected with mode evaluation from a company perspective are examined, and an evaluation framework is developed.

REFERENCES

Bartlett, C.A. and S. Ghoshal (1989), *Managing Across Borders: The Transnational Solution*, Boston: Harvard Business School Press.

Benito, G.R.G. and L.S. Welch (1994), 'Foreign market servicing: beyond choice of entry mode', *Journal of International Marketing*, **2**(2), 7–27.

Burgel, O. and G.C. Murray (2000), 'The international market entry choices of start-up companies in high-technology industries', *Journal of International Marketing*, **8**(2), 33–62.

Calof, J.L. (1993), 'The mode choice and change decision process and its impact on international performance', *International Business Review*, **2**(1), 97–120.

Clark, T., D.S. Pugh and G. Mallory (1997), 'The process of internationalisation in the operating firm', *International Business Review*, **6**(6), 605–23.

Hill, C.W.L., P. Hwang and W.C. Kim (1990), 'An eclectic theory of the choice of international entry mode', *Strategic Management Journal*, **11**, 117–28.

Johanson, J. and F. Wiedersheim-Paul (1975), 'The internationalization of the firm – four Swedish cases', *Journal of Management Studies*, **12**(3), 305–22.

Luostarinen, R. (1979), *Internationalization of the Firm*, Helsinki: Academiae Oeconomicae Helsingiensis, Helsinki School of Economics.

Luostarinen, R.K. and L.S. Welch (1990), *International Business Operations*, Helsinki: Export Consulting KY.

Petersen, B., L.S. Welch and K.V. Nielsen (2001), 'Resource commitment to foreign markets: the establishment patterns of Danish firms in South-East Asian markets', in S. Gray, S.L. McGaughey and W.R. Purcell (eds), *Asia-Pacific Issues in International Business*, Cheltenham, UK and Northampton, MA, USA: Edward Elgar, pp. 7–27.

Reid, S.D. and P.J. Rosson (1987), 'Managing export entry and expansion', in P. Rosson and S. Reid (eds), *Managing Export Entry and Expansion: Concepts and Practice*, New York: Praeger, pp. 3–18.

Welch, C.L. and L.S. Welch (2004), 'Broadening the concept of international entre-preneurship: internationalisation, networks and politics', *Journal of International Entrepreneurship*, **2**(3), 217–37.

Welch, L.S. (1999), 'Outward foreign licensing by Australian companies', in P. Buckley and P. Ghauri (eds), *The Internationalization of the Firm: A Reader*, 2nd edn, London: International Thomson Business Press, pp. 219–44.

2. Theoretical approaches

INTRODUCTION

Whenever a company ventures abroad, decisions have to be made regarding how its business activities in a foreign market should be conducted and/or how its linkages to a foreign actor should be organized. Foreign operation methods can be defined as the institutional/organizational arrangements that are used in order to conduct an international business activity, such as the manufacturing of goods, servicing customers, sourcing various inputs – in fact, undertaking any business function (for example, as depicted in a value chain). In principle, the alternatives are plentiful, ranging from various types of trade arrangements, often in some form of exporting organization, to investments in manufacturing operations in wholly owned subsidiaries.

While the theoretical number of foreign operation methods can be very large (Petersen et al., 2004), as a starting point the decision can usefully be broken down to two main dimensions: (i) location, that is, where a certain activity takes place, and (ii) governance, that is, how that activity is organized.

Based on these two dimensions, a simple exposition of the range of alternatives is given in Figure 2.1, which for simplicity assumes a set of three countries: A, B and C. Also, following much of the literature, a distinction is made between three main ways of organizing interdependencies across value activities: via market transactions, through various contracts or performing activities in-house. Finally, the scheme depicted in Figure 2.1 takes into account inward as well as outward internationalization options. In all, this gives six main internationalization alternatives, of which three describe various ways of organizing inward internationalization, and an additional three describe outward internationalization alternatives. For example, inward internationalization encompasses sourcing through arm's-length import transactions, sourcing through a long-term supply relationship, or internal transfers within a vertically integrated multinational enterprise. Similarly, outward internationalization could involve either direct exporting to the end customer, or licensing to a foreign manufacturer that served its local market, or internal transfers of technology, capital and inputs to a subsidiary unit in the foreign location.

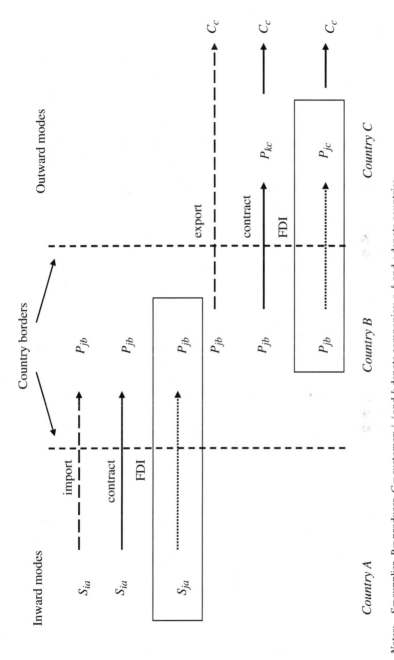

Notes: S = supplier, P = producer, C = customer; i, j and k denote companies; a, b and c denote countries

Figure 2.1   A simple scheme of foreign operation methods

Decisions about how to operate abroad are important. In the short run, how a company chooses to operate in a given foreign market is likely to have considerable impact on the revenues from and costs of being involved in that market, and the company's exposure to the risks and uncertainties of operating there. Equally important is that such decisions have effects on the more long-term considerations regarding the degree of various types of risk, the degree of strategic and operative control, the level of resource commitment and the opportunities for development of a firm's capabilities and network connections. Foreign operation mode choices have there-fore, rightly, been considered as strategic decisions of utmost importance (Anderson and Gatignon, 1986; Hill, Hwang and Kim, 1990).

Several theoretical perspectives have been used to explain companies' choice of foreign operation methods. Since such decisions can be fairly complex in their very nature and because researchers with quite different theoretical and methodological backgrounds have examined them, the lit-erature on foreign operation methods is rather heterogeneous.

Broadly speaking, one can make a distinction between two main appro-aches: a so-called 'economics–strategic' stream, and a behavioural, or process-oriented, stream that could be loosely termed the 'international-ization process'. Numerous theories and models can be placed within each of these two broad streams, some of which are at odds with each other, but most are not. In practice, many researchers draw from both literature streams in their research. Nevertheless, although the various strands in the literature are perhaps better considered as being complementary rather than competing, a unifying all-encompassing framework of the factors that may have an impact on such decisions has yet to be presented (Benito and Welch, 1994; Datta, Herrmann and Rasheed, 2002; Malhotra, Agarwal and Ulgado, 2003). In the following, we present the best-known theories and frameworks within these two streams in some detail.

ECONOMIC APPROACHES

The 'economics–strategic' stream of literature is usefully summarized in the works of Anderson and Gatignon (1986), Hill et al. (1990) and Hennart (2000). The principal line of reasoning in this approach is that choice of foreign operation method is essentially a question of finding the appropri-ate (or, as argued, the 'optimal') degree of control – which again has a bearing on risk exposure and firms' degree of strategic flexibility – over foreign operations, given internal and external contingencies. Although economic approaches to choice of foreign operation method are rooted in economic theory they differ from traditional international trade theory reasoning in international economics. The theory of international trade (i) takes countries as the unit of analysis, (ii) assumes immobile production factors but mobile goods, (iii) predicts that trade patterns based on comparative advantage would suggest that there should be more trade (or investment) the more dissimilar the countries, (iv) assumes competitive markets, and (v) takes resource endowments largely as given. Instead, economic international business theories posit that (a) firms and people trade, not countries, (b) production factors move, for example, capital and technology, but also people, (c) there are cross-flows of goods (intra-industry trade) as well as capital between countries, and similar countries tend to trade most between themselves, (d) many industries/markets are imperfectly competitive, and (e) many critical resources are created, not given. The economics-based international business stream of literature includes principally market imperfections theory, organizational economics theories such as internalization and transaction cost theories, strategic behaviour theory, resource-based theory and the eclectic framework.

Market Imperfections

The market imperfections theory first proposed by Hymer (1960), and later developed and tested by, among others, Kindleberger (1969), Gruber, Mehta and Vernon (1967) and Horst (1972), was one of the first attempts at explaining the international operations of companies at the firm level. The then dominant view of international trade, the Heckscher–Ohlin theory, was based on the assumption of competitive markets and did not really consider the micro-level actors actually carrying out trade transactions across national borders. Firms' internationalization, if at all looked at, had simply been seen as derived from country-level comparative advantages. In contrast, Hymer (1960) took the firm as the centrepiece of attention when trying to explain why foreign firms, which *ceteris paribus* would have been at a competitive disadvantage (owing, for example, to lack of knowledge about the foreign environment) vis-à-vis indigenous firms, nevertheless could successfully compete in their local markets. He observed that foreign firms were even frequently able to drive indigenous firms out of their home markets. According to Hymer, the existence of multinational companies demonstrated that competition often was imperfect as a firm, to become multinational, had to possess an advantage (or a set thereof) that at least cancelled out its initial handicap when competing against local firms. In other words, firms had to have some sort of monopolistic advantages in order to venture abroad, especially when they chose to be physically present in a foreign location such as when setting up a manufacturing unit there.

Market imperfections that lead firms to make foreign direct investments could be (i) imperfections in product markets, such as brand names and marketing skills, (ii) imperfections in factor markets, such as proprietary technology and exclusive access to resources, (iii) economies of scale and learning, which lead to cost declines that essentially affected firms' ability to survive, and (iv) politically created imperfect competition, for example subsidies, concessions and other policy instruments that attract and/or positively discriminate against certain firms.

Given that firms have the benefit of advantages like those just mentioned, they can obviously use them when entering foreign markets. Moreover, such proprietary advantages may become key drivers of internationalization, since firms have an incentive to exploit them as much as possible for further expansion abroad. From the perspective of this theory, the choice of foreign operation method is driven by the nature of the proprietary advantage of the company. However, the range of foreign operations methods considered is constricted. The theory essentially looks at this choice as a question of outlining under what conditions companies would choose to operate in a foreign location through an equity mode, that is, foreign direct investment, instead of producing at home and then exporting the good to customers elsewhere.

A modern variant of market imperfections theory is the resource-based view, which posits that, when valuable firm resources and capabilities are heterogeneous and relatively immobile, firms gain a competitive advantage that results in superior performance (Barney, 1991; Peteraf, 1993; Wernerfelt, 1984). Firms may acquire and/or develop a wide variety of valuable resources, including financial, physical, technological, human, organizational, informational, legal and relational, which can subsequently be put into use when developing, producing and marketing their product offer domestically as well as abroad. Several international business scholars have recently taken a resource-based perspective on the choice of operation mode and argue that the best way for a given firm to operate in a foreign market should depend on the characteristics of its key resources (for example, Andersen, 1997; Madhok, 1997; Madhok and Phene, 2001). For example, if the specific advantage of a company is its superior knowledge, which in turn is often based on tacit information, the company is likely to prefer operating abroad through a hierarchical governance structure such as a wholly owned subsidiary. That arrangement not only gives the company a satisfactory level of control over the use of a key resource, it also provides an organizational set-up that facilitates the transfer of tacit knowledge, which normally requires a supportive, long-term and close relationship between the individuals involved (Kogut and Zander, 1993; see also Box 2.1).

BOX 2.1   A STUDY OF MODE CHOICE IN THE HOTEL
          INDUSTRY

For many service firms that want to enter foreign markets a key question
is not really one of choosing between equity and non-equity modes, but
how to choose between different non-equity modes, for example, licensing, franchising and management service contracts (MSC), for organizing
their operations in foreign markets. Non-equity modes in particular are
widely used in service sectors such as hotels and restaurants. Even
though contractually based, various non-equity modes can differ substantially in many respects. For example, in the hotel industry franchising
involves primarily the leasing of a brand name and some marketing
support and training, whereas an MSC gives substantial strategic and
managerial control over the hotel operations. Using a resource and capability based perspective, Erramilli, Agarwal and Dev (2002) argue that
selecting an MSC would be more likely the better the availability of potential partners in the host country, the greater the competitive advantage
generated by 'imperfectly imitable' capabilities, and the greater the cultural
distance to the host country, but that franchising should be the expected
choice the greater the availability of qualified managerial staff and the
more developed the host country (and hence its institutional and legisla-
tive support for franchising contracts). They then tested the propositions
on data collected through a survey among managers of 139 hotel operations in 49 different countries. Using logistic regression models the propositions were generally supported by the data. The study demonstrates that
there are noteworthy differences across modes, even within one category
of operation modes. Moreover, the findings are generally consistent with
the idea that tacit knowledge, which is difficult to codify, is more likely to
be transferred internally (see, for example, Kogut and Zander, 1993) or as
in the study by Erramilli et al. (2002), in the manner that most closely
emulates an internal transfer.

Shared control modes, such as a joint venture, are typically associated with
a higher risk of unwanted dissemination of valuable knowledge, whereby the
other partner might access, and then exploit, the knowledge for its own business purposes without sharing the resulting proceeds. Conversely, firms
moving into unknown areas, new types of technology, and/or new lines of
business, need to improve their resource or capability bases. While the need
to protect existing firm-specific advantages remains important, it needs to be
counterbalanced by the call for new capabilities and, sometimes drastic,
transformation of firms' resource base (Madhok, 1997). Collaboration with
other firms may then make sense both in terms of accessing the required
complementary assets and resources and in order to reduce the risks associated with moving into unfamiliar areas, activities and businesses.

Transaction Cost and Internalization Theories

Transaction cost reasoning has been a leading perspective on foreign operation mode choice for more than two decades, either in its general Williamsonian version (Teece, 1986; Williamson, 1979, 1985) or in versions that were developed by international business scholars who explicitly attempted to explain the existence, organization and behaviour of multinational firms (Buckley and Casson, 1976; Hennart, 1982; McManus, 1972; Rugman, 1986). The central tenet of transaction cost theory is that firms choose governance structures in order to promote asset utilization while safeguarding against hazards (Williamson, 1985). In the context of international business, the key proposition of transaction cost theory is that multinational firms evolve as a response to market imperfections for various types of cross-border transactions (see, for example, Buckley and Casson, 1976). The starting point taken is that markets, by means of the price mechanism, provide efficient outcomes if competition is strong. Yet, in a complex and uncertain world populated by economic actors who have incomplete information, are only rational in a limited way and may have opportunistic tendencies, positive transaction costs are likely to exist. These costs are the costs of drafting, negotiating, monitoring and enforcing an agreement between economic actors (Williamson, 1985). The presence of positive transaction costs in the market provides an incentive to organize transactions within hierarchical structures – given, of course, that bureaucratic costs are less than the costs resulting from deficiencies in the market. Basically, the multinational enterprise is a firm that finds it efficient to integrate business functions across national boundaries.

In what circumstances are firms likely to integrate activities, or in other words, when and why are markets likely to fail? According to transaction cost theory, one key issue is whether the cross-border transactions involve specific assets, that is, sunk investments that make it difficult to switch from one party to another. Typical cases of asset specificity include location specificity (locating a unit nearby another, for example in order to reduce transportation costs) and physical asset specificity (for example, specially designed production machinery, for which great costs would be incurred if modified for other uses than the one it was originally designed for). In such instances, arm's-length (market) transactions and/or contracts with independent actors may not provide sufficient protection and/or incentives to comply with original agreement, and as a consequence firms choose to perform the activities in-house.

Uncertainty is another key issue. If all future eventualities and contingencies were known beforehand, it would be possible for parties to plan ahead and handle their interdependencies through comprehensive contracts.

Uncertainty, that is, the inability to know about and predetermine all future eventualities, increases the costs and risks of relying on contracts, both because contracts may have to be more detailed and because contracts, even highly detailed ones, remain incomplete and hence open to interpretations, renegotiations and haggling between the parties. Uncertainty points on the one hand to the need for being flexible, and on the other hand to the need for coordination. In both instances, performing activities in-house may be the preferred option.

A third important matter is the frequency of transactions. Specialized governance forms such as the foreign organization of a given firm often carry relatively high fixed costs due to setting it up and administering it, and such costs would to a large extent be independent of the volume of transactions involved. However, once the administrative set-up (for example, the hiring of personnel, the development of appropriate routines and so on) is in place to handle an activity, the subsequent variable costs tend to be rather low. In contrast, a market transaction usually has minimal fixed costs attached to it, but transacting parties have to take on its costs (for example in terms of searching for relevant transaction parties, negotiating a deal and ensuring that the elements of the deal are fulfilled) each time a transaction is carried out. Setting up a contract will also incur costs, but because contracts usually involve repeated transactions over an agreed period of time, there are likely to be some scale effects to contracting, and hence the ratio of variable-to-fixed costs can be assumed to lie between the extremes of market transactions and in-house operations. On the basis of such considerations, Buckley and Casson (1981) developed a simple model for the choice between using the market (exporting), contracting (licensing) or performing an activity within the firm (hierarchy). The focal variables in the model are (i) the costs (C_i) of exporting, contracting, and FDI, respectively, and (ii) the size of the market and the resultant scale of operations, Q. Given the cost conditions depicted in Figure 2.2, exporting is the lowest-cost alternative up to scale Q^*. Contracting gives the lowest costs if volume is in the range Q^*-Q^{**}, and FDI represents the lowest-cost option for volumes beyond Q^{**}. In extension, the model is useful in terms of suggesting when it would be rational for a firm to switch from one way of operating in a market to another as a function of growth in the market. Obviously, integration in the form of setting up its own subsidiary in a foreign country makes sense only if the market is rather large from the outset, or if the market develops positively over time, thereby accommodating a volume that supports a subsidiary operation.

Integration, however, is a matter of degree; the question is not simply whether to integrate or not, but to what extent one should integrate a foreign operation (Anderson and Gatignon, 1986; Benito, 1996; Gatignon and Anderson, 1988; Gomes-Casseres, 1989; Hennart, 1991; Sanchez-Peinado

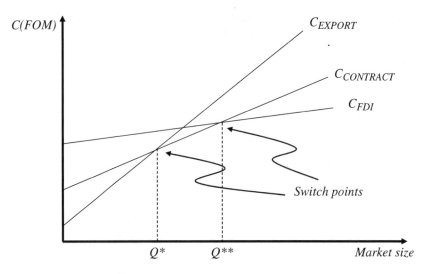

Source: Adapted from Buckley and Casson (1981).

Figure 2.2   A cost-based view of mode choice

and Pla-Barber, 2006). While many companies without doubt may have incentives to keep some degree of control over certain assets and activities, they may recognize that very tight control by means of complete ownership is not really required, and/or that insisting on full control entails its own problems in the sense that one forgoes the potential benefits of teaming up with others. The hallmark of an equity joint venture is that it combines the services of assets held by two or more separate firms (Buckley and Casson, 1988; Hennart, 1988).

From a transaction cost perspective, a necessary condition for a joint venture to exist is that markets for intermediate goods (such as know-how, raw materials, parts and components) held by both potential partners simultaneously fail. If not, the parties would simply coordinate their interdependence through market exchange or through a contract. Making the parties co-owners of the venture reduces the incentives for opportunistic behaviour such as charging inflated prices or supplying inferior goods (Hennart, 1991). Both parties should have an interest in maximizing the profits of the venture because they are paid for their contribution in the form of a share of the profit actually made by the venture. However, as noted by Hennart (1988, 1991), the presence of failing markets for intermediate goods is not sufficient for joint ventures to emerge. Opportunism can also be lowered if one of the parties takes full control, for example through acquisition of or merger with the other party. In fact, one basic problem with partial ownership is that the incentives for a firm to contribute to the venture are not as strong as when it has full ownership (Gomes-Casseres, 1989).

Because complete integration comes at a cost, joint ventures are sometimes an efficient way of organizing. This seems to be the case in two instances (Buckley and Casson, 1988; Hennart, 1988). First, a joint venture is likely to be the preferred choice when the non-marketable assets are a small and inseparable part of the total assets held by both potential partners. Second, a joint venture may also be the preferred alternative if a merger or complete acquisition increases management costs to unacceptable levels, which is particularly likely to happen if cultural differences between parties are very great. A joint venture may then provide an avenue for bridging cultural gaps (Gatignon and Anderson, 1988; Hennart, 1988). The bottom line in transaction cost theory is nevertheless that a high level of control is crucial if valuable specific assets are present. Thus, when a Multinational Enterprise (MNE) exploits types of knowledge and goodwill, which are difficult to protect, it is less likely to accept partial ownership of a foreign subsidiary. Likewise, when the link to a subsidiary involves sourcing from (or supplying to) the subsidiary intermediate goods that otherwise would be transferred through channels prone to market failure, an MNE is likely to insist on full ownership.

A theory that is closely related to transaction cost theory is agency theory, which focuses on the information asymmetries that exist between principals (chiefly the owners of a company) and agents (those acting on the principal's behalf, such as managers, employees, and/or external actors such as intermediaries); for a review, see Thompson (1988). Information asymmetries, which are particularly pronounced in international business contexts, cause both pre-contractual and post-contractual problems. The pre-contractual problems concern the principal's problems in knowing the true qualifications and shortcomings of prospective agents. Post-contractual problems are those related to controlling the actions of agents in order to mitigate shirking. These are classic problems in economics (Jensen and Meckling, 1976), and the international business literature has dealt with a range of applications of agency theory, in particular exporter–intermediary relations (Petersen et al., 2000).

Monitoring the performance of foreign sales agents is difficult, both because agents are at a distance and because they are likely to have information (for example about the market) which they do not necessarily share with the principal (Nicholas, 1983). Thus agency problems are often seen as a strong motivator for internalizing foreign sales activities (Anderson and Coughlan, 1987; Casson, 1987), although such greater commitment is often only made after some time as sales volumes become sufficiently large to support a local subsidiary (see Buckley and Casson, 1981), and the

exporting company develops necessary knowledge about a given market and
how to conduct operations there. Without such knowledge it is difficult to
evaluate the competence and commitment by which the intermediary performs a given task. If the intermediary assigns poor sales results to non-
controllable, adverse exogenous factors, the exporting company will find it
hard to prove that explanation wrong. Also the company will not know with
any degree of certainty whether more capable intermediaries in fact are
available, which could replace the current ones. However, as an exporting
firm accumulates knowledge about foreign markets and develops skills in
managing and dealing with foreign intermediaries, its ability to detect
an intermediary's actual shortcomings and shirking proclivities should
increase accordingly. Stated differently: as the control capability of the
exporter improves, an intermediary should as a result become more exposed
to the risk of replacement. Moreover, the accumulation of market knowledge implies discovering and learning about other local intermediaries that
are believed to be superior – along a range of characteristics, including capabilities, enthusiasm and trustworthiness – to the current intermediary.
Unless such superior intermediaries are contractually bonded to competing
firms, current intermediaries will be at some risk of being replaced.

Rivalistic and Strategic Behaviour

Industry characteristics shape firm strategies and constrain the strategic
options open to firms (Ghoshal, 1987; Porter, 1986). Knickerbocker (1973)
observed that, in oligopolistic industries, firms tend to move in tandem to
preserve industry stability and, if one competitor internationalizes, others
are prone to follow. Oligopolies typically exist in industries that have
reached a mature phase in the industry life cycle, and in which competition
commonly is regarded as a zero-sum game. Firms attempt to minimize the
risks and uncertainties associated with their businesses and generally dislike
actions that disrupt the status quo. Because sales and market shares lost to
competitors often have direct effects on the bottom line, firms try to match
the behaviour and activities of their rivals. The initiation of cross-border
activities represents a potentially important change in the competition
arena and, whereas firms operating in industries with large numbers of
incumbents would not necessarily feel compelled to react, firms in oligopolistic industries tend to respond vigorously to a competitor's moves.
Internationalization can then be a direct countermove to competitors internationalizing, thereby creating a chain of interdependent moves and coun-
termoves (Yu and Ito, 1988). Sometimes the entry of one of the industry
incumbents into a foreign market unleashes a chain of subsequent entries
by other incumbents, thereby establishing a follow-the-leader pattern of

foreign market entries (Knickerbocker, 1973). Sometimes the initiating move is undertaken by foreign firms entering a market previously dominated by domestic firms, which in turn leads these firms to launch counterattacks on the national markets of the entrants (Graham, 1978).

The international strategy literature also addresses industry-related characteristics in the global integration/local responsiveness framework in terms of various pressures in the firms' competitive environment (Prahalad and Doz, 1987; Bartlett and Ghoshal, 1989). This approach regards the issue of foreign operation methods primarily as a question of the level of control that is needed in order to coordinate global strategic action (Hill et al., 1990). In contrast to a so-called multi-domestic strategy, where all or most of the value chain takes place in every country, a key feature of a global strategy is that the value chain of the firm is configured in such a way that value added at each stage is maximized (Hout et al., 1982; Porter and Fuller, 1986; Yip, 1989). In the presence of location-specific scale economies this leads to the breaking up of the value chain so that the various activities are conducted in different countries (Yip, 1989).

As pointed out by Hill et al. (1990), achieving coordination of an interdependent global manufacturing system seems to require a high degree of control over the operations of subsidiaries located in different countries. The various foreign units must accept centrally determined decisions as to what, how much, and at what price they should produce. Such terms do not constitute a suitable basis for cooperation and are hardly likely to be accepted by any alliance partner.

In a similar vein, when an industry is highly concentrated globally, competitive moves may be taken on the basis of strategic objectives that go beyond the narrow calculus of choosing the most efficient mode of operation in a particular market (Doz, 1986; Hill et al., 1990). For example, a company may undertake an aggressive entry into the home market of a competitor in order to induce the latter into a fervent defence of its home market position. The rationale behind such an entry is not profitability in a strict sense (as it often involves fierce price competition), but it may nevertheless be consistent with maximization of global profits. The loss taken on operating in the home market of the competitor is simply part of the cost of deterring the competitor from entry elsewhere. To the extent that firms in industries with a limited number of players actually engage in such games, it follows that firms will prefer to have a high degree of control over the behaviour of their subsidiaries, partly because competitive moves have to be coordinated but also because certain subsidiaries are likely to run at a loss (which probably will not be acceptable to a venture partner). In sum, companies are likely to have a pronounced preference for wholly owned subsidiaries if they pursue global strategy and/or the configuration of an industry is one of global oligopoly.

Combining strategic and internalization approaches, Hill et al. (1990) argue that the decision can be seen as driven by a set of three main groups of variables: strategic factors, environmental factors and transaction cost factors. First, strategic variables, such as the extent of scale economies and global concentration, have an impact on the appropriate level of control. For example, firms that pursue global strategies are more likely to insist on high-control modes, such as fully owned subsidiaries, owing to their need to coordinate operations tightly in dispersed locations. Second, environmental variables influence the resource commitment (and hence the strategic flexibility) aspect of foreign operation modes. For instance, when country risk is high and/or cultural distance is large, firms are expected to select low-resource commitment modes so that resources may be reallocated at a low cost. Finally, the value and nature of firm-specific assets have implications for how much dissemination risk (that is, the extent to which contract partners may appropriate valuable assets without consent) the firm can accept. The more valuable the assets (say, know-how) the greater the probability that the firm will take extra precautions safeguarding them, and hence choose an operation mode involving low dissemination risk, such as a fully owned subsidiary.

The Eclectic Framework

Although all the foregoing theories provide significant insights into companies' choice of foreign operation methods, each one really gives only a partial view of such choices. Dunning (2001) argues that they are individually incomplete and that they cannot satisfactorily explain either the choice of foreign direct investment over exporting or licensing or some other type of interorganizational set-up, or the choice of where to locate the various value activities. As an alternative, John Dunning has over the years developed the so-called 'eclectic framework' (Dunning, 1981, 1988, 2001), which usefully synthesizes the various strands of the other theories. Dunning's framework is based on three main sets of factors that are regarded as necessary in order to explain the choice of foreign operation method, ranging from export operations to foreign direct investment. The three factors are ownership (O) factors, location (L) factors and internalization (I) factors, hence the often used OLI acronym for the framework. The framework encompasses market imperfections and resource-based theory (the ownership factor), international trade and location theory (the location factor) and transaction cost theory (the internalization factor). Box 2.2 presents an empirical study based on the framework.

As shown in Figure 2.3, the basic reasoning proposed by the framework is as follows. First, the ownership factor is about whether the firm controls

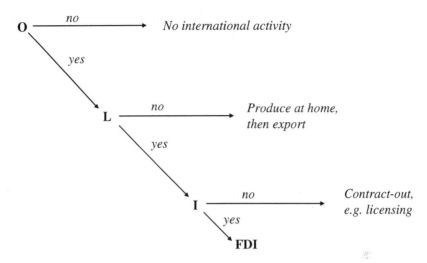

Figure 2.3 A decision tree for FDI, based on the OLI framework

certain assets that give it a competitive advantage over indigenous firms. Given the additional costs of operating in a foreign environment, such an advantage is necessary in order for the firm to compete on a par with local firms. Without it, the firm would simply not be able to survive in a competitive foreign context. Second, the location factor brings up whether certain assets controlled by the firm are best put into use in parts of the world beyond the firm's 'country of origin'. The issue here is whether a necessary condition for foreign production is met. If there were no foreign location advantages, the activity (for example, manufacturing) would be carried out in the home country of the firm and the product then exported to customers elsewhere. The location factor is hence not crucial for whether or not the firm would internationalize, but decisive for whether the servicing of a foreign market is carried out via exports or through local production. Third, the internalization factor points to the organization of an activity: does the best use of assets involved in performing a given activity require that these assets be internally transferred? A positive answer to this question is a necessary condition for conducting activities in-house.

A Simple Formalization of the Choice of Foreign Operation Method

The reasoning of economics approaches to choice of foreign operation methods is straightforward to formalize. We take as a starting point that the firm has three main strategic options when deciding how to service a

---

BOX 2.2   AN EXAMINATION OF THE OLI FRAMEWORK

To what extent and how do location, ownership and internalization factors influence the choice of foreign operation method? To examine the soundness of the so-called OLI framework, Agarwal and Ramaswamy (1992) investigated the entries of 97 US-based equipment leasing companies into three countries: the UK, Japan and Brazil. The study covered a variety of entry modes, ranging from 'no involvement', via exporting, licensing and joint venture, to a wholly owned venture in a given host country. Based on the OLI framework, the explanatory variables were categorized into the three main groups: (i) ownership advantages including firms' ability to develop differentiated products, firm size and experience, (ii) location advantages, such as market potential and investment risk, and (iii) contractual risk, dealing with, internalization advantages. The study was conducted as a mailed questionnaire survey where all variables were measured by multiple items, which were then combined into scales. The results, which were generally supportive of the OLI framework, suggest *inter alia* that internationalization of any kind hinges on firms' ability to develop differentiated products, but that equity modes are preferred over exporting or licensing in high-potential markets. Also, while wholly owned subsidiaries are the preferred choice of large, multinational firms, especially in markets with higher potential, firms tend to stay away from wholly owned subsidiaries when the risks (contractual as well as investment risks) are high.

---

foreign market: (i) it can export to the market on an arm's-length basis, (ii) it can contract another firm to carry out a certain set of activities in that market, or (iii) it can directly invest in the market by setting up its own subsidiary and hence conduct the activities in-house. The strategic options (S) of exporting versus contracts versus foreign direct investment can be denoted S_{exp}, S_{con}, S_{FDI}, respectively. The goal of the firm is to maximize its expected profits, max $E[\pi(S)]$. Profits are given as the net result of operations after costs have been subtracted from revenues, and if production (or activity) costs as well as transaction (or organization/agency) costs are taken into account, the firm will seek to maximize:

$$\pi(S) = R(S) - [c(S) + t(S)],$$

where $R(S)$ = revenue of option S_i, $c(S)$ = production cost of option S_i, and $t(S)$ = transaction cost of option S_i.

Obviously, FDI would be preferred only if $\pi(S_{FDI}) > [\pi(S_{exp}), \pi(S_{con})]$. This may happen if the revenues generated by the focal firm are greater if the market in question is serviced by a subsidiary operated by the firm than if the firm exports to that market or lets a contractor conduct the operations there. Formally, this means that the following condition is met:

$$R(S_{FDI}) > [R(S_{exp}), R(S_{con})].$$

As suggested by the notions of market imperfections and ownership advantages, superior revenues can be due to the competitive conditions, for example that the focal firm enjoys some degree of market power, which can be sustained over some time because of entry barriers. The basis of such market power can be prior investments in brands, design, technology, product development capabilities and so on. Revenues can also be higher for the FDI option because the firm operates on its own and therefore does not have to share profits with an external party.

The FDI option may also be preferred on the grounds of lower production costs, due, for example, to lower input costs or lower wages in the foreign location. This entails the following condition:

$$c(S_{FDI}) < [c(S_{exp}), c(S_{con})].$$

Finally, as pointed out by internalization and transaction costs theories, the options may differ in terms of their transaction cost outcomes. Making an FDI is certainly not without costs. Nevertheless, setting up a subsidiary controlled by the firm may enhance the coordination of actions across markets, facilitate the monitoring of operations and, because the interests of the parties involved are more aligned with each other, also help in reducing the bargaining costs that often arise between parties. The third possible condition for making a FDI is hence:

$$t(S_{FDI}) < [t(S_{exp}), t(S_{con})].$$

BEHAVIOURAL APPROACHES

In contrast to the 'economics–strategic' stream with its strong emphasis on rational decision making, the internationalization process approach to foreign operation mode decisions takes as a starting point that a framework of unconstrained rationality performed, as if by unitary entities, provides limited understanding of the way firms actually make decisions. Instead, the internationalization process approaches view such decisions through the lenses of limited rationality and organizational learning processes (Cyert and March, 1963; Simon, 1955, 1979). Process perspectives also tend to take a more holistic approach in which the operation mode dimension is only one of several aspects of internationalization (Welch and Luostarinen, 1988).

As pointed out by Carlson (1975), firms' expansion beyond the borders of their home countries is in many ways 'unnatural', and is not likely to happen in the absence of driving forces such as a saturated home market or unsolicited orders from abroad. International expansion represents a voyage into unknown territory. Such decisions are for most firms, but particularly for those with limited international experience, characterized by considerable perceived uncertainty. This uncertainty stems from general lack of knowledge about the workings of particular foreign markets (customer behaviour, institutional and legal frameworks and so on), as well as lack of knowledge about how to run specific business operations in unfamiliar contexts. Typically, such knowledge is 'fuzzy', and acquiring such knowledge is often a lengthy process since it involves developing it by 'learning-by-doing', and institutionalizing it in a company.

The Internationalization Process Perspective

Based upon the behavioural theory of the firm, models of a gradual internationalization process were proposed by Johanson and Vahlne (1977, 1990), Johanson and Wiedersheim-Paul (1975) and Luostarinen (1979), and further developed by Hedlund (1994) and Vermeulen and Barkema (2002), among others. Their research underlines the importance of experiential knowledge and suggests an expansion pattern where the firm is gradually moving along the governance or organizational dimension as well as the location dimension. Specifically, as depicted in Figure 2.4, firms move over time towards (1) higher commitment operation modes and (2) more distant countries in cultural or psychic distance terms.

In the initial phases of their internationalization, few firms are prepared and willing to commit resources to foreign operations. Without appropriate experience and knowledge, decision makers will inevitably have a strong sense of risk and uncertainty, which again is likely to constrain the range of operation modes that are considered. Conversely, the greater the depth of knowledge and experience in foreign markets, the more confident a firm tends to be about making commitments, and about its judgment of the degree of exposure to risk.

In their influential article on firms' internationalization, Johanson and Vahlne (1977) suggested that there is an interplay between accumulation of knowledge, on the one hand, and firms' actions, on the other. Commitment decisions are based on the knowledge that firms already have. Knowledge is crucial in order to identify and assess problems and opportunities, which in turn drive the decisions that are made. In the decision-making process, the

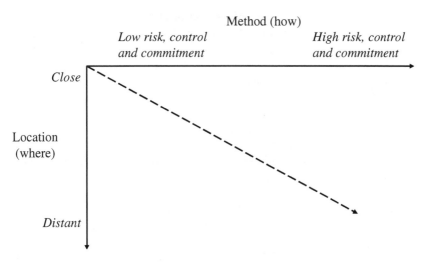

Figure 2.4   Dimensions of international expansion

identification of appropriate alternative courses of actions and their evaluation hinges on the knowledge that is available about relevant parts of the market environment, such as customers, competitors and suppliers, and about the performance of the various activities undertaken by the firm. Much of the knowledge on hand is so-called 'objective knowledge' (or, rather, information) of a fairly general kind, which can be treated more or less like a commodity and which can be taught and/or bought. Nevertheless, the most important and relevant type of knowledge is so-called 'experiential knowledge' that is primarily learned through personal experience with actual operations in foreign markets, hence providing an important feedback loop in the process.

The seminal study by Johanson and Wiedersheim-Paul (1975), who examined the internationalization moves of four major Swedish firms (Sandvik, Atlas Copco, Facit, Volvo) since their foundation provided evidence that suggested a distinctive pattern of internationalization. First, they reported that there was, generally, a high correlation between the sequence of (initial) entry into a market and the 'psychic' distance to the home country (Sweden) and that market. However, 'psychic' distance was somewhat less important for establishment of manufacturing subsidiaries, possibly because such establishments usually came quite late in firms' internationalization, after they had already operated abroad for some time. Also their findings indicated that 'psychic' distance was a stronger factor than market size in explaining companies' choice of location. Finally, Johanson and Wiedersheim-Paul (1975) reported that the speed of internationalization increased over time.

Since Johanson and Wiedersheim-Paul's (1975) study, a considerable number of empirical studies have provided additional support for the notion of internationalization as a gradual learning process; Leonidou and Katsikeas (1996) provide a fine overview. It appears that many firms follow distinct stages of development in their internationalization. In terms of their choice of location, firms tend to enter countries successively according to how similar (or, conversely, how psychic or culturally distant) they are to their own home countries. In terms of foreign operation modes, firms tend to increase their commitment step by step, a common pattern for manufacturing firms regarding modes of operation being: (1) no regular export or other types of international activities, (2) export via a foreign intermediary (for example, agents or distributors), (3) establishment of a sales subsidiary, and (4) production in a foreign country.

Despite the intuitive and commonsensical appeal of the basic ideas in the process perspective on firms' internationalization, the empirical support for the theory is far from conclusive. For example, empirical tests have not uniformly supported the gradual move into culturally more distant countries (Benito and Gripsrud, 1992; Mitra and Golder, 2002). A possible explanation is that some companies internationalize in order to lower their production costs, to get closer to suppliers, and/or to obtain agglomeration benefits, and such locations simply are in distant countries. The economic motivation behind an internationalization decision may hence sometimes override concerns about lack of knowledge about given locations. Studies have also shown that firms may leapfrog stages in the establishment chain, for a variety of reasons, including competitive motives (Petersen and Pedersen, 1997), avoidance of costs involved in switching between modes of operation (Benito, Pedersen and Petersen, 2005), and entrepreneurial action (Andersson, 2000).

Some critics argue that the internationalization process approach has been overly deterministic, and emphasize that firms have options for strategic choice both regarding the countries and markets they want to enter and when selecting the modes of operation. Critics also point out that several studies over the last decade have reported that an increasing number of firms internationalize much more rapidly and in more adventurous ways than seems to have been common in the past. A significant number of firms did not slowly build their internationalization, which could appear to contradict earlier studies of firms' internationalization (Johanson and Vahlne, 1977, 1990; Johanson and Wiedersheim-Paul, 1975). Instead, these firms turned international shortly after their inception (see, for example, Andersson and Wictor, 2003; Madsen and Servais, 1997). A variety of labels have been applied to characterize these firms, including Born Globals (for example, Andersson and Wictor, 2003;

Knight and Cavusgil, 1996; Madsen and Servais, 1997; Moen, 2002), International New Ventures (McDougall et al., 1994) and Instant Exporters (McAuley, 1999).

In what was one of the first studies about Born Globals (Rennie, 1993), the McKinsey consultancy company reported that Born Globals in Australia typically shared the following features: they were small, usually established by active entrepreneurs, often as a result of significant break-throughs in process or product technology, which were put into use to develop a unique product idea or a new way of doing business. The management of the companies tended to regard the world as its marketplace right from the outset, with exports beginning only a couple of years after the establishment of the firm.

Several factors have contributed to quicker internationalization, more diverse internationalization patterns and the proliferation of Born Globals, International New Ventures and Instant Exporters. Among external factors, the following should be mentioned:

- the emergence of world-wide market niches;
- rapid technological change, which requires going beyond local markets in order to reap scale economies;
- developments in communication and transportation technologies have made it easier for firms to stretch their boundaries;
- psychic distance has been reduced through increased globalization.

Internal factors are also important, in particular:

- Some owners and/or managers have extensive international experience. Having prior knowledge and experience helps in reducing psychic distance to specific markets. It also increases absorptive capacity (that is, the ability to appropriate and use new knowledge), which in turn makes the actors more able to accumulate and use new knowledge about internationalization;
- Increased competition requires more proactive and strategic internationalization behaviours.

Alongside the focus on Born Globals, there is an increasing awareness of the potential importance of entrepreneurs in firms' internationalization. A number of studies have found that entrepreneurs' attitudes towards international activities, and their motivation, orientation, experience and networks have a positive impact on the international operations of firms (Andersson, 2000; Andersson and Wictor, 2003; Bloodgood et al., 1996; Ibeh and Young, 2001; Kuemmerle, 2002; Madsen and Servais, 1997;

McDougall et al., 1994; Moen, 2002; Oviatt and McDougall, 1994, 1997; Preece et al., 1999; Welch and Welch, 2004).

A focal issue for international entrepreneurship and internationalization researchers alike is how perceived risk affects the way individuals and companies approach international activities (Welch and Luostarinen, 1988), but according to Welch and Welch (2004) there are noteworthy differences between the two. Companies unavoidably take on risk as they enter a foreign market and develop international operations, but at the same time they seek various ways to minimize their exposure to risk. Among entrepreneurship researchers, the focus has tended to be on the way different actors act when facing risk. For example, risk taking can be regarded as an important aspect of an entrepreneurial orientation, especially in the context of the internationalization of small and medium-sized companies that are often expected to behave cautiously when venturing abroad. Some companies take steps that others do not, simply because of audacious and influential actors in them. The centre of attention for internationalization researchers has not so much been attitudes towards risk *per se*, but more how risk is related to other factors that also influence internationalization behaviours. For example, perceived risk is likely to change as a result of experience in a particular country and/or with a particular mode of operation and/or relationships with certain actors, and such changed perceptions of risk provide an impetus and/or hinder subsequent commitment to foreign operations.

The Network Approach

Although the views on the importance of various factors as well as their assumptions regarding the degree of rationality involved in decision making clearly vary, both the 'economics–strategic' approach and the 'process' (or 'behavioural') approach take primarily into account factors internal to the firm – given, of course, environmental contingencies such as legal and political issues in the countries of interest. In recent years, increasing attention has been given to the view that 'no firm is an island' (Håkansson and Snehota, 1989), but that its past, its existing activities and its future potential for strategic manoeuvres are largely a reflection of its links to other actors. The network approach maintains that an integral part of the internationalization process is the establishment, nurturing and expansion of relationships – and thereby networks – in foreign markets. It is almost inconceivable that foreign market penetration can in fact take place without building relationships with a wide range of organizations and individuals: in particular, customers, intermediaries, financial institutions and government officials. From a network perspective, the knowledge a firm has about foreign markets, and the opportunities open to the firm in these markets, extend beyond the boundaries of the firm itself; it is principally contained in the network that the firm has been and will be able to develop, and anchored by key actors within them (Benito and Welch, 1994).

Formal as well as informal contacts between people provide the basic mechanism through which relationships are created and maintained. Naturally, relationships vary in kind and quality. Of particular importance are those that, over time, create a sense of trust and mutual dependence between the actors. Especially in cases where a foreign market is perceived as being complex, different and very 'distant', without trustworthy connections to 'insiders' in the market, decision makers are not likely to be willing to operate in the market with any high degree of commitment. Of course, even though it may reduce the risk exposure in the short term, becoming too entangled with other actors may also restrict the opportunities open to the firms in the future.

The network perspective is pertinent in order to explain the phenomenon of rapid and adventurous internationalization. Born Globals are usually more specialized and niche-oriented than other exporters, and their products tend to be either more customized or more standardized (Knight and Cavusgil, 1996; Madsen and Servais, 1997). The seemingly less predictable location patterns often observed in their expansion patterns suggest that the activities of Born Globals are strongly influenced by the past experience of the founders and partners, that is, the entrepreneurs, and by customer-related and supplier-related factors, either directly or through interaction. Compared to other firms, Born Globals often rely on complementary resources and competencies, which are sourced from other firms, and their distribution channels frequently depend on mixed structures, or hybrids, that involve network partners, strategic alliances and joint ventures (Madsen and Servais, 1997; Crick and Jones, 2000). The risk of entering foreign markets is managed by exploiting simultaneous trade-offs between entry mode commitment, country risk and foreign revenue exposure in each country (Shrader et al., 2000).

Inward–Outward Connections

As pointed out earlier in this chapter, firms' internationalization comprises inward operations as well as outward operations (see Figure 2.1). Internationalization research has so far had a strong bias towards outward operations, such as exporting and the establishment of foreign sales and manufacturing subsidiaries, whereas the reverse side of these activities, such as importing and sourcing activities, has received considerably less attention. Even less is known about the potential linkages between activities that

---

BOX 2.3   INTERNATIONALIZATION WITHOUT CHANGE OF FOREIGN OPERATION METHOD

According to internationalization process models firms typically change the ways they operate in foreign markets as they gain experience from operations abroad. In particular, if their foreign operations are reasonably successful it is expected that firms over time deepen their commitments abroad, normally by changing from export-oriented operations (which are undertaken from the firms' home base) to carrying out activities in foreign locations, either in a wholly owned venture or in cooperation with a local partner. However, exceptions to this notion of incremental internationalization can be found and some companies internationalize without ever changing their foreign operation method. In a study of the Australian conglomerate CSR, Welch and Welch (2004) describe how that company's sugar division held on to exporting as their mode of operation for a period of more than 75 years. CSR's allegiance to exporting did not imply stagnant internationalization. Despite sticking to the same operation method, CSR enjoyed considerable success in their internationalization in terms of trade volume as well as the number of markets served. According to Welch and Welch (2004) the development of relationships and networks at home as well as abroad – not only with customers but also with actors in the political and regulatory spheres – were crucial factors behind the success of CSR's internationalization. Furthermore, their study demonstrates that understanding modes of operation may require going beyond traditional labels: considerable variation can be found within one type of foreign operation mode, even for the same company, as time passes. In the case of CSR, the company followed a strategy of network investments and relationship commitment that effectively 'stretched' its foreign operation method, but without changing it.

---

are outward-oriented and those that are inward-oriented. In a study of a large number of Finnish small and medium-sized companies, Korhonen, Luostarinen and Welch (1996) found that a majority of the studied companies began their international activities on the inward side rather than on the outward side, thus pointing to the potential importance of inward activities as a springboard to outward activities. Typical inward operations were imports of physical products like raw materials, machinery and components. Imported services, like installation, testing, servicing and maintenance, were also common, although at a lower level compared to physical products.

The connection between inward and outward activities and how it affects the internationalization process of the firm has been identified primarily through research on specific business operations such as licensing, subcontracting and counter trade. Welch and Luostarinen (1993) provide several examples of such instances and argue that the inward–outward connections may be important even at the very early stages of international development for many companies. They also suggest that the connections often are broad, go across operation modes and may develop from either inward or outward sides at different stages of international development for many companies. The evidence, while limited, indicates that inward activities may provide a good opportunity to learn about foreign trade techniques, foreign operation characteristics and ways of using different operation modes. By active use of this knowledge, the firm should be in a better position to undertake outward operations in a foreign market. However, as pointed out by Karlsen et al. (2003), a real challenge is to deal with the barriers that exist within firms regarding effectively transferring and using the knowledge that has been generated by inward activities. In their study of the evolution of Norwegian timber company Moelven's operations in Russia, Karlsen et al. (2003) report that Moelven was relatively successful in using knowledge and personal and network relations developed through inward activities (such as import of timber) when it subsequently ventured into outward-oriented activities in Russia, including a turnkey project and the setting up of a jointly-owned production facility there for exports to other European markets. An important reason why so many connections between inward and outward activities were identified in Moelven was the perceived strategic importance of Moelven's purchasing function. However, Korhonen (1999) argues that inward and outward processes are frequently poorly linked, particularly because the purchasing function typically has tended to be viewed as a clerical function of modest strategic importance and which therefore has limited authority in many companies.

The research on inward–outward linkages connects well with recent avenues in studies of firms' internationalization. First, it goes some way to answer why some companies seemingly internationalize very rapidly: thanks to previous inward activities companies may already have developed the knowledge and relations needed to move on swiftly with outward operations. Second, it answers another intriguing question that has been raised by recent research on firms' internationalization: why is the level of unsolicited orders so high in the initiation of international operations? The fact that many firms develop international operations via various forms of importing activities opens up a wide range of potential links through which information relevant to outward operations might be transferred. Third, the interaction between inward and outward internationalization is related to, and possibly dependent on, the concurrent evolution of formal and informal business networks. The network approach provides a useful framework for understanding the way in which inward–outward connections emerge and develop. Obviously, the focal linkages are not just with external actors. Also important are intro-company relations, where cross-functional communication and personal relationships are necessary in order to build a strong internal network within which inward–outward connections may emerge.

SUMMARY

Given the importance of foreign operation method decisions, it is not surprising that the extant literature on the subject is large and multifaceted. Despite the numerous theoretical and empirical contributions, two main approaches can readily be identified: one that is rooted in an economics and strategic approach to business behaviour, and another that builds on a learning and decision-making perspective of organizations. There are noteworthy differences between the approaches. First, while the former assumes that decision makers are rational at least in a semi-strong sense, the latter takes as its starting point that bounded rationality is a more accurate description of economic actors' decision-making capabilities. Second, whereas economics-based approaches focus on discrete decisions (for example, an entry into a given country at a certain point) and as a result tend to be static, researchers taking a behavioural approach emphasize that internationalization is an evolutionary organizational process and are more apt to take a longitudinal and holistic view of the processes involved. Third, the approaches differ in their views of what are relevant units of analysis. Transactions, resources/assets and firms (their boundaries) are at the core of economics-based analyses. Conversely, individuals (entrepreneurs), actions, organizations, and linkages between actors, are considered as focal in behavioural approaches.

REFERENCES

Agarwal, S. and S.N. Ramaswamy (1992), 'Choice of foreign market entry mode: impact of ownership, location and internalization factors', *Journal of International Business Studies*, **23**(1), 1–27.
Andersen, O. (1997), 'Internationalization and entry mode choice: a review of theories and conceptual frameworks', *Management International Review*, **37**(Special Issue 2), 27–42.
Anderson, E. and A.T. Coughlan (1987), 'International market entry and expansion via independent or integrated channels of distribution', *Journal of Marketing*, **51**(1), 71–82.
Anderson, E. and H.A. Gatignon (1986), 'Modes of foreign entry: a transaction cost analysis and propositions', *Journal of International Business Studies*, **17**(3), 1–26.

Andersson, S. (2000), 'Internationalization of the firm from an entrepreneurial perspective', *International Studies of Management and Organization*, **30**(1), 63–92.

Andersson, S. and I. Wictor (2003), 'Innovative internationalisation in new firms: Born Globals – the Swedish case', *Journal of International Entrepreneurship*, **1**(3), 249–76.

Barney, J.B. (1991), 'Firm resources and sustained competitive advantage', *Journal of Management*, **17**(1), 99–120.

Bartlett, C.A. and S. Ghoshal (1989), *Managing Across Borders: The Transnational Solution*, Boston: Harvard Business School Press.

Benito, G.R.G. (1996), 'Ownership structures of Norwegian foreign subsidiaries in manufacturing', *International Trade Journal*, **10**(2), 157–98.

Benito, G.R.G. and G. Gripsrud (1992), 'The expansion of foreign direct investments: discrete rational location choices or a cultural learning process?', *Journal of International Business Studies*, **23**(3), 461–76.

Benito, G.R.G., T. Pedersen and B. Petersen (2005), 'Export channel dynamics: an empirical investigation', *Managerial and Decision Economics*, **26**(3), 159–73.

Benito, G.R.G. and L.S. Welch (1994), 'Foreign market servicing: beyond choice of entry mode', *Journal of International Marketing*, **2**(2), 7–27.

Bloodgood, J.M., H.J. Sapienza and J.G. Almeida (1996), 'The internationalization of new high-potential U.S. ventures: antecedents and outcomes', *Entrepreneurship. Theory and Practice*, **20**(4), 61–76.

Buckley, P.J. and M.C. Casson (1976), *The Future of the Multinational Enterprise*, London: Macmillan.

Buckley, P.J. and M.C. Casson (1981), 'The optimal timing of a foreign direct investment', *Economic Journal*, **91**(361), 75–87.

Buckley, P.J. and M.C. Casson (1988), 'A theory of cooperation in international busines', in F. Contractor and P. Lorange (eds), *Cooperative Strategies in International Business*, Lexington: Lexington Books.

Carlson, S. (1975), *How Foreign is Foreign Trade?* Acta Universitatis Upsaliensis, Studia Oeconomicae Negotiorum 11, Uppsala.

Casson, M.C. (1987), 'Multinational firms', in R. Clarke and T. McGuinness (eds), *The Economics of the Firm*, Oxford: Basil Blackwell.

Crick, D. and M.V. Jones (2000), 'Small high-technology firms and international high-technology markets', *Journal of International Marketing*, **8**(2), 63–85.

Cyert, R. and J.G. March (1963), *A Behavioral Theory of the Firm*, Englewood Cliffs, NJ: Prentice-Hall.

Datta, D.K., P. Herrmann and A.A. Rasheed (2002), 'Choice of foreign market entry modes: critical review and future directions', *Advances in International Management*, **14**, 85–153.

Doz, Y. (1986), *Strategic Management in Multinational Companies*, Oxford: Pergamon Press.

Dunning, J.H. (1981), *International Production and the Multinational Enterprise*, London: George Allen and Unwin.

Dunning, J.H. (1988), 'The eclectic paradigm of international production: a restatement and some possible extensions', *Journal of International Business Studies*, **19**(1), 1–31.

Dunning, J.H. (2001), 'The key literature on IB activities: 1960-2000', in A.M. Rugman and T.L. Brewer (eds), *The Oxford Handbook of International Business*, Oxford: Oxford University Press.

Erramilli, M.K., S. Agarwal and C.S. Dev (2002), 'Choice between non-equity entry modes: an organizational capability perspective', *Journal of International Business Studies*, **33**(2), 223–42.

Gatignon, H. and E. Anderson (1988), 'The multinational corporation's degree of control over foreign subsidiaries: an empirical test of a transaction cost explanation', *Journal of Law, Economics and Organization*, **4**(2), 305–36.

Ghoshal, S. (1987), 'Global strategy: an organizing framework', *Strategic Management Journal*, **8**(5), 425–40.

Gomes-Casseres, B. (1989), 'Ownership structures of foreign subsidiaries: theory and evidence', *Journal of Economic Behavior and Organization*, **11**(1), 1–25.

Graham, E. (1978), 'Transatlantic investment by multinational firms: a rivalistic phenomenon?', *Journal of Post-Keynesian Economics*, **1**(1), 82–104.

Gruber, W., D. Mehta and R. Vernon (1967), 'The R&D factor in international trade and investment of United States industries', *Journal of Political Economy*, **75**(1), 20–37.

Håkansson, H. and I. Snehota (1989), 'No business is an island: the network concept of business strategy', *Scandinavian Journal of Management*, **4**(3), 187–200.

Hedlund, G. (1994), 'A model of knowledge management and the N-form corporation', *Strategic Management Journal*, **15**(5), 3–90.

Hennart, J.F. (1982), *A Theory of Multinational Enterprise*, Ann Arbor: University of Michigan Press.

Hennart, J.F. (1988), 'A transaction cost theory of equity joint ventures', *Strategic Management Journal*, **9**(4), 361–74.

Hennart, J.F. (1991), 'The transaction costs theory of joint ventures: an empirical study of Japanese subsidiaries in the United States', *Management Science*, **37**(4), 483–97.

Hennart, J.F. (2000), 'Transaction cost theory and the multinational enterprise', in C.N. Pitelis and R. Sugden (eds), *The Nature of the Transnational Firm*, 2nd edn, London: Routledge.

Hill, C.W.L., P. Hwang and W.C. Kim (1990), 'An eclectic theory of the choice of international entry mode', *Strategic Management Journal*, **11**(2), 117–28.

Horst, T. (1972), 'Firm and industry determinants of the decision to invest abroad: an empirical study', *Review of Economics and Statistics*, **54**(3), 258–66.

Hout, T., M.E. Porter and E. Rudden (1982), 'How global companies win out', *Harvard Business Review*, **60**(5), 98–108.

Hymer, S.H. (1976), *The International Operations of National Firms: A Study of Direct Foreign Investment*, Cambridge, MA: MIT Press (originally presented as the author's thesis, Massachusetts Institute of Technology, 1960).

Ibeh, K.I.N. and S. Young (2001), 'Exporting as entrepreneurial act – an empirical study of Nigerian firms', *European Journal of Marketing*, **35**(5/6), 566–86.

Jensen, M.C. and W.H. Meckling (1976), 'Theory of the firm: managerial behavior, agency costs and ownership structure', *Journal of Financial Economics*, **3**(4), 305–60.

Johanson, J. and J.-E. Vahlne (1977), 'The internationalization process of the firm – a model of knowledge development and increasing foreign market commitments', *Journal of International Business Studies*, **8**(1), 23–32.

Johanson, J. and J.-E. Vahlne (1990), 'The mechanism of internationalization', *International Marketing Review*, **7**(4), 11–24.

Johanson, J. and F. Wiedersheim-Paul (1975), 'The internationalization of the firm: four Swedish cases', *Journal of Management Studies*, **12**(3), 305–22.

Karlsen, T., P. Silseth, G.R.G. Benito and L.S. Welch (2003), 'Knowledge, internationalization of the firm and inward–outward connections', *Industrial Marketing Management*, **32**(5), 385–96.

Kindleberger, C.P. (1969), *American Business Abroad: Six Lectures on Direct Investment*, New Haven: Yale University Press.

Knickerbocker, F.T. (1973), *Oligopolistic Reaction and Multinational Enterprise*, Boston, MA: Harvard Business School.

Knight, G.A. and S.T. Cavusgil (1996), 'The born global firm: a challenge to traditional internationalization theory', *Advances in International Marketing*, **8**, 11–26.

Kogut, B. and U. Zander (1993), 'Knowledge of the firm and the evolutionary theory of the multinational corporation', *Journal of International Business Studies*, **24**(4), 625–45.

Korhonen, H. (1999), *Inward–Outward Internationalization of Small and Medium Enterprises*, Helsinki: Helsinki School of Economics and Business Administration.

Korhonen, H., R. Luostarinen and L.S. Welch (1996), 'Internationalization of SMEs: inward–outward patterns and government policy', *Management International Review*, **36**(4), 315–29.

Kuemmerle, W. (2002), 'Home base and knowledge management in international ventures', *Journal of Business Venturing*, **17**(2), 99–122.

Leonidou, L.C. and C.S. Katsikeas (1996), 'The export development process: an integrative review of empirical models', *Journal of International Business Studies*, **27**(3), 517–51.

Luostarinen, R.K. (1979), 'Internationalization of the Firm', doctoral dissertation, Helsinki School of Economics.

Madhok, A. (1997), 'Cost, value and foreign market entry mode: the transaction and the firm', *Strategic Management Journal*, **18**(1), 39–61.

Madhok, A. and A. Phene (2001), 'The co-evolutionary advantage: strategic management theory and the eclectic paradigm', *International Journal of the Economics of Business*, **8**(2), 243–56.

Madsen, T.K. and P. Servais (1997), 'The internationalization of born globals: an evolutionary process?', *International Business Review*, **6**(6), 561–83.

Malhotra, N.K., J. Agarwal and F.M. Ulgado (2003), 'Internationalization and entry modes: a multitheoretical framework and research propositions', *Journal of International Marketing*, **11**(4), 1–31.

McAuley, A. (1999), 'Entrepreneurial instant exporters in the Scottish arts and crafts sector', *Journal of International Marketing*, **7**(4), 67–82.

McDougall, P.P., S. Shane and B.M. Oviatt (1994), 'Explaining the formation of international new ventures', *Journal of Business Venturing*, **9**(6), 469–87.

McManus, J. (1972), 'The theory of the international firm', in G. Paquet (ed.), *The International Firm and the Nation State*, Don Mills, Ont.: Collier Macmillan Canada.

Mitra, D. and P.N. Golder (2002), 'Whose culture matters? Near-market knowledge and its impact on foreign market entry', *Journal of Marketing Research*, **39**(3), 350–65.

Moen, O. (2002), 'The born globals: a new generation of small European exporters', *International Marketing Review*, **19**(2), 156–75.

Nicholas, S. (1983), 'Agency contracts, institutional modes, and the transition to foreign direct investment by British manufacturing multinationals before 1939', *Journal of Economic History*, **43**(3), 675–86.

Oviatt, B.M. and P.P. McDougall (1994), 'Toward a theory of international new ventures', *Journal of International Business Studies*, **24**(1), 45–64.

Oviatt, B.M. and P.P. McDougall (1997), 'Challenges for internationalization process theory: the case of international new ventures', *Management International Review*, **37**(Special Issue 2), 85–99.

Peteraf, M.A. (1993), 'The cornerstones of competitive advantage: a resource-based view', *Strategic Management Journal*, **14**(3), 179–91.

Petersen, B. and T. Pedersen (1997), 'Twenty years after – support and critique of the Uppsala internationalization model', in I. Björkman and M. Forsgren (eds), *The Nature of the International Firm*, Copenhagen: Copenhagen Business School Press.

Petersen, B., G.R.G. Benito and T. Pedersen (2000), 'Replacing the foreign intermediary: motivators and deterrents', *International Studies of Management and Organization*, **30**(1), 45–62.

Petersen, B., G.R.G. Benito, L.S. Welch and C.G. Asmussen (2004), 'Mode configuration diversity: a new perspective on foreign entry mode choice', paper presented at 2nd Annual JIBS/AIB/CIBER Conference on Emerging Research Frontiers in International Business Studies, MSU, East Lansing, Michigan, 16–19 September 2004.

Porter, M.E. (1986), *Competition in Global Industries*, Boston, MA: Harvard Business School Press.

Porter, M.E. and M.B. Fuller (1986), 'Coalitions and global strategies', in M.E. Porter (ed.), *Competition in Global Industries*, Boston, MA: Harvard Business School Press.

Prahalad, C.K. and Y. Doz (1987), *The Multinational Mission: Balancing Local Demands and Global Vision*, New York: Free Press.

Preece, S.B., G. Miles and M.C. Baetz (1999), 'Explaining the international intensity and global diversity of early stage technology-based firms', *Journal of Business Venturing*, **14**(3), 259–81.

Rennie, M.W. (1993), 'Born global', *The McKinsey Quarterly*, **4**, 45–52.

Rugman, A.M. (1986), 'New theories of the multinational enterprise: an assessment of internalization theory', *Bulletin of Economic Research*, **38**(2), 101–18.

Sanchez-Peinado, E. and J. Pla-Barber (2006), 'A multidimensional concept of uncertainty and its influence on entry mode choice: An empirical analysis in the service sector', *International Business Review*, **15**(3), 215–35.

Shrader, R.C., B.M. Oviatt and P.P. McDougall (2000), 'How new ventures exploit trade-offs among international risk factors: lessons for the accelerated internationalization of the 21st century', *Academy of Management Journal*, **43**(6), 1227–47.

Simon, H.A. (1955), 'A behavioral model of rational choice', *Quarterly Journal of Economics*, **69**(1), 99–118.

Simon, H.A. (1979), 'Rational decision making in business organizations', *American Economic Review*, **69**(4), 493–513.

Teece, D. (1986), 'Transaction cost economics and the multinational enterprise: an assessment', *Journal of Economic Behavior and Organization*, **7**(1), 21–45.

Thompson, S. (1988), 'Agency costs of internal organization', in S. Thompson and M. Wright (eds), *Internal Organization, Efficiency and Profit*, Oxford: Philip Allan.

Vermeulen, F. and H.G. Barkema (2002), 'Pace, rhythm and scope: process dependence in building a profitable multinational enterprise', *Strategic Management Journal*, **23**(7), 637–53.

Welch, L.S. and R.K. Luostarinen (1988), 'Internationalization: evolution of a concept', *Journal of General Management*, **14**(2), 34–55.

Welch, L.S. and R.K. Luostarinen (1993), 'Inward–outward connections in internationalization', *Journal of International Marketing*, **1**(1), 44–56.

Welch, C.L. and L.S. Welch (2004), 'Broadening the concept of international entrepreneurship: Internationalisation, networks and politics', *Journal of International Entrepreneurship*, **2**(3), 217–37.

Wernerfelt, B. (1984), 'A resource-based view of the firm', *Strategic Management Journal*, **5**(2), 171–80.

Williamson, O.E. (1979), 'Transaction-cost economics: the governance of contractual relations', *Journal of Law and Economics*, **22**(2), 233–61.

Williamson, O.E. (1985), *The Economic Institutions of Capitalism*, New York: Free Press.

Yip, G.S. (1989), 'Global strategy. . .in a world of nations?', *Sloan Management Review*, **30**, 29–41.

Yu, C.M. and K. Ito (1988), 'Oligopolistic reaction and foreign direct investment: the case of the U.S. tire and textiles industries', *Journal of International Business Studies*, **19**, 449–60.

PART II

Modes of operation

3. Franchising

INTRODUCTION

Over the last three decades, franchising has moved from being viewed as a relatively exotic form of international business operations to one which is taken more seriously as its use has spread across industries and countries and been used as an important means of internationalization by many companies. The potential of international franchising has been brought into focus by the high-profile global success of companies such as McDonald's, KFC and Body Shop, which have used franchising as a major part of their expansion strategies. In the advanced countries, franchising has reached a high level of use in the retail sector: in some countries constituting as much as 50 per cent of retail activity. While retailing has been the most obvious area of franchising growth, it has spread into diverse areas of business activity, particularly in the services sector, but also in manufacturing, so that there is almost no area where franchising is not represented – including banking and university education. It is, therefore, somewhat surprising that franchising has received relatively limited treatment in the international business literature. Where it is dealt with, it is often in a simplistic way, ignoring its links to other operation methods, or it is placed in the 'similar to licensing' box, or even treated as the same as licensing. In contrast, this chapter will provide a comprehensive treatment of franchising and its place as a method in international business activity: including its characteristics, international patterns of expansion, diverse roles, links to other modes, international triggers and processes, reasons for its use, franchisor and franchisee perspectives, problems in its use and the impact of governments.

FRANCHISING DEFINED

In its simplest form, franchising has a long history, stretching back to the times, for example, of businesses operating under royal patronage. Around the beginning of the 20th century, franchising began to grow through its extensive use in three industries, involving motor vehicle dealerships, the retailing side of the oil business and soft drink bottling.

Franchising in this version has been called 'first generation franchising', 'simple franchising' or 'product and tradename franchising' – the latter defined by the International Trade Administration (1987, 1) as '. . . an independent sales relationship between supplier and dealer in which the dealer acquires some of the identity of the supplier. Franchised dealers concentrate on one company's product line and to some extent identify their business with that company'. The simplicity of this form is in contrast to the more complex variety of franchising which has characterized much of the growth of franchising over the last 40 years, and been associated with the better known company examples such as McDonald's. It has been variously referred to as 'second generation franchising', 'system franchising' and 'business format franchising', the latter defined by the US International Trade Administration (1987, 3) as 'characterized by an ongoing relationship between franchisor and franchisee that includes not only the product, service and trademark, but the entire business format – a marketing strategy and plan, operation manuals and standards, quality control, and continuing 2-way communication'. It is of note that the major oil companies have been converting their retail operations to a business format franchised basis, from their earlier use of product and tradename franchising.

As this definition indicates, the franchisor transfers a full business system that enables a franchisee, after training, to start operating an independent business, but under the guidance of the franchisor's overall business model and framework, typically with a strong marketing emphasis, within an active, continuing relationship. Thus the franchisor remains heavily involved in the continuing operations of individual franchisees. It is usual for the business format franchisor to undertake advertising and other major forms of promotion for the franchise chain, register trademarks and generally defend the intellectual property of the business. Given the comprehensive nature of the knowledge, skills and business system transfer from franchisor to franchisee, training forms a critical part of the transfer process to, and establishment of, franchisee businesses. Training programmes may last as long as nine months (for example McDonald's). For franchisors, training is a key step in ensuring the consistency of operations in diverse locations and cultural contexts. Alongside control of overall marketing programmes, and contractual requirements as to the level of services and quality of product, the franchisee, although operating as an independent business, does so within a highly constrained framework. In some cases, the franchisor will be responsible for key supplies to the franchisee and for elements such as the information technology hardware, software and network connections.

FRANCHISING V. LICENSING

As already indicated, there is considerable confusion regarding the difference between licensing and franchising, and in reality it is sometimes difficult to draw a line between these two foreign operation forms. For our
purposes, the difference, particularly with regard to business format franchising, lies in the degree of control: in licensing, this lies more in the hands
of the licensee, whereas in business format franchising the individual franchisee is highly restrained, especially in terms of marketing strategy and
promotion. Franchisees are part of an overall system and must operate
within it and are driven by it, whereas licensees tend to be in a position to
set many of the parameters of the operation: often licensing takes place to
an existing business which sets many of the boundaries to the use of what
is licensed. Nevertheless, licensing, as a form of foreign operation, has been
moving in the direction of franchising, with licensing packages generally
becoming more rounded, including stronger marketing components.

THE FRANCHISING PACKAGE

As already noted, and illustrated in Figure 3.1, the package which is transferred from franchisor to franchisee in business format franchising tends
to be relatively broad, potentially encompassing a wide range of transfer

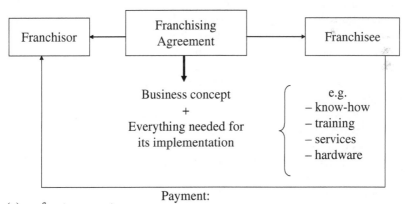

Payment:
(a) up-front payment
(b) up-front payment + royalties (% of sales or charge on supplies)
(c) other mark-ups and contributions (e.g. rent, finance charges)

Source: Adapted from Luostarinen and Welch (1990, p. 75).

Figure 3.1 The franchising package

components, at the outset and on a continuing basis. It should be stressed that this range varies considerably among franchising companies so that it is difficult to describe a standard pattern; for example, McDonald's transfers a comprehensive package, including a demanding training programme, and is highly involved with franchisees on a continuing basis, whereas Benetton takes a relatively minimalist approach to the point where some have questioned whether Benetton can be said to be using franchising.

There is considerable variation also in the types of payment made by franchisees to franchisors. The general form is an up-front franchise fee as well as a capital contribution towards fixtures and fittings and other set-up costs. In Australia, average start-up costs across all industries in a recent survey were found to be $A78 000 (retail 262 500), including an average initial franchise fee of $A30 000, varying from 0 to $A140 000 (Frazer, Weaven and Wright, 2006). Then there is usually an ongoing royalty payment expressed as a percentage of sales made by the franchisee. The royalty payment often includes a promotional levy: for example, an early study of British franchising found an average royalty rate of 10.7 per cent, composed of a 3.2 per cent promotional levy and 7.5 per cent basic component (Churchill, 1982). The 2004 Australian survey of franchising found an average royalty of 6 per cent of gross sales (ranging from 1 to 15 per cent), with an added 3 per cent of gross sales when an advertising or marketing levy was applied, as in most cases (Frazer and Weaven, 2004). Beyond the general pattern there are cases of up-front franchise fees being charged without an ongoing royalty; in some cases this implies an expectation of little or no continuing involvement, indicative of a very simple form of franchising arrangement. In other cases, returns are generated through other means than a simple royalty. For instance, Benetton does not charge an ongoing royalty as a proportion of sales but rather generates an effective royalty through its margin on the provision of product to Benetton franchisees. Some franchisors, although charging a royalty, add to their returns from the franchising relationship, as shown in Figure 3.1, through additional charges on franchisees for various services provided (such as assistance with finance or property), perhaps by mark-ups on supplies or charging rent on property leases. McDonald's has generated a significant proportion of its returns in the past through rental charges on its franchisees (Love, 1986).

Franchising contracts tend to be longer than those in licensing arrangements: in the US, the bulk of contracts in early research were revealed to be for more then ten years, with many for 20 years or more (International Trade Administration, 1987). McDonald's utilizes franchising contracts of 20 years' duration: the first contract renewal in Australia did not take place until 1994, McDonald's having entered the market in the early 1970s (Hudson, 1994). In the Australian context, recent evidence points to a move to shorter duration contracts – mainly five years or less (Frazer and Weaven, 2004).

FRANCHISING IN INTERNATIONAL OPERATIONS

While franchising appears straightforward as a business method in the above exposition, in the international context the situation when using franchising in other countries is far more complex (Petersen and Welch, 2000). While some franchisors do expand internationally by directly setting up each individual franchisee in foreign countries (so-called 'direct franchising'), at least during the early establishment phase, this is not the main path of internationalization by companies using franchising. Clearly, the management demands of a growing number of franchisees in foreign locations force franchisors to consider other organizational vehicles to handle franchising development and management. However, some companies point to the advantages of this approach as a way of experimenting in a foreign market and getting a direct 'feel' for the foreign market and its prospects, before making a major commitment to the market. Direct franchising is, of course, more feasible when countries are geographically and culturally close, such as the northern US and Canada, or Norway, Sweden and Denmark, or Australia and New Zealand.

As Figure 3.2 shows, there are three other main forms of set-up in foreign markets that are used by franchisors as a basis for eventual franchising. Studies in different countries indicate that *master franchising* (earlier called 'master licensing') is the most used path by companies engaging in international franchising – well above other approaches in recent surveys in Australia and New Zealand (Frazer, Weaven and Wright, 2006; Paynter and Everett, 2003). In master franchising, an independent foreign company is licensed to establish, develop and manage the franchising operation in the foreign market (may involve some company-owned units as well). Typically, the master franchisee pays an up-front fee (often substantial for well-known franchises) and a continuing royalty based on sales in the foreign market, effectively sharing the continuing royalty paid by each sub-franchisee with the franchisor (for example, an 11 per cent royalty paid by the sub-franchisee might be shared as follows: franchisor, 4 per cent, master franchisee, 7 per cent).

For companies embarking on international expansion, master franchising is attractive because of the lower costs relative to other forms of foreign market penetration: the master franchisee undertakes the establishment and management of franchisees in the designated region, often the whole country. The franchisor only has to deal directly with the master franchisee.

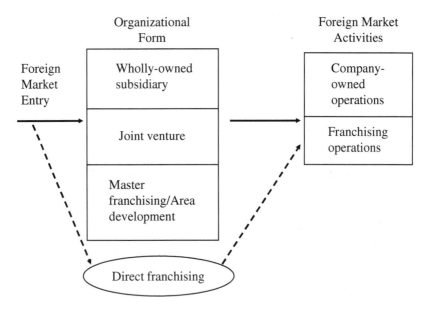

Organizational Form   Foreign Market Activities

Foreign Market Entry

Wholly-owned subsidiary		Company-owned operations
Joint venture		Franchising operations
Master franchising/Area development		

Direct franchising

Source: Adapted from Petersen and Welch (2000, p. 481).

Figure 3.2   Paths to international franchising

As a result, it becomes more feasible for the franchisor, with limited resources, to expand on a broader and faster basis in international markets. At the same time, the franchisor is able to tap into the local knowledge and networks of the master franchisee. Problems with this method revolve around finding a suitable partner, building an effective relationship, achieving and sustaining knowledge and other transfers, and obtaining an acceptable level of control over operations despite the inevitable dependence on the master franchisee. While it may be easy to find partners for well-known franchises, this is not the case for many franchising businesses, particularly those starting out in the international arena.

A variant of the master franchising system, although far less used in the international arena, is the *area development* method. This method involves licensing of an independent foreign company to establish and manage individual units in an assigned area within the foreign market. Unlike master franchising, these are owned rather than sub-franchised units, although royalty arrangements between the licensee (area developer) and licensor operate in a similar way to master franchising.

Franchisors often use joint ventures as a way of setting up in a foreign market before establishing franchising activities. There may be considerable variation in the equity level that the franchisor takes in the foreign joint venture – from minority to majority stakes. There will normally be some type of licensing arrangement between the licensor and the joint venture to cover the retention of intellectual property rights by the licensor while providing a right to use them by the joint venture. There are cases where the licensor obtains a minority share in the joint venture without making any capital contribution. Effectively, the licensor is exchanging royalty payments (as in master franchising) for a share of profits expected to flow from the joint venture. Clearly, the capital contribution of the foreign joint venture partner is an important attraction of this approach. For example, the Australian pizza delivery chain, Dial-a-Dino's (later acquired by Pizza Hut), entered New Zealand in 1987 via a joint venture: it acquired a one-third interest in the New Zealand operation without any capital contribution, in exchange for the transfer of the franchising package, including associated intellectual property rights (Welch, 1989). In addition, the joint venture partner is able to provide a range of other potential benefits in the foreign market, such as local knowledge, useful connections and a general understanding of how to develop a business within the market in question. Of course, much of the success of the arrangement depends on the relationship between licensor and joint venture partner, and while still reliant on the performance of the local, generally there is more scope for control over operations than in the master franchising situation.

The reasoning behind the use of joint ventures is illustrated in the way McDonald's approached the Japanese market. McDonald's entered Japan quite early in its internationalization via a joint venture arrangement that was seen to be important in delivering local market (particularly cultural) knowledge. Despite the perceived attractiveness of the Japanese market, McDonald's felt that it was not equipped to undertake operations by itself, and was conscious of the extent of differences when compared to the US market (Love, 1986). The McDonald's joint venture operation in Japan has been one of its most successful, achieving a high level of market penetration and, until recently, being highly profitable over many years.

The fourth main form of organizational set-up for international franchising is that of the wholly-owned subsidiary, as shown in Figure 3.2. This approach has been extensively applied by major global companies such as McDonald's as a basis for their use of franchising. As with direct franchising, this form ensures a high level of control over the development of foreign operations, without the constraint of having to work with a local partner. Unlike direct franchising, though, the subsidiary provides an on-the-ground presence that can be the basis of building key resources in the foreign market, particularly training and developmental, and responsive marketing capabilities via local and expatriate staff. It does of course come at a price, and tends to be viewed as the high-cost option by companies seeking to build international franchising operations, so that it is less used than other approaches.

COMPANY-OWNED V. FRANCHISING OPERATIONS

While direct franchising inevitably means franchising in the foreign market, this is not necessarily the case with the other entry forms. Figure 3.2 illustrates the choice that companies make between using company-owned or franchising operations as the means of foreign market expansion. It is quite common for entrant firms to start with company-owned outlets as a way of better assessing what elements of the franchising system need to be adjusted for differences in the foreign market before a full roll-out, and of experimenting with changes. Company-owned outlets also can be used as 'flagship' operations, serving as a marketing vehicle and model for potential franchisees, and as training centres. Beyond these initial steps, in the expansion phase, quite varied approaches have been used, even within the same company. For example, in Norway, McDonald's operates through a 50:50 joint venture with a Norwegian company, having 62 outlets at the beginning of 2003, of which 50 were franchised and 12 company-owned (Fuller, 2003). The bulk of McDonald's outlets in Japan are company-owned and run (Hutton, 1998). Likewise, in the UK, the emphasis has remained, over a long period, on company-owned operations rather than franchising, in stark contrast to the situation in France and Australia, where franchising is the dominant form of operations. There were early supply-chain problems for McDonald's in the UK, and there was a concern to maintain tight control over operations, which was seen to be facilitated by the company-owned emphasis. In 1990, out of 338 outlets in the UK, only 14 (4.1 per cent) were franchised (Churchill, 1990). By 1994, there had been a stronger move towards franchising: of 550 outlets 95 (17.3 per cent) were franchised. The head of European operations for McDonald's, in an address to attendees at the Finnish annual franchising conference (14.2.95), said that the best results for the company came from franchised stores, not company-owned ones. Over its total global operations in 2004, about 70 per cent of McDonald's restaurants were franchised.

In contrast, virtually all of Subway's outlets are franchised: there was only one company-owned site in 2006, used as a 'testing facility'. At the beginning of 2003, KFC had 800 outlets in China of which only ten were franchised: the rest were fully or partially company-owned. Despite the high entry cost for franchisees, the company receives many applications. According to the head of KFC China, 'what we're doing now is planting the seeds, to start franchising with a lot of experiments' (McGregor, 2003, 14). The UK-based Body Shop has a majority of company-owned operations in the UK, Ireland and the Americas, whereas franchising is overwhelmingly used in the rest of Europe and the Asia–Pacific region.

There is a mix of explanations for this disparity, including the business and franchising 'climate' in the foreign market: for example, legal and financial; the ability of the company to finance expansion. Franchising is a low-cost method of expansion; the lower cost of franchising supports the goal of rapid expansion; owned operations are viewed as delivering higher returns (particularly in high traffic sites); and ownership delivers greater control but with greater risk. The Australian arm of the US-based Krispy Kreme doughnut chain (initially a joint venture but later bought out by the Australian partner) uses only company-owned outlets, in contrast to the US parent which uses a mix of franchised and company-owned outlets. Its justification is this: 'To be more effective, we have to own the stores so that we can control the product and run the company under one structure' (Ooi, 2005). The founder and owner of the Malaysian chain, England Optical, explained that his company's late switch into franchising in 1998 (it began operating in 1979) was due to the perception that franchising represented 'a way of expanding his business with minimal expense' (Jayasankaran, 2003, 36). Similarly, Jollibee, the fast-food chain based in the Philippines, has noted that 'the franchise strategy has kept Jollibee's overseas capital spending to less than 5 per cent of total costs' (Luce, 1996, 10). However, the perspective on this issue may vary depending on the organizational form employed in the foreign market: with joint ventures and the master franchising form there are effectively two perspectives, the entrant firm's and local partner's. The local partner's resource base and local knowledge may be decisive in the choices made.

INTERNATIONALIZATION VIA FRANCHISING

Figure 3.2 above demonstrates that the path to franchising in a foreign market may not be a simple one: it could be a significantly lagged step in foreign market penetration and is typically embedded in a more complex foreign operation mode package within each market. In the following section we will place franchising in the broader context of a company's internationalization, encompassing issues of domestic versus international operation, the process of international entry and development via franchising, reasons for franchising use versus other forms of foreign operation, foreign market choice, and franchising package adaptation in foreign markets.

In an overall sense, companies involved in international franchising generally have developed their franchising systems first within domestic markets before moving into international activity. This is not surprising given the demands of building and trialling the franchise system, and of making adjustments to market outcomes and the experience of appointing, training and managing dispersed franchisees. This process is handled more readily in a local environment where it is easier to maintain oversight and react quickly to emerging issues. The initial focus, therefore, tends to be strongly domestic, although it is interesting that, in Australian research, some franchisors indicated that they were interested in international possibilities from the outset of operations, revealing an ambition to become the 'McDonald's of' their field (Welch, 1990). However, research indicates that franchising companies on average spend less time in domestic operations before their first international move as compared to exporting companies.

INTERNATIONAL ENTRY: PROCESS AND INFLUENCES

As with exporting companies, franchisors' approach to international possibilities is heavily affected by their preceding domestic experience, including package development, and the type, success and extent of growth and expansion. Indeed, Australian research revealed a strong drive for growth and expansion among franchisors, with the potential to spill over into international interest – in a sense the ultimate seal of approval of entrepreneurial franchising endeavour (Welch, 1990). One Australian franchisor described the expansion ethos as follows: 'I had the fire in my belly and had to move quickly, I couldn't wait' (Bedpost – bedding retail chain). He later admitted that he had 'let too many franchises too quickly' (O'Hare, 1992). Widespread expansion is a confirmation, a validation of the original idea, but it has the practical effect of increasing the basis of income generation and becomes an important part of the sales message to potential new franchisees. Having a widespread network of franchised outlets, in diverse locations within a country, along with associated promotional activities, inevitably increases the likelihood of contact not just by locals, but also by interested foreigners. A New Zealand businessman became interested in the Australian pizza delivery chain, Dial-a-Dino's (see above), as a result of seeing one of its delivery vehicles with an outsized red telephone on top making a call. Long-standing research shows that inquiries or approaches by potential franchisees, frequently unsolicited, are one of the main factors (often overwhelmingly so) in

BOX 3.1   SUBWAY'S APPROACH TO FOREIGN MARKET
ENTRY

For the US-based international franchising chain, Subway, reliance on
foreign franchisee interest as a basis for international expansion is virtually enshrined in company policy. According to the company website
(accessed 13/5/06): 'How does the SUBWAY chain select new countries to
expand into? [answer] The SUBWAY chain does not select new countries
to expand into. In a way, they choose us. . . . If an individual approaches
the chain from a country where there are no SUBWAY restaurants, the
development team will work with that person to provide assistance in
opening their first SUBWAY restaurant.' Its initial foreign entry in 1986 was
typical of this pattern, and contrary to the more normal foreign market
expansion pattern it was in Bahrain! But that was not by design. The initial
interest came from an Italian who wanted to open a Subway outlet there.
Don Fertman, the director of franchise sales, commented: 'We had no idea
what we were going to do because we had never done any international
franchising before. So we said, well, let's bring him to headquarters and
have him stay here a really long time and learn everything he possibly can
about Subway and send him over there and let him get that first store open.
And he did . . . international investors tend to come to Subway as a result
of hearing about the company. We advertise in a number of international
publications like the international edition of the *Wall Street Journal*, the
International Herald Tribune, airline publications and in-flight programmes.
People hear about us that way or when they visit the United States or one
of the other 75 countries we are in. We give them all of the information we
can about Subway and say, "Look, you are from this country. We don't know
a whole lot about your country, but you do. Here's our concept. What do you
think? Do you think it will work?" And if they think it will we say, "Go ahead
and do it"' (Larson, 2004, 5). In an overall sense, though, over 70 per cent
of new franchises are purchased by existing franchisees.

franchisors stepping toward international involvement (Walker and Etzel,
1973; Hackett, 1976; Walker, 1989; Welch, 1990; McCosker and Walker,
1992; Frazer, Weaven and Wright, 2006). For example, in Walker's (1989)
study, 88 per cent of US franchisors had indicated that they 'recruited
[foreign] franchisees' via unsolicited inquiries.

Domestic expansion by franchisors appears to affect the potential to
internationalize in a number of ways. Perceived domestic limits to growth
emerged as a factor in international entry in both US and Australian
studies (Hackett, 1976; Welch, 1990). At the same time, when questioned
as to the reasons why companies had not moved internationally, studies
indicated that the focus on domestic expansion and the perception of
ample scope for domestic expansion were of prime importance (Aydin and

Kacker, 1990; McCosker and Walker, 1992; Walker, 1989). During domestic expansion franchisors are being exposed to a wider range of situations and contexts, and undergoing learning on a number of fronts: including coming to terms with managing franchising operations on a larger and more dispersed basis: what could be termed 'internationalization at home' (Welch and Wiedersheim-Paul, 1980). Franchising package refinements are made, training programmes introduced, site selection processes organized, promotional techniques expanded and franchisee selection techniques developed. Where successful, inevitably confidence builds and expansion horizons are raised. An Australian franchisor (photographic supplies retail chain) described to one of the authors how the idea to go to New Zealand arose: the top executive group were discussing the next expansion move within Australia, focused initially on a move across the country to Western Australia. Other major parts of the country had already been successfully penetrated. In the midst of the discussion, one of the team asked, 'Why not go to New Zealand?' Following on successful domestic expansion, this was viewed as a relatively small next step, effectively on a par with the move to Western Australia, and was actioned first. In the 2006 survey of Australian franchising, 45.6 per cent of franchisors with international operations indicated that domestic market success was a reason for international expansion – the third most important factor mentioned (Frazer, Weaven and Wright, 2006). As expressed by a number of franchisors in earlier Australian research, 'we have succeeded in a tough market like Australia, I can't see any reason why we should not succeed in other markets' (Welch, 1990).

Regardless of the array of potential influences pushing a franchisor toward international activity, as shown in Figure 3.3, their impact on whether action is taken, and the nature of that action, depend on how they are perceived by the key decision maker/s within the franchising company. Research indicates that the personal drive of the entrepreneur who starts the franchising business is often crucial in domestic expansion and the move into international operations. This is in line with research on export activity in the fields of internationalization and entrepreneurship, which stresses the dominant role of the key decision maker/s' background experience, interests and attitudes in driving companies into the international arena (Andersson, 2000; Welch, 2004). In a study of the internationalization of US franchisors it was concluded that 'the attitudes of a firm's managers, as opposed to the firm's individual characteristics, are stronger indicators of the firm's likelihood to franchise on an international basis' (Kedia et al., 1994, 65).

For a number of cases in Australian research, an important part of the formative process of franchisors was their business activity as franchisees

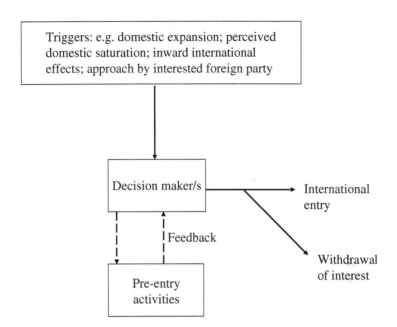

Figure 3.3 Influences on international entry

of international chains; that is, inward international franchising preceded outward activity. Not surprisingly, this affected the individuals' preparation for their ultimate outward move as franchisors. At a basic level they learned about franchising systems from experienced operators, but also they were introduced to the international potential of franchising concepts (Welch, 1990). Other preceding inward international activities were shown potentially to expose franchisors to international prospects; for example, foreign suppliers of equipment had urged some Australian franchisors to look at foreign markets for their systems. In three cases this was the principal stimulus to the attempt to set up internationally. In essence, this mirrors the findings in exporting research showing the importance of inward international activities, in many instances, to the start of outward steps (Korhonen et al., 1996). For the suppliers of equipment, there is a vested interest, possible increased international sales, in the franchisor achieving international success.

Once a franchisor becomes interested in international possibilities, the types of response have been shown to vary widely, from limited exploration of the prospects to substantial and committed effort to achieve international entry. In the case of Dial-a-Dino's (see above), having received the unsolicited approach by a New Zealand businessman, and responding positively, it was a matter of actioning the steps required to fulfil the arrangement agreed to. However, even in this seemingly straightforward example, there was much to be done before New Zealand entry was achieved. This is in contrast to the normally far simpler process for an exporter of responding to an unsolicited export order. In general, for franchisors, there are many decisions to be made and different types of action to be undertaken before foreign market entry:

- What organizational form should be used in the foreign market, or is direct franchising appropriate? Establishment of a foreign subsidiary may be a costly and demanding first step, taking a considerable period of time to put into effect.
- Even if there is an approach by an interested foreign party, negotiations on the precise form of the arrangement will be necessary, with various legal steps required, communication with relevant parties and the preparation of legal documents.
- If not already undertaken, intellectual property protection in the foreign market is essential. In Australian research, cases were found of franchisors allowing their New Zealand franchisees to register the company's trademark, effectively handing over ownership of a key element of the franchising system (Welch, 1990).
- What to include in the franchising package? At the outset this may be a demanding issue for the franchisor: for example, should the package be altered in some way to take account of cultural and other differences?
- With or without an unsolicited approach by an interested foreign party, the franchisor may want to cast a wide search net, seeking the most appropriate partner to handle the franchise system.
- Foreign market research and testing and modification of package components normally will be required.
- Use of consultants in planning various steps involved in foreign entry.
- Evaluation of sources of supply within the foreign market.

These steps, individually and collectively, may take a considerable period of time to carry through, and there is no certainty about outcomes. Negotiations could turn sour or foreign market research might reveal unattractive prospects: whatever the preceding reasons for interest in international franchising, feedback from the various pre-entry actions represents an important new input into the decision-making situation, as illustrated in Figure 3.3. In Australian research, there was wide variation in the time taken to achieve international entry once the attempt to do so had begun. In some cases, deals were settled within six months of a foreign approach.

At the other extreme, one company had taken a number of steps, including foreign market investigations and the purchase of land in one target market, over a period of ten years without making a final commitment to international operations (Welch, 1990). In fact, the company, Bob Jane T Marts (tyre retailing), re-focused on the domestic market with new expansion plans for rural areas and other smaller urban centres. For franchisors, the initial exposure of foreign market prospects, particularly via an unsolicited approach, is hard to resist. Many speak of the way in which they responded, quickly and positively, to the international openings. For instance, Anita Roddick, co-creator of the Body Shop chain, has commented: 'For the first couple of years we more or less opened wherever anyone asked if they could open a shop. I don't think we said no to anybody, though now we have to say no to nearly everybody.' Later caution and care in foreign market activity is typical. A rapid response to an unsolicited approach does hold the risk of making an inappropriate choice of partner – of effectively having the decision made for the franchisor. There are dangers on the other side, of course, of being cautious and taking a long time to effect foreign entry:

- Competitors may arise. A unique concept could be copied and the foreign market pre-empted by a competitor – local or foreign.
- If a potential foreign partner's approach is rejected or held off, that party may simply seek an alternative partner – again, locally or in another foreign market.
- Over time, domestic market issues may come to re-occupy attention to the detriment of the foreign options.

OTHER PATHS TO INTERNATIONAL FRANCHISING

While the domestic to international franchising path is undoubtedly the dominant one, many examples exist of different paths, and domestic franchising may not necessarily provide the formative base. For example, Scandinavian Health Systems (producer of equipment and software for health studios) started in Norway in 1986, supplying the local market. In 1990, it made its first move into franchising in Sweden, not Norway. It was used as a test market for the development of the franchising system, including experimentation and package development (Framnes and Welch, 1992). Of course, these countries are physically (common border) and culturally close.

Early Australian research exposed a small number of cases where companies had extended existing international retailing operations (owned) by adding franchised units without the benefit of domestic franchising (Welch, 1990). The Swiss shoe manufacturer, Bally, had set up manufacturing facilities in the UK, sold to independent retailers and established a small number of its own shops before turning to franchising. Apparently, an important factor in this switch was the input of new management staff with franchising experience (Dnes, 1992). After acquiring the Italian retail chain, Fersina, the French company, Elf Atochem, converted five of the 32 retail stores to a franchising basis (Baroncelli and Manaresi, 1997). Clearly, franchising is not the path to international entry in these cases; playing an extension role, or representing a new stage in the development of international strategy, is preferable. In Bally's case there was a concern to reduce their reliance on independent retailers, but general concerns in the different examples revolved around the desire to accelerate foreign market expansion while minimizing the capital demands of doing so.

A study of the paths to international franchising in the Danish clothing and footwear industries revealed an array of diverse and sometimes complex patterns of evolution (Petersen and Welch, 2000). This included non-franchising domestic sales, exporting, foreign contract manufacturing, upstream and downstream foreign direct investments, and international retailing via company-owned outlets before international franchising. For two of the companies analysed in detail, Carli Gry and InWear, business format franchising was added to existing international retail operations, and was 'now seen as the way to grow' and as 'low risk and low investment' (Petersen and Welch, 2000, 493). However, the move could not be seen as transformational. The companies stressed the importance of the preceding retailing activity in building a base of systems (such as information technology) and foreign market experience and knowledge. Franchising, as a way of operating, was not viewed as difficult to learn. The foreign subsidiaries that had already been established provided the organizational base for setting up and managing franchisees; in the main, they were responsible for the local choice between company-owned or franchised outlets. While making the move into franchising, it was not a case of wholesale adoption. In the end, the step into international franchising was not a large one, compared to companies using it as a starting point of international activity. It was relatively incremental, and was viewed as such: it was only one part of a much larger set of international operations. It is of note, however, that in the order of international business operation development, business format franchising, what could be considered a low commitment mode, was used after high-commitment direct investments, at the end of process, contrary to the 'normal' pattern (Petersen and Welch, 2000). In contrast, franchising appears to have been far more important for the retail side of the clothing sector in France, and companies have used this

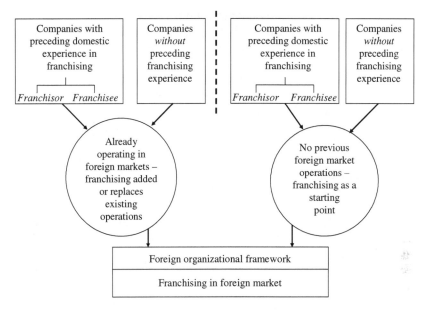

Source: Adapted from Welch (1989, p. 388).

Figure 3.4 Potential paths to foreign franchising

experience in the development of international franchising activities, along more traditional lines (Lewis, 1993).

The Danish examples demonstrate that the difference in paths to international franchising may well breed quite different perspectives on its demands, on how it is used and its role in international development. As Figure 3.4 illustrates, there is a wide range of types of experience preceding the move into international franchising. Combined with the different organizational forms noted in Figure 3.2 above, it is clear that international franchising is far from being a simple, unitary form of international operations (except with direct franchising), making comparison to other modes and their international paths difficult, contrary to the way it is often presented in the international business literature.

GLOBAL PATTERNS OF FRANCHISING TAKE-UP

As noted earlier, so-called 'first generation' franchising has a long history, but expanded worldwide rapidly during the late 19th and early 20th centuries. The more influential form of business format franchising has been a post-World War II phenomenon, with its genesis in the US. By the early 1990s, business format franchising for US companies was growing ten times faster than product and tradename franchising (Hoffman and Preble, 1993). While much of the franchising focus has been on the major fast food chains (US-based initially) that have grown so rapidly and expanded so widely, and noticeably, the global penetration of mainly business format franchising has been distinguished by its extent in terms of the range of countries but also by the range of industries and the size of businesses it has engendered (see, for example Hoffman and Preble, 1993). Throughout the growth process there has been a continual pushing out of the boundaries of areas where business format franchising has been used, involving all business sectors. It is difficult now to find an area where business format franchising has not been tried. Bendigo Bank in Australia has made extensive use of franchising, especially in rural areas, while examples have begun to appear even in the university sector. The spread of franchising has reached the stage where it is in important part of economic activity and employment in many countries. In Australia, the franchising sector has been estimated to contribute about 12 per cent of GDP (based on Frazer and Weaven, 2004). In a US study, franchised businesses were estimated to generate an economic impact equivalent to almost 10 per cent of private sector GDP and an even higher proportion of employment (International Franchise Association, 2004). Overall, the rapid move to prominence of franchising in international business activity says a great deal about the underlying rationale of the business method and its expansion ethos.

While US franchisors were undoubtedly the drivers of early global growth, the picture has become very much more dispersed now. US companies initially concentrated on high-income countries with well developed retail and service sectors. Cultural similarity was also a factor, except for Japan, although entry arrangements there were such as to leave development and management substantially in the hands of Japanese companies via master franchise and joint venture deals. In 1985, almost 70 per cent of the foreign outlets of US franchisors were located in just four countries: Canada, Australia, the UK and Japan (Welch, 1989). Even at that time, though, US franchisors were widening the spread of countries entered. In the 1990s, there was acceleration in this process, with Asian and European (non-UK) countries becoming particularly important. Notable too was the wider dispersion of operations by culture and income level of recipient country, as shown in Figure 3.5. For example, by 2006, McDonald's had spread to 119 countries with more than 30 000 restaurants (company website, 13/5/06). Subway had penetrated 84 countries by 2006, with 25 728 outlets (company website, 13/5/06). Figure 3.5 attempts to depict a general

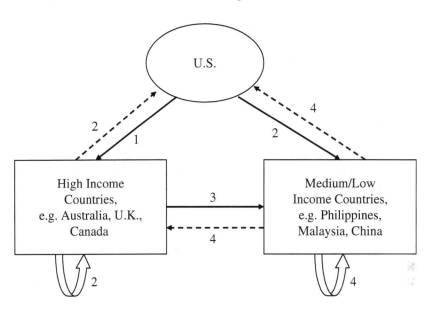

1–4: broad order of movement

Figure 3.5   Pattern of global franchising spread

order of franchising spread in the global arena: it should be stressed that there are individual examples that do not fit the general pattern; for example, Jollibee started in the Philippines in the 1970s, and was an early participant in franchising's global spread.

In high-income countries where US franchisors built operations it was not long before local copies of the US concepts began to emerge, with adaptations for the local market context, and for innovative local concepts to be developed, employing business format franchising along the lines of the US models, for example Body Shop in the UK and Dial-a-Dino's in Australia. Their growth soon spilled over into international operations, and the US market was an obvious target country of early interest for many non-US franchisors. Thus the reverse pattern of franchising into the US began in earnest quite early. As with US franchisors, geographical proximity and cultural similarity seemed to be important in early patterns of international spread, such as New Zealand for Australian franchisors, and Sweden and Denmark for Norwegian franchisors (Framnes and Welch, 1992; Welch, 1990). Added to this more diverse mix of international franchisors were those from less advanced countries, as illustrated in Figure 3.5. Again, there have been many examples of local companies quickly following entrant foreign firms into franchising, even preceding them in some cases, and then turning to the international arena.

Malaysia's Marrybrown Family Restaurant (fried chicken) began operations in 1981 and by 2004 had more than 100 outlets in Malaysia, China, India, Sri Lanka and the Middle East (Hookway, 2003, company website 28/9/04). Another Malaysian chain, England Optical, had over 120 outlets in Malaysia in 2004, with operations in Cambodia and China (called E-Optics) (Jayasankaran, 2003, company website 28/9/04). A new doughnut chain in the Philippines, called Go Nuts Donuts, began operating in December 2003 with its operation and products deliberately modelled on the US chain Krispy Kreme, rather than other imported versions (such as Dunkin Donuts). This is despite the fact that Krispy Kreme had not yet entered the Philippines: nevertheless, it was well known as a result of visits to the US by many residents of the Philippines. The rapid success of Go Nuts Donuts has already led to a number of inquiries about foreign franchising possibilities (Winn, 2004).

In China, an early response to entry by the major franchising chains came in the form of the establishment of a duck restaurant chain, Quan Ju De. Although having operated at a prime Beijing site since 1864, it decided to establish a chain of restaurants in 1994, based on franchising principles 'inspired' by new competitors like McDonald's (Huus, 1996). Perhaps the most surprising aspect of the chain's development was the speed of its international entry: already in 1994 it set up restaurants in Houston, Los Angeles and Guam, on a joint venture basis. Its franchising activities have struggled since the early expansion. 'Of the 50 restaurants that bear the Quan Ju De name in China, 41 are franchise businesses over which the Beijing-based Quan Ju De has little control. Several others are copycat operations that imitate the Quan Ju De logo to attract customers . . . Quan Ju De has successfully sued one imposter, forcing it to close down' (Young, 2004, 2). As a result of its experiences it intends to open only company-owned restaurants. As these examples illustrate, local franchisors and their international activity have burgeoned in countries as diverse as the Philippines, Malaysia and China, pointing to a future pattern of dense global use and inter-country flows of business format franchising. Particularly with retail franchising, the visibility and openness of operations, combined with the increased global movement of people, have increased the likelihood of early foreign reaction to innovation in franchising concepts in whatever country they arise.

The use of franchising concepts seems to have become less constrained by national boundaries, what might be considered a new level of globalization, judging by some of the examples which have emerged in different countries. One successful Australian ice cream and frozen yoghurt chain, with operations in New Zealand, in many Asian locations and in the UK (over 80 foreign outlets in 2004), is called New Zealand Natural. Its logo, promotional images and the livery of its stores give every indication of a New Zealand base, trading on the idea of that country's natural and healthy image. Another Australian ice cream chain is Royal Copenhagen Ice Cream: it uses the colours of the Danish flag in its logo and store presentation and refers to its ice cream as Danish ice cream, projecting a strong Danish image. The US-based Outback Steakhouse chain of restaurants, with operations in 21 countries in 2004 (mainly company-owned rather than franchised), uses a strong Australian theme in menus, store layout, and so on.

INFLUENCES ON FRANCHISING TAKE-UP

The analysis so far has stressed some of the forces encouraging, and paths that have been used by, companies in employing franchising as a form of international operations, at the individual and company level. However, there have been broader forces at work which have stimulated interest in franchising at micro levels; in part it has been a case of success feeding on itself. There has been a rising global tide of interest in, and publicity about, franchising, as reflected in the many examples referred to in the business press and media in general. McDonald's was probably the earliest and strongest example of this, even leading to the regular use of the 'Big Mac Index' of purchasing power parity of exchange rates by the international news magazine the *Economist*. When the company opened its first outlet in Moscow in 1990, the event was covered in a blaze of global media coverage. Such processes helped to create worldwide interest in the franchising method on the part of both potential franchisors and franchisees. This was occurring at the same time as many economies were moving out of socialist frameworks, such as in Eastern Europe, providing a more amenable environment for the move into franchising systems. More recently, China has moved from a relative hostile position on franchising to one which is now supportive, and enacted regulations to remove major restrictions. By the mid-1990s, various Chinese government authorities were supporting the staging of international franchise exhibitions.

Governments generally have played a part in supporting the global development of franchising in a variety of ways, including assistance to outward internationalization by local chains. As an illustration, 'Singapore's Local Enterprise Technical Assistance Scheme has facilitated the creation of more than 200 franchises . . . while the country's International Franchise Enterprise Program has been instrumental in assisting more than 100 franchise companies to export their systems' (Paynter and Everett, 2003, 1).

The Malaysian government's Ministry of Entrepreneur Development has actively promoted the development of home-grown franchising businesses: by 2003 there were more than 300 local franchise businesses in Malaysia (Aziz, 1996; Hookway, 2003; Jayasankaran, 2003). However, the impact of governments has probably been more important where it has acted to create a more amenable environment for franchising to function.

An important reason for the growth of franchising use globally has been the growing pool of potential franchisees attracted by the characteristics of this business method: that is, providing independence for the franchisee but within an established and supported business system. During the 1990s many executives receiving 'golden handshakes' and, seeking to start their own businesses, were adding to this pool of potential franchisees, and were in a strong position to finance a move into franchising (Stirling, 1991). Another important group within the franchisee pool that emerged in the 1980s was the trading companies. Looking to expand business beyond what was often low-margin trade in commodities they began to consider opportunities in the service sector, and franchising was seen as one possible route into this area by bringing well-established systems into foreign markets where they were already operating, or into their home market. For example, Japanese trading companies were involved in this process, and were responsible for a number of foreign franchise systems being brought to Japan. For instance, Mitsui set up a service business division in 1986, acquired the rights to the US-based El Pollo Loco chain in 1987 and opened the first restaurant in Japan in 1988 (*Focus Japan*, 1989). Similarly, Jardine Matheson, the Hong Kong-based trading company, acquired franchise rights to Pizza Hut, Sizzler restaurants and 7-Eleven in various parts of the Asia–Pacific in the 1980s and early 1990s.

While the activities and promotion by international franchising chains in diverse markets has been partly responsible for the growth of interest in franchising and the growing global pool of potential franchisees, the growing number of franchisees also contributes to the development of future franchisors. Franchisees are trained in the use of a franchising system, working with an international chain, and the knowledge and perspective gained are sometimes applied by franchisees in the creation of their own systems, ultimately moving into the international arena themselves in some cases. The Australian franchising chain, Wendys Supa Sundaes, was established in the 1980s by two partners who had been franchisees of an international chain for five years before starting the Wendys Supa Sundaes operation. At the time of start-up of the first Wendys Supa Sundaes outlets they were still running three Wimpy's hamburger restaurants (Welch, 1989). Despite problems with the name (similarity to Wendy's, the US hamburger restaurant chain) the company began international operations in

New Zealand in 1989 under the Wendys Supa Sundaes name, which many New Zealanders would have been familiar with as a result of visits to Australia. A variant of this step is when the franchisee acquires the franchisor, and automatically internationalizes, as in the case of the takeover of the US owner of the 7-Eleven international chain by its Japanese franchise owner. In another example, the Australian operator of Gloria Jean's Coffees acquired the international rights and operations (but not US) of its US-based franchisor in 2005, obtaining master franchises in 14 countries immediately from the deal, which it has since extended (Walker, 2006).

Much of the growth of business format franchising in diverse markets over the last three decades has been driven by the development of local chains in response to the entry of high-profile foreign chains. For example, in terms of number of franchisors, local chains dominate the franchising scene in Australia and New Zealand, constituting 82 per cent in New Zealand and 93 per cent in Australia (Frazer, Weaven and Wright, 2006; Paynter and Everett, 2003). The New Zealand situation is quite instructive: one might expect greater foreign impact in such a small market, particularly given its proximity to Australia. It is indicative of the ability of local businesses to learn and apply franchising techniques quickly, and adapt them to the local context. From a start in 1987, the South African restaurant chain, Nando's, with its distinctive spicy flame-grilled chicken, has expanded to a diverse mix of countries, including Sri Lanka and the UK, using company-owned and franchised outlets (see company website). The success of Jollibee, a local fast food chain in the Philippines, in outcompeting McDonald's, and of achieving significant international penetration, is illustrative of the way in which this is happening in developing countries as well, not just the high-income countries (Luce, 1996; Winn, 2004). Jollibee also demonstrates that a local response may occur even before the well-known chain begins operating in a particular market: by the time McDonald's entered the Philippines in 1981, Jollibee had already established 11 outlets.

The development of such local chains has provided the option for internationalizing franchisors of accelerating international growth even further by acquiring and converting already established local chains. For example, McDonald's had been slow in penetrating the Italian market (only 26 outlets) so in 1996 it undertook its largest acquisition to that time of the 80 outlet Burghy fast food restaurant chain (Hill and Tomkins, 1996). The takeover not only removed a major competitor (Burghy had assiduously copied McDonald's in its operations and achieved considerable success) but McDonald's saved itself the often lengthy and difficult task of obtaining planning approval for the opening of new restaurant sites, particularly in historic centres. Both Burger King and the Belgian fast food chain,

Quick, had also been involved in bidding for Burghy. Similarly, Pizza Hut in 1989 acquired the Australian pizza delivery chain, Dial-a-Dino's, which had expanded rapidly during the 1980s via franchising to the point where it was the market leader in delivery pizza (110 outlets in 1989), and had operations in three countries: New Zealand, Japan and the UK. Through acquisition, Pizza Hut accelerated its Australian expansion (they were geographically complementary), removed its major competitor and ensured market leadership. In 2000, Pizza Hut bought the New Zealand franchised operations of Eagle Boys Dial-a-Pizza (58 outlets and market leader) from its Australian-based owner. In both cases, the outlets were fully converted to Pizza Hut operations.

The growth of franchising also brought on board a range of support service firms over time, such as banks and consulting firms, that further facilitated growth. For example, many banks added specialist franchise lending units. As franchisors' activities developed, there was greater publicity and media attention on franchising, especially when McDonald's started in a new country, which fed further interest in it as a business concept. In addition, the increasing global movement of people, for business, tourism, migration or family reunion, has been a factor in moving franchising concepts and systems between countries, and at a faster rate. The various contributors to global franchising growth noted above are summarized in Figure 3.6.

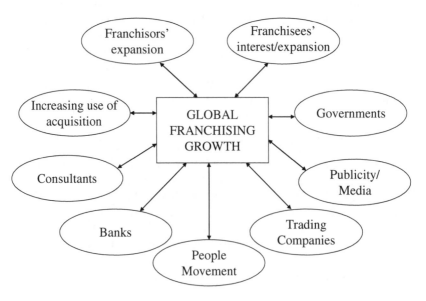

Figure 3.6   Contributors to global growth of franchising

FRANCHISEE PERSPECTIVES

As noted already, the receptive global environment of potential franchisees explains much of the growth and spread of franchising, and the ability of franchisors to use franchising as a means of international business development. Such receptivity does not appear to differentiate clearly between local and foreign-based origins, although the ability of the well-known and publicized international chains, such as McDonald's and Subway, to generate a steady stream of applicants is indicative of differentiation between well-known and less well-known concepts. The importance of unsolicited approaches by potential foreign franchisees in triggering international activity by franchisors is suggestive of the advantages of the chains with significant international spread in generating local or foreign franchisee interest, especially given the increased international movement of people. Nevertheless, as noted earlier, many local chains have succeeded in the face of strong international competition, such as Jollibee in the Philippines and Dial-a-Dino's in Australia (before takeover), so that the international connection of itself does not seem to be a decisive factor in franchisee choice of franchisor.

In addition, beyond the well-known international chains, other foreign chains may be far less familiar to potential franchisees than local equivalents. The experience of the US chain, Tippy's Taco House, is instructive: in the late 1980s, it sought to enter the UK market via a master franchising arrangement. After about two and a half years of trying it was still without a partner interested enough to pay the up-front fee to secure the UK rights. The Texas (US) operation had franchised just 25 restaurants at the time, of which only 16 had been opened. The leading video rental chain in the US at the time, West Coast Video, also struggled to sell franchises in the UK, so it switched back to a company-owned emphasis in order to kick-start its UK operations (AP-Dow Jones, 1988).

Various studies reveal a relatively consistent set of main reasons, or perceived characteristics, stressed by franchisees as to why they apply to become franchisees, to local or international chains, and remain with a chosen franchise operation (for example, McCosker, 1990; Peterson and Dant, 1990; Withane, 1991): (a) proven business format, (b) established name (goodwill), (c) support of the franchisor (quick start-up), (d) cooperative marketing, (e) initial/ongoing training, and (f) independence.

In McCosker's study, franchisees were asked reasons for taking up a franchise in the first place, as well as current perceived advantages of franchising. The main difference was for 'known name/ready made business' which rose in importance from 53 per cent at the outset to 91 per cent after operations had been proceeding; 'support of the franchisor' increased from 28 per cent to 50 per cent; and, somewhat surprisingly, 'independence' did not register at all with franchisees initially but was stressed by 41 per cent based on experience. The frequently publicized feature of a lower failure rate for franchised businesses, as against small businesses in general, was not mentioned in these studies, but is often stressed in franchising promotion, seminars and the like. A number of studies provide confirmation of the lower failure rate, although there is some variation in outcomes (Luostarinen and Welch, 1990; Frazer and Weaven, 2004).

The advantage of being an independent small firm as a franchisee, yet being linked to the size and scale advantages of a large chain, such as in purchasing inputs and promotion, also failed to be mentioned specifically, but is often referred to in franchising publications and forums, and may well have been subsumed in the broad factor 'franchisor support'. In regard to 'franchisor support', an advantage of large international chains is the ability to tap into a wide range of knowledge and solutions, arrived at in different cultures, in servicing individual franchisees in diverse locations. McDonald's often stresses the value to the company of the contribution of ideas by franchisees in their system on many aspects of its operation, including new product concepts. The large international chain would seem to offer a telling combination of well-known international brand name, marketing and operational expertise from other markets, with national advertising in the host market, providing instant visibility and goodwill for a potential franchisee. It seemingly solves a major concern for a start-up firm: how to get started and achieve market impact. Of course, the international name of a franchisor does not guarantee success in individual foreign markets: the large US-based Wendy's hamburger chain failed in both the UK and Australia in the 1980s and withdrew from both markets, although returning to the UK in the early 1990s.

An additional factor, financing support of the franchisee, has become more important in a widening range of countries. This support has come in the form of external institutions (such as banks) increasingly targeting franchising, as well as some franchisors stepping into this role. In the 2006 survey of Australian franchisors, 22 per cent indicated that they provided financing to franchisees if required – either directly or via third parties (Frazer, Weaven and Wright, 2006). Research (for example, Peterson and Dant, 1990) has also shown that franchisees are sometimes prepared for the role through previous employment with a franchisee or franchisor. One Australian franchisor, Bob Jane T Marts, even had it as a deliberate policy, encouraging future franchisees and their training through managerial roles within the operation.

BOX 3.2   WHY FRANCHISING? THE PERSPECTIVE OF ONE
FRANCHISEE

Individuals from diverse backgrounds are attracted to the idea of taking up
a franchised business. Their interest continues to sustain the growth of
franchising. What sparks that interest? An indication is given by the experience of one franchisee of the Australian chain Wendys Supa Sundaes
(soft serve ice cream and other fast food items). It is instructive that the
person concerned, Ken Love, before taking up the franchise, had been the
manager of the Franchise Services section of Westpac, one of the four
large banks that dominate the banking sector in Australia. In that position
he had an ideal opportunity to observe the performance of various franchising operations in Australia. He was 'responsible for deciding whether
the bank would provide finance for franchised businesses' (Stirling, 1991,
70). On the basis of that experience, he concluded: 'in general, franchise
loans are far less risky than independent ones, citing as evidence the fact
that not one bad debt [related to franchising loans] had been written off in
the past five years at Westpac' (ibid.). Perhaps even more telling was the
fact that, after 23 years in the banking business, he was prepared to resign
and strike out on his own as a franchisee, and was followed soon after-
wards by his deputy in the bank, who also joined Wendys as a franchisee.
Love commented that 'franchising was appealing because of the reduced
element of risk' (ibid.).

FRANCHISOR PERSPECTIVES

In preceding sections, aspects of the reasoning and process that explain the
extensive use of this method of operating in widespread global markets
have been referred to, particularly in terms of initial international activity
via franchising, and links to other modes. In the following section, we
examine reasons given by companies as to why they have been using franchising in international operations, how this has been accomplished and
issues in its implementation (foreign market selection; package adaptation;
legal issues and so on).

In summary, reasons for the use of international franchising, initially or
subsequently, include the following:

- domestic use and related expansion processes, which may involve preceding experience as a franchisee of an international chain, or lead
  to perceived domestic saturation;
- approach by interested foreign party, often unsolicited;
- foreign supplier of inputs encourages international expansion;

- strong interest in international activity by entrepreneur/founder, manager;
- franchising as a way of expanding rapidly or accelerating expansion;
- lower capital demands of international expansion via franchising, capitalizing on the franchisee's financial contribution;
- demonstration effect of highly publicized inward and outward international movement of franchising chains;
- means of tapping into the motivation and local knowledge of franchisees.

In explaining why it has used franchising as its method of achieving international expansion, Benetton has emphasized four main contributory factors: captive distribution network – sell only Benetton goods; no financial commitment – franchisees arrange all their own finance; hastens expansion; and removes the need to oversee day-to-day performance (Bruce and Reed, 1987).

Taken at face value, franchising would seem to be the ideal solution to the question of how to achieve internationalization, using franchisees to shoulder much of the burden and risk of the process. However, it is perhaps not surprising that there have been many cases of franchisee failure, disaffection and legal action against Benetton, especially in the US.

Early US research stressed the importance of franchisee motivation as a factor in the use of franchising by companies in the domestic context, although clearly the factor has similar relevance in the international context (Luostarinen and Welch, 1990). In a sense, through franchising a company is 'buying' motivation, which has been deemed to be more effective – a franchisee owning an independent business – than operating with company-owned outlets and with company-based employees. At an international level, a franchising chain offers the prospect of tying an independent local operator with a well developed franchise package, of combining the benefits of skill, knowledge and product/service development centralization, of inputs from diverse locations and contexts, with operational decentralization. Seemingly, the best of both worlds in international management is achieved.

The low cost and rapid expansion benefits of franchising in foreign markets are consistently and strongly stressed by franchisors, perhaps even more so than in the domestic context given the additional costs of international operations. These benefits are further facilitated when master franchising or joint venture paths are employed, minimizing set-up and on-going costs, as only one party in the foreign market may have to be dealt with, and this partner is responsible for the franchising roll-out in the foreign market. This has facilitated the ability of many franchisors to achieve rapid entry and penetration in a multitude of foreign markets in a relatively short period of time compared to other methods of operation.

Subway and Benetton are illustrative of the rapid international growth and expansion potential of franchising, the latter having reached into markets as diverse as Cuba and Syria, with operations in 120 countries in 2004 (see company website). An Australian franchisor, Cartridge World, a printer cartridge refilling chain, made its first international move in 2000. By 2006, it had expanded to 23 countries, with 1189 outlets through an emphasis on master franchising.

The expansion potential of franchising has been further facilitated by the practice in some cases of so-called 'piggybacking'; that is, setting up within or attached to an outlet of another operation. An example is the placement of an ice cream outlet within an existing fast food restaurant. In 2004, Dunkin' Donuts announced an agreement with Wal-Mart to set up outlets within Wal-Mart stores in the US, some of which would be in combination with Baskin-Robbins ice cream facilities. Many franchises of clothing chains, such as Stefanel in Europe, have been set up within department stores. When such activity is linked to an existing chain which has multiple locations in a country, it may allow widespread establishment, at much lower cost, in a very short time. Clearly, the choice of franchised versus company-owned outlets will have a major impact on the international growth and expansion potential of a company, and its affordability. Likewise, as noted earlier, acquisition of an existing chain within another country enables extremely rapid expansion, but it may come at a high cost, particularly when a bidding war is involved, as in the case of the acquisition of the Italian Burghy chain by McDonald's (Hill and Tomkins, 1996). Overall, the rise to prominence of business format franchising use in international business in such a short period of time is a testament to the power of the method in stimulating growth and expansion.

IMPLEMENTATION ISSUES

Rapid growth, of course, does provide its own set of problems, particularly implementation and control issues. There is an inevitable concern about the control of franchisee activities beyond the initial flush of elation when local, and then foreign, franchisees take up a company's franchise system. The strength of the franchising concept, tapping into the motivation and the self-interest of the independent businessperson, also provides a continuing potential source of tension. With a relatively standardized franchise package, and through training and contractually stipulated guidelines, franchisors typically try to ensure that franchisees, though notionally independent, conform consistently to the template laid down for them. Consistency of store layout, presentation, service, and quality and range of products are seen as critical to the customer appeal of the chain, and its marketing approach. The operations manual that a franchisee is expected to conform to is a key part of the effort to generate consistency among franchisees. In the end, though, the franchisor depends on franchisee commitment and performance in ensuring ultimate success of the venture.

A frequently quoted example of the problems flowing from poor control is the former Wimpy hamburger chain in the UK: in the 1970s, poor service and quality problems in a number of the outlets eventually threatened the viability of the whole chain (*Economist*, 1985). The problem for franchisors is that inadequate performance at one outlet tends to produce a judgment by customers about the chain as a whole. Product quality problems were also a major problem at Wimpy's Finnish operation, causing it to withdraw from that market (Luostarinen and Welch, 1990). In a study of US international franchisors, Walker (1989) found that respondents rated the maintenance of adequate control as the biggest challenge in international expansion. McDonald's has been known to take a strong line on this issue, as exemplified in its treatment of an early Parisian franchisee: '[the Parisian franchisee] put bernaise sauce in the Big Macs, hid straws and napkins under the counter and let his restaurants degenerate to a filthy condition, resisting McDonald's request that he step into line. When the matter eventually arrived in court the franchisee claimed that his behaviour was appropriate to the local market, the French being "dirty" people. However, the court, whilst possibly amused by such claims, recognized McDonald's entitlement to terminate his franchise to protect its goodwill' (Connors, 1984, 32–3). 'Dunkin' Donuts chose to terminate its contract with Russian franchisees that were selling vodka and meat patties in contravention of their contracts' (Alon and Banai, 2000, 106).

Control problems may be such as to cause franchising companies to question the appropriateness of the franchising strategy, at least in problem markets, leading to a stronger emphasis on company-owned operations instead. For example, Tie Rack, a UK-based international retail chain, in the early 1990s had problems with some of its franchisees (standards of operation and payments), and eventually terminated their franchises. The head of the company later commented about franchising that 'when it works it works very well because you have a highly motivated group . . . [Tie Rack] could not always control its franchisees and now prefers to open new stores in the UK under its own management' (Gourlay, 1994, 13).

FRANCHISOR–FRANCHISEE RELATIONSHIPS

While franchisees may be highly motivated and enthusiastic at the outset, especially after a sustained period of training, there is an inevitable waning of this enthusiasm as the practical realities of developing the franchised business are faced over the medium to long term. At the same time there is an inevitable questioning of the benefits of the franchise connection as often monthly royalty payments are made. A life cycle analogy has been used to describe the pattern of the franchisor–franchisee relationship over time: moving from dependence (of the franchisee) through growth to adolescence, rebellion and finally resolution, characterized by compromise or a severing of the relationship (Justis and Judd, 1989). Franchisors often refer to the quality of the franchisor–franchisee relationship as a key variable in success and sometimes refer to it as 'like a marriage'. While the importance of the initial selection process is often stressed, the need for the franchisor to continually demonstrate benefits from the franchise connection, such as new products, promotions, transfer of new techniques and continued interaction, is seen as vital to positive relationship maintenance and effective franchisee performance. When disaffected franchisees respond by taking legal action against the franchisor, as many have done against Benetton, they have the capacity to do considerable damage to the chain as a whole in a given country and far beyond, in a world where publicized cases are often readily globalized through global media connections or via the Internet.

FRANCHISEE SELECTION

Given the criticality of franchisee performance for the success of franchising ventures, the choice of franchisee emerges as one of the key decisions made by the franchisor or its foreign partner. On the one hand, research shows that many franchising deals in the international arena are triggered by unsolicited approaches (see above; for example, Walker, 1989). On the other hand, although franchisors often admit that early franchisee choices tended to be hasty responses to approaches by interested parties, typically they become more careful and systematic over time, forcing franchisees to undergo significant tests and training before being offered a franchise. In part this process is a way of trying to ensure that appropriate and committed franchisees are selected in the first place, thereby minimizing the extent of problems in long-term franchisor–franchisee relationships. In the 2004 survey of Australian franchising, companies were asked how they recruited their international franchisees. In order of importance, the responses were (multiple responses allowed):

- 'Advertised in overseas country (38.6 per cent)
- Responded to request from potential franchisee (34.1 per cent)
- Used an agent to recruit (20.5 per cent)
- Enquiry from exhibition/trade shows overseas (18.2 per cent)
- Enquiry from exhibition/trade shows in Australia (11.4 per cent)'
  (Frazer and Weaven, 2004, 52).

MARKET SELECTION

Various studies of patterns of market spread in international franchising reveal a strong impact of cultural or psychic distance factors, particularly in the earlier stages of internationalization, not unlike that found for exporting companies (Welch, 1990). Companies clearly find foreign market penetration easier and faster to accomplish in locations that are familiar (legal systems, business practices and so on) and geographically close, for example when moving from the US to Canada, or from Norway to Sweden or Denmark. For Australian franchisors, as expected, New Zealand has remained by far the most important host country. While earlier surveys revealed the UK and US as important, the most recent survey shows they have been joined by a number of Asian countries (Singapore, Malaysia, Hong Kong, and even China), indicating a reduction of the general impact of psychic distance over time (Frazer, Weaven and Wright, 2006; McCosker and Walker, 1992; Welch, 1990). Nevertheless, similarity to the Australian market was cited as the main factor in choice of foreign market by Australian franchisors in 2006 (Frazer, Weaven and Wright, 2006). New Zealand franchisors, at an earlier stage of internationalization, have concentrated on Australia, then the US, Canada and the UK, with little involvement in Asia (Paynter and Everett, 2003). Of course, the global spread of franchising has created a more positive environment for franchising in culturally and economically diverse markets, facilitating cross-cultural expansion. The move to a more supportive environment in China is illustrative of this development. The general growth of franchising has created a more 'franchising-literate' business community (including banks), with a range of facilitating institutions, such as franchisors' associations, and with government assistance in different forms in many countries.

PACKAGE AND MARKETING ADAPTATION

International operations expose another basic tension in the use of franchising: while there are strong reasons for maintaining a standardized

franchise package and associated marketing, market differences inevitably call for a variety of modifications in order to better fit target market
circumstances. Empirical research confirms the reluctance of franchisors
to make any substantial modifications (Hackett, 1976; McCosker and
Walker, 1992; Walker, 1989). For example, Walker (1989) found that
about two-thirds of US international franchisors surveyed made no
adjustment in their marketing strategies for foreign markets. For those
that did, this was almost evenly spread between modifications of promotion, product offering and pricing. Only six companies had altered their
company or brand name in foreign markets. Kentucky Fried Chicken (as
it was) changed its name to Sanders in Brazil because of the difficulties in
pronunciation experienced by the Brazilians (Luostarinen and Welch,
1990). In the early 1980s, Taco Bell, the large US-based, Mexican-ori-
ented restaurant chain, entered Australia under the brand Taco Amigo
because the Taco Bell brand was already in use by an Australian company.
The venture failed, for a variety of reasons, but Taco Bell returned under
its own name in the 1990s when the Australian user of the name sold the
business and it switched to another name (Hornery, 1998). The concern
on the part of franchisors to minimize alterations is not just a question of
cost, important though this consideration is; it is about achieving a consistent image in the marketplace, of transferring and applying the accumulated knowledge and skills that have evolved in using a franchise
system in other locations, that are built into the different elements of
the franchise package, such as the operations manual and accounting
systems, and training methods. Thus companies will often talk up the
extent of changes for different markets, but they tend to be in areas that
do not change the core components of the package, but alter aspects such
as, for fast food operators, menus, internal décor in stores, advertising and
promotion.

Inevitably, there are bound to be cases where cultural and market
differences will confront international franchisors with the question of
whether they are prepared to make more substantive changes in their
systems in order to penetrate particular markets. In order to achieve
acceptable standards in its initial Moscow outlet, McDonald's had to
become involved in expensive upstream investments and associated activities, such as a large food processing plant (cost $40 million), rather than
follow its normal policy of utilizing independent suppliers (Peel and
Nicholson, 1990). The Australian chain, Wendys Supa Sundaes, initially
explored US market possibilities as its first international move, but was
confronted by the problem of similarity of the name to Wendy's, the US
fast food chain. It considered changing the name to Cindy's, but in the end
decided that this change would be too disruptive for the operation and

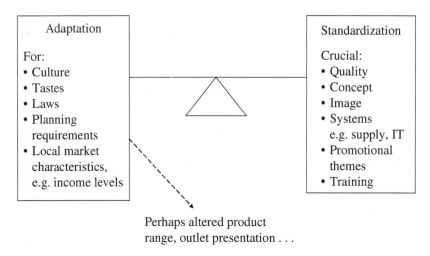

Figure 3.7 Franchisors' balancing act in different foreign markets

switched its interest to other markets, achieving initial foreign entry in New Zealand.

If franchisors do not make adjustments for the local context, they risk competitive responses that are more finely attuned to the local cultural and market environment, as with Jollibee in the Philippines, which even taunted McDonald's with slogans such as: 'smells and tastes delicious, not bland', responding to the local preference for hamburgers with strong taste (*Business Asia*, 1990, 172). Jollibee also introduced a far wider range of menu items, including spaghetti with a sweet and spicy topping, which forced McDonald's to introduce spaghetti into its menu as one of the first countries in its global operations where this happened. The dilemma facing international franchisors is depicted in Figure 3.7: while there are core elements of the franchise package that are often considered sacrosanct, it is frequently difficult to avoid the local demands for adaptation in many foreign markets. It is a difficult balancing act, and franchisors typically seek to make adjustments that are at the surface level rather than substantive, such as product range and internal outlet décor, in effect, to both standardize and adapt. McDonald's was not impressed with the attempt by one local government authority in Melbourne, Australia to force it to change its golden arches to green to better fit the environment after strong opposition from local residents. The difficulties of the standardization/adaptation balancing act are illustrated in the recent experience of McDonald's: see Box 3.3 below.

BOX 3.3   McDONALD'S STRUGGLES WITH
STANDARDIZATION/ADAPTATION

As franchisors become more and more dispersed in their global activities, the demands of achieving appropriate adaptation to the differences (culture and so on) in various foreign markets, while at the same time maintaining control and consistency in its key package components, systems and marketing themes tend to become more pronounced. Some of the recent problems experienced by McDonald's can be traced back to its handling of this issue. When the incoming CEO, Jack Greenberg, took over in 1998, in order to rebuild damaged relationships with franchisees he gave them more power to determine aspects such as changes in menu and marketing details. However, this decentralization, promoting local adaptation, had an effect on the 'main pillars of McDonald's brand: service, quality and cleanliness' (*Economist*, 2001, 72). With falling customer satisfaction ratings in the US, the company was forced to address these problems, setting up 'a new layer of management to monitor quality and impose tougher standards on franchisees' and simplifying its menu (ibid.). This was an attempt to move the company back towards a more centralized control model with greater standardization of core package elements. However, this process was overtaken by a further threat in the form of a growing concern and related negative publicity about obesity and the contribution of fast food to this growing epidemic in developed countries. The company rushed to add salads and other healthier options to its menus, resulting in more complex and costly operational requirements in dealing with fresh and perishable foodstuffs, although recent sales and profit data indicate this move has been a success in the marketplace (*Economist*, 2004). Nevertheless, it still confronted the choice between allowing franchisees sufficient freedom to respond to local circumstances, even at the risk of falling standards, and tightening controls even further, at the risk of adaptability and performance in some foreign markets, in order to ensure overall quality and standards are maintained. The vice president of restaurant innovation at McDonald's has said that the company 'was built on a strong foundation of a core menu that we took around the world, but we need to make sure we are more locally relevant . . . taste profiles and desires are changing' (Grant, 2006, 28). What would you have recommended to McDonald's?

LEGAL AND REGULATORY ISSUES

In early research on the internationalization of US franchisors, the area of government regulation and legal restrictions was noted as the major problem in establishing foreign operations (Hackett, 1976; Walker and Etzel, 1973). However, Australian research revealed a very different perspective for Australian franchisors: they did not see this as an important constraint on international expansion (Welch, 1990). Whatever the emphasis in thinking, though, it is clear that there are significant legal and regulatory hurdles to be surmounted in order to effect international entry. It is, therefore, not surprising to find that franchisors in the 2004 Australian survey of franchising indicated that the two main sources of assistance in international expansion are, firstly, Australian lawyers and, secondly, foreign lawyers (Frazer and Weaven, 2004). As well, lawyers may have an influence on the choice of entry medium, as related by the founder of an Australian company, Granite Transformations, an international franchised kitchen refurbishment business which entered the US in 2000: 'Their first meeting was with a US attorney specialising in franchising, who convinced them that master franchising would be a mistake because of the potential for litigation . . . [the founder said] franchisors in the US have limited recourse, other than terminating the agreement, if the master franchisee is not supporting franchisees or is failing to fully exploit opportunities in the territory. It requires a great deal of trust and commitment' (Walker, 2004, 57).

US franchising companies have struggled, some unsuccessfully, to deal with the idiosyncrasies of the Russian legal system (Alon and Banai, 2000). This is one of the realities of international expansion, dealing with the varying requirements and complexity of different legal systems. While some countries have specific regulations covering franchising (for example, the US and Canada), this is not the case for most countries. As a result, franchising is covered within broader commercial laws, while other laws, such as those dealing with competition, intellectual property, taxation and international trade, also are likely to be pertinent, and there may be limitations on royalty rates. For example, franchisors have been prosecuted in Australia under the country's competition laws regarding misleading representation of the state of their franchise operations and likely returns to potential franchisees. There was considerable debate in Australia about whether to introduce separate legislation to cover franchising, but in the end it was decided that existing laws were adequate, and an industry 'code of practice' was developed to deal with some of the specifics of franchising and to regulate conduct. Overall, there has been an improvement in the global legal climate covering franchising, including an easing of legal restrictions on the right to use franchising in countries where previously it had been difficult, providing greater certainty for would-be franchisors. There has been sustained growth of franchising in China since the passing of its first franchise law in 1997, which signalled government support for franchising. Further clarifying laws that apply to foreign franchisors were passed in 2005, although the legal status of master franchise arrangements remains in doubt, creating a legal bias in favour of joint ventures and wholly owned enterprises as the foundation for franchising development (Terry, 2006).

Some of the legal pressure on franchisors has been coming from disaffected franchisees. There have been many examples of franchisees taking legal action, frequently on a collective basis, against franchisors in a wide array of countries. Benetton is a high-profile case of a company subject to legal action by franchisees, particularly in the US. Site location, exaggerated claims, lack of profitability and lack of promised franchisor support are common issues inspiring franchisee action. As chains grow in size, the threat of a large number of franchisees taking joint action, with the increased collective means to finance legal action, becomes a powerful potential threat. Australian research has shown a high level of disputation between franchisors and franchisees: '35 per cent of franchisors reported that they had been involved in a substantial dispute with a franchisee over the previous 12 month period' (Frazer, Weaven and Wright, 2006, 56). However, only 14 per cent of the disputes had ended up in litigation at that point. Franchisor-initiated actions (mainly around system compliance) were slightly higher than those initiated by franchisees. Overall, the number of franchisees in dispute with franchisors represented less than 2 per cent of the total number of franchisees.

Illustrative of the conflicting pressures and legal responses, often played out in the local media, is the experience of the international chain Midas in Australia: 'International muffler business and franchisor Midas has a mutiny on its hands, as about 30 franchisees are expected to take class action against the local master franchisor . . . At the heart of the dispute are moves by Midas to terminate franchise agreements with some franchisees' (Switzer, 2004). In general, the Australian situation appears to be illustrative of the greater preparedness by franchisees to take legal action against perceived wrongful performance or non-performance by the franchisor that harms the franchisee's business. A Franchisees Federation was set up in 1991 in Australia to give collective voice to the concerns of franchisees before the government and franchisors (Forman, 1992). Governments worldwide have been subject to varying pressure by franchisees to provide extended forms of protection for their interests within and beyond existing legal frameworks, in areas such as termination due to alleged 'breach of contract'. In general, the trend has been towards increasing legal protection for franchisees in different jurisdictions.

LACK OF PROFILE IN FOREIGN MARKETS

In the literature on international franchising, there is extensive treatment of the activities of the large international chains, notably McDonald's, Pizza Hut and KFC. In the franchising industry, the major players have acted as role models for many emerging franchisors, and they have undoubtedly acted as a stimulus to international franchising activity. The marketing thoroughness, careful establishment of supply lines and preparedness to wait for appropriate sites in new foreign markets by McDonald's is frequently noted. This was typified in their start-up in Moscow and in their approach to operations in China, where the company spent five years undertaking preliminary research, locating partners, planning store fit-outs and menus, and establishing supply networks – the latter being particularly important in the Chinese context (McGurn, 1997; Peel and Nicholson, 1990; Thornton, 1995). Impressive as these steps seem, they are far removed from the situation of a small company moving into the international arena with limited finance and a relatively unknown franchise concept, in contrast to the profile and capital base of McDonald's, so that the role model relevance quickly breaks down.

The lack of international profile accentuates the difficulties of achieving international entry. It is difficult to sell an unknown quantity to potential franchisees. Typically, a profile has to be built from scratch, whether by the franchisor or its foreign partner, within constrained marketing budgets. 'The franchise name and image are important for ultimate success and it may take some time for [these] to be developed' (Luostarinen and Welch, 1990, 87). Even Allied Domecq, owner of the Baskin-Robbins (ice cream) and Dunkin' Donuts chains, in recognition of the reality that although 'strong brand name recognition can help the company make a sale . . . it takes time to build a reputation . . . [therefore it] waived the franchise fees for its initial Baskin-Robbins investors in Russia but will eventually charge some as it develops greater brand name recognition and acceptance by consumers' (Alon and Banai, 2000, 111). Consider the difficulties of marketing the Mad Barry's, franchise-based, Australian home improvement retail chain in foreign markets: it is perhaps not surprising that the name was eventually changed to Barry's.

TIMING OF FOREIGN MARKET ENTRIES

Research in various countries, as noted above, shows that many franchisors enter foreign markets as a result of being approached by a foreign party interested in acquiring the rights to the franchise system for a country or region – typically before the franchisor has become interested in or initiated steps to effect entry to the market/s involved. In such circumstances, the franchisor is confronted by the difficult question of whether to respond positively to the approach and start the process of foreign market entry, in association with the interested party. The issue is even more difficult to deal with when it involves the first international market entry by the franchisor – even worse if it is still in the early stages of developing, testing, refining and proving the franchise system in the domestic market. The franchisor is undoubtedly better equipped for international operations with a settled franchise system and relatively standardized components. Lawyers stress the potential dangers of offering an unsettled franchise system in many legal jurisdictions, given the range of disclosure requirements and information quality standards demanded.

Ultimately, it is more difficult to sell a relatively experimental concept to foreign franchisees. Nevertheless, franchisors admit that it is hard to dismiss such approaches, no matter how early they arrive in the process of domestic expansion. They represent confirmation of the franchising idea, of the entrepreneurial venture and personal fulfilment. Also there is often a concern that the interested foreign party will look elsewhere if rejected. However, as noted earlier, to go ahead may require many practical steps to implement the decision, not the least being, importantly, trademark registration in the country concerned, and may take considerable time, with potentially adverse outcomes. Obviously, for franchisors that have already established international operations, responding to unsolicited foreign approaches can be more readily handled given that they have dealt with many foreign entry issues already and can apply accumulated expertise. At the same time, research indicates that international experience tends to lead to greater caution in responses to external approaches, including greater time and care in the evaluation of potential partners.

With or without unsolicited foreign approaches, the timing and rate of foreign market entries is related to the entry forms used in different countries, and the decision about franchised versus company-owned outlets. A combination of master franchising (or joint ventures) and franchising of individual outlets should allow faster penetration of more foreign markets in a given period of time than through subsidiary establishment and greater emphasis on company-owned outlets.

CONCLUSION

The extent of global penetration of the franchising method has meant that it is difficult to dismiss as a potentially important means of achieving internationalization. It has become dispersed in use across the globe, in countries that vary widely by income levels and culture. While the major chains are still dominant, they are being challenged in many quarters. As franchising has been applied in diverse locations, with many locally grown products, this has been followed by their emergence as international players. Many companies have used franchising successfully and see it as a powerful means of achieving low-cost, rapid international growth. However, the analysis of franchising as a method of international operations has shown that its use is anything but straightforward. At the outset, there is the question of the form of foreign market entry, even with franchising in the foreign market as the chosen expansion means. Direct franchising is difficult to sustain as a long-term path to franchising. Having settled on the form of entry, companies have been shown to operate with quite varied policies regarding the choice between franchised and company-owned outlets, from market to market. The company-owned path, though, effectively negates the low-cost, rapid growth reasoning frequently expressed for the initial choice of franchising. While McDonald's has a strong emphasis on developing local suppliers, there are many examples of franchising being used as a 'trojan horse' for exporting activity (for example, Benetton), and even McDonald's is involved in exporting as local reliable sources are being developed or in the face of short-term supply problems (Love, 1986; Thornton, 1995).

As a result, the use of franchising occurs in the context of a sometimes complex mix of modes, and is a powerful illustration of the mode combination and configuration demands in reality that face companies, rather than the simplistic, unitary mode choice framework presented in much of the literature on international business operations. Nevertheless, whatever the overall mode setting, franchising has characteristics that continue to make it interesting to companies seeking to start or expand international activities, and, more particularly, to the growing global throng of potential franchisees. In the end, the ability to tap into the motivation and local knowledge of franchisees has made franchising a mode that is taken more seriously – beyond the 'exotic' tag that might have applied two decades ago – as shown in its adoption by companies already heavily involved in international operations by other means. At this stage, though, the principal path to international franchising starts from a domestic franchising base.

REFERENCES

Alon, I. and M. Banai (2000), 'Franchising opportunities and threats in Russia', *Journal of International Marketing*, **8**(3), 104–19.
Andersson, S. (2000), 'The internationalization of the firm from an entrepreneurial perspective', *International Studies of Management and Organization*, **30**(1), 63–92.
AP-Dow Jones (1988), 'UK's franchise guinea pigs', *Australian Financial Review*, 24 August, 36.
Aydin, N. and M. Kacker (1990), 'International outlook of US-based franchisors', *International Marketing Review*, **7**(2), 43–53.

Aziz, A.K.A.A. (1996), 'Official blessing for franchising in Malaysia', *Franchise International*, Fall/Autumn, 51.

Baroncelli, A. and A. Manaresi (1997), 'Franchising as a form of divestment: an Italian study', *Industrial Marketing Management*, **26**, 223–35.

Bruce, L. and C. Reed (1987), 'The bright new worlds of Benetton', *International Management*, November, 24–35.

Business Asia (1990), 'Jollibee dominates market by catering to local tastes', 14 May, 172.

Churchill, D. (1982), 'Franchising: rewards and independence', *Financial Times*, Section 3, 28 October.

Churchill, D. (1990), 'Battle of the burgers all set to sizzle', *Financial Times*, 1 February, 9.

Connors, J.A. (1984), 'Legal aspects for prospective franchisors', *The Chartered Accountant in Australia*, March, 30–34.

Dnes, A.W. (1992), *Franchising: A Case Study Approach*, Aldershot: Avebury.

Economist (1985), 'Franchising: fast and fashionable', 5 January, 61–2.

Economist (2001), 'Where's the beef?', 3 November, 72.

Economist (2004), 'McDonald's turned around – Big Mac's makeover', 16 October, 61–3.

Focus Japan (1989), 'Trading companies form joint ventures for new services', April, 3.

Forman, D. (1992), 'Franchising offers rich rewards for the canny', *Business Review Weekly*, 18 December, 52–4.

Framnes, R. and L.S. Welch (1992), 'Entering international markets via franchising: the Norwegian experience with comparisons to Australia', in O.H.M. Yau and W.F. Shepard (eds), *Problems and Prospects in International Business*, Proceedings of the AIBSEAR Conference, Brisbane, 21–24 June, 599–602.

Frazer, L. and S. Weaven (2004), *Franchising Australia 2004 Survey*, Griffith University: Franchise Council of Australia and Australian Trade Commission.

Frazer, L., S. Weaven and O. Wright (2006), *Franchising Australia 2006 Survey*, Griffith University: Franchise Council of Australia.

Fuller, J. (2003), 'Say cheese Theo', *Finansavisen*, 29 January, 10–11.

Gourlay, R. (1994), 'Bring on the clones – how franchising can help companies grow', *Financial Times*, 12 April, 13.

Grant, J. (2006), 'Maccas savours exotic flavours as market matures', *Australian*, 10 February, 28.

Hackett, D.W. (1976), 'The international expansion of US franchise systems', *Journal of International Business Studies*, **7**(1), 65–75.

Hill, A. and R. Tomkins (1996), 'McDonald's buys Italian restaurant chain', *Financial Times*, 22 March, 21.

Hoffman, R.C. and J.F. Preble (1993), 'Franchising in the twenty-first century', *Business Horizons*, **36**(6), 35–43.

Hookway, J. (2003), 'Franchising with frills', *Far Eastern Economic Review*, 13 March, 34–6.

Hornery, A. (1998), 'Next: the purple tower of taco', *Sydney Morning Herald*, 5 November, via website: http://www.smh.com.au.

Hudson, T. (1994), 'From ski slopes to the Big Mac heights', *The Age*, 15 August, 25.

Hutton, B. (1998), 'Fast food group blows a McBubble in slow economy', *Financial Times*, 8 May, 24.

Huus, K. (1996), 'Too many cooks', *Far Eastern Economic Review*, 2 May, 74–6.

International Franchise Association (2004), 'Franchises provide big boost to nation's economy', *International Franchise Association Website*, http://www.franchise.org/resourcectr/bigboost.asp, accessed 10/8/04, 1–3.

International Trade Administration (1987), *Franchising in the Economy 1985–87*, Washington, D.C.: US Department of Commerce.

Jayasankaran, S. (2003), 'Malaysia's optical chain eyes the franchising prize', *Far Eastern Economic Review*, 13 March, 36.

Justis, R.T. and R.J. Judd (1989), *Franchising*, Cincinatti, OH: South-Western Publishing.

Kedia, B.L., D.J. Ackerman, D.E. Bush and R.T. Justis (1994), 'Determinants of internationalization of franchise operations by US franchisors', *International Marketing Review*, **11**(4), 56–68.

Korhonen, H., R. Luostarinen and L. Welch (1996), 'Internationalization of SMEs: inward–outward patterns and government policy', *Management International Review*, **36**(4), 315–29.

Larson, P. (2004), 'Opening doors to emerging economies', *International Franchise Association Website*, http://www.franchise.org/intl/News/Prjf6.asp, accessed 10/8/04, 1–6.

Lewis, M. (1993), *Selling Textiles and Clothing in France: The Franchise Route*, Textile Outlook Market Report No. 2636, London: Textiles Intelligence Limited and Economist Intelligence Unit.

Love, J.F. (1986), *McDonald's: Behind the Arches*, New York: Bantam.

Luce, E. (1996), 'Taste of success', *Financial Times*, 31 May, 10.

Luostarinen, R.K. and L.S. Welch (1990), *International Business Operations*, Helsinki: Export Consulting KY.

McCosker, C.F. (1990), 'Preparation and perceptions of Australian franchisees . . . and their afterthoughts', *Accounting Forum*, **14**(2), 97–114.

McCosker, C.F. and B.J. Walker (1992), 'International expansion by Australian franchisors', paper presented at the 12th Babson College Entrepreneurship Research Conference, Fontainebleau, France, June.

McGregor, R. (2003), 'China swallows fast food at an ever more rapid rate', *Financial Times*, 20 January, 14.

McGurn, W. (1997), 'Burger boom' and 'Think locally', *Far Eastern Economic Review*, 20 November, 66–8 and 69.

O'Hare, N. (1992), *Bedpost*, MBA Project, Melbourne: Monash University.

Ooi, T. (2005), 'Giving stick to retirement', *Australian*, 19 December, 27–8.

Paynter, J. and A.M. Everett (2003), 'Exporting New Zealand's franchise systems', in ANZIBA Conference Proceedings (on CD-Rom), 7–8 November, 2003, Dunedin, New Zealand.

Peel, Q. and M. Nicholson (1990), 'Mac attack in Pushkin Square', *Financial Times*, 31 January, 14.

Petersen, B. and L.S. Welch (2000), 'International retailing operations: downstream entry and expansion via franchising', *International Business Review*, **9**(4), 479–96.

Peterson, A. and R.J. Dant (1990), 'Perceived advantages of the franchise option from the franchisee perspective: empirical insights from a service franchise', *Journal of Small Business Management*, **28**(3), 46–61.

Stirling, P. (1991), 'Middle managers find new home', *Business Review Weekly*, 28 June, 70–73.

Switzer, P. (2004), 'Midas facing a franchise rebellion', *The Australian*, 20 July, 27.

Terry, A. (2006), 'Mass market appeal', *Business Review Weekly*, 19–25 January, 48–51.

Thornton, E. (1995), 'McManaging supplies', *Far Eastern Economic Review*, 23 November, 76.

Walker, B.J. (1989), *A Comparison of International vs. Domestic Expansion by US Franchise Systems*, Washington, D.C.: International Franchise Association.

Walker, B.J. and M.J. Etzel (1973), 'The internationalisation of US franchise systems', *Journal of Marketing*, **37**(2), 38–46.

Walker, J. (2004), 'Branching out', *Business Review Weekly*, 23–9 September, 57.

Walker, J. (2006), 'Franchises – overview', *Business Review Weekly*, 19–25 January, 32–9.

Welch, L.S. (1989), 'Diffusion of franchise system use in international operations', *International Marketing Review*, **6**(5), 7–19.

Welch, L.S. (1990), 'Internationalization by Australian franchisors', *Asia Pacific Journal of Management*, **7**(2), 101–21.

Welch, L.S. (2004), 'International entrepreneurship and internationalisation: common threads', in L.-P. Dana (ed.), *Handbook of Research on International Entrepreneurship*, Cheltenham, UK and Northampton, MA, USA: Edward Elgar, pp. 137–49.

Welch, L.S. and F. Wiedersheim-Paul (1980), 'Domestic expansion – internationalization at home', *Essays in International Business*, No. 2, December, 1–31.

Winn, H. (2004), 'Fast-food frenzy', *Far Eastern Economic Review*, 29 July, 44–6.

Withane, S. (1991), 'Franchising and franchisee behavior: an examination of opinions, personal characteristics, and motives of Canadian franchisee entrepreneurs', *Journal of Small Business Management*, **29**(1), 22–9.

Young, E. (2004), 'Franchising in China: a dead duck', *brandchannel.com website*, http.www.brandchannel.com/features_effect.asp?pf_id=89, accessed 10/08/2004, 1–3.

4. Licensing

INTRODUCTION

Licensing is a foreign operation mode that covers a wide range of activities, users and diverse roles. The span of users extends from individual inventors, often without a base of operations, to large multinationals, utilizing licensing within a broad mix of modes. As in franchising, both licensees and licensors have played an active part in the development of a vibrant international market for licensing deals. While licensing tends to be associated with technological advance and its exploitation, it covers far more than technology, including the commercial rights to use famous names, symbols and entertainment vehicles. Licensing is an important means of penetrating foreign markets, often used by smaller firms as the sole means for early international forays. It may be employed, though, in a variety of roles in international operations, for example in support of managerial control objectives regarding a company's foreign subsidiary. When used for control purposes, it tends to be within a mix of modes, often including foreign direct investment (FDI). In fact, the bulk of licensing, as measured by licensing revenue, occurs as internal transfers within the subsidiary networks of multinationals rather than between independent entities. In global terms, licensing has been estimated by UNCTAD (2006) as being worth $US91 billion in total in 2005 – a reduction of 20 billion on 2004. Its significance, as measured by sales generated by licensing, would be far greater: using a 5 per cent of sales royalty basis, the total would amount to $US1820 billion. In addition, unrecorded cross-licensing activities amongst multinationals are known to be important, so that the recorded total may well be a significant understatement of the true state of affairs.

While earlier research indicated that licensing tended to be viewed as a residual or secondary strategy for achieving internationalization (Luostarinen and Welch, 1990), the perspective has shifted somewhat since then, partly as a result of the emergence of the knowledge-based view of the firm, ensuring that licensing, both into and out of the firm, would be regarded as being of greater strategic significance. Likewise, Smith and Hansen (2002, 372) have argued: 'In a knowledge economy, IP [intellectual property] moves from a legal matter to a strategic issue.' As well, the publicized, increased use of licensing by many large multinationals, such as by

IBM and Texas Instruments, has acted to raise the consciousness and consideration of licensing's place in international operations (Grindley and Teece, 1997). For example, after a change in policy in the early 1990s to use licensing as a way of generating increased revenue from its intellectual property portfolio, rather than concentrating on the defensive role of the portfolio, IBM was able to increase its licensing revenue from $US500 million in 1994 to about $US1.5 billion in 1999 – around 20 per cent of company profits (*Economist*, 2000, 80). A McKinsey survey found an expectation among the bulk of executives of increased buying and selling of licences in the future, and almost half were anticipating a large increase in revenue from licensing (Cukier, 2005).

Nevertheless, licensing continues to be used at times by companies to penetrate foreign markets because of perceived constraints on the capacity to employ other modes of operation. For example, in a study of Norwegian companies with operations in the Indian market, not including simple exporting, licensing was found to be important: only one company was using a wholly-owned subsidiary whereas almost a quarter were operating solely via licensing, and 42 per cent were using joint ventures. This outcome appeared to be a response to the perception by the Norwegian firms that they were not well equipped, in terms of cultural knowledge and Indian experience, to undertake high commitment modes (Tomassen et al., 1998).

Despite the positive, or secondary, reasons for adopting licensing as a way of operating in foreign markets, it is not universally accepted as an

---

BOX 4.1   TWO ENDS OF THE LICENSING SPECTRUM

Milk discovery
Researchers at the University of Melbourne discovered a peptide in milk that can be used to coat teeth and reverse early tooth decay. Importantly, it can be used as a food additive in averting tooth decay, and is 'set to be added to everything from mouthwash to chewing gum . . . one of the most successful trials was with chewing gum' (Brook, 1999, 1). Initial licence fee payments earned the university $A1.1 million. The discovery, called Recaldent, was the outcome of 15 years of research.

Microsoft licensing deal
'Microsoft and Citrix, a developer of software that enables Windows software applications to be shared among multiple terminals, yesterday announced a licensing agreement under which Microsoft will pay an initial $US75m. in fees, and up to $US100m. in royalties, for use of Citrix's WinFrame technology' (Kehoe, 1997, 25).

appropriate mode; in fact, many companies are strongly opposed to the idea of licensing, some as a result of their own negative experience with using the mode. Typically, it involves a long-term commitment to a foreign partner, about whom little may be known beforehand. By its very nature, it involves the transfer of knowledge and skills with the aim of creating the capacity in another entity to reproduce what the licensor is doing, in whole or part. Inevitably, there is a concern: are we simply creating a future competitor, whatever the legal defences? There are enough 'horror' stories around, repeated in various forums and literature, dealing with international operations in general and licensing specifically, to ensure that this concern is maintained (see THECO example in Box 4.2). Japan and other East Asian economies were heavy users of government-supported inward licensing during the post-World War II period as a means of obtaining key technologies to help rebuild and build industries, leading to many examples of companies arising to compete with and even dominating former licensors (Davidson, 1979). Allied with this competition concern is the worry that licensing will be just a vehicle for accessing important technology by the licensee, without even honouring the terms of the agreement and paying agreed-upon fees. For individual inventors and small firms, after perhaps having spent many years developing the technology in question, without strong enough financial backing to obtain legal redress and with limited foreign operation options, licensing accordingly is sometimes viewed as a very high-risk path.

BOX 4.2   FEAR OF CREATING A COMPETITOR

The rise of a Thai producer of air conditioning components, Thai Heat Exchange Company (THECO), through initially licensing in, is the type of story that causes so many companies to reject licensing.

1967: THECO is founded as an importer of automobile air conditioning components;

1972: starts production of components under licence from a US firm John E. Mitchel;

1978: the licensing agreement expires, but THECO continues production independently, and begins exporting to Singapore;

1980: begins exporting to Malaysia;

1981–8: exporting spreads to Hong Kong, Taiwan, Indonesia, India, Pakistan, Bangladesh, China and the Middle East;

1991: forms a joint venture with an Indonesian company to produce air conditioning components for the Indonesian market;

1992: joint venture established with Sanden International (Japan).

Source: Hunsongtham (1993).

While there are many cases of companies licensing to other firms in domestic markets, taken overall, most licensing is carried out on a cross-border basis (Luostarinen and Welch, 1990). In the main, this is because companies are, not surprisingly, less prepared to license domestic competitors or potential competitors than similar foreign companies that are seen, rightly or wrongly, as less likely to intrude on the domestic market as a result of using the licensed technology. As well, licensing that is internal to multinationals is driven by cross-border considerations to do with the functioning of their global subsidiary networks.

The above discussion of licensing demonstrates that there are many different perspectives on licensing and its use in international operations. It is therefore important to examine the many aspects of licensing in order to provide a clear basis for its consideration as a form of foreign operations, on its own, as well as in combination with other forms. We will define licensing, analyse its nature and content, its various roles, reasons for its use, its implementation, problems, success factors, impact on internationalization and long-term considerations.

LICENSING: DEFINITION AND CONTENT

As noted in the previous chapter, there is considerable confusion around the definition of licensing and in drawing the line between franchising and licensing. A starting point in clarifying the nature of licensing is the following definition. Licensing involves the sale of a *right to use* certain proprietary knowledge (so-called 'intellectual property') in a defined way. The intellectual property may be registered publicly, for example in the form of a patent or trademark, as a means of establishing ownership rights. Or it may be retained within the firm: in the form of know-how it is commonly based on operational experience. Know-how for licensing purposes may include commercial and administrative knowledge as well as technical knowledge. The licensing agreement is the legal agreement setting out what is to be transferred from licensor to licensee and under what conditions. (Adapted from Luostarinen and Welch, 1990, 32.)

The first point to stress in this definition is that licensing does *not* involve the sale of the intellectual property, in whatever form, only the rights to its use. For instance, Disney might license the right to use the Mickey Mouse trademark to another company, say to a fast food franchise for a particular promotion, but is highly unlikely to sell the trademark, a valuable asset, to the other company.

Forms of Intellectual Property

There are many forms of intellectual property that may be included in licensing arrangements. It should be noted that the types of intellectual property, and issues surrounding their development and protection, are not exclusive to licensing – they are relevant to operation modes in general. For example, companies embarking on international franchising are consistently warned about the importance of protecting their intellectual property in relevant foreign domains as part of the planning for international entry. While there is a range of main forms of intellectual property where legal protection may be available, there is considerable variation between countries as to relevant laws, regulations and institutions governing their administration. In overall systems the main variation is between those countries using common law (based on legal precedent, for example US and UK) and those using code law (set of legislated rules or codes, for example Continental Europe). In code law countries, the first to register a trademark has priority, whereas in common law countries it is the first to use the trademark in practice. However, individual country differences, even within overall systems, remain substantial. For example, although Thailand adopted the code law system in 1925, this was on top of elements of English law and a Hindu framework stretching far back in time. Thus Pearson (1993, 158) had this advice for a licensor entering Thailand: '[do not assume] the same legal issues upon which he has had advice in his home country can be resolved in the same way in Thailand. Thai law blends features of the English law with the European civil law system and adds some uniquely Thai ingredients, with a blend that is all its own'.

Differences between the US and Japanese approaches to patent law and practice are substantial, and are illustrative of the country-by-country variations in intellectual property systems that internationalizing companies have to cope with. In general, the Japanese system stresses technology sharing whereas the US system aims to protect individual inventors. Patent applications remain secret in the US until the patent is granted, whereas they are made public after 18 months in Japan. The Japanese system is much slower in investigating and granting patent claims than in the US system. In determining priority, the US uses a first-to-invent rather than a first-to-file principle, the latter being the dominant pattern in the rest of the world (Spero, 1990). The issue of patents on computer software and business methods has created a division between the US and Europe: they are currently ruled out in Europe, but allowed in the US, although some companies have been able to achieve software patents by arguing on the grounds of technical effects (*Economist*, 2000, 2003a).

Legal establishment of ownership rights in a public form, apart from copyright and trade secrets, normally is undertaken through a statutory authority within the relevant government, which evaluates aspects such as uniqueness, effectively granting ownership under certain conditions if, for example, uniqueness is proved, while requiring public disclosure of the protected intellectual property. However, alongside national oversight of intellectual property there has been an evolving multilateral system, providing for international standards and registration systems that are coming to play a larger role in intellectual property protection. It remains to be seen whether this global system will supplant national systems, but it undoubtedly offers the prospect of a simplified, one-stop shop for intellectual property protection in the future, with considerable benefits to companies undertaking licensing or other methods of international operations. In defining the various forms of intellectual property, we shall refer to those used by the World Intellectual Property Organization (WIPO), a branch of the United Nations, which is the principal body administering the emerging world system. For a comprehensive account of WIPO and its role in the development of a global intellectual property system and its administration, see http://www.wipo.int.

Within the World Trade Organization, the Agreement on Trade-Related Aspects of Intellectual Property Rights (TRIPS) further ensures that member states are required to adhere to minimum standards of intellectual property protection, forcing many countries to alter relevant laws. For example, in 1999, India began to implement an undertaking to the WTO to introduce patent protection on products in a number of areas, including pharmaceuticals and agricultural chemicals, where previously only process patents were permitted – against strong local opposition (Nicholson, 1999). In both China and India, there has been rising concern about intellectual property protection for local firms as they face competition in local and foreign markets, as well as wanting to become more attractive to multinational companies for the establishment of research and development facilities, for which the strength of the local intellectual property regime, or lack of it, has been considered to be an important factor in investment decisions. Since joining the WTO, China has been under greater pressure to improve the quality of its intellectual property protection regime. In what was considered a landmark case, in 2003, the Danish toymaker, Lego, won a case against a Chinese company over copies of Lego's products: 'Lego, renowned as a vigorous defender of its intellectual property rights, said this was the first time the Chinese legal system had delivered a judgement confirming copyright protection of industrial design and applied art' (MacCarthy, 2003, 18). The Chinese manufacturer was forced to halt production, and hand over copied products and relevant manufacturing

equipment for destruction by the authorities. However, the Chinese authorities recently overturned an earlier decision granting a patent on Viagra:
'. . . after a group of Chinese drug makers filed a petition arguing that
Viagra's active ingredient, sildenafil citrate, failed to fulfil the "novelty
requirement" of Chinese patent law' (FEER, 2004, 27). Again, as in other
countries, local interpretation of intellectual property laws is always bound
to generate divergent outcomes across countries.

Patents

A patent is defined by WIPO (2004) as 'an exclusive right granted for an
invention, which is a product or process that provides a new way of doing
something, or offers a new technical solution to a problem . . . [it] provides
protection for the invention to the owner of the patent . . . for a limited
period, normally 20 years'. Proof of novelty or uniqueness is the major
issue in the registration process. WIPO has been seeking to simplify and
develop uniform standards for submissions of patent applications culmi-
nating in an international standard accepted by signatories under the terms
of the Patent Co-operation Treaty (PCT) that it administers. It is possible
to lodge an international patent application (via the relevant national
patent authority) and have it searched and assessed for its international
validity. However, a successful outcome of this process does not mean a
world patent, even though that is the ultimate goal of the evolving world
system. Even in the European Union, 'although many patents are awarded
centrally by the European Patent Office . . . national courts have the final
say over a patent's validity' (*Economist*, 2003a). Once the PCT process is
completed, companies have to decide which countries they want to enter
and make the required applications under each set of national rules, and
paying relevant fees. Individual countries differ on precisely what constitutes 'novelty' and so maintain their own standards, despite the emerging
harmonization of international standards. WIPO argues that the international search and evaluation process facilitates examination within the
different national jurisdictions.

Patents are an important part of licensing activity. However, they do
expose a company's technology to public view. As a result, companies often
seek to obtain patent protection, but at the same time to leave out key parts
of the technology and thereby make it as difficult as possible for others to
access and utilize the technology, while avoiding the strictures of the patent
regime. In the mid-1990s Dell, the US computer assembler and retailer,
began to build a patent portfolio around unique aspects of its method of
doing business. When asked about whether the patents had been useful the
vice-president of intellectual property replied: 'They make people go away.

In this business that's what counts' (*Economist*, 2000, 79). The representative of an Australian company involved in developing advanced engine technologies, Orbital Engine Corporation, has commented that the company 'tried to make it as tough as possible for its competitors by giving them lots of patents to study. There is also potentially patentable material which we leave out so our competitors don't know how all of our patents fit together'. In a similar vein, a director of Memtec, an Australian company with a multitude of patents in the area of sewage treatment and micro-filtration processes, stated: 'we have laid a minefield of patents so anyone who wants to get into the micro-filtration area will have great trouble' (Smithers, 1992).

A factor in the closer attention to a company's patent portfolio has been the increasing resort to litigation regarding infringement of patents. It was reported that 'after Microsoft had to pay IBM $US30 million in a patent infringement suit Bill Gates sent a memo round to employees saying that the solution was "patent as much as we can"' (*Economist*, 2000, 79). However, it was an earlier court case that started a re-examination of the significance of patents, involving Polaroid and Kodak. After a long battle in US courts, Kodak was convicted of infringing Polaroid's patents in instant photography technology. The court decision required Kodak to pay a large financial penalty (about $A1 billion) and to close down its instant photography business. The result of the case led to 'an increased preference at many corporations for patenting inventions rather than keeping them as trade secrets' (Perry, 1986, 80). Nevertheless, in Australian research there were companies who even boasted about their ability to 'invent around' any patent in their field (Welch, 1993). Thus, dealing with such issues, and devising an effective patenting strategy, have increasingly come to be viewed as an important part of overall business and technology strategy, as well as playing a significant role in licensing. Grindley and Teece (1997, 8) concluded that 'one of the most significant emerging business developments in the last decade has been the proactive management of intellectual capital by innovating firms'.

Grindley and Teece (1997) also refer to the growth of cross-licensing among multinationals as an indicator of the re-thinking occurring on intellectual property strategy, with consequent effects on the approach to licensing. Nokia's approach is a case in point. In an address regarding Nokia's strategy in 1994, Sari Baldauf, the head of the Cellular Systems division at the time, indicated that, under an overall aim of intellectual leadership in the field, it had embarked on a programme of heavy investment in technological development, along with the construction of an extensive portfolio of patents, in contrast to an earlier lack of emphasis on patents. There were two important elements to this approach: a recognition that a company 'can't cover everything' and that Nokia needed 'patents in a portfolio to swap' that is, patents were seen to provide a basis for accessing others' technology, through cross-licensing.

In many situations in foreign markets, patents are critical to potential licensees being prepared to consider the technology. For Australian firms in the US, patents were viewed as a sign of 'technological respectability', so that patenting was viewed as an essential precursor to the licensing process (Welch, 1993). Companies that are involved in patenting and intend to include patents as part of their licensing package face a number of difficult decisions when embarking on international activity. Initially there is the choice of markets to target and therefore to seek to have patents registered: it is difficult in advance of experience to decide on the range of markets, and there is a limited time that domestic patenting provides priority in the international arena – generally only a year, or 30 months if undertaken via the Patent Cooperation Treaty. Particularly for smaller firms, the cost of widespread patenting is often a major constraint on how far international patenting can proceed, given that it is still the case that companies have to pay for patent protection on a country-by-country basis. In Australian research, licensors estimated that the protection of intellectual property, of which the registration of patents was the major form, represented 25 per cent of total licensing costs, with a further 3 per cent of the total involving intellectual property defence (Welch, 1993).

Small firms face the additional concern about whether they would be able to sustain or defend a case of patent infringement against another company or companies in different legal jurisdictions, particularly in the US legal system. The example of Bath Scientific, a small UK company with only 25 staff at the time, is instructive. In 1992, 50 per cent of its total sales of a moving probe system were being made to the US market. A US competitor alleged infringement of three of its patents and brought legal proceedings against Bath Scientific. The cost of the initial defence was $US250 000, which was roughly equal to total profits for 1992, and the company was looking at the average for a 'normal patent case' taking around six years to be finalized in the US (Dodwell, 1993). In Australian research, one of the authors investigated a small company with only 36 employees in the area of building supplies which had obtained patent protection for one of its inventions in the US as a forerunner to licensing. Within six months it found that its patent was being infringed by a large US multinational. When confronted by the Australian company, a representative of the US firm admitted that it had expropriated the invention and merely invited the Australian firm to undertake court proceedings against it, commenting: 'before the case is ever finalized you will be bankrupt'. The Australian firm withdrew from the attempt to license, and ceased patenting altogether, although still undertaking technological development. This is in contrast to the ability to persist with legal action as in the cases of Polaroid, noted above, and of Honeywell, which won a judgment in 1992 of $US96 million against Minolta for infringing its patents on the autofocus process in cameras. Honeywell spent six years and $US14 million in legal fees to achieve this outcome (Bremner and Neff, 1992).

Trademark

This is defined by WIPO as 'a distinctive sign which identifies certain goods or services as those produced or provided by a specific person or enterprise . . . A trademark provides protection to the owner of the mark by ensuring the exclusive right to use it to identify goods or services, or to authorize another to use it in return for payment. The period of protection varies, but a trademark can be renewed indefinitely beyond the time limit on payment of additional fees'. The scope of what can be registered as a trademark has been broadening and includes, individually or in combination, letters, words, phrases, shapes, logos, pictorial features, and even smells and sounds. In a recent example of the broad reach of trademarks in Australia, BP has won a case in the Federal Court preventing the petrol retailing operation of supermarket chain, Woolworths, from using a similar shade of green to that of BP's outlets. The judge found that 'customers identified BP's service stations by the colour green alone, independently of the shield', and were therefore entitled to protection under the Trade Marks Act which in 1995 included colours for the first time as a separate protectable element of trademarks (Carson, 2004). When the law was changed in many countries in the mid-1990s, Coca-Cola was one of the first to register the contour shape of its bottle, first introduced in 1915 (Rice, 1995). The Internet and the registration and protection of domain names have been an arena of strong activity on the trademark front in recent times. For example, a small Australian company called Absolut Beach sold swimwear via the Internet, but was successfully sued for trademark infringement and had its website shut down by the owners of the Absolut Vodka name (IP Australia, 2002).

Under WIPO, international registration of a trademark is now possible for a large number of countries (60 in 2004) that are signatories to the relevant international treaty. However, there has been a substantial difference in the approach to trademark law, as noted above, between common law and code law countries. Under common law (countries such as the UK, US and Australia), ownership rights have been determined to apply to the person or company that employs the trademark first, with registration

acting in a confirmatory role. In contrast, for code law countries, ownership
is determined according to who registers first, as in most of Europe and
Japan. However, there has been a trend towards greater emphasis on
registration in common law countries. For example, under a revision of the
US trademark law in 1988, it became possible to apply for registration
of a trademark on the basis of a 'bona fide intention to use' the trademark (Cohen, 1991, 48). Canada similarly switched from a common law
approach to one where the first to register gains priority provided there is
an intention to use. Ultimately, whatever the system, rights are confirmed
through use of the trademark; in Japan, cancellation of rights occurs after
three years of non-use.

There has been increasing global recognition of the commercial value of
trademarks, which has been reflected in their greater importance in licensing agreements, but also they have come to be more highly valued because
of the longevity of protection that they provide. Many companies consider
trademarks as a relatively cheap form of intellectual property protection:
by the mid-1990s, the UK-based company ICI had about 15 000 registered
trademarks. For a licensee, where a market has been developed under the
licensor's registered trademark, to strike out alone, beyond the licensing
arrangement, means the extra cost of building a market anew under a
different trademark, and the risk that the licensor will enter the market
with the benefit of its already established trademark – critically, its brand
name.

Designs

An industrial design is defined by WIPO as 'the ornamental or aesthetic
feature of an article. The design may consist of three-dimensional features,
such as the shape or surface of an article, or of two-dimensional features,
such as patterns, lines or color'. The emphasis is on the visual appearance
of the product or artefact. Examples are in houseware, jewellery, textiles
and architectural structures. 'In most countries, an industrial design must
be registered in order to be protected, under industrial design law . . . to be
registrable, the design must be "new" or "original", [and] protection is
limited to the country in which protection is granted.'

Mask Work

Under the 1984 US Semiconductor Chip Protection Act, a new type of
intellectual property protection was established, applying to semiconductor chip development. 'Creators of mask work are given exclusive rights
over the reproduction, importation, distribution, and sale of the mask

work for a ten-year period. The mask work must be original and must be registered within two years of its creation' (Jain, 1996, 15).

Copyright

Copyright is a form of protection where normally official registration is not required. It applies to the right of creators of literary and artistic works to control and exploit their work. It covers literary works, music, art, sculptures, photographs, films, computer software, advertisements, databases and technical drawings. These rights are automatic upon creation and protected under the Berne Convention, administered by WIPO, to which most countries are party, and are supported by other international treaties, including TRIPS (Trade-Related Aspects of Intellectual Property Rights) which operates under the auspices of the WTO. The general rule is that protection lasts for the creator's lifetime and at least 50 years thereafter. The rights are international in character, although legal protection is provided by national copyright laws.

Trade Secrets

In addition to the above forms of intellectual property that provide protection but imply disclosure, undisclosed information and technology, defined as trade secrets, may be protected through a legal defence in court that all measures were taken to ensure that the information was not available to outsiders, and that the information was taken and used without the approval of the company concerned (Jain, 1996). Texas Instruments pursued legal action against two former employees who had copied computer files before leaving their jobs. It took six years and went to an appeals court that upheld the convictions against the two men as having stolen trade secrets. 'The question of whether they had actually used the information was never raised; the company had only to show that they had neither requested nor received permission to copy the files' (Lyons, 1992, 70). Australian steel producer, BHP, took legal action against former executives in the US who were trying to set up in competition with BHP in the coated steel market there. The court indefinitely extended an injunction on the former employees from using BHP trade secrets, while maintaining an injunction that prevented the company set up by the former employees from operating in the industry for seven years (Peers, 1992). Cases of a similar character in Australia have proved more difficult to prosecute, with the courts making a distinction between general knowledge that an employee is entitled to carry beyond the employing company and specific, company confidential information. Some companies have sought to extend protection through copyright laws, demanding that all training and other relevant documentation be returned by employees on departure (Lyons, 1992).

Know-How

In general, a major part of the intellectual property that is the basis of licensing is unable to be protected: it does not satisfy the test of uniqueness or novelty, but nevertheless is a critical part of the knowledge that a licensee needs to put technology into practice. Referred to as know-how, it is the type of working knowledge that a company typically develops in the process of applying new technology, or manufacturing a newly invented product. Much of it is tacit knowledge. Different studies indicate that know-how is viewed by licensees as the most important part of licensing packages, in essence because it is the type of working knowledge gained through experience that enables a licensee to implement the licensed technology more rapidly and effectively without repeating the costly mistakes of development and application incurred by the licensor. In line with comments about patenting strategy noted above, Pengilley (1977, 201) has stated that 'In a great number of patents, the patent does not necessarily tell anybody how the invention will work in a practical manner in actual operation. This disclosure is something different. It is "know-how" . . . a US survey showed that about 50% of US patents studied had to be supplemented by "know-how" details before the patent became viable. Persons in industry with whom I have discussed this statistic give the uniform reply that they feel it overstates the position; that is they feel that far fewer inventions would be workable in the absence of "know-how" details.' Commercial know-how, related to marketing and management aspects, also has become increasingly important for licensees, as they seek to ensure not just effective technological implementation but also marketplace success, and are therefore interested in anything learned through the licensor's marketing activities in other markets which might be of assistance.

The importance with which know-how tends to be generally regarded, in contrast to the mixed perspectives on patents, is reflected in the outcomes of a study of a small number of Canada-based multinational firms. Out of 14 companies, 13 indicated that patent protection was not a major concern in foreign market entry decisions, and that patents did not 'provide an effective protection against opportunistic behavior by partners'. In contrast, 13 of the 14 said that 'know-how would be difficult for others to copy even if they had access to the patent', while 'the tacitness of know-how provides effective protection against opportunistic behavior by others' (Madhok, 1996, 349). This is in line with earlier research in Finland and

Australia which indicated a preponderance of know-how relative to patents in licensing deals, in terms of content and income generated (Luostarinen and Welch, 1990; Welch, 1993). This research likewise revealed that having know-how which was important to the ability of the licensee to absorb the technology being transferred, and was difficult for competitors to readily copy, gave licensors a greater sense of confidence about embarking on a licensing programme. This confidence was further enhanced when the know-how was linked to patented technology. In reality, there is little legal constraint on a competitor independently developing and using the same know-how. It is seen to be valuable, which is why companies are so concerned about the potential departure of key individuals who may be agents of know-how transfer to other companies.

IP IMPLICATIONS FOR INTERNATIONAL LICENSING

The discussion of the various forms of intellectual property that form the basis of licensing activities gives a clear indication that, while licensing is often perceived as a relatively simple and cheap way to embark on international operations, this is not necessarily the case: obtaining adequate and sufficiently widespread protection of intellectual property assets necessarily slows and complicates international licensing, and may be too costly for many small firms. From application to successful granting of patents and trademarks in Japan can take seven and three years, respectively. In an earlier Australian study of the use of licensing in international operations by mainly SMEs, for 57 per cent of respondents licensing was the sole starting point in activity in the foreign market in question, although most had previously engaged in exporting to other markets (Carstairs and Welch, 1982). For these companies, licensing was seen as a relatively low-cost way of exploiting the unique technology they had developed. In general, companies are tending to take IP issues more seriously, whether for licensing or other operation forms, and to view intellectual property in strategic terms. Reflecting the change in perspective, Rabino and Enayati (1995, 23) have argued: 'the strategic *use* of intellectual property assets can be a competitive weapon'. In many large companies positions have been created at the upper echelons of management with responsibility for intellectual property, carrying titles such as 'Head of Intellectual Capital' or 'Chief Knowledge Officer'.

The increased IP consciousness, and its consideration within company strategy, has had the spin-off effect in many companies of leading to a broadening and strengthening of IP within licensing packages (see

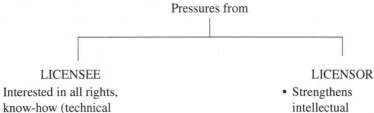

Pressures from

LICENSEE	LICENSOR
Interested in all rights, know-how (technical and commercial) that contribute to the most rapid and effective technology transfer and market penetration	• Strengthens intellectual property against infringement • Broadens the basis of income generation • Makes the package more readily marketable

Figure 4.1   Broadening of licensing package

Figure 4.1). On one side there is the concern on the part of licensees that they have the full array of intellectual property assets to assist the implantation of the technology and ultimate marketing of the end-product. On the licensor's side, a well rounded licensing (IP) package provides greater protection against infringement: the sum is greater than the individual parts; given the mutual reinforcement that normally occurs among the parts, the strengthened protection means that a licensor tends to be more confident about opening up the package to scrutiny in the marketing process, and a higher royalty should be more readily negotiable given the breadth of the package.

In countries where incoming companies are concerned about the potential loss of technology through licensing or other operation arrangements, further steps are sometimes taken to protect IP. For example, in the study of Norwegian firms in India, one approach taken was to not send the latest version of the company's technology. The sales manager of one company remarked: 'We have to be a bit pragmatic with regard to licence agreements and technology transfer to countries like India. The risk of larceny is, of course, always existing, but you have to take this risk if you want to enter a perceived promising market . . . Besides that, the next generation of technology is always our own and back in Norway' (Tomassen et al., 1998, 12). Similarly, companies have used a variety of approaches to protect their IP in China beyond the official system, such as transferring outdated rather than state-of-the-art technology; withholding crucial components, such as source code; restricting access to key internal documentation; and setting up monitoring systems to notify cases of IP infringements (Tackaberry, 1998). The approach of the Japanese company Kyocera is another illustration of the extended efforts made to protect key intellectual property when manufacturing in other countries, as described by their technology and strategy manager: 'Workers in its overseas plants are told precisely how to mix materials from Japan with local ones, but are given no idea what the ingredients are. When a part breaks on an advanced machine overseas, Kyocera's Japanese engineers disassemble and repair it in privacy, so that none of the local workers can take a good look' (*Economist*, 2004, 67).

WHY INTERNATIONAL LICENSING? THE LICENSEE'S PERSPECTIVE

It is clear that there is widespread use of licensing by the full range of companies in their international operations. What drives the adoption and continued use of licensing? In the initiation of licensing deals, licensees frequently play the principal role in the process: in some studies they are shown to be the primary initiators (Ford, 1988; Lowe and Crawford, 1984). The case below, in Box 4.3, of an Irish company is provided as an example of licensee-initiated licensing, showing that an unsolicited approach may be the result of a process begun some time beforehand, and may be a key plank of the technology-seeking company's business development strategy, but for the company possessing the technology it may involve a new, unconsidered departure from its planned operations.

There are various reasons for companies to be seeking technology in the international arena, many that are explained by the particular circumstances of individual firms, such as in the Plastronix case. However, an important general factor is the competitive pressure that companies face to develop new products as rapidly and as cheaply as possible – in part reflecting the shortening of product life cycles. Also, by obtaining new technology, companies may be able to enter new and promising market areas. At an international business seminar in Australia in 2002, the head of a company involved in brokering technology deals, including licensing, described how a multinational mining company had approached another company that also set up technology deals, saying, roughly, 'we have $70 million to spend, how can we get into biotechnology?' Glaxo Wellcome's activity as a purchaser of technology illustrates how importantly the search for sources of new technology is regarded by large and small firms, frequently generating licensing outcomes: 'Like its peers, Glaxo spends around a fifth of its budget buying other people's ideas – particularly from

---

BOX 4.3   A CASE OF LICENSEE-INITIATED LICENSING

Research reveals that licensing activity is initiated frequently by potential licensees seeking specific technology. The following case is an example of this process, providing insight into how a licensee might arrive on the doorstep of a company with the relevant technology, offering a licensing deal or some other arrangement in order to gain access to the technology. The company in question is Plastronix, part of the Irish diversified group, Killeen Investments, which began as an assembler and distributor of Toyota vehicles, and among other investments had added an engineering division. As part of a search for new business opportunities in 1980, in view of the rise of computer manufacturing and related electronics products, options for supplying this growth sector were examined. A large market was identified for the plastic mouldings or boxes into which the electronic equipment was inserted. Given the company's inexperience in the field, its first task was to locate the technology that might provide the basis for setting up a manufacturing operation. Potential sources were seen as likely to have been in the US, Europe or Japan, and accordingly a search process was initiated. As a part of this process, the Tokyo office of the Irish Development Authority (IDA) was brought into play to look for options in Japan. In the course of discussions with the IDA, a company with the relevant technology was identified: Munekata, a manufacturer of injection moulding tools and precision plastics for the electronics industry. In December 1981, a meeting with Munekata was arranged, with a formal introduction, by the IDA. Munekata initially responded negatively to the idea. Subsequently, Plastronix enlisted the support of Toyota in a second attempt to come up with an acceptable arrangement, putting forward three main options: an equity joint venture, a licensing agreement with an option of conversion to a JV at a later stage, or a technology collaboration/licensing agreement. After lengthy negotiations, a renewable seven-year technical collaboration agreement was signed, leading to a manufacturing start-up in Ireland in 1984 (Cullen, 1986). Subsequently, Munekata took over the Irish operation (in the late 1980s), then sold it back to an Irish company in 2002 (a management buy-out), and reverted to a technical collaboration agreement as the basis for a continuing relationship.

---

small biotech firms . . . Lamivudine/3TC was invented by a Canadian biotech firm, Biochem Pharma, which licensed it to Glaxo in 1990' (*Economist*, 1997, 66). Whatever the reason, a choice is faced as to how to achieve the goal of new technology in the form of new products or processes. Figure 4.2 illustrates these choices – overall, to make, buy or cooperate.

The 'make' choice involves the company in undertaking the requisite research and development (R&D) in order to generate (perhaps) the desired

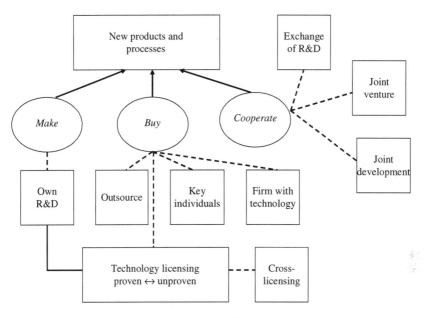

Source: Adapted from Luostarinen and Welch (1990, p. 37).

Figure 4.2   Licensing and new products/processes

technology. To take this path is to involve the firm in the cost, risk (of failure) and time to achieve an uncertain outcome. As it is, much of the research that is carried out is wasted because the work has already been carried out elsewhere, and is subject to patents: estimates reach as high as 30 per cent as to the research that is wasted because of this. Rabino and Enayati (1995, 22) refer to the case of a company that developed a new product and did achieve a patent on their invention, but also found out that patents were held on other parts of the product, so they could not go ahead with production. A problem is the sheer amount of new, patented technology emerging each year: there were 355 000 patent applications filed with the US Patent Office in 2002, and the Office was dealing with a backlog of about half a million applications (*Economist*, 2003b). Given the high cost and failure rate of technology development projects, it is not surprising that companies continue to seek alternative paths to desired new technology. Even where technology licensing is used, if the technology is relatively unproven, considerable further R&D may be required to bring the technology to a practically usable state with a marketable end-product.

Amongst the alternative approaches is a broad group which has been labelled 'cooperate' in Figure 4.2. The high costs and risks in technological development are particularly evident where attempts are made to achieve major advances or leaps in technology, creating a strong incentive to share the costs with other companies. This might occur through joint development, exchange of R&D or through the establishment of a joint venture company to carry out the R&D. An example of the cooperation route to technical development is the Kone–Toshiba alliance noted in Chapter 12.

The third main path is to 'buy' the technology, using a number of different techniques. An obvious method is to buy the company that is developing, or has already developed, the desired technology. During the dot.com boom of the early 2000s this was a path favoured by many companies seeking to get started in this area. It has been heavily used also by companies seeking to become involved in the biotechnology sector. In many cases, this may not mean full takeover but will be undertaken initially in the form of a minority share: perhaps only 10–15 per cent, as a way of opening up a window on what is happening in the company in question, with a view to ultimately increasing the stake if technological outcomes look promising. Technological development begins with the ideas of people, and one way of accessing new technology is to acquire the people that can change technology. If people have developed the new technology while at other companies, acquiring the people and the technology may not be straightforward: many firms have been trying to prevent this occurring through the application of legal constraints on relevant individuals taking the technology elsewhere, with varying success.

Increasingly, rather than developing the desired technology themselves, firms have been resorting to outsourcing of the R&D, effectively purchasing a technological outcome. As part of the general trend in outsourcing, some of the work has gone to lower-cost locations, such as India in the information technology field. The Australian company Mayne Group has contracted an Indian pharmaceutical company, Intas, to develop a generic anti-cancer drug rather than trying to do the work itself, bypassing some Australian regulatory restrictions and accessing a lower-cost environment in the process (Matterson, 2004). A US investigation concluded that outsourcing, foreign and local, constituted about 25% of total R&D spending in the US (Studt and Duga, 2001).

Finally, amongst this broad mix of approaches shown in Figure 4.2 is the licensing option. Instead of outright purchase of the technology, a company is seeking the right to use already developed technology under certain conditions; that is, the company is not free to exploit the technology without constraint. For example, there may be a strict geographical limit on the range of exploitation under the terms of the agreement. As well, there is a wide spectrum in the extent to which the technology that is being accessed has actually been proved, technologically and in the marketplace. In general, licensees show a preference for technology that is fully proven, thereby minimizing the time and costs of applying the technology. However, there are cases where companies have a clear idea of the technology required and how it might be used, often within an existing context, such that they will only need the raw technology, even if it is in a relatively undeveloped state. In such situations, those seeking the technology – potential licensees – may have a far clearer idea of how the technology can be applied than its owner, and, as a result, be far more active and committed in pursuing the licensing deal. The high level of US patent applications noted above is an indication of just how much new technology is continually coming on stream, much of which would be in an unproven state.

Cross-licensing is a sub-set of licensing which has been growing in importance as a way of accessing technology: effectively the rights to use the desired technology are purchased in whole or part through the exchange of technology that the purchaser possesses; that is, it necessarily implies preceding technological development and resulting ownership of outcomes. The head of strategic planning at BHP's steel division in the early 1990s indicated that the key consideration in its approach to obtaining technology was whether the relevant technology was critical to the division's operations. If not, they would seek to buy the technology. If it were deemed to be critical, the division would seek to develop it via internal R&D, or would outsource the task. Overall, it is evident that the strong demand for licensing deals arises out of broad processes whereby companies are using licensing as one of a range of options in response to the pressure to continually upgrade or diversify their technology, and improve performance in the marketplace.

ADOPTION AND USE OF LICENSING: THE LICENSOR'S PERSPECTIVE

As noted already, licensing is used extensively by the largest multinationals, but also it is employed by individual inventors and very small firms; in other words, its usage covers a wide range of types of firms. Inevitably, there is also a long list of reasons, often differing, across these different groups, as to why licensing is utilized in international operations, separately, or as part of broader operation packages. Individual inventors typically have a limited range of foreign operation options available, and licensing tends to feature strongly for them, whereas large multinationals tend to be better placed to fit licensing into broader packages, with a wider set of objectives. As well, there has been a shift in the way licensing has been regarded in a

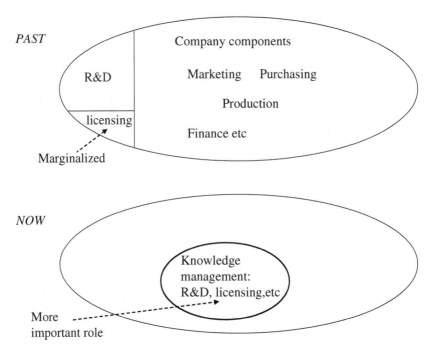

Figure 4.3   Changing strategic view of licensing

general sense in recent years: along with intellectual property it has
come to be viewed in more strategic terms by companies, rather than being
a 'fringe' concern, as illustrated in Figure 4.3. In this section we will seek
to unravel the different perspectives on why and how licensing is employed,
to provide a basis for understanding its role in international business
operations.

Earlier research indicated that licensing was not seen as a front-line
method for penetrating foreign markets. Its adoption, in the main, was as
a residual or secondary strategy, when, for various reasons, companies
were constrained from using other, more preferred, methods of operation.
In an Australian study of outward foreign licensing by mainly small and
medium-sized enterprises (SMEs) in almost no case did companies refer
to 'positive' reasons for adopting licensing as a form of foreign operations; rather, 'negative' factors, mainly constraints on using other operation methods such as exporting and foreign direct investment, were
stressed (see Table 4.1; Carstairs and Welch, 1982). While undoubtedly
there has been a general shift in the way licensing is regarded, for many
companies it is still a 'second choice' method in international operations

Table 4.1   Why outward international licensing? An Australian study

Reason given	% of firms
High shipping costs	53.5
Tariff and non-tariff barriers	41.9
High Australian production costs	25.6
Problems in selling goods overseas (e.g. distributors)	23.3
High risk in foreign investment	18.6
Lack of finance	11.6

Source: Carstairs and Welch (1982, p. 35).

(Tomassen et al., 1998). In the machine-tool industry, Davies (1995, 941) concluded that 'in general licensing is chosen as a "second-best" option for use where constraints dictate the course of action'. This is not to say that licensing was regarded as unhelpful in foreign market penetration. In the study of Norwegian firms in India it was evident that licensing was not a 'residual' strategy but part of an overall objective of long-term penetration of the Indian market by the companies concerned (Tomassen et al., 1998).

The genesis of outward licensing in many cases is the act of first becoming a licensee. Given the drive to obtain technology, it is not surprising that for many companies the first experience of licensing is in becoming a licensee. While not a focus of the study, a number of companies in Australian research stressed how inward licensing had facilitated their eventual outward licensing activity. The inward contribution came in the form of licensing-specific knowledge, networks and raised awareness of the international possibilities of licensing (Welch and Luostarinen, 1993). This is in line with growing research that emphasizes the importance of inward–outward connections in explaining internationalization (see, for example, Karlsen et al., 2003).

Licensing Linked to other Modes

Overall statistics regarding licensing show that it is extensively, if not predominantly, used in association with foreign direct investment rather than as a unique, individual mode, involving independent (that is, unconnected) organizations. In terms of aggregate international licensing payments, the proportion paid between parts of affiliated entities is as high as 80 per cent (Clegg and Cross, 2000; UNCTAD, 2003/6: based on German, Japanese and US data). US balance of payments data regarding royalties and licensing fees reveal that payments between affiliates constituted 74.5 per cent of receipts and 81.8 per cent of payments in this category for 2003. In this context, licensing clearly is not the mainstream penetration mode. It tends to serve a supporting role to foreign direct investment, aimed at achieving other objectives (see strategy section for a discussion of mode combinations including licensing). Apart from assisting in foreign market penetration, licensing can contribute to more effective control over the foreign unit, especially when the investment is in the form of a minority joint venture. A licensing agreement may encompass many aspects of business activity and knowledge, including managerial and marketing considerations, thus extending the reach of control. This possibility was important to a number of Australian firms in Malaysia when local laws at the time restricted the level of foreign equity in local operations to less than 50 per cent.

Licensing also represents a basis for transferring funds between different parts of a multinational's subsidiary network, rather than relying on the most direct form of profit remittance. Again, this may be more important to the multinational when a joint venture is involved and its profit remittance policy is constrained by concerns such as the need to fund expansion projects. The cost incurred by the subsidiary through the payment of royalties under a licensing agreement has the additional effect of reducing the amount of profit at the subsidiary, and therefore reducing the extent of liability to local taxation. Effectively, licensing can serve as a means of transferring taxation liabilities from high to low taxation regimes within a multinational's network of countries with divergent taxation systems. Taxation administrations in various countries have begun discussions with each other with the aim of restraining such techniques. Recently, the Australian Taxation Office has been focusing on licensing as an international funds transfer vehicle. The issue has come to the fore as a result of an Australian court's decision that Unisys Australia was liable to pay an extra $A89 million in tax based on royalties paid to the parent corporation in the US under a licensing agreement: it was viewed as constituting a transfer pricing arrangement. The case, and the issue, have become the subject of talks between the US Inland Revenue Department and the Australian Taxation Office (Riley, 2004). Clearly, the rationale for licensing in this case has little to do with its potential role in penetrating foreign markets.

Licensing also may be linked to project operations, such as in the building of large industrial complexes, covering the transfer of required technology during the construction phase and in ongoing operation of the relevant facility. Again, licensing plays a supportive, though nonetheless important, role to the primary project activity. Licensing establishes agreed-upon ownership of technology by the project provider, and a basis and schedule for its transfer, and can be an important means of generating additional returns from the project.

Stepping-Stone Strategy

Although licensing tends mainly to be used as a starting point in the pene-tration of individual foreign markets, nevertheless it is employed often in other positions in companies' chain of operations over time in certain markets (Welch, 1993). In fact, it can serve as an important link or stepping-stone between modes at any stage; for example, in some of the cases noted above it provided a link between exporting and foreign direct investment. The experience of Foster's, the Australian beer and wine multinational, in penetrating the UK market illustrates this positioning. It began exporting beer to the UK in the late 1970s. Having identified the market potential through exporting, it felt that it needed another form of operations if it were to develop the market: exporting was a high-cost method given the weight factor, ensuring that Foster's beer would stay as a premium priced, niche product rather than tapping into the mass market. At that point, the company was unprepared to make a major commitment by setting up its own manufacturing operations, so it went into a licensing arrangement in 1981 with the local brewer, Watney, Mann and Truman, to produce Foster's for the UK market. However, by 1986, it had begun a more aggressive inter-national strategy of penetrating foreign markets via acquisition, to acceler-ate expansion and to be in stronger control of the development of the Foster's brand. As a result, it switched from the licensing arrangement to acquisition of a major UK brewer, Courage, in 1986 to form the centre-piece of its UK operations.

For manufacturers that have begun exporting to relatively distant markets, such as from Europe or the US to Australia, if business develops, questions often arise, particularly for those companies selling industrial products, around the servicing of their products and customers. The need for quick delivery, frequent customer contact, constant monitoring of product performance and the need to fix breakdowns and the like quickly place considerable demands on foreign companies without local facilities. Rather than setting up a costly service and support operation for what may be a small market initially, licensing sometimes is viewed as a way of effectively 'purchasing' a manufacturing and servicing base, with invest-ment for manufacturing a future option depending on the growth of sales and the nature of the licensing arrangement.

Figure 4.4 demonstrates the fact that licensing can fit into a stepping-stone role in various stages of foreign market penetration and between different modes, even after foreign direct investment. While less common,

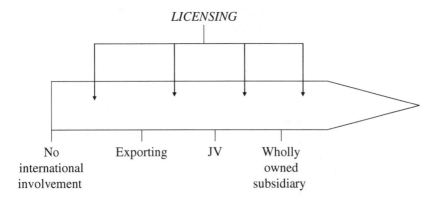

Source: Adapted from Luostarinen and Welch (1990, p. 41).

Figure 4.4   Licensing as a 'stepping stone'

the latter situation may be used when a company wants to scale back its activities in a certain market, but maintain a presence and a continuing income stream despite reduced involvement. For example, an Australian firm, Schiavello Commercial Interiors, acquired a New Zealand manufacturer in 1990, but found that sales did not develop as expected through to 1992, so it sold the business, but entered into a licensing agreement with the acquirer and exported components for the licensed products. In a study of 209 outward foreign licensing arrangements by Australian companies, 12 (5.7 per cent) were found to have been preceded by foreign direct investment (Welch, 1993, 223).

In a study of Swedish companies, Svensson (1984, 223) found instances where licensing was being used as a stepping-stone strategy, although this was 'seldom intended from the beginning but emerged as the firm's financial resources and management, production and marketing skills increased. In some cases the transition to other modes of penetration implied that co-operation with the original licensees was terminated. In other cases the original licensee became a joint venture partner or was acquired by the licensor'. For smaller companies with limited resources to undertake any degree of foreign market activity, licensing often seems to be an attractive option, with another party carrying out the tasks and incurring the costs of market development, with the prospect of an income stream that contributes to further technological and market expansion – which is why so many companies use licensing as an initial foreign market penetration mode. Mode switching tends not to enter consideration at this stage. However, licensing can be, and has been, employed as a perceived low-risk form of market experimentation, before making a deeper commitment in some other form, whether intended or not. Clearly, there are many possibilities regarding when and how licensing might be used in a stepping-stone role, although the ability to benefit from this potentially flexible contribution does depend on the structure and functioning of the licensing arrangement as a springboard to mode switching (Petersen et al., 2000).

Accessing Blocked Markets

While it is becoming less common for foreign markets to be fully blocked to products from other countries as the impact of WTO rules strengthens in the global trading environment, there is still a variety of import restrictions, involving both tariff and non-tariff barriers, which are applied in a range of product and service areas by different countries and make it difficult for foreign firms to penetrate the markets in question. For example, tariffs and import restrictions were stressed by Norwegian companies as reasons why they did not pursue exporting in penetrating the Indian market, and therefore turned to other methods, including licensing. The sales manager at one company commented: 'Export to India was out of the question – it was impossible to compete with Indian firms, or foreign firms established in India, due to extremely high tariff barriers' (Tomassen et al., 1998, 11). In Australian research, there were cases of companies, having penetrated certain foreign markets via exports initially, then facing the subsequent application of import restrictions (Welch, 1993). Being unprepared at that stage to set up direct investment operations, they switched to licensing as a way of ensuring a continuing presence in the relevant markets. The licensing option could be particularly viable if a company has built a market position around its trademark and technology, making it an attractive prospect to potential licensees. As well, if the licensee's operations and marketing activities are carried out under the licensor's banner, a base is being maintained, or even expanded, for a potential future switch in operation modes, depending on the construction of the licensing arrangement. An Australian study of outward licensing deals found that 18.2 per cent were preceded by exporting activity in the foreign markets in question (Carstairs and Welch, 1982, 36).

Licensing as a 'Trojan Horse'

Various studies show that licensing use often brings additional benefits beyond the licensing deal itself that can significantly enhance the basis for its adoption. Licensing may be the mainstream penetration mode, but it has the potential to open up other possibilities, accessed through broadened mode activity. In some cases this is a by-product of the initial negotiations regarding the licensing arrangement, an intended feature of the overall arrangement. In others, it will be the outcome of an evolving relationship between licensor and licensee. When a positive relationship evolves between the two parties, it is almost inevitable that they will explore expanded business possibilities beyond the formal licensing arrangement. Australian and Finnish research has shown that exports by the licensor to the licensee under the umbrella of the licensing arrangement were very common, frequently generating more revenue than that from the licensing deal itself (Luostarinen and Welch, 1990; Welch, 1993). Effectively, licensing can act as a 'Trojan horse', creating the basis for the supply of components, equipment or materials to a licensed foreign manufacturing operation. Ongoing licensor–licensee interaction might lead to divergent forms of cooperation: examples found in research were of the licensor importing products from the licensee that contributed to its product range, and of the licensor and licensee joining for a project in a third market. Of course, the most striking form of licensor–licensee cooperation is in cross-licensing deals, which have been a growing and important feature of the licensing landscape, as noted earlier, with companies seeking to obtain others' technology by offering 'interesting' technology in exchange. In the case of the cross-licensing deal between Sanyo and Kodak, this was preceded by a lawsuit brought against Sanyo by Kodak over alleged infringement of some of its patents – clearly, not born out of cooperation! Kodak withdrew its lawsuit and instead agreed to license the patents in exchange for Sanyo licensing its patents, both in the area of digital photography (Kodak press release, 2/9/01). A US study of licensing deals across a range of countries found that 'cross licensing firms enjoy superior profitability compared to firms that receive or give licenses' (Gleason et al., 2000, 431).

Residual Technology/Markets

The residual or secondary approach to licensing noted above is evident when companies use it to serve foreign markets that are considered less important for various reasons: their size, prospects, distance (cultural and physical), or simply in terms of strategic priorities. Licensing is viewed as being suitable because of its perceived low cost and low ongoing commitment to activities in the foreign market, thereby allowing the company to concentrate on more important markets. Similarly, companies sometimes create new technology in the process of solving manufacturing or other operational problems, but the technology is subsidiary, or unconnected, to their area of business so they are not prepared to exploit the technology as a new venture. Through licensing, however, it is still possible to obtain a return from the new technology. A large Australian mining company, MIM (now part of Swiss-based Xstrata), began selling processing technology in this manner, although in its case foreign income grew to the point where it made a substantial contribution to total R&D costs.

Taken overall, it is evident from the above discussion that licensing is adopted as a method in international business operations for a variety of reasons, and used in divergent roles, some as a mainstream foreign market penetration vehicle, others in support of different modes, as a part of broader packages. A key driving force in the adoption of licensing is the relentless global search for sources of new technology by large and small companies. Sometimes the particular use of licensing is intended from the outset, but often it develops over time, as companies better understand through experience how to extract its range of potential contributions to internationalization more effectively.

INTERNATIONAL LICENSING: IMPLEMENTATION AND PROCESS ISSUES

Pre-agreement

It has already been identified that much of the international licensing that occurs is driven by the activity of licensees, so that many of the preliminary phases (such as search and promotional activities) leading to deals being concluded are short-circuited. Even with an unsolicited approach by a potential licensee, often with a draft licensing agreement to hand, there is much to be settled. Of course, there are some companies that are prepared to sign an agreement with little or no investigation because they have a limited view of international prospects, and are happy to contemplate a future royalty stream involving little work on their part. The Plastronix–Munekata case, in Box 4.3 above, viewed from Munekata's perspective, demonstrates how much may be involved after the unsolicited approach by a potential licensee. The experience of an Australian inventor shows how difficult it can be sometimes to readily accept an offer, no matter how attractive it seems. The Australian was exhibiting at a trade fair in the United States, when approached by a team, including lawyers, from a large US multinational with the offer of a licensing deal, and draft agreement to sign. He said he felt 'overwhelmed', returned to Australia, undertook a year of market research and advertised his technology in relevant US trade magazines, then finally signed with the original interested party. For most companies, the offer of a licensing deal will be followed by negotiation, research regarding the potential licensee, and discussions with lawyers and, perhaps, consultants on intellectual property, taxation and foreign market requirements. In a study of predominantly small firms in the US licensing in and out, it was found that, where external help was sought, it was mainly in the area of legal negotiations (Fu and Perkins, 1995). It is common for negotiations to take at least six to nine months, during which the tone and setting of a possible future relationship is established, and there is much to be settled, with no certainty of an agreement being reached.

Timing of Foreign Push

For companies that have chosen licensing as a way of penetrating foreign markets, there are many hurdles to overcome before even reaching the negotiation stage. At the outset, there is the question when it is appropriate to take new concepts or technology into the international marketplace. A general principle is that the marketing process is easier with proven technology – technically finalized and with already established market acceptance. This is why some research shows surprisingly high rates of licensing of relatively mature technology (Lowe and Crawford, 1984; Welch, 1993). Given that widespread evidence shows a low rate of *technical* causes of failure of new products that have entered the marketplace, but a relatively high failure rate due to lack of market acceptance, potential technology recipients are looking to be convinced about likely market attractiveness of the technology. However, in industries where technology is changing rapidly, it may be necessary to move quickly to exploit new technology, even before completion of the final development and testing stages. As Figure 4.5 shows, such technology is less valuable to a potential licensee as much remains to be done after access to the technology is obtained, including further development and market introduction, with all the additional costs and risks to be incurred. The importance of this consideration, though, is related to the technological and marketing ability of the recipient firm to implant the new technology: a close fit may enable the recipient firm to apply quickly and easily even relatively raw technology (Welch, 1985). In a similar way to franchising, it takes considerable time for the licensor to assemble the licensing package and secure the requisite intellectual property protection, in its various forms, in chosen markets, well ahead of any marketing steps.

FOREIGN MARKETING: FINDING LICENSEES

Companies utilize a wide variety of avenues to seek out licensing customers: personal networks of key staff; government-based networks and services; trade shows; Internet-based sources and databases; advertising and promotion in trade and business journals, magazines and newspapers; relevant seminars and conferences; and external consultants. Fu and

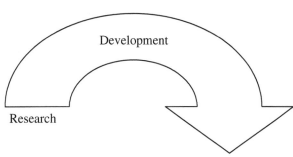

Early: less valuable to licensee as much remains to be done

Commercialization

Late: more valuable to licensee as development, production and marketing problems should have been dealt with

However, depends on:
• Technical and marketing ability of technology recipient
• Rate of change of technology

Source: Adapted from Luostarinen and Welch (1990, p. 52).

Figure 4.5   Technology cycle

Perkins (1995) found that, for licensors, the most important sources of licensing prospects were personal acquaintances, word-of-mouth informal leads and trade shows. A licensing consultant based in Germany has observed: 'My experience over 25 years has shown that the most successful way to find licensing partners abroad is to kindle the interest of a member of management or of the technical department of prospective partners . . . to accomplish this, the best medium . . . is the technical and industrial press . . . most serious inquiries and about 80% of the licence contracts resulted from editorial publication in trade magazines' (Marx, 1996, 9). With increasing use of the Internet in all aspects, its importance as a means of finding, contacting and communicating with potential licensees should increase, although the question of intellectual property protection may constrain the rate of progress (Petersen and Welch, 2003).

CONSTRAINTS ON MARKETING ACTIVITY

Figure 4.6 summarizes the range of factors that constrain the approach by companies to the marketing of licensing arrangements to prospective

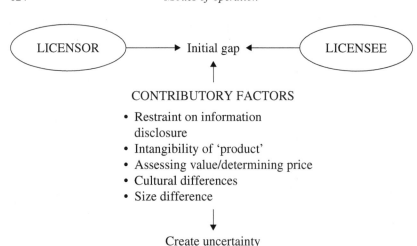

CONTRIBUTORY FACTORS

- Restraint on information disclosure
- Intangibility of 'product'
- Assessing value/determining price
- Cultural differences
- Size difference

Create uncertainty

- This may be diminished by licensing knowledge/experience;
- Strong licensing package;
- Relevant foreign market experience/networks.

Source: Adapted from Luostarinen and Welch (1990, p. 50).

Figure 4.6   Exchange impediments

clients, and the moderating factors acting to facilitate exchange. A major constraint on companies and individuals in the marketing of the technology they have developed is the concern about appropriation of the technology, without compensation, by those showing an interest in it. Even though there has been a global strengthening of IP protection systems, those depending on the quality of these systems are all too aware of their frailties in practice, especially individual inventors and small firms. Relative size is a consideration: small firms and individual inventors tend to be particularly wary about information disclosure when dealing with large multinationals. This concern is reinforced in situations where there is a dependence on secrecy (or confidentiality) agreements in pre-licensing contact. It is always difficult to sell new technology and its benefits, and build a relationship, when the first step is to demand that a potential partner sign a secrecy agreement.

The constraint on information disclosure makes it difficult for the prospective client firm to assess the viability and value of what is being offered. Marx (1996) argues that the stress on secrecy is a major obstacle to licensing, and that companies overestimate the uniqueness of the technology on offer anyway. This is often exacerbated by the intangibility of the 'product' on sale: it may be little more than a set of drawings or blueprints.

Particularly when the technology has not yet appeared in the marketplace, uncertainty is further accentuated by the difficulty of determining an appropriate price, by both sides to the exchange. In addition, there are the normal gaps between the parties created by cultural and other national differences, such as technical standards. Taken together, these factors generate considerable uncertainty in how the marketing of licensing deals in foreign markets is approached by many companies and individual inventors, and is matched by similar uncertainty for many of those who are targets in the marketing process.

As noted in Figure 4.6, there are a number of factors that may act to moderate or even remove the sense of uncertainty in pre-licensing contexts. On the licensor's side, having a strong, well protected licensing package generates greater confidence about opening up the technology for inspection, and making it easier for a prospective licensee to assess what is being offered. Research also indicates that, as companies gain experience in licensing in foreign markets, they become more adept at handling the pre-licensing process, and more confident about handling initial information disclosure and deal structuring issues (Welch, 1993). Inevitably, too, the activity in other markets provides a clear demonstration of the technology's worth and marketability to purchasers in new markets, thereby further easing uncertainty. Companies stress the importance of the learning process in successful licensing. In situations where the licensor has had preceding operations in the market in question, there should be a reduction in uncertainty, even more so when this has involved contact or joint activity in some form with the eventual licensee. As noted earlier, a licensee with a clear idea of the technology on offer and where it would fit into that company's activities, as well as having previous licensing-in experience, tends to approach the pre-licensing stage with greater assurance.

SELECTION OF LICENSEES

Having found one or more interested and interesting potential licensees in a foreign market, the critical next step is to choose the most appropriate partner to negotiate a deal with. In Australian research, experienced licensors stressed this step as the most important of all. Because of the longevity of the bulk of licensing arrangements, a bad choice can have a significant, long-term negative impact, and removal of a non-performing partner may be legally awkward. For instance, Pearson (1993, 159) has argued that, in the Thai context, 'it is often difficult to terminate licensing agreements if there is a problem. It is better to allow the agreement to lapse'. Many of the individuals engaged in marketing new technology, especially those from small firms or individual inventors, are focused on the technology and what it will do, whereas the key to licensing success from a licensor's standpoint is a licensee effectively exploiting the technology in the foreign market: 'the success of the licensor depends on the success of the licensee . . . the licensor is not so much selling a "product", its technology, but rather seeking a partner for a long term relationship' (Luostarinen and Welch, 1990, 54). Consequently, it makes sense for a licensor to spend time and take care in the selection process, which is difficult in situations where the approach has come from an interested buyer. This may involve talking to customers, suppliers and the like that are interacting with the company in focus, that is, going beyond the company profile and its financial position, as well as engaging in personal contact with relevant company staff, with consequent demands for visits and network establishment. Mottner and Johnson (2000) point out how important yet difficult selection is in transitional and emerging economies because of the problems of finding and evaluating licensing candidates. Some companies in the Australian research took as long as two to three years to carry through this phase, reflecting just how critically it was regarded (Welch, 1993).

In their evaluation of licensee candidates, the Australian licensors were able to describe the types of partners to avoid, but found it difficult to give clear guidelines on what constituted an ideal licensee. Some of the candidates to avoid that they mentioned were firms making a competitive product; the leader in the field; those that had already invested substantial sums in seeking to develop what the licensor had achieved; and firms with inadequate marketing and production capacity. There was a general concern expressed by small firms about becoming lost in larger firms' activities. On the positive side, licensors expressed the ideal licensee as something like the following: a licensee where the business emanating from the licensed technology could be considered important enough to invest substantial effort to ensure success. This could be a firm seeking growth. The possession of an appropriate marketing infrastructure and resources by the licensee was stressed, while companies often referred to the need for a good fit between the two parties' operations, particularly at a technical level.

NEGOTIATION

While the licensor might have found a suitable licensee candidate, there is another substantial hurdle to be overcome: the negotiation of the terms of an agreement that is acceptable to both parties. This can take considerable time, and is typically the start of a higher level of communication between the parties. At this point, licensors have to deal more directly with the idiosyncrasies of a foreign legal and business system, and cope with cultural differences, including the vagaries of cross-cultural communication and, perhaps, language barriers. Communication breakdown and disagreements can easily lead to early failure, although from the licensor's perspective this stage provides a means of testing what is to come. The negotiation phase does not just involve coming up with the basis of agreement, but is an important building block in the future relationship. Pushing for the highest possible payment and most favourable terms can easily sour the relationship from the outset: Australian licensors emphasized the importance of being seen to 'be reasonable'. As noted earlier, the offer of a comprehensive, well protected licensing package, proven in technological and marketing terms, strengthens the hand of the licensor in negotiations. A study of licensing by US firms found that the most important factor driving the price or return from licensing was the 'amount of technical and other services provided to licensees' (Root and Contractor, 1981). As well, Australian licensors indicated that the greater the extent of knowledge about the foreign market, and more particularly the likely market impact of the technology in question, the better equipped they were to argue for an acceptable agreement and payments.

THE LICENSING AGREEMENT

There tend to be different positions on the place of the formal licensing agreement in the licensing relationship, depending on cultural background. In some cultures, the agreement is viewed as a statement of intent rather than a precise set of guidelines governing action. For licensing agreements in Thailand, Pearson (1993, 159) has noted: 'Business agreements are founded on trust and understanding, and there is an expectation that if a business is not going well the parties will not look to the letter of their agreement, but will sit down and talk about it. Your agreement therefore needs to establish a "middle path" between Western certainty and Eastern flexibility.' In a similar vein, Australian licensors stressed that a tight legal document could never ensure that licensing worked in practice, and depended on the development of trust and a positive working relationship between the parties. As it is, no licensing agreement is able to cover all future contingencies, so that the parties must call on the quality of the working relationship at some stage to deal with emerging issues. However, in both contexts there is agreement on the importance of the formal agreement as a reference point for the parties through time. An effective relationship between licensor and licensee is built on informal, personal relations, but people move and memories dim as to what was agreed to, so in some situations it is necessary to return to the formal document that encapsulates the intention of the parties.

AGREEMENT CONTENT AND TERMS

There is a wide variation in the content and structure of licensing agreements, depending on many factors, such as the industry; the nature of the technology or intellectual property being licensed, such as a cartoon figure versus complicated new industrial equipment technology; the negotiation process; the legal context and role of lawyers; the licensing experience and attitudes of both parties; and the country context. Ultimately, the content is determined by what is negotiated. In one case involving a small New Zealand licensor and large Australian licensee, the head of the New Zealand company said he did not want lawyers involved in the drawing up of the licensing agreement. As a result, he penned a short, simple version of what the parties had agreed to, and that became the formal agreement. A representative of the licensee indicated that lawyers could drive 'the proverbial truck through the legal loop-holes' in the agreement, but it worked anyway because of the value of know-how flowing through the arrangement which would be more costly than the licensing fees to replicate. It is, therefore, difficult to describe a standard form of licensing agreement. Nevertheless, the types of clauses commonly used in agreements, as shown in different studies and presentations, include those covering the following:

- the licensing package components – a description of the rights to be transferred;
- payment terms;
- obligations of both parties in the arrangement, for example by the licensor in respect of the steps taken to transfer effectively the technology, including training; and by the licensee with regard to marketing and other actions to advance the interests of the licensed business;
- restrictions;
- intellectual property protection obligations;
- performance clauses;
- grant-back rights to technology developed by the licensee in the course of using the original, transferred technology: it is common for these to be assigned back to the licensor;
- exclusive or non-exclusive right to a territory(ies) – country or region;
- duration of agreement;
- dispute settling arrangements, including the national law or arbitration body to apply.

PAYMENT TERMS

While each licensing case has its own set of unique considerations that may require specific contractual provisions, payment demands represent a key general concern that is often at the heart of licensing negotiation difficulties and compliance problems, and there are differing perspectives on how best to approach the subject. The two main forms of payment are an up-front lump sum when the agreement is signed, or in stages shortly thereafter; and an on-going royalty based on sales or production (as measured, for example, by ex-factory price). These are commonly applied in combination. When a licensor is faced with conditions of uncertainty of outcomes related to the licensee's operations or their business context, there is a strong temptation to seek as much revenue as possible in an up-front form. Whether this can be achieved in negotiations is always questionable: at the least, it makes the process more problematic. High up-front fees inevitably place early financial demands on the licensee, before operations occur, and it may take some time to implant the new technology and put a marketing infrastructure in place, further exacerbating financial commitments sometimes well before revenue begins to flow. This is why some companies, in the interests of the long-term viability of the licensee, waive not only up-front fees but also royalty payments for periods of 12–18 months, particularly in developing countries and emerging economies.

Rather than focusing solely on fees generated via the licensing agreement, companies may be able to obtain revenue from the licensing connection through sales of machinery, equipment, materials and the like. In the end, successful licensing as an international operation form depends on successful, performing licensees, and the fees being charged are a factor in this. In a study of inward licensing by Swedish companies, Svensson (1984) found a moderate royalty to be a positive element in assisting the early introduction of the object of the licensing activity to the marketplace, and profitability. Royalty rates in licensing agreements show large variation: in Australian research, the range was from 2 to 15 per cent. A starting 'rule-of-thumb' often used in the Australian context was 5 per cent of output or a sales indicator, but this was adjusted in the bargaining process, or for situations such as when technology was changing rapidly (adjusted upwards) and there were distinct industry differences. Ultimately, for the parties to be committed to the licensing relationship, there has to be clear mutual benefit for both, and a high payment by the licensee may simply become the incentive to get around the terms of the agreement after post-agreement transfers have been completed.

PERFORMANCE CLAUSES

A major concern for licensors is how to ensure that licensees operate
effectively and generate worthwhile returns. One approach to dealing
with this concern has been the insertion of performance clauses in many
licensing agreements. Performance clauses are an attempt to provide a
legal basis for requiring a licensee to perform to what is deemed to be
a minimum acceptable standard. Examples are the requirement to pay a
minimum level of royalties and to maintain given quality standards.
The minimum royalty clause is important as a way of ensuring that the
licensing agreement is not used by the licensee simply as a means of closing
down the introduction of competitive technology to the market in question. This is precisely what happened to an Australian company that
licensed a British company in the same field: the agreement was for 15
years without a minimum performance clause. The British company did
not apply the technology and was not legally obliged to do so. Not surprisingly, the Australian company had a very negative view of licensing,
but a major part of the problem was the agreement that had been negotiated. However, there are limits on what requirements can be placed in a
licensing agreement, for example, via the inclusion of a clause requiring
the best endeavours of a licensee to promote the sale of a product. The
judge in an Australian court case commented: 'the inventor must take [the]
contracting party as he finds him. He cannot expect from a small company
the same expenditure and production as from a large and powerful
company. He cannot expect from an old-fashioned and financially embar-
rassed company that which he should receive from a better equipped and
more flourishing concern' (Wray, 1983).

POST-AGREEMENT TRANSFERS

The licensor has a strong vested interest in the licensee quickly and
effectively taking and using the technology to be transferred. While the
licensing agreement provides a general framework for the process of transferring licensed components to the licensee, its effectiveness will depend on
more than what is set down in the agreement. This is related to the technological and marketing capacity of the licensee to receive and apply the technology to be transferred, as shown in Figures 4.7 and 4.8.

The extent of departure from its existing base determines the amount
and type of learning that will be necessary for the licensee to become oper-
ationally capable. In turn, this will influence the nature of flows between the
parties (the greater the gap, the greater the flows), the type of activities this

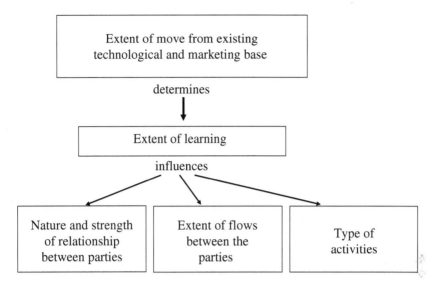

Source: Adapted from Killing (1980, p. 40).

Figure 4.7   Flows to licensee?

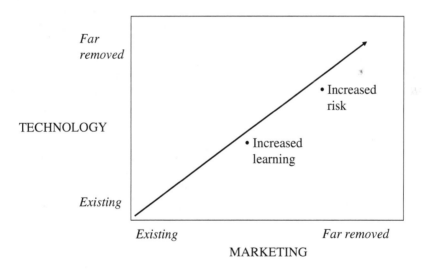

Source: Adapted from Killing (1980, p. 39).

Figure 4.8   Licensee competence?

Table 4.2   Licensing profitability

		Licence object within or closely related to licensee's technology	
		YES	NO
Licence object within or closely related to licensee's market	YES	18/25* (72%)	7/10* (70%)
	NO	0/2	1/9*

Note: * Number of profitable cases over total number of cases in each cell.

Source: Svensson (1984, p. 79).

will entail (training, interaction of personnel and so on) and the extent and type of relationship that will be necessary to support these processes. As Figure 4.8 illustrates, the further the licensee has to move away from its competence base, both technologically and in marketing terms, the greater the risk that the licensed venture will not succeed. As well, because of the greater help required by the licensee, the costs that will be incurred by the licensor in the transfer process will be greater, unless there is a clear-cut arrangement set down in the licensing agreement to cover such additional expenses, often more extensive than anticipated. In many cases, adaptation of the transferred technology and marketing techniques will be required in order to fit local conditions better. At issue then is which party should undertake the necessary adaptation, and pay for it. Ultimately, success of the transfer depends on the commitment by both parties to the process, often in ways that can never be fully anticipated in advance and covered within the licensing agreement. It is interesting to note that, in a rare study of its kind, Svensson (1984) found that the success of the licensing activity was far more related to marketing compatibility of the two parties' operations than technological fit, as shown in Table 4.2. It shows that, while marketing closeness differentiated profitability of the Swedish licensing cases examined, technological closeness had no such impact.

LONG-TERM INTERACTION AND AGREEMENT COMPLETION

Past research has shown that, having successfully completed the transfer process to licensees, licensors find it easy to downgrade their involvement,

Table 4.3   Relative licensing costs (Australian research)

Overall cost distribution:
25% protection of intellectual property
47% establishment of agreement
29% maintenance costs

Main establishment costs:
45% communication
28% training of licensee's personnel
23% search for licensees
10% adaptation & testing of equipment for licensee

Maintenance costs:
65% back-up service for licensee
11% defence of intellectual property
10% audit
7% ongoing market research

Source: Welch (1993, p. 88).

sometimes to the point where little or no contact occurs other than around the payment of royalties, or at the instigation of the licensee (Welch, 1993). Of course, this is more likely in situations where licensing is regarded as a residual or secondary form of international operations. However, in the long run, a lack of continued active commitment to the licensee's operations may be detrimental to the licensor's interests. Svensson (1984) found that continuous cooperation between licensor and licensee was critical to the long-run profitability of the licensing cases he examined. Wiedersheim-Paul (1982, 20) concluded that 'the reason for success or failure of licensing activity had little to do with the licensing object itself but rather depended on the patience of the parties in building a long-term relationship for mutual benefit'. Clearly, there are costs involved in a more active approach by the licensor, as evidenced by Australian research indicating that 'maintenance costs' represented 29 per cent of total licensing costs (see Table 4.3). Almost two-thirds of these costs were back-up services to the licensee, including technology updates, further training and personnel transfers – both ways. The other main maintenance costs were incurred in undertaking audits, defence of intellectual property, and ongoing market research – in the licensee's market. The latter may seem surprising, but the companies doing this were concerned to stay in touch with the way the market was evolving and so be better informed about the licensing operation and better placed to decide on the nature of future activities. Staying close to the licensee had the benefit of enabling the licensor to exert

greater subtle control over operations. This was further enhanced by the
continuing transfer of upgraded technology and marketing information
and programmes as they came on stream: contract violation by the licensee
risked not only legal action but also the loss of this continuing flow of
technology.

As noted earlier, by maintaining close contact and building a positive
relationship with the licensee, more opportunities are likely to arise for
wider cooperative activity in the same market or further afield. Perhaps
most importantly of all, through continued active involvement, and positive relationship development, the licensor is more likely to have widened
mode options at the completion of the initial term of the licensing agreement, including renewal of the licensing agreement or an altered mode
arrangement with the licensee. Where the licensor has been able to negotiate an option-to-buy clause within the original agreement, takeover of the
licensee may be a relatively straightforward exercise, although a licensing
arrangement could still be carried forward as part of a broadened mode
package. Anticipating such options, and trying to allow for them when
licensing is first approached, is a difficult exercise for most companies, given
that the licensing contract typically runs for a period of around seven years,
and ten years is not uncommon.

In Australian research, although there were only 11 cases where the
existing licensing arrangement was terminated, they provide some insight
into the circumstances surrounding the end of licensing. Some licensees
were unwilling to renew the agreement, in other cases market results were
unsatisfactory, but the most important reason referred to was 'problems
with the licensee', such as unsatisfactory performance. These issues led
most of the licensors to suspend operations in the host country altogether;
some switched to exporting, while one company maintained licensing
activity but with a different licensee (Carstairs and Welch, 1982, 41).
Preceding this stage, the major problems in licensing stressed by companies in the study were lack of control and information flow with regard to
the licensee's operations. At the same time, many of the licensors were able
to work around the constraints of the licensing mode to obtain an acceptable measure of influence on their licensees, but this required commitment
and involvement.

CONCLUSION

Analysis of the nature of licensing and its use has exposed a mode of
international business operations which plays multiple roles and is difficult to characterize at times, displaying almost chameleon qualities. In

comparative assessments of modes it is often depicted as being a low-risk, low-commitment mode, and that is how many companies perceive it, particularly those starting out on international operations with limited resources to support the new venture. However, other companies see licensing as a high-risk activity, with the potential to create a competitor and lose control of the technology, and as a result are generally reluctant to use licensing. For licensing to be effective, it does require active involvement and commitment by the licensor, which comes at a price, so that even the label of low commitment needs to be qualified. As it is, the demands of intellectual property protection, for broad licensing packages, in an array of countries, are often beyond the budgets of many small firms, without considering what may be demanded in defending intellectual property rights in some legal jurisdictions such as the US.

While often touted as a mode for small firms, and frequently used by them, it is large multinationals that have been using licensing more extensively, and in creative ways, in recent times, and they are clearly not driven by the resource constraint concerns that typically afflict small firms. Licensing has come to be viewed in more strategic terms in the wake of the rise of the knowledge-based view of the firm, interest in the related potential of cross-licensing, an increased concern about intellectual property protection, and a growing recognition of the revenue-generating qualities of licensing as a result of some high-profile cases involving large multinationals. Whether small or large, though, the experience of diverse companies demonstrates a wide range of useful roles that licensing is able to play in supporting or leading the internationalization activities of companies. It is often used in support of foreign direct investment, or as a stepping-stone between different modes through time, or as a first-time means of testing the potential of certain foreign markets. Whatever the purpose, between independent parties its success depends on the choice of partner, the content of the licensing arrangement and the way in which the ongoing licensor–licensee relationship is handled.

REFERENCES

Bremner, B. and R. Neff (1992), 'From the mind of Minolta – oops, make that Honeywell', *Business Week*, 24 February, 28.

Brook, S. (1999), 'Milk discovery gives scientists $1m smiles', *The Australian*, 10 June, 1.

Carson, V. (2004), 'Business big shot', *The Australian*, 27 October, 36.

Carstairs, R. and L.S. Welch (1982), 'Licensing and the internationalisation of smaller companies: some Australian evidence', *Management International Review*, **22**(3), 33–44.

Clegg, J. and A.R. Cross (2000), 'Affiliate and non-affiliate intellectual property transactions in international business: an empirical overview of the UK and USA', *International Business Review*, **9**(4), 407–30.

Cohen, D. (1991), 'Trademark strategy revisited', *Journal of Marketing*, **55**(3), 46–59.

Cukier, K. (2005), 'A market for ideas: a survey of patents and technology', *Economist*, 22 October, 1–20.

Cullen, J. (1986), 'Case study: international collaboration', *Les Nouvelles*, **21**(3), 17–21.

Davidson, W.H. (1979), 'Trends in the international transfer of the US technology to Pacific nations', in F. Choi et al. (eds), *Proceedings of the Academy of International Business: Asia–Pacific Dimensions of International Business*, College of Business Administration, University of Hawaii.

Davies, H. (1995), 'Intra-firm versus licensed transfers of machine-tool technology', *International Journal of Technology Management*, **10**(7/8), 941–54.

Dodwell, D. (1993), 'Patent troubles create trauma and cost', *Financial Times*, 27 January, 7.

Economist (1997), 'Glaxo – coping with unwellcome news', 26 April, 65–6.

Economist (2000), 'The knowledge monopolies: patent wars', 8 April, 79–82.

Economist (2003a), 'Software patents: a ticking bomb', 6 September, 57–8.

Economist (2003b), 'Patents – inventive ideas', 8 November, 63.

Economist (2004), 'Protecting the family jewels', 26 June, 67.

Far Eastern Economic Review (2004), 'Viagra loses patent protection', 29 July, 27.

Ford, D. (1988), 'Develop your technology strategy', *Long Range Planning*, **21**(5), 85–95.

Fu, S. and D.S. Perkins (1995), 'Technology licensors and licensees: who they are, what resources they employ, and how they feel', *International Journal of Technology Management*, **10**(7/8), 907–20.

Gleason, K.C., I. Mathur and M. Singh (2000), 'Operational characteristics and performance gains associated with international licensing agreements: the US evidence', *International Business Review*, **9**(4), 431–52.

Grindley, P.C. and D.J. Teece (1997), 'Managing intellectual capital: Licensing and cross-licensing in semiconductors and electronics', *California Management Review*, **39**(2), 8–41.

Hunsongtham, V. (1993), *Internationalisation Process of Thai Heat Exchange Co., Ltd.*, MBA project, Graduate School of Management, Monash University, Australia.

IP Australia (2002), *Smart Start*, Australian Government.

Jain, S.C. (1996), 'Problems in international protection of intellectual property rights', *Journal of International Marketing*, **4**(1), 9–32.

Karlsen, T., P.R. Silseth, G.R.G. Benito and L.S. Welch (2003), 'Knowledge, internationalization of the firm, and inward–outward connections', *Industrial Marketing Management*, **32**(5), 385–96.

Kehoe, L. (1997), 'Microsoft in licensing deal', *Financial Times*, 13 May, 25.

Killing, P. (1980), 'Technology acquisition: license agreement or joint venture', *Columbia Journal of World Business*, **15**(3), 38–46.

Lowe, J. and N. Crawford (1984), *Innovation and Technology Transfer for the Growing Firm*, Oxford: Pergamon Press.

Luostarinen, R.K. and L.S. Welch (1990), *International Business Operations*, Helsinki: Export Consulting KY.

Lyons, M. (1992), 'How to protect trade secrets', *Business Review Weekly*, 15 May, 70–71.

MacCarthy, C. (2003), 'Lego wins landmark Chinese court victory in piracy lawsuit', *Financial Times*, 21 January, 18.

Madhok, A. (1996), 'Know-how-, experience- and competition-related considerations in foreign market entry: an exploratory investigation', *International Business Review*, **5**(4), 339–66.

Marx, R. (1996), 'Licence to make money abroad', *Financial Times*, 3 September, 9.

Matterson, H. (2004), 'Mayne push to lead Indian drug trial', *The Australian*, 21 May, 23.

Mottner, S. and J.P. Johnson (2000), 'Motivations and risks in international licensing: a review and implications for licensing to transitional and emerging economies', *Journal of World Business*, **35**(2), 171–88.

Nicholson, M. (1999), 'India complies on patent laws', *Financial Times*, 11 March, 6.

Pearson, R. (1993), 'Licensing basics for Thailand', *Les Nouvelles*, **28**(4), 158–62.

Peers, M. (1992), 'Ex-employees settle secrets row with BHP', *Australian Financial Review*, 8 October, 23.

Pengilley, W. (1977), 'Patents and trade practices – competition policies in conflict', *Australian Business Law Review*, **5**(3), 172–203.

Perry, N.J. (1986), 'The surprising new power of patents', *Fortune*, **113**(13), 57–60.

Petersen, B. and L.S. Welch (2003), 'International business development and the Internet, post-hype', *Management International Review*, **43**(special issue no. 1), 7–29.

Petersen, B., D.E. Welch and L.S. Welch (2000), 'Creating meaningful switching options in international operations', *Long Range Planning*, **33**(5), 688–705.

Rabino, S. and E. Enayati (1995), 'Intellectual property: the double-edged sword', *Long Range Planning*, **28**(5), 22–31.

Rice, R. (1995), 'Coca-Cola is the first real thing', *Financial Times*, 11 September, 6.

Riley, J. (2004), 'ATO, IRS talk on transfer pricing', *The Australian*, 22 June, 30.

Root, F.R. and F.J. Contractor (1981), 'Negotiating compensation in international licensing agreements', *Sloan Management Review*, **22**(2), 23–32.

Smith, M. and F. Hansen (2002), 'Managing intellectual property: a strategic point of view', *Journal of Intellectual Capital*, **3**(4), 366–74.

Smithers, P. (1992), 'Patents as an aggressive tool against rivals', *The Age*, 30 April, 19.

Spero, D.M. (1990), 'Patent protection or piracy – a CEO views Japan', *Harvard Business Review*, **68**(5), 58–67.

Studt, T. and J.J. Duga (2001), 'R&D growth continues amid softness in economy and high-tech sector', *R&D Magazine*, website: www.rdmag.com, 1–8, accessed 14/3/01.

Svensson, B. (1984), *Acquisition of Technology through Licensing in Small Firms*, Linkoping: Department of Management and Economics, Linkoping University.

Tackaberry, P. (1998), 'Intellectual property risks in China: their effect on foreign investment and technology transfer', *Journal of Asian Business*, **14**(4), 1–38.

Tomassen, S., L.S. Welch and G.R.G. Benito (1998), 'Norwegian companies in India: operation mode choice', *Asian Journal of Business and Information Systems*, **3**(1), 1–20.

UNCTAD (2003/6), *World Investment Report 2003/6*, New York and Geneva: United Nations.

Welch, L.S. (1985), 'The international marketing of technology: an interaction per-spective', *International Marketing Review*, **2**(1), 41–53.

Welch, L.S. (1993), 'Outward foreign licensing by Australian companies', in P. Buckley and P. Ghauri (eds), *The Internationalization of the Firm: A Reader*, London: Academic Press, pp. 64–90.

Welch, L.S. and R. Luostarinen (1993), 'Inward–outward connections in interna-tionalization', *Journal of International Marketing*, **1**(1), 44–56.

Wiedersheim-Paul, F. (1982), 'Licensing as a long run relation', *Working Paper 1982/2*, Centre for International Business Studies, University of Uppsala, Sweden.

World Intellectual Property Organization (WIPO) (2004), *About Intellectual Property*, http://www.wipo.int.

Wray, R.W. (1983), 'Best-efforts clauses – a review', *Les Nouvelles*, **18**(1), 46–50.

5. Management contracts

INTRODUCTION

Amongst the array of foreign operation methods used by companies, management contracts are probably the least researched and certainly not in the front line of consideration when alternatives are being evaluated, except in a limited number of industries with a history of using them – for example, in the hotel sector and in the airline industry (Welch and Pacifico, 1990). When Philippine Airlines ran into financial troubles in the late 1990s, it turned to the German airline Lufthansa for assistance in managing the operation, under the terms of a management contract (*Australian*, 1998). In a large global study of foreign operation mode choice by hotels, Contractor and Kundu (1998) found that management contracts were the most important individual mode used, constituting 37 per cent of total foreign hotel arrangements. Franchise agreements made up a further 28.4 per cent of the total. There has been a growing number of examples of hotel chains, such as Starwood, InterContinental and Hilton, selling their property and switching to managing rather than owning hotels, with management contracts playing an important part in this shift (Beltran, 2005; *Economist*, 2005; Yee, 2005).

In the most substantive research on the topic, Brooke (1985a, 1985b) estimated the global value of management contracts to be about 10 per cent of that for licensing. There is no way of verifying this estimate as there are no official statistics on a country-by-country basis or globally, or major studies that allow meaningful extrapolation. It is often difficult to separate management contracts from the normal provision of management services and from increasingly outsourced arrangements for the provision of management functions: for example, accounting, research and human resource management. Brooke (1985a) found cases of management contracts being confused with licensing arrangements.

Management contracts are often readily confused with management consulting, which typically involves the provision of management advice, but without a direct managerial role in the implementation of the advice or in overall management of the client organization. There are of course cases where this does occur, and there is some anecdotal evidence of a limited trend in this direction as recipients of managerial consulting services try to ensure that they represent more than expensive 'advise and run' situations.

In contrast, management contracts are about longer-term managerial involvement, about running a foreign organization or a part of it – on a contractual basis, for a set period of time. They are also distinguished from franchising and licensing in that they involve not just selling a method of operating a particular business, but require the contractor actually to undertake the implementation process within the foreign organization. As a result, the contractor has more direct control over know-how transfer, foreign business activities and the ultimate outcomes generated by the client organization. Licensing and franchising represent more arm's-length arrangements in which the foreign licensee or franchisee implements the transferred package, albeit with guidance. In strategic terms, of significance is the fact that the management contract places the contractor on the inside of the recipient organization, putting it in a unique position to influence a range of short- and long-term decisions from which the contractor has the potential to benefit, and to block competitive activity.

Management contracts came into focus in the 1960s as many newly independent nations were seeking ways of developing local industries through foreign involvement but without ceding ownership to foreign entities as in direct investment. The management contract allowed governments to contemplate non-ownership options such as a turnkey project followed by a management contract that ensured the transfer of technical know-how and management expertise, with appropriate training, so that locals ultimately could be equipped to run their own operation (Gabriel, 1967). In some cases this was somewhat urgently required when already established foreign operations were acquired or expropriated by the local government. A further boost to the demand for management contracts came with the rise of OPEC and the quadrupling of the price of oil in the early 1970s. As a result, many oil-rich countries had substantial new inflows of income and foreign currency reserves that enabled them to finance new development expenditures in a range of industries. Again, management contracts were viewed as supporting this process by acting as a means of know-how transfer without ownership. Support also emerged at the United Nations for the management contract form, and it developed a manual that countries could apply in negotiating management contract deals. In a more recent example, the Water Authority of Jordan signed a four year 'license (effectively a management contract) . . . to manage the distribution of water without the loss of government ownership and control' (Al-Husan and James, 2003). The aim of the Jordanian government was to raise the managerial and technical skills of staff, and efficiency of the overall operation. Management contracts also came to be used in diverse ways in the developed countries, for example, in the tourism, hospitality and retailing sectors, such as in the case of the hotel chains noted above (Kacker, 1986).

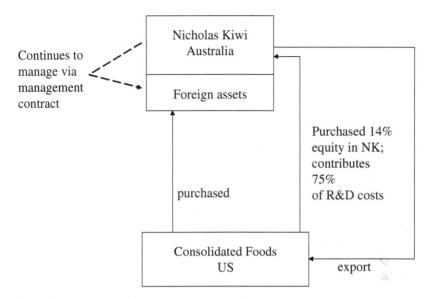

Figure 5.1 Nicholas Kiwi's management contract

An unusual case that illustrates the diverse scope of management contracts involved the Australian multinational Nicholas Kiwi, a producer of pharmaceuticals and shoe cleaning products. As shown in Figure 5.1, its foreign assets were acquired by the US-based multinational, Consolidated Foods (owner of Sara Lee), in 1985. However, Nicholas Kiwi continued to run these foreign operations for Consolidated Foods under the terms of a ten year management contract. Consolidated Foods also acquired a 14 per cent equity interest in the restructured Nicholas Kiwi entity, and paid for 75 per cent of the company's R&D costs, and was a channel for a significant level of product exports by Nicholas Kiwi (Whitmont, 1985).

In this chapter, in the process of analysing the nature and use of management contracts in international business operations, we aim to bring this method into more mainstream consideration as a viable alternative to other methods: in its own right, but also as an accompaniment to other modes in broader penetration packages, and as a means of linking and maintaining foreign market operations over time. The analysis reveals a method which is surprisingly versatile, with a capacity to contribute to long-term market development goals, in spite of the fact that, at its heart, it involves an attempt to transfer know-how and build a set of skills in the recipient organization that should allow it to dispense with the contractor's role.

DEFINITION

A management contract has been defined by Pugh (1961, 49) as: 'an arrangement under which operational control of an enterprise (or one phase of an enterprise) which would otherwise be exercised by the board of directors or managers elected or appointed by its owners is vested by contract in a separate enterprise which performs the necessary managerial function in return for a fee'. Although with many variants, in simple terms it involves management of a foreign firm, or part thereof, on a contractual basis. As defined, it is sometimes referred to as a 'pure' management contract in that there is no equity connection between the contracting parties, or other mode linkages – i.e., there is a clear separation between ownership and management (Luostarinen and Welch, 1990). As Figure 5.2 illustrates, frequently it refers to a tripartite arrangement in which the foreign contractor provides the managerial function, for a negotiated fee, to an enterprise that is owned by a client organization, the party to the contract (the contractee). The client firm (contractee) provides ownership and the necessary resources to enable the enterprise to operate. The contract enterprise pays relevant costs associated with its activities and the foreign-based management function. Sometimes the management contract is a simpler two-way arrangement only, wherein the contractor is engaged to manage the contractee. The duration of the contract can be quite variable, ranging from two to 20 years in Brooke's research; he also found renewal to be quite common (Brooke, 1985a, 6). In the case of Starwood's property sale to Host Marriott, linked to a licence and management contract to cover a continuing management role, the initial contract is for 20 years, but with the

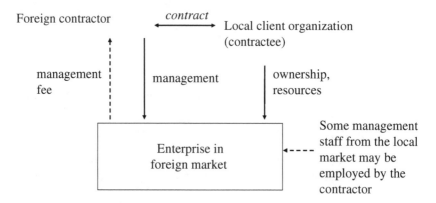

Source: Adapted from Brooke (1985a, p. 5).

Figure 5.2   Pure management contract

option of two ten-year extensions, at Starwood's discretion! (Beltran, 2005). Effectively, this is a 40-year commitment.

MANAGEMENT CONTRACTS AS A CONNECTED FORM

Research indicates that management contracts are not mainly used in the pure form noted above, but rather are utilized in connection to a variety of other mode forms, frequently as part of an equity arrangement between the contractor and contractee (Brooke, 1985b). As such, the management contract may not be the primary foreign market penetration vehicle being used by a company, but rather it may be acting in a supportive role, in a similar way to that noted in many licensing arrangements, and the management fee may be of subsidiary concern. Some of these connections are shown in Figure 5.3. Although each management contract has its own specific provisions, in general they tend to ensure that the contractor has a high level of control over the management process in the foreign organization – the contractee. This may be a particularly important aspect for companies that consider they have insufficient control through another mode, or other modes which are the primary focus of foreign market penetration.

The case of Nicholas Kiwi and Consolidated Foods outlined above demonstrates how management contracts can become part of quite complex mode packages, although the combination of inward foreign direct investment (from the Australian perspective) and an outward management

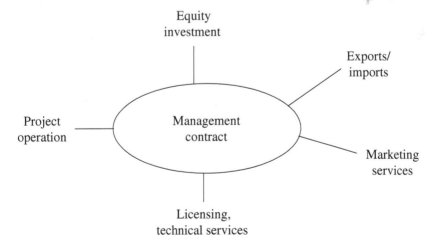

Figure 5.3   Management contract connections

contract is somewhat unusual. More typical is the use of a management contract alongside a joint venture or minority equity as a unidirectional package, providing an enhanced control and revenue-generating function. When a manufacturing facility is involved, the package commonly will include different types of exports. For the contractee, equity involvement by the contractor is often seen as a way of ensuring that the contractor is committed to a successful outcome for the operation, while increasing its financial base. Brooke (1985a) found examples of the use of management contracts alongside other contractual forms, such as licensing and different types of technology transfer arrangements. Although licensing deals often include transfers of managerial know-how, they lack the depth of managerial control that management contracts can provide. Management contracts represent a more effective arrangement for limiting the leakage of transferred technology outside the recipient organization. Further, they have been used often in connection with long-term importing arrangements, as a way of ensuring the security, reliability and quality of key supplies that are provided to the contractor by the contractee.

Research also shows that management contracts are frequently used with project operations, as a follow-up to ensure that the constructed facility – factory, mine, transport system and so on – functions successfully after completion, and that the essential know-how to operate and maintain it, and the associated business activities, over the long term are transferred to local staff. As well, the continuing association through the management contract may lead to additional exports and/or imports for the contractor. In a similar manner to that of project operations, consultancy, marketing or other services can be a forerunner to management contracts (Brooke, 1985a). Foreign customers have an opportunity to experience what the service provider is able to deliver and may therefore seek to extend and embed the contribution, including the transfer of relevant capabilities to local staff. Clearly, management contracts can play a useful role in linking modes over time, of providing a continuing position in the foreign market that can form an effective springboard to other modes, in switching situations, or into extended mode packages.

AGREEMENT CONTENT

The exact nature of each management contract agreement varies, depending on the nature of the management task, the concerns of the contractor and contractee, and the negotiation process. Inevitably, too, the range of transfers from the contractor to the client organization typically will extend beyond the formal contract terms: as management staff move and perform their managerial and technical roles they bring with them a potential to contribute a wide range of useful services over and above that which has been contracted. This may be connected to their personal and business networks which are activated to provide useful market knowledge, contacts and the like in helping their own activities or those of local staff. Whether specifically included in the contract or not, contact between foreign and local staff tends to involve an informal training role, necessarily so if the local firm is to function effectively. In an overall sense, the contractor may provide substantial assistance to the local firm if it is well known, with a strong and positive reputation in the international arena. This may contribute to enhanced goodwill for the local firm and support for various functions, such as the attempt to access international finance.

Perhaps the main difference in management contracts is whether they are concerned with the overall management of the firm – running the local operation – or only managing a specific function or group of functions within the recipient organization. For example, Goekjian (1980, 6) presents the example of a management contract to run a sugar refinery, which covered the full range of managerial functions:

The Management Company shall have full and exclusive authority for the management of the Refinery and shall supervise all services connected with the operation of the Refinery, including . . .
(1) production
(2) office management
(3) financial accounting
(4) cost accounting
(5) purchase or requisition of raw materials or finished products
(6) inventory control
(7) hiring of personnel and payroll records
(8) sales
(9) engineering services relating to production
(10) maintenance, repair and replacement of plant equipment including utilities, and
(11) supply of technical information.

Some contracts are far less comprehensive in scope, dealing with a specific area where the local firm may be particularly weak and in need of external assistance to build local managerial competence – for example, in accounting and finance or information systems. This is not a case of outsourcing of a business process, which will be covered in the next chapter, as there is an objective of the local firm ultimately taking over the relevant business function, while the activity is performed directly 'in house', although, with the evolution of IT systems, what is internal and external to the firm is becoming increasingly blurred.

A termination clause is normal in contracts to cover events which make contract completion untenable. These can be unforeseen events such as strikes or government action, or developments within the discretion of the owner of the contract venture, such as non-payment of fees or lack of provision of financial and other resources that are critical to the effective functioning of the venture. A more detailed coverage of types of management contracts and their content is provided by Brooke (1985b) and the UN Centre on Transnational Corporations (1983).

PAYMENTS

There are three main elements of the payments which may be used with management contract arrangements, apart from those which may apply to connected operation forms, such as joint ventures, that could be the primary income source:

1. *Basic fee.* This is the management fee which is charged for the provision of the basic management service to the client organization. It may be a fixed fee, irrespective of outcomes, or related to some company activity variable such as production.
2. *Incentive payment.* It is not uncommon for an additional incentive payment to be offered to the contactor. This tends to be related in some form to the profitability of the client firm – typically a percentage of the profit outcome. In the Asian hotel sector during the early-to-mid-1990s, management contracts negotiated by international chains (for example, Hyatt and Hilton) included basic management fees of up to 3.5 per cent of total revenues as well as incentive payments of 6–10 per cent of gross operating profits. After the 1997 financial crisis, contract payments were pushed more in the direction of incentives: with basic fees as little as 1 per cent while incentive payments were raised to as high as 12 per cent (*Economist*, 1999). As the name implies, incentive payments have been used as a way of motivating the contractor to work for the best possible results in the client firm. Effectively, the profit link brings the management contract operation closer to that of the joint venture form, without a continuing involvement through equity. In a study of management contracts involving public enterprises in developing countries it was found that the successful (financial performance) management contracts relied more on success fees, whereas failures relied more on fixed fees (Shaikh and Minovi, 1995).
3. *Additional services payments.* Contractors often charge for what are defined as additional services associated with the main management

activity. These might be in the area of marketing, for example through the contractor's international network or for training above an agreed level that is part of the basic contract. Training is one of the problem areas for contractors as it can be very costly if it is open-ended: there is never enough as far as the contractee is concerned. As a result, many contractors have found that the most appropriate way of dealing with this issue is to separate it and charge an additional amount for the training service, forcing the contractee to decide what level of training it wants, and can afford.

CONTRACT DURATION

As noted earlier, there is wide variation in the length of management contracts found in empirical research: five to ten years in Swedish research (Sharma, 1983), and even longer for many arrangements in the hotel sector (*Economist*, 1999). The length seems to be related, in part, to the perceived nature of the management task and of the demands of the learning process from the client firm's perspective. In the hotel sector, though, the long-term contracts appear to have been related to the objective of client firms, for example in the tourism business, to connect to the branding and international market network benefits of international hotel chains, creating long-term dependent connections rather than shorter management and know-how transfer arrangements (Stewart, 1992). The longevity of some of the hotel contracts, some for as long as 25 years, aligned them more closely with long-term FDI forms. Sharma (1983) found that renewal of management contracts after completion was common, when outcomes were viewed as being successful.

WHY MANAGEMENT CONTRACTS? CONTRACTEE'S PERSPECTIVE

Management contract arrangements have arisen because they fill a need for the client firm. At a basic level, this is typically related to a deficiency of managerial and technical experience and skills in running a particular type of organization and its business activity. For example, the Ethiopian government advertised for bids to run the country's main bank (government-owned, conducting the bulk of the country's banking business) in 2001, under the terms of a management contract. The aim was to raise the standards of the bank's operations by adopting international best practices. Frequently, this arises because the contractee is moving into a new area and establishing a new business, perhaps preceded by a major project in which the facilities that form the basis of the new business are constructed. With respect to developing countries, it has been noted that 'management contracts are often combined with licensing agreements in order to complement the transferred licensed technology with the expertise to use it' (UNCTC, 1983, 4). Also, there are situations where a previously foreign-owned firm is acquired by a local company as a going concern, but the change of ownership is associated with a withdrawal of key expatriate staff, so that the new owner is faced with the question of whether to seek to employ replacements on an individual basis or to opt for a more packaged solution via a management contract. As alluded to above, the management contract may be viewed as a means of establishing a link with a well established international operator in the field, as in the hotel sector, with all of the spillover advantages that come with that connection: for example, providing immediate local and international market recognition. In some cases, it is these surrounding benefits that will be crucial in generating interest in the management contract form.

While foreign direct investment normally implies a highly packaged operation form, with equity at its heart, management contracts allow the recipient organization effectively to unbundle this package – to obtain key management skills without ceding ownership, as illustrated in Figure 5.4. This latter characteristic is sometimes very attractive to potential contractees,

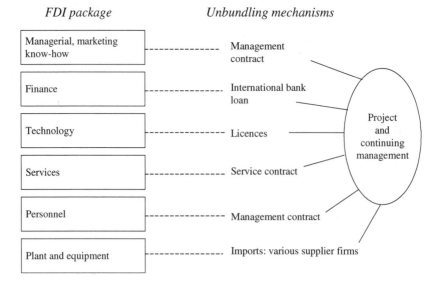

Figure 5.4   Foreign direct investment unbundled

and especially so for many local governments, with the prospect of eventually dispensing with foreign participation altogether. The concern has been particularly evident in many countries that have sought to create their own airline, often owned and supported by the national government (Welch and Pacifico, 1990). For many newly independent nations, having a national airline was often seen as one way of making a statement about that status. An example is the small Pacific island of Vanuatu, which persuaded the Australian airline Ansett to enter into a management contract as the basis for the establishment of Air Vanuatu. With power over the use of their countries' air space, local governments possess a means to put pressure on major airlines to support the push for a local airline. Management contracts provide a path to this objective, often associated with aircraft leasing, a link to a sophisticated reservation system and other services. For Air Vanuatu, the management contract arrangements with Ansett were very comprehensive, including provision and coordination of catering and crew requirements, training, access to Ansett's computer reservation network, accounting and marketing services, as well as aircraft leasing. Vanuatu had virtually no ability to provide any of these services itself, but the government was concerned to extend the provision of airline services to the country to ensure the development of its tourism sector. The example of other countries that had gone down this road, such as Fiji and its management contract link to the Australian airline Qantas, was an important factor in interest in the management contract form amongst newly independent South Pacific nations.

THE CONTRACTOR'S PERSPECTIVE

Earlier use of management contracts by companies in their foreign operations tended to be a response, like licensing, to the perceived constraints, often driven by government action, in using other operation modes. In the Ansett case, there was a strong internal push to internationalize at the time, which was reflected in the development of its globally oriented aircraft leasing business (Welch and Pacifico, 1990). Ansett was a major Australian domestic airline and international airline services were a natural step, but this was prevented by the monopoly on Australian-based international airline services held by the government airline Qantas at the time. As a result, Ansett had to pursue other foreign expansion options, and management contracts came into the evaluation mix because of their known record of use in the international airline industry, with a capacity to link the operation to its evolving aircraft leasing business. While forceful local government action is less likely in the current global environment, particularly in its most extreme form of expropriation, as a factor in pushing foreign companies to consider the use of alternatives such as management contracts governments are still important in the setting of the local business environment. This is not just in terms of local regulations regarding foreign direct investment and other operations, but also in regard to their effect on political and business risk – for example, on the level of corruption. In conditions of high perceived risk, management contracts represent a way of operating without a high level of exposure to the local environment, in contrast to foreign direct investment. In some cases, management contracts have been used by the contractor as a way of ensuring secure supplies of imports, or of guaranteeing the quality and reliability of key supplies, from the client organization.

At the least, a management contract enables the contractor to establish or maintain a foreign market position, with the potential to extend this involvement as its own experience and ability to operate develop through the management contract-related activity. Inevitably, because the contractor is directly engaged in the foreign market through management of the client organization, there is a higher degree of knowledge transfer, in all forms, to the contractor than would apply in more arm's-length arrangements such as licensing, and more extensive personal and business network development. Therefore the contractor should be better positioned to engineer, for example, a step up in involvement, in whatever form, or a pull out from the market altogether, as shown in Figure 5.5.

As noted above, management contracts are frequently, if not preeminently, used in association with, or following, other modes. For example, FedEx negotiated a management contract with its 50:50 joint venture partner in China when this operation was established in 1999 (see Box 12.3). FedEx had used a representative office and agents prior to this

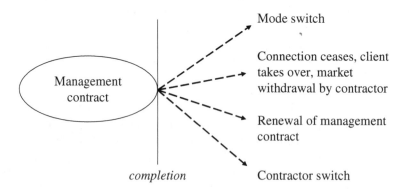

Figure 5.5   After completion of the management contract

arrangement. From FedEx's perspective, the management contract was to ensure day-to-day control of the operation. In such cases, in a similar way to the use of licensing, the management contract clearly has a role subsidiary to the main mode, the joint venture, although it was important in creating a preparedness by FedEx to go ahead with the joint venture form, thereby accessing a range of perceived advantages, such as the reduction of overall venture risk and utilization of the connections and market experience of its Chinese partner (Petersen and Welch, 2003). When management contracts are used following a turnkey project, they may serve a number of purposes, including maintenance of market involvement and influence, generation of additional returns and ensuring that the project functions successfully after completion, therefore enabling it to be used as a reference project by the builder in other project bidding situations. Alfa Laval's use of a management contract after the completion of its first turnkey project in Saudi Arabia (see Figure 5.6) is illustrative of the range of potential benefits that may be obtained (Sharma, 1983).

The Swedish multinational, Alfa Laval, built a turnkey dairy farm and milk processing plant in Saudi Arabia in 1977. It was hoped that this would be a forerunner of other, similar projects in Saudi Arabia and other parts of the Middle East. Therefore, it was important that the project operate

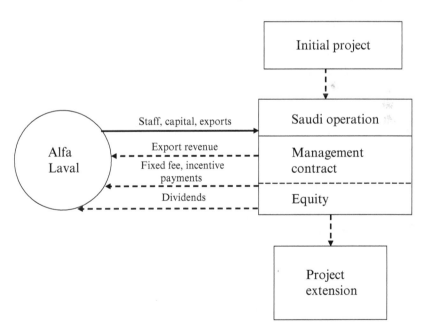

Figure 5.6   Alfa Laval in Saudi Arabia

successfully after completion as a basis for future marketing activity. For this purpose the management contract arrangement was ideal as it involved sending managerial and technical staff to direct operations, and carry out appropriate training. Alfa Laval took an equity interest of 12.5 per cent in the contract venture, which meant a seat on the board of directors. Overall, the control of the contract venture was relatively high. The returns under the management contract were a fixed management fee plus an incentive payment, tax free, of 6 per cent of profits in year one, rising to 10 per cent in year five. Also, the arrangement led to exports by Alfa Laval to the contract enterprise, involving the supply of equipment, spare parts and software to the contract venture. Effectively, in this setting, a captive market for exports was created. Following the success of the operation from the local firm's perspective, it was decided to undertake a major extension of the original facilities in 1981. Competitive tenders were not called: Alfa Laval was the only contender for the new project. Its position was facilitated not only by the success of the first project but also by the key roles played by its own staff, under the terms of the management contract, on a continuing basis: it had the benefit of being an insider to deliberations and decisions from which it stood to benefit. Clearly, Alfa Laval used the management contract as a way of generating short- and long-term benefits, financial and strategic. The management contract made an important contribution to the company's long-term market positioning in the region.

In the case of Air Vanuatu noted above, the choice of a management contract as a way of internationalizing by Ansett was not because of a first line preference for this mode but rather because of the Australian government's policy of allowing only one provider of Australia-based international airline services to and from Australia. Nevertheless, the role of management contracts was seen as important in that they provided a basic building block for international activities, generating experience and learning (for example, systems development) in international airline operations. This was gradually applied as the company bought equity shares in other international airlines, supporting its burgeoning, associated aircraft leasing activities. Again, like Alfa Laval, Ansett used management contracts as an important stepping stone in its evolving international expansion strategy.

RISKS

Despite the obvious contributions that management contracts can make to a company's capacity to internationalize, like all the other modes they carry a set of risks for the implementing firm.

Developing Future Competitors

Whatever the basic reason for entering into management contract arrangements, contractors face the potential threat that, if they have been successful in transferring relevant technology and skills to the contractee, and helped to build a marketing infrastructure, the contractee ultimately might be able to act as a competitor in other markets – regionally and even globally. In many instances that is part of the rationale for the recipient using the management contract mode. However, the fact that so many management contracts are re-signed, and are for long periods, indicates a range of broader considerations, particularly performance, which the contractor is seen to be critical in ensuring. Given that the contractor is on the inside of the contract venture, managing the operation, it is in a strong position to engineer outcomes that limit potential competition: a stronger position than, for example, with licensing.

Control

As noted already, one of the strengths of the management contract form is that it normally delivers a high level of operational control of the contract venture to the contractor. However, this is not total control, as in a wholly-owned direct investment. Ultimate control of the operation is in the hands of the client organization: its ownership of the contract venture means that it is in a position to influence the strategic direction of the company, and even to determine its viability through the extent of provision of financial and other resources. In the Alfa Laval case, its minor equity position gave it one position on the board of directors, and thereby a voice in board decisions, but that was all.

Financial Viability

It is normally the responsibility of the owner of the contract venture to provide sufficient resources – for example, initial and working capital – to enable the venture to carry through its operations. Consequently, the financial viability of the owner to undertake this role becomes an important issue for the contractor.

Government Interference

In many situations in developing countries where management contracts are used, the local government is involved in initiating and supporting the arrangements because of the perceived importance of the activity to the national interest, as in the Ethiopian government's role in the banking management contract noted above. Because of the strong government interest, inevitably there is a potential for interference in the contract venture's activities and policies, in some cases to the detriment of outcomes. Governments have political concerns that do not always align with the profit motive of companies. This was evident in a number of instances in Africa during the apartheid era in South Africa when governments of other nations restricted potentially profitable business with South Africa. There are many areas, though, where conflict might arise, including the rate of indigenization of the contract venture's management and operations, that is, the speed with which local staff take over from foreign staff; import policy; export policy; and the use of local suppliers.

Mismatched Expectations

In a more general sense, there is a risk of mismatched expectations between the contractor and the triumvirate of contractee, owner and local government about the contribution by the contractor and outcomes. This was evident in the case of Ansett's establishment and development of Air Vanuatu under a management contract arrangement (Welch and Pacifico, 1990). The government of Vanuatu was heavily involved in the venture, and was part of generally inflated expectations on the Vanuatu side about levels of training, and commitment of resources at all levels by Ansett, especially on the ground in the small Pacific island of Vanuatu. The government viewed it as more akin to an aid project. For its part, Ansett was concerned about commercial realities, about the profitability of the venture, and committed itself accordingly. In the end there was considerable ill-feeling on the Vanuatu side about the contribution of Ansett. The chairman of Air Vanuatu, reflecting a general perception, felt that the company had been 'ripped off unmercifully by Ansett' and the contract was not renewed (Davis, 1987, 13).

SOME IMPLEMENTATION ISSUES

As the Air Vanuatu example illustrates, the success of a management contract arrangement is dependent on the effectiveness of the unfolding implementation of the various elements of the management activity and related operations. As various practical problems emerge, much depends on how they are handled, which in turn depends on the quality of the relationship between the contracting parties, and the staff sent to manage the contract venture. Important issues include staffing and relationship building.

Staffing

Perhaps the most important issue for both parties to the contract is that of staffing. The quality of the staff sent by the contractor to manage the contract venture is critical to outcomes. The management contract is a highly human resource-intensive mode of operation. For example, in the case of the management of the Water Authority of Jordan, referred to above, the French multinational with the task sent a total of 'fifty to sixty expatriates . . . Six of these, each of them directors, were appointed for periods of between two and four years . . . the remainder . . . middle management . . . for more than one year' (Al-Husan and James, 2003). Additionally, some staff were sent on a short-term basis to solve specific problems. This company's approach was to emphasize expatriates in the management of new projects during the initial stages of operations, but there was a Jordanian government condition as well that expatriate managers be used. Inevitably, such demands create a range of concerns for the contractor. As Figure 5.7 shows, at the outset there is the question of the availability of suitable managerial and technical staff, with relevant experience, skills, technical knowledge and cultural sensitivity. Appropriate language skills could be a key aspect of the ability to perform in the contract venture (Marschan-Piekkari et al., 1999). Such staff could be

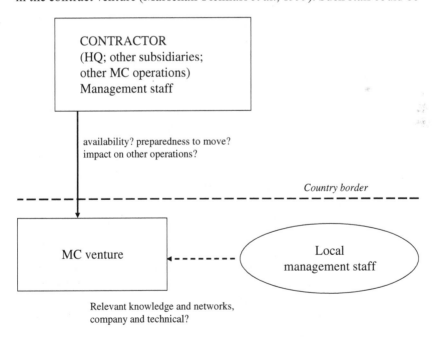

Figure 5.7   Staffing of MC venture

drawn from headquarters or from subsidiary and other operations of a multinational, but might not be readily available. An early Finnish study of management contracts found that companies using management contracts were larger than those using licensing, the latter making lower demands on staff availability (Oravainen, 1979). Companies are understandably reluctant to release large numbers of valuable staff for extended periods in foreign locations.

Even if there are appropriate staff within the multinational's far-flung operations, there is a further question as to their preparedness to move. It would not be surprising to find a reluctance among Western staff to move to a location such as Ethiopia, or Iraq. In the face of this question of staff availability, a seemingly obvious solution is to hire new staff that have the relevant background, and transfer them to the contract venture's location, or hire them within the country in question, thereby removing expatriation-related costs. However, research indicates that this is not a straightforward exercise because of the lack of familiarity of outside staff with a company's knowledge base, internal and external networks, methods and routines. Use of outside staff appears to increase the risk of failure of contract ventures (Holly, 1982). The employment of local staff in managerial roles in the contract venture faces an additional barrier in the local perception that management know-how lies elsewhere and is introduced by foreign, not local, staff: if the management know-how is available locally there is no need to use a foreign company.

Building Relationships, Handling Disputes

The management activity in the contract venture is carried out through, and relies on, a network of relationships, internal and external to the operation, that have to be established and maintained. It has been argued that, in cases of dispute between the contractor and contractee, the legal provisions in the contract provide limited protection; in the end it is the quality of the relationship which is critical (Holly, 1982). This is particularly so when the contract venture is supported by the local government. The contractor undoubtedly is in a powerful position at the outset of the contract as a result of being in possession of the key know-how, skills and foreign networks that the contract venture seeks. As the venture proceeds, though, subtle changes occur as a result of the learning process within the contract venture – through training, on-the-job experience and knowledge sharing. The power balance begins to shift with these processes, in favour of the contractee, as the local staff become less reliant on foreign staff, so that it is more difficult for the contractor to impose its will in the face of local opposition. As well, there is the natural desire and expectation that locals will increasingly take over positions held by foreign staff, and this is a potential source of conflict. It is a delicate balancing act for the contractor: bringing locals into managerial roles over time but not at a rate such as to interfere with the effective functioning of the venture. It will never be fast enough to satisfy the locals, particularly the local government, and this is accentuated if the government is involved in some way in the venture.

This issue is connected to that of training, and similarly there will never be enough training to satisfy the ultimate objective of indigenization of management, so there is a balance that has to be struck between the cost and the amount of training. In the Jordanian Water Authority case, there was a large training component in the contract, leading to the creation of a separate training department and a big jump in the amount spent on training (Al-Husan and James, 2003). As noted earlier, this issue is often dealt with by separating the training component of the management contract, exposing its cost and having the contractee accept some of the financial responsibility for the extent of formal training.

LONG-RUN INTERACTION AND POST-COMPLETION STRATEGY

Once the management contract's objectives of technology transfer and management training have been completed, it might be assumed that the end of the contract would mean the end of the contractor's involvement. The fact that so many management contracts are subject to renewal would seem to indicate a broader complexity of processes. As with licensing, depending on the type of relationship established between contractor and contractee under the terms of the management contract, there is a potential for a widening of activities and contractor involvement. Through the management contract, as the cases such as Alfa Laval, examined above, demonstrate, the contractor is placed in a unique position to build an understanding of the foreign market concerned, to assess the viability of a deeper commitment, and to build conducive relationships with key players in various network positions in the foreign market. Because of its direct role in the contract venture, the contractor is in a better position to understand the needs of both the contract venture and the local owner, and thereby to devise extension arrangements that fit the local situation. Thus it is not surprising that short-term management contracts often turn into long-term arrangements such as joint ventures. The contractor may prefer an alternative arrangement to a continued management contract because of a concern to move valuable management staff to other important roles within the company's global activities, perhaps in promising emerging markets.

As an initial market entry form, a joint venture might have been viewed as entailing unacceptable risk and uncertainty, whereas, after the management contract experience, the contractor has a clear basis for evaluating whether an increased commitment is justified or not, with much of the uncertainty removed. Of course, such options depend on a positive outcome for the contract venture, from all parties' perspectives. Where governments are heavily involved in the venture, a successful outcome may well be seen as one which involves the disconnection from the foreign contractor, with full independence for the local operation as an important political goal from the outset. In cases where the contractor has built in a relatively high level of dependence by recipient enterprise on the contractor's global system – for example its brand name, marketing prowess and network, and knowledge development capacity – it could be difficult for the contractee, even with political pressure, to countenance dispensing with the contractor altogether.

CONCLUSION

Analysis of management contracts demonstrates that this under-researched mode of international business operations has much to contribute, either as an individual mode or as part of a broader mode package. Also, it has been shown to be potentially useful, like licensing, as a stepping stone to deeper foreign market commitment or as a critical link between operations over time, by providing the means for a company to build or maintain its market position. Perhaps more so than other forms of operation, apart from some foreign investment situations, management contracts normally require a strong commitment of managerial and technical staff (not necessarily in numbers) to the foreign venture. For companies without previous experience of using management contracts, or without current involvement in equivalent forms of foreign management activity, this may be the most difficult practical aspect to cope with. There is always a question mark regarding the availability of suitable management staff who are prepared to undertake relatively long-term foreign assignments, in sometimes demanding environments, and the problem is accentuated for inexperienced firms that have to undergo a substantial learning process across a number of fronts. A management contract might seem to be an effective mode solution for a particular foreign market compared to other modes, but as a single, isolated step in a company's overall foreign activities, it may not be justified because of the steep initial learning costs and the difficulties of fulfilling the terms of the contract with regard to the provision of management staff.

Notwithstanding such caveats, management contracts have been used creatively and successfully by many companies in diverse foreign market situations, and are an important component of the mode arsenal of firms, deserving of more serious examination than has tended to be the general pattern in the past, at the least as an accompaniment to other modes, enhancing overall penetration packages, particularly in the area of additional control delivered by direct involvement in running a foreign venture. While franchising and licensing have risen to greater prominence in the last two decades, management contracts have tended to languish as a subject of interest in both academic research and in the popular business press.

REFERENCES

Al-Husan, F.B. and P. James (2003), 'Cultural control and multinationals: the case of privatized Jordanian companies', *International Journal of Human Resource Management*, **14**(7), 1284–95.
Australian (1998), 'Lufthansa flies to rescue of PAL', 2 June, 27.
Beltran, E. (2005), 'Starwood to sell hotel properties to Host Marriott', *Wall Street Journal (Asia)*, 15 November, 6.
Brooke, M.Z. (1985a), 'International management contracts', *Journal of General Management*, **11**(1), 4–15.
Brooke, M.Z. (1985b), *Selling Management Services Contracts in International Business*, London: Holt, Rinehart and Winston.
Contractor, F.J. and S.K. Kundu (1998), 'Modal choice in a world of alliances: analyzing organizational forms in the international hotel sector', *Journal of International Business Studies*, **29**(2), 325–58.
Davis, M. (1987), 'Ansett "ripped us off" says Air Vanuatu Chairman', *Age*, 8 June, 13.
Economist (1999), 'Asia's hotels – empty rooms? So what?', 5 June, 63–4.
Economist (2005), 'Hotels – budget room', 19 March, 64.
Gabriel, P.P. (1967), *The International Transfer of Management Skills: Management Contracts in Less Developed Countries*, Boston, Mass.: Harvard University.
Goekjian, S.V. (1980), *Management Contracts*, UNCTC Advisory Report, EGY/TP/80-02.
Holly, J. (1982), 'Management contracts', in M.Z. Brooke and P.J. Buckley (eds), *Handbook of International Trade*, Brentford, UK: Kluwer, 3.7, pp. 1–14.
Kacker, M. (1986), 'Coming to terms with global retailing', *International Marketing Review*, **3**(1), 7–20.
Luostarinen, R.K. and L.S. Welch (1990), *International Business Operations*, Helsinki: Export Consulting KY.
Marschan-Piekkari, R., D. Welch and L. Welch (1999), 'Adopting a common corporate language: IHRM implications', *International Journal of Human Resource Management*, **10**(3), 377–90.
Oravainen, N. (1979), *Suomalaisten Yritysten Kansainvaliset Lisenssi – ja Know-How – Sopimukset* (International Licensing and Know-How Agreements of Finnish Companies), Helsinki: Helsinki School of Economics, FIBO Publications No. 3.
Petersen, B. and L.S. Welch (2003), 'Foreign operation mode combination strategy', in EIBA Conference Proceedings (on CD-Rom), 11–13 December, Copenhagen, Denmark.

Pugh, R.C. (1961), *The Promotion of the International Flow of Private Capital*, New York: UN Report E-3492.

Shaikh, H. and M. Minovi (1995), 'Management contracts: a review of international experience', CFS Discussion Paper 108, World Bank, May.

Sharma, D.D. (1983), *Swedish Firms and Management Contracts*, Uppsala: Acta Universitatis Upsaliensis (16).

Stewart, A. (1992), 'Hotel contracts under fire', *Business Review Weekly*, 24 July, 65–7.

UN Centre on Transnational Corporations (1983), *Management Contracts in Developing Countries: An Analysis of Their Substantive Provisions*, New York: United Nations, ST/CTC/27.

Welch, L.S. and A. Pacifico (1990), 'Management contracts: a role in internationalization', *International Marketing Review*, **7**(4), 64–74.

Whitmont, T. (1985), 'A grounded Kiwi is set to fly again', *Australian Financial Review*, 19 November, 15.

Yee, A. (2005), 'Host Marriott to buy Starwood property', *Financial Times (Asia)*, 15 November, 18.

6.   International subcontracting

INTRODUCTION

International subcontracting, as a form of international operations, offers considerable potential for internationalizing companies, and has come to the forefront of options considered by companies in recent times. However, the potential of international subcontracting has tended to be viewed most strongly in terms of its contribution to overall cost reduction rather than its ability to enhance the development of international operations. The cost reduction and employment effects of international subcontracting also have made it a controversial method, with widespread coverage of issues connected with its use – in business and popular media outlets. The clamour about loss of jobs from the advanced economies such as the US has led to widespread political activity in these countries with the objective of attempting to restrain the growth of international subcontracting. On the other hand, this has been counterbalanced by lobbying activity by governments and industry associations of recipient countries attempting to maintain the growing pattern, for example in defence of Indian companies in the IT field (Hiebert and Slater, 2003; Shankar, 2003). Much of the public debate echoes that seen in earlier times when the effects of so-called 'cheap imports from low-wage countries' began to appear, prompting calls for tariff and other forms of protection in the advanced countries to save industries such as textiles, clothing and footwear.

The current debate has been sparked by the move of international subcontracting into the services area, in some cases encompassing jobs regarded as high skill and knowledge, typically considered to be the province of the advanced countries, for example in the case of the transfer of research and development activities (R&D) to India in the IT and pharmaceutical sectors. As an illustration, the Australian company Mayne Group has 'contracted an Indian pharmaceutical manufacturer to make what it hopes will be a leading generic anti-cancer drug' (Matterson, 2004, 23). Companies in the IT sector such as Hewlett Packard have been closing some of their R&D units in Australia and moving the activity to India (Mackenzie and Denton, 2002). Perhaps the ultimate example of international subcontracting was seen when half a million school leaving certificate examination papers were sent to India for marking (*Australian*, 2005a). In addition, the spread of international subcontracting in the manufacturing sector has continued apace, building on a long-established base of activities and operators, now including brokers or intermediaries, and consultants, that have come to provide a managerial service in out-sourcing to companies, effectively resulting in outsourcing of the out-sourcing activity, in a way similar to the function of freight forwarders in solving the transport needs of exporters (*Economist*, 2001). In a recent Delphi study of a global panel of experts regarding international business that considered corporate strategies for the next decade, there was an overwhelming consensus about the importance of outsourcing (Czinkota and Ronkainen, 2005). Overall, the growth of international subcontract-ing in international business activity has been spectacular, judged by dis-parate pieces of evidence, particularly in the services area, albeit from a low base, although it is difficult to say with any precision just how large it is because of definitional problems and the fact that official balance of payments statistics do not separate out an international subcontracting component in either goods or services sections (Edwards, 2004; UNCTAD, 2004).

In the midst of the debate regarding the cost and employment effects of international subcontracting (or international outsourcing/offshoring), it is easy for the international operation aspects to be lost or overlooked, whereas that is the focus of this chapter. We will analyse the nature of inter-national subcontracting, reasons for its use and the various ways in which this method can contribute to companies' internationalization, as well as the demands of successful implementation; compared to other operation forms, but, again, also in association with other operation methods. One of the major problems in analysing international subcontracting is the fact that it overlaps with exporting and importing and foreign direct investment in many situations (see Figure 6.1), so we shall initially attempt to clarify what the term means, in its various forms.

DEFINITION

Given that there is no consistent definition of international subcontracting, or other terms that are used interchangeably with it, such as international outsourcing, we shall attempt initially to clarify the basic concept and applications that have evolved. A useful starting point is the definition of international subcontracting used by Sharpston (1975, 94): 'all export sales of articles which are ordered in advance and where the giver of the order arranges the marketing'. Other earlier definitions included the

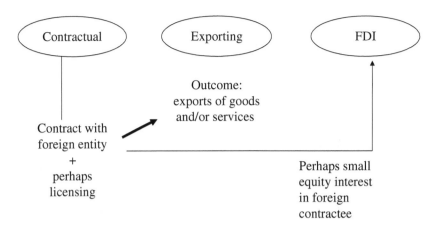

Figure 6.1   International subcontracting: mode connections

BOX 6.1   OUTSOURCING OF THE OUTSOURCING PROBLEM

As companies contemplate moving to the outsourcing of a range of production activities that they carried out in-house previously, they are often faced with significant organizational, coordination and supply-chain questions. These include where to have the good or service produced, which company to use in the foreign location, and what are the specific demands of importing/exporting operations in the different countries involved. Quality assurance is a major issue (with significant supervisory demands: see Box 6.2), as is timely shipping of the different parts and the final product, along with handling the bureaucracies of various countries and payment systems. Answering these questions is a demanding research exercise, particularly for companies with limited international experience. For example, a European clothing company might be considering sourcing material from China and India, zippers from Taiwan, and having the final sewing taking place in Vietnam. Even this simplified case involves considerable demands on coordination, monitoring and general management of the subcontracting activity ultimately to fulfil the changeable tastes of European markets. Finding and locking in quality suppliers can be difficult. It is not surprising, therefore, that intermediaries like the Hong Kong-based company Li and Fung have arisen to become specialists in handling the various steps in the international subcontracting chain, solving the outsourcing practicalities for its client firms – allowing companies to outsource the outsourcing problem. The extent of the perceived need and demand for this service is indicated by the growth and size of Li and Fung's operation, with about 6000 staff and 65 offices in 38 countries at the beginning of 2005.

Source: Economist (2001, pp. 62–3) and company web site, accessed 12/1/2005.

constraint that it should involve a contractual arrangement, while there were conflicting views on whether the supply operations of multinational subsidiaries back to the parent ought to be included (Michalet, 1980). Effectively, the subcontracting activity means that the principal arranges for an activity that it might have carried out itself, and may even currently be doing, to be undertaken instead by another party in a foreign location. A key element, as stressed in the original Sharpston definition, is that the principal handles the marketing and distribution of the output – in whatever market that might be. The output might be in the form of components or parts that are assembled into a final product by the principal, or it might be in the form of a final product that is sold directly into the end-market/s. A legitimate question in this context is: how much of this is different from simple importing/exporting, perhaps via a subsidiary operation, and thereby just the enactment of the FDI form within a multinational's dispersed global network, utilizing various subsidiaries to generate the most cost-effective operations?

From an operation method perspective, the essence of international subcontracting is the utilization by a company of another entity's facilities, or service provision capacities, rather than its own, as a base to serve foreign markets, or home markets as a form of inward operations. In its pure non-FDI form, this would mean not having to make a major commitment to foreign facilities; the company's only formal commitment is that set down in the terms of the contract with the foreign contractee (or subcontractor), that is, it could be a one-off arrangement, or a longer-term relationship. As a result, international subcontracting could then be defined as a low-commitment operation, similar to licensing, but with greater control, and responsibility, through retention of the ultimate marketing role. The rise of companies such as Nike, Reebok and Adidas in the sporting goods field is illustrative of how powerful the control of marketing can be in building successful global operations, alongside a reliance on international subcontracting activities.

The ability to utilize subcontracting as a foreign operation method has been facilitated by the development of companies specializing in the provision of a subcontracting service to other companies: for example, carrying out the production activity at the behest of other companies. In the electronics sector, a prime example is the specialist contract manufacturer Flextronics (see Table 6.1), which is a large multinational in its own right, with facilities in many countries, and an ability to respond rapidly to the production needs of client companies such as Microsoft, Alcatel, Siemens and Hewlett-Packard (Shameen, 2003). The buying power of large multinationals means that they can apply significant pressure on contract manufacturing companies' location and investment policies. A case in point

Table 6.1   Some characteristics of Flextronics International

---

- Singapore-based
- Sales of almost US$14 billion in 2002
- 87 plants in 27 countries
- Largest manufacturer of cellphones; 16% of global production
- Largest fabricator of printed circuit boards
- Makes printers for HP and Epson; copiers for Xerox; personal digital assistants for Casio
- 'Idea is to make products in the cheapest location closest to the end customers'
- Moving up value chain by doing its own design work

Source: Shameen (2003, pp. 32–5).

Table 6.2   International outsourcing versus offshoring

		Internal or external sourcing	
		Within firm – captive/tied	*External to firm – untied (outsourced)*
Production location	*Local*	1. Production in-house, at home	2. External supplier in home market
	Foreign (offshore)	3. In-house in foreign market (own operation: captive offshoring)	4. External supplier in foreign market (international subcontracting)

Source: Adapted from UNCTAD (2004, Table 10, p. 25).

is the Taiwan-based sports shoe manufacturer Yue Yuen. It is a major supplier to firms such as Nike and Reebok from large production operations in China. In the mid-1990s, 'Nike began to worry that trade friction between China and Washington could trigger a disruption in supply to the US market. So, at Nike's behest, Yue Yuen opened assembly lines in Java, Indonesia' (Sender, 1998, 63–4).

Two recent reviews of international subcontracting, with a focus on its rise in the services sector, have attempted to deal with the definitional issue as it applies to the terms 'outsourcing' and 'offshoring' (Edwards, 2004; UNCTAD, 2004). Table 6.2 encapsulates the approach taken in both reviews. In simple terms, offshoring refers to the foreign placement of production activity (goods or services) that is, production is carried out in a foreign location. As shown in Table 6.2, cells 3 and 4, offshoring can be

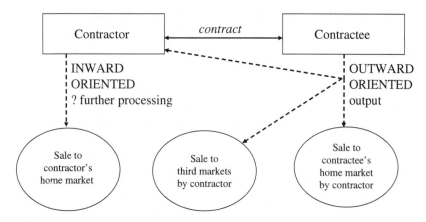

Source: Adapted from Luostarinen and Welch (1990, p. 116).

Figure 6.2   Destinations of subcontracted output

carried out either in-house, as a tied or captive form of operations via the firm's own subsidiary, or through the use of an external supplier in the foreign market. Thus cell 4 can also be referred to as international out-sourcing (or offshore outsourcing).

A further factor to be considered in understanding international sub-contracting (or its variants noted above) is the destination of the con-tracted output, as a prelude to the marketing process undertaken by the contractor. As noted in Figure 6.2, the three basic options are selling into the home market, or into the contractee's home market or into third markets. Further processing or assembly in a different location may precede marketing of a final product. In foreign operation terms, foreign output which is imported to sell in the contractor's home market would necessarily not be included as a way of servicing foreign markets. Clearly, this would exclude much of what is included in normal definitions of, and statistics regarding, international subcontracting. A complication, though, is the fact that often the contracted product which is imported by the contractor is subject to further processing or final assembly, and then re-exported. At another level, it also can be argued that the contracted imports of cheap components, or even final products, may be critical to the viability of a company's overall international operations. However, the international subcontracting activity is not a direct form of foreign market servicing.

After assessing the various perspectives on the issue of defining interna-tional subcontracting as a foreign operation mode, the following points can be made about international subcontracting:

- It involves the use of a foreign entity on a contractual basis to generate the goods and/or services which the contractor then takes over for the marketing and distribution role.
- The end-product (including services) of the subcontracting activity may be aimed at the market of the contractee and/or third markets, referred to as *outward-oriented* subcontracting, or at the contractor's home market, called *inward-oriented* subcontracting (as in Figure 6.2).
- Foreign production and service-generating activities carried out through the subsidiaries of multinationals are normally excluded from definitions of international subcontracting. Basically, if the activity is handled within the firm, it is not international subcontracting, and this is the position we take. Nevertheless, this is a 'grey' area. Foreign production by the multinational might have all of the characteristics of subcontracting, and may even have been a direct follow-up to initial subcontracting to an independent operator, perhaps by takeover of the independent firm. There have been many examples of this emerging in the Indian IT sector, such as with General Electric (Slater, 2003). It has been estimated that, 'if data for India are indicative, perhaps as much as 60% of offshored IT-enabled services takes place within TNCs [transnational corporations]' (UNCTAD, 2004, p. 26). These activities, which are part of FDI operations, are akin to international subcontracting when an important part of the purpose of the owned foreign facility is to supply one or more parts of the company's wider international network.

    There will be cases, of course, where the foreign subsidiary outsources part of its activities to local or other foreign firms, which, from the viewpoint of the parent and some researchers, constitutes international subcontracting (Michalet, 1980). While having built up its own operations in a number of industries in India, including its largest R&D centre outside the US, General Electric also maintains a still significant level of subcontracting to independent Indian firms (Slater, 2003). An even more awkward definitional question arises when the contractor takes a small, minority equity interest in the subcontractor (contractee). While not 'within the contractor firm', the equity interest does provide a basis for influencing the operations of the subcontractor. Rather than attempting to draw a precise line between subcontracting and an alliance or FDI in such situations, we view this as a case of the expected overlap in operation modes, as noted in the introductory chapter.
- The broader the definition of international subcontracting, especially if it includes the activities of MNC subsidiaries, the greater its aggregate amount and extent in measured international business activity.

DRIVERS OF INTERNATIONAL SUBCONTRACTING DEVELOPMENT

Cost Differences

While there are many factors which have been involved in the growth of international subcontracting, difference in costs, especially labour costs, has probably been the major single stimulus, and has remained so through the spread of subcontracting in manufacturing and now in the services sector. Companies involved in international subcontracting consistently stress the cost savings that it has generated for them. Whatever the reality, it is a view strongly embedded in the thinking of many within manufacturing, as illustrated in an exchange described in an interview with Nicolas Hayek, the former head of Swatch: 'Not so long ago, I was in the United States for a meeting with the CEO of one of your big companies. We were discussing a joint venture to produce a new product we had developed. He saw what the product could do, he reviewed the design, and he got very excited: "Great, we'll make it in Singapore." His people had done no research or calculations at all. It was a reflex' (Taylor, 1993, 100). In services, lower costs have been stressed in various studies as the main reason for 'offshoring'. 'Cost savings of 20–40% are commonly reported by companies that have experience in offshoring' (UNCTAD, 2004, p. 28). In industries such as clothing and footwear, where labour costs remain an important component of costs (in the 20–30 per cent range) differences in labour costs become a large factor in the use of international subcontracting (Navaretti et al., 2001). Table 6.3 shows the extent of difference between manufacturing labour costs in some of the advanced countries and those in some of the less advanced countries. The most striking difference is between those at the top and China, which readily explains much of the attraction of China as a destination for subcontracting activities and foreign direct investment.

Footloose Subcontractors

The importance of these cost differences in location decisions is shown in the readiness of contractors to move to new locations when former sites are subject to increases in labour costs. This was most apparent in Taiwan and South Korea, early sites for internationally contracted production of clothing and footwear, where highly efficient, large-scale producers of these products developed, dominating world trade in these sectors for a period in the 1970s and 1980s. With the rise of China and other far cheaper locations, however, activity quickly shifted out of these countries. However, Taiwanese and South Korean companies play a significant role as investors

Table 6.3   Average hourly wages, manufacturing workers (US$, 2003)

Country	Hourly wage
Germany	29.91
US	21.97
UK	20.37
Japan	20.09
Australia	20.03
Korea	10.28
Brazil	2.67
Mexico	2.48
China	0.64 (estimate)

Source: US Bureau of Labor Statistics.

in manufacturing facilities in the new locations, retaining their position as subcontractors to companies like Nike and many large retailers, but providing product from cheaper foreign bases. An example was Indonesia in the late 1980s, which benefited from 'rapid wage increases in Korea and Taiwan . . . [resulting] in an influx of investors from both countries to Indonesia' (Munthe and Hukom, 1993, 10). Their impact was considerable in a short period of time – generating an increase in exports of footwear out of Indonesia from US$23 million in 1987 to 994 million in 1991 – driven by much lower labour costs. Reebok began sourcing from Indonesia in 1989, ordering three million sports shoes at first, rising to 24 million in 1992. One of the companies set up to produce sports shoes was a joint venture between Indonesian entrepreneurs and HS Industries of South Korea, the latter holding a 60 per cent interest: see Figure 6.3. All production was exported, with major sports goods companies such as Reebok and Puma as well as large retailers as customers. Quality control of production was overseen by six Reebok and four Puma inspectors (Munthe and Hukom, 1993).

The 'footloose' characteristic of subcontracting activity in the textiles and clothing industries was illustrated also in the rapid transfer of work to the countries of central Europe after the demise of socialism at the end of the 1980s. By 1994, subcontracting had made substantial inroads in all four countries, constituting a large or dominant share of total exports of textiles and clothing in each case: the Czech Republic (49.6 per cent), Slovakia (50.7 per cent), Hungary (69.4 per cent), and Poland (79.9 per cent). Stimulated by the growth of subcontracting, Poland's exports of textiles and clothing had reached $US2.13 billion by 1994, demonstrating how rapidly subcontracting could be built up and affect the recipient economy.

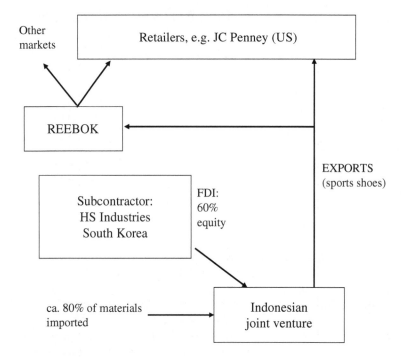

Source: Adapted from Munthe and Hukom (1993).

Figure 6.3   Internationalization of subcontractors

Of course, over time, with a rise in local costs, contractors can just as readily move elsewhere (*Business Central Europe*, 1995).

Subcontracting and Advanced Technologies

The impact of cost differences on subcontracting has been felt in a wide range of industries, not just relatively standardized manufactured products. Even products incorporating sophisticated, advanced technologies have become subject to the inroads of outsourcing, as witnessed in its massive growth in the electronics sector. This began to emerge at quite an early stage. An example was the IBM personal computer soon after its appearance in the early 1980s. Even at that stage, about three-quarters of its production was outsourced to suppliers in South Korea, Japan and Singapore (Luostarinen and Welch, 1990). More recently, while Taiwan dominated global production of notebook computers at the end of the 1990s, via subcontracting to companies such as IBM and Hewlett Packard, by the end of 2004 the bulk of this activity had already been moved to China. The chairman of Taiwan's Ho

Tung group expressed prevailing sentiment in this way: 'If you don't go to China, others will, and the first to suffer will be you' (Miles, 2005, 9).

It has been estimated that about 20 per cent of global manufacturing of high-technology products in the electronics sector, such as mobile telephones, personal digital assistants and network base stations, is carried out by contract manufacturers, many with globally dispersed production sites, constituting about $US84 billion in total global business (Shameen, 2003). As shown in Table 6.1, contract manufacturers like Flextronics have become powerful global players in their own right, in a sense riding on the wave of international outsourcing growth, and have begun to develop advanced design capacities, moving up the value chain, offering an advanced service to clients beyond the basic manufacturing function. Japanese firms have been able to enter commercial aircraft production as subcontractors, providing key parts of Boeing aircraft. About 70 per cent of Boeing's latest aircraft, the 787, is to be manufactured outside the company (*Economist*, 2005a).

The growth of international subcontracting in products incorporating more sophisticated technology has also gone hand-in-hand with the development of companies' more comprehensive provision of systems solutions to industrial customers. Systems solutions involve combinations of hardware and software elements, sometimes quite complex, designed to satisfy the particular needs of individual customers. They represent a 'problem-solving package' (Luostarinen and Welch, 1990). The industrial needs of companies typically vary from case to case, generating the need for customization of the overall system: for example, the communication system within mines. However, 'costs would be far too excessive if the solution was so customised that many new component parts had to be produced. Rather, to keep costs manageable in the hardware area, yet staying flexible, sets of standardised interchangeable parts need to be developed, which can be mixed and matched to different requirements. At the same time, by standardising the component base, it is possible to reduce costs through economies of scale in production or by subcontracting' (ibid., p. 119). This is illustrated in Figure 6.4. For systems suppliers, the aim is to minimize as much as possible the customized component of the system, thereby keeping overall costs to a manageable level, with international subcontracting playing an increasingly important role in this task.

Impact of Reduced Trade Protection

As world trade is freed through various protection-reducing measures in different industries, including both goods and services, the cost differences

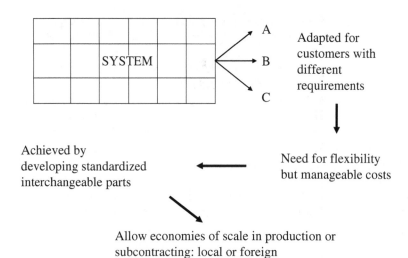

Source: Luostarinen and Welch (1990, p. 121).

Figure 6.4   Systems development and subcontracting

between countries are more readily able to be acted upon. This is perhaps being most starkly exposed with the demise of the Multilateral Agreement on Textiles and Clothing at the end of 2004: see Table 6.4. China is seen to be well placed to increase its already dominant share of world trade in clothing, although India is also predicted to be a major beneficiary of the removal of the system of quotas. The WTO estimated that China's share of US clothing imports would rise to 50 per cent in 2005 as a result of the removal of quotas, up from 16 per cent in 2002, while India's share was expected to reach 15 per cent, rising from a minor position of just 4 per cent in 2002 (Nordas, 2004). Not surprisingly, affected manufacturers in the US have been lobbying the government to introduce measures to restrain the expected surge of Chinese imports. They have already been successful in having growth ceilings applied in some product areas, under the terms of a special provision introduced as part of China's WTO admission permitting such restraints until 2008. The head of US retailer JC Penney's purchasing unit has commented that 'he will monitor how Washington applies safeguards to limit Chinese exports, so that he isn't caught having ordered products that will be barred from entering US ports' (Hiebert, Murphy and Vanderwolk, 2004, 32). Even Chinese authorities have become concerned about a too-rapid rise in Chinese exports of clothing producing a protectionist backlash. In the first quarter of 2005 there was a large jump in Chinese clothing exports which generated such a high level of protest in the

Table 6.4   Textile and clothing quotas

Characteristics of quotas

- 31/12/2004: WTO's Agreement on Textiles
  and Clothing expires: end of system of quotas
- World Bank economists estimate that China will
  control 45 per cent of global exports by 2005
- Pakistan clothing producer Balal Ahmad sees the
  lifting of quotas as 'the opportunity of a lifetime'.
  Ahmad's factories produce 12–18 million knitted
  shirts a year for companies such as Levi Strauss,
  JC Penney and Calvin Klein
- Attempts to reinvent quotas in high-income
  countries such as the US expected

US and Europe that China voluntarily introduced export taxes on a range of clothing products (*Economist*, 2005b).

Reduced Transport and Communication Costs

Clearly, protection enacted by governments in its various forms has the capacity to restrain trade in goods and services, whereas its reduction, or removal in some cases, becomes an important contributor to the development of international subcontracting. In a similar way, reductions in the cost of transport and communications act as a facilitator of trade and thereby international subcontracting. Put simply, a large increase in transport costs would kill off much of the type of globally dispersed subcontracting of production of different product parts organized by Li & Fung (see Box 6.1). Even today, with significantly lower real transport costs across the main forms compared to 20 years ago, many products are still subject to limited international subcontracting because of high transport costs per unit of value of the product (Edwards, 2004). 'Foamex International, the world's biggest supplier of [poly]urethane foam (which goes into car-seats and mattresses), has 67 different factories and distribution outlets in America . . . the firm's chairman points out that transporting a product that is 95% air is not economic' (*Economist*, 1998, 86).

While lower transport costs have played their part in the rise of international subcontracting in manufacturing, the fall in communication costs has been more dramatic, particularly with the arrival of cheap telecommunications which have rapidly opened up a range of services subcontracting possibilities to countries such as India, with their low cost of educated workers.

The growth of the IT sector has been a major contributor to these emerging possibilities – in part benefiting from the cost-reducing effects of international subcontracting in the manufacture of IT hardware products – as exemplified by the fall in prices of personal computers. The huge reduction in costs of computer equipment has enabled the diffusion of their use into widespread locations, in both consumer and industrial markets. Within the IT field, perhaps the most important single development with implications for services subcontracting has been the rise of the Internet, its rapid global spread, and its impact on communication costs. It has procured a dramatic reduction in the cost of transferring large amounts of data between remote locations, the output of many service activities such as market research and document processing. As important, though, has been the Internet's effect on the organization of many work tasks carried out within companies, such as dealing with customers and suppliers, handling promotional activities, and coordinating inter-unit operations. It has sensitized companies and workers to working with others on a remote basis, and in combination with the restructuring of work, has created a basis for companies to consider more readily the outsourcing of some of these activities, particularly given the perceived cost implications of so doing. Edwards (2004, 4) notes McKinsey research indicating that 'already, 16% of all work done by the world's IT services industry is carried out remotely, away from where these services are consumed'.

There is little doubt that there will be substantial continued growth of international subcontracting in the services sector in the foreseeable future, across a broadening range of activities, and in the face of, at times, virulent political opposition. At the same time, the benefits of being close to one's customers will remain, as evidenced by the moves of a number of the successful Indian IT subcontractors to set up in the US and other markets of their main customers. For example, Satyam Computer Services, the fourth largest Indian software exporter, has established development centres in the US, Europe, Japan and Singapore (*Australian*, 2005b).

The Role and Impact of Retailers

Large retailers in various countries have played a substantial role in stimulating the growth of international subcontracting, perhaps most obviously in the textiles, clothing and footwear industries. This has been stressed in a recent WTO report, in which it is argued that it has reached the stage where 'the retailers in the clothing sector increasingly manage the supply chain of the clothing and textiles sectors' (Nordas, 2004, p. 1). Retailers have a direct impact through the size of their foreign purchases: for example, imports from China into the US by Wal-Mart, the world's largest retailer, worth about $US15 billion, represented about 10 per cent of China's total annual exports to the US at the time (*Economist*, 2004c). Clearly, the bulk of these imports was destined for the US market, with some re-exports to Canada and Mexico. However, Wal-Mart also organizes production by sub-contractors in China for supply to its various international retail sites, including China itself. In general, retailers have such a powerful effect on manufacturers in countries such as China, Vietnam and Indonesia because of their bridging function between manufacturer and ultimate consumer. Production is carried out according to the retailer's specifications, deter-mining designs and styles in line with the needs, preferences and fashion trends of the local market where the retailer is located. The retailers drive the marketing process. As such, foreign subcontractors do not have to understand the retailer's market, do not have to undertake foreign market research, or puzzle about required product adaptations as is a normal requirement in international marketing. This is why contracted production for the retailers represents such an attractive way of getting started in inter-national trade for companies in low-wage developing countries. Effectively, market acceptance of production, provided it conforms to the retailer's specifications, is the problem taken over by the retailer.

Yue Yuen, now the world's largest producer of sports footwear, stresses the role of US retailers in getting it started as an international sub-contractor. About five years after starting operations, the company was approached to start producing cheap in-house brand sneakers for US retailers. One of the company's founding four brothers, Chi Neng Tsai, has commented that 'we knew nothing about foreign trade then . . . we didn't even know what a letter of credit was' (Sender, 1996, 51). The role of retail-ers in generating increased international subcontracting is illustrated in Figure 6.5.

The impact of retailers on international subcontracting goes far beyond the direct effects noted above. Their use of foreign subcontractors means that they are not using local manufacturers. This inevitably creates pressure on domestic manufacturers (as shown in Figure 6.5) to compete for this business, to develop responses in a way that ensures their viability. Defensive responses include the following:

- lobbying activity with government representatives to restrict the inflow of subcontracted products, as with clothing imports from China into the US under the new trade regime;
- changes in production systems, such as the extension of automated processes and use of robots, in an attempt to reduce costs and become more price-competitive with imports. For example, 'Canon, Japan's leading office equipment maker, is planning to automate as

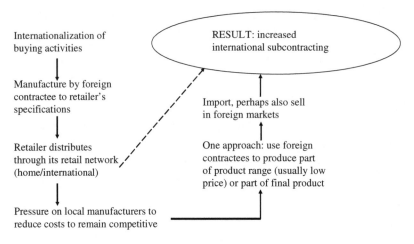

Internationalization of
buying activities

Manufacture by foreign
contractee to retailer's
specifications

Retailer distributes
through its retail network
(home/international)

Pressure on local manufacturers to
reduce costs to remain competitive

RESULT: increased
international subcontracting

Import, perhaps also sell
in foreign markets

One approach: use foreign
contractees to produce part
of product range (usually low
price) or part of final product

Source: Adapted from Luostarinen and Welch (1990, p. 118).

Figure 6.5   Retailers and international subcontracting

much as a quarter of its domestic manufacturing over the next three
years as part of reforms aimed at maintaining production in Japan'
(Nakamoto, 2004, 20);

● for many companies it is not possible to compete directly with the
lower-priced imports, so they have attempted to develop their own
low-cost foreign sources of supply, with the aim of becoming competitive at the lower-priced end of their product range, thus further
contributing to the growth of international subcontracting. At the
same time, many of these companies have tried to maintain or
enhance their offering at the higher-priced end of their range – to
compete more strongly on the basis of non-price features such as
technology, design and style as a way of ensuring long-term viability.
An example is the South Korean shoe manufacturer, Sungho
Industrial, which responded to low-priced competition by moving
the bulk of its production to China in the 1990s, setting up two factories there. However, 'high quality boots, that need sophisticated
needlework, are still made in Pusan' [South Korea] (Min, 2003, 32).
The president of the company has added that a further stage of its
strategy is the attempt to build its own brand name within the global
market over the next five to ten years. Already, it has exported its
high-end climbing boots to seven countries, including the US,
Canada and Japan. A recent development by the company is 'Digital
Shoes . . . customers can receive made-to-measure shoes in three days

– the time it takes from foot measurement at any of Sungho Industrial's stores to home delivery' (ibid., 30).

The effect on home manufacturers of retailers sourcing offshore is similar to that on foreign subcontractors when retailers, or other contractors, shift their sourcing to other, cheaper, locations, as in the Sungho Industrial case. The initial choice is often brutal: move or go out of business. Sometimes, though, manufacturers have seen the change coming well before it affects them directly and have developed defensive responses well in advance – even preceding retailers into new subcontracting locations in some instances.

Free Trade Zones

A further stimulant to the growth of international subcontracting (and foreign direct investment) has been the establishment of free trade zones (FTZs) in many countries. It is difficult to judge just how important their stimulus effect has been, and they are the subject of considerable questioning as to the benefits for the countries within which they are established, as the following comment by the General Secretary of the Congress of South African Trade Unions illustrates: 'In no country has it been shown that free trade zones are a real path to development. Investment comes and goes, usually leaving little behind once it has gone' (Perman et al., 2004, 4). Free trade zones come in various forms, and different terms are used for them, for example export-processing zones, free ports, and maquiladoras, the free assembly plants mainly clustered around the border between the US and Mexico. Whatever they are called, the characteristics are relatively consistent (see Figure 6.6): within the zones there are special incentives, such as tax holidays and relief from import duties, provided the end-product is re-exported, and reduced bureaucracy and concentrated infrastructure. For example, an advertisement for the new Special Economic Zone at Navi Mumbai (New Bombay) stressed the following features:

- minimal red tape and bureaucracy,
- functions like a foreign territory,
- 100 per cent corporate tax holiday for ten years,
- 100 per cent foreign ownership of an investment permitted,
- free repatriation of profits.

Dubai has set up a free trade zone aimed at outsourcing companies in the IT sector, called Dubai Outsource Zone. The zone 'will provide a comprehensive infrastructure and environment for outsourcing companies to set

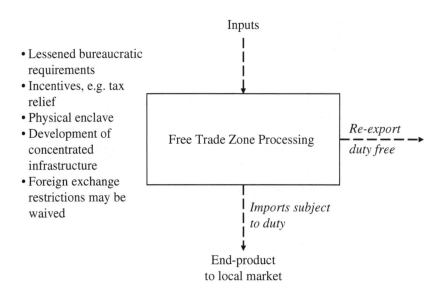

• Lessened bureaucratic
  requirements
• Incentives, e.g. tax
  relief
• Physical enclave
• Development of
  concentrated
  infrastructure
• Foreign exchange
  restrictions may be
  waived

Inputs

Free Trade Zone Processing

Re-export duty free

Imports subject to duty

End-product
to local market

Figure 6.6   FTZ characteristics

up global or regional hubs servicing the worldwide market . . . DOZ's offering includes 100 per cent exemption from taxes' (*Australian*, 2004, IT Business, 2). Apparently, the WTO Agreement on Subsidies and Countervailing Measures, which came into force in 2003, has had some effect in constraining the use of export subsidies associated with FTZs by some WTO members, although there are let-out clauses for the less developed countries (Perman et al., 2004).

The aims of countries setting up the zones have been to attract foreign direct investment, create employment and encourage technology transfer and skill development. Based on an investigation that it conducted, the International Labour Organisation concluded that, globally, there were 5174 zones in 2004, employing just under 42 million workers. This was an increase from 500 in 1995 and 176 in 1986. The greatest number of zones was in China, with over 2000, employing about 30 million workers (Perman et al., 2004). While it is questionable whether the free trade zone format is sufficient to encourage foreign direct investment in the first place, once having decided to set up in the country concerned, they do represent an opportunity for companies to lower the costs of the activity compared to non-zone options. For some this will assist in the provision of an enhanced outsourcing service to client companies. The zone incentives may also sway the choice between investment options in different countries.

BENEFITS: MORE THAN COST SAVINGS

It is clear from the analysis so far that there is an array of forces encouraging the development of international subcontracting, cost difference being a key factor, but many broader influences have been at work, such as the impact of retailers and lowering of protection. For individual companies, the reasons for using international subcontracting as a form of foreign operations are more extensive: for instance, while cost differences are important, there are many other considerations that come into play in companies' decision making. Indeed, the UNCTAD (2004) report on the use of 'offshoring' in the services sector stresses the positive benefits that many companies have derived beyond cost reduction: 'many of the pioneers offshored to access skills and to improve the quality of services provided' (p. 28). Companies outsourcing call centres and IT services to India have been able to access workers who are typically better educated than those in the source countries. As a result, it is claimed that the precision and quality of work is improved by the transfer of this work, with higher rates of customer satisfaction and greater precision and quality of work such as software development.

This is in line with earlier studies of the benefits of using foreign sources of supply. For example, using a survey of purchasing professionals in the US, Birou and Fawcett (1993, 34) concluded that 'international sourcing's greatest benefit is that it provides access to lower priced products. This result is consistent with price being reported as the primary catalyst [in other studies] that brings firms into the international market . . . The availability of higher quality goods and access to product technology were also considered to be important benefits'. Another survey of US purchasing professionals even found that, 'unlike most of the earlier studies which indicated that lower price was the most important factor in selecting overseas suppliers, these respondents list *better quality* as the most important factor', closely followed by price (Min and Galle, 1991, 14). In both studies, sources included European countries, Japan, newly industializing countries (such as South Korea) and less developed countries. While this reflects the regard held for sources such as Japanese and West German companies in the sample, it was seen also as a reflection of 'the shift in emphasis on quality . . . [resulting in] the ongoing push for improved quality at source' (ibid.). More than a decade later it is clear that considerable effort now goes into the process of assuring quality and outcomes generally from the outsourcing activity, whether by the contractor directly or through an intermediary such as Li & Fung (see Box 6.1 above). Nike, Reebok and Puma, for example, put substantial resources into ensuring quality standards, such as by placing staff at subcontractor factories, as in the case of sourcing from

Indonesia noted above. There is no doubt that companies like Nike, that have been using international subcontracting for long periods now, have become more adept, with accumulated experience, in ensuring quality meets the standards demanded by their markets.

For the individual company, there are not only potential cost and even quality benefits from international subcontracting; as an operation mode (in its non-FDI form) it involves far lower cost and commitment in establishing a foreign production base as a means of servicing global markets. As noted earlier, the commitment may be as little as a single order at the outset, although companies using subcontracting on a widespread basis tend to look for greater assurance by establishing more long-term relationships with their subcontractors. In Nike's case, it has built a network of suppliers to which it passes on the outcomes of its research where it is considered that it will improve their efficiency, from which it will ultimately benefit as well. Building such a network of subcontractors is seen to provide another benefit: greater flexibility. 'One of [Nike's] competitive advantages is that it can respond to changes in fashion faster than its rivals: rearranging what each supplier does on its network, Nike can change its product mix almost overnight' (*Economist*, 1992, 81). It can also add suppliers as a way of increasing capacity. In a general sense, this is one of the most important aspects of subcontracting: it can make a company better equipped in responding to changes in its international environment, including shifts in government policy, political risks and changes in business climate in individual countries. Inevitably, too, non-investment subcontracting means that the contractor is not hostage to the circumstances of a particular country. By utilizing another company's facilities in a foreign market, the contractor is able to penetrate the market, and leave more rapidly compared to foreign direct investment and some other forms of foreign operation. To the extent that companies increase their level of international subcontracting it should be expected that they will be more prepared to engage in partial de-internationalization (Benito and Welch, 1997).

International subcontracting allows companies to extend their existing product range. While this often means an ability to offer products in the low-price range, sophisticated subcontractors in some cases may be a source of new and more advanced products. For example, subcontractors both design and manufacture mobile handsets for more recognized companies. Advantages of using these subcontractors for the established handset makers are that 'it helps them fill gaps in their product lines quickly and cheaply; it saves money on research and development; and it means the [subcontractor] takes on some of the business risks associated with fluctuations in component supply and end-user demand. Northstream, a Swedish consultancy, predicts that the proportion of handsets produced by [subcontractors] will grow from 9% in 2002 to around 30% by [2005]' (*Economist*, 2004b, 66). Taiwanese subcontractors in the electronics sector have been competing for business by putting resources into product innovation in order to make themselves more attractive to foreign contractors (Dean, 2004).

THE IMPORTANCE OF MARKETING AND BRAND STRENGTH

Whether subcontractors are used as a way of extending a company's product range or to produce its core products, the ability to carry this out without creating a future competitive threat in the subcontractor depends heavily on the contractor's strength in the marketplace, particularly its brand strength. Nike and Reebok no longer undertake any manufacturing on their own part, but recognize the critical importance of maintaining their market position, investing heavily in research and development, advertising and promotion. The extent of this investment is such as to make it difficult for subcontractors to attempt to move up the value chain and become direct competitors with Nike and Reebok in the marketplace using their own brands. As Figure 6.7 illustrates, a strong brand and associated marketing activity provide an umbrella or hat under which international

Figure 6.7   Subcontracting and marketing

subcontracting is able to flourish, putting companies in a stronger position to decide on the optimal mix and form of domestic activities and foreign subcontracting operations.

In general, international subcontracting enables companies in advanced countries to strengthen their competitive ability in all markets, with the ability to combine advanced technology, design and styling with lower foreign costs of production, typically by accessing lower labour costs. This is further buttressed by their control over marketing and distribution. As the global reach of subcontractors has extended, this has made it easier for many contractors to source output closer to their end-markets, facilitating faster responsiveness to market shifts and reduced transport costs. In essence, subcontracting can provide a powerful basis for penetrating global markets, one which has come to be used increasingly by internationalizing companies, across both goods and services.

CONSTRAINTS, PROBLEMS AND STRATEGIC ISSUES

The above analysis would seem to indicate that, given the positive forces working in favour of international subcontracting, both at the company level and in the broader global business and economic environment, there is an almost matchless argument for companies to choose this mode, where feasible, over and above other mode options. The tide clearly seems to be flowing strongly in its direction. However, as noted in Box 6.1 above, as a background to the rise of outsourcing intermediaries, there is an array of practical and cross-cultural issues that have to be dealt with that can generate significant problems and costs and make international subcontracting uneconomic at times. They have even led some companies to engage in *insourcing*, where previously subcontracted operations are brought home and back within the company. For example, Japanese companies Kenwood (mini-disc players) and Aiwa (mini-stereo systems) have moved previously subcontracted production home; in Aiwa's case, 'the development of new technology in Japan was the trigger for moving production home' (*Economist*, 2004a; Moffett, 1996, 63). A recent survey by Deloitte in the Australian IT sector found that respondents were negative about their out-sourcing experiences and almost half indicated that expected cost savings did not eventuate. As a result, some companies were taking services back in-house (Mills, 2005). In the following section we examine the various aspects that raise questions about the attractiveness of the mode, and outline the strategic risks that companies may expose themselves to, with sometimes 'life-threatening consequences'.

ADDITIONAL COSTS INCURRED

In a review of international versus domestic outsourcing within the retail sector, Liu and McGoldrick (1996, 28) listed the benefits of domestic sourcing as including 'the shorter lead and transit times, the ability to monitor closely the total production process and the lower costs in terms of management time and communications'. They concluded 'that retailers in general would pay a premium of around 15 percent for goods provided by domestic suppliers'. A similar conclusion was reached in a review of outsourcing to eastern Europe by west European firms in the garment industry, emphasizing the advantages of fast response times to changes in the industry compared to suppliers from China (*Economist*, 2005c). Such conclusions expose the reality that, despite the potential cost savings through international subcontracting, there are also costs and organization problems incurred in the activity that are not always obvious at first sight. For example, the PC maker Compaq Computer, now part of Hewlett Packard, in the early 1990s subcontracted part of its notebook PC production to the Japanese company, Citizen. There were 'all kinds of difficulties, in design, manufacturing, cost and quality . . . the head of corporate operations at Compaq . . . concedes that it would have been cheaper to make computers in-house' (*Economist*, 1995, 67). In a survey of purchasing professionals with offshore sourcing experience in the US, Frear, Metcalf and Alguire (1992, 11) found that 'problems with performance, delivery, and technical capabilities existed for more than 50 percent of the respondents'. This is in line with the findings of a number of other studies (Min and Galle, 1991; Birou and Fawcett, 1993). Liu and McGoldrick (1996, 18) classify the range of constraints on international sourcing as either 'hard' or 'soft' costs, including,

'Soft:

- transit time
- political risks
- trade barriers
- culture
- language
- quality control
- supervision procedures

Hard:

- international transport costs
- inland freight

- insurance
- tariffs
- export taxes
- foreign exchange costs
- rejects
- letters of credit
- damage in transit.'

Clearly, in combination these cost factors can easily accumulate to the point where foreign contracted output becomes more costly than the local outsourced or in-house product. For products with relatively low unit value but high weight or large mass – for example, with polyurethane products, as noted above – transport costs alone may be enough to make international outsourcing uneconomic. In many cases, even within textiles and clothing, where outsourcing is so pervasive, rapid response and reliable service can matter more than simple cost comparisons, as noted above. This is particularly so where the product is highly fashion-sensitive and there is a need for a rapid response to a change in market tastes. In such circumstances retailers are loath to carry large inventories, pushing the burden on to suppliers' response systems. This has opened up non-price ways of competing with offshore contract suppliers. A study of manufacturers in the US clothing sector found that, in responding to low wage costs in foreign locations, companies were seeking to emphasize the benefits of speed, flexibility and information technology. Customers were being linked to direct on-line ordering options and automated inventory and distribution systems, creating rapid response times, and overall responsiveness that foreign producers would find difficult to match (Abernathy et al., 1999). As it is, technological improvements can quickly alter the cost equation and other aspects in favour of local outsourcing and in-house manufacturing, as illustrated in the case of Aiwa, noted above.

ASSURING QUALITY AND TIMELY DELIVERIES

While the case of Flextronics, noted in Table 6.1, might give the impression of sophisticated subcontractors able to be readily tapped at a moment's notice, with the ability to deliver from a plant nearby, this is far from the true situation for most subcontractors, and contractors may have to play a part in developing the efficiency (such as delivery effectiveness) and quality of foreign manufacturers first in order to derive the benefits of acceptable low-cost supplies. An example is the support provided by Toyota to its subcontractors in Thailand. It established the Toyota Co-operation Club for subcontractors. 'Club members are provided with advice and training in a large number of areas – including in quality assurance *Kaizen* steps (steady improvements), cost *kaizen* processes, and quality control circle activities. They are also encouraged to improve, on a voluntary basis (*Jishiuken*), the quality, cost and timeliness in delivery of their products and services as well as to learn from each other and to cooperate among themselves' (Wattanapruttipaisan, 2002, 82).

While Toyota may be able to handle the demands of such an exercise, the time, cost and risk would be beyond the capacity of most contractors. The weaker the technical and managerial foundation of the subcontractor, the greater the need for assistance via technology transfer and training, and the higher the costs involved. Weaknesses will not always be obvious prior to the establishment of the contractual relationship. In the latter part of the 1990s, Nokia experienced rapid growth in market demand for its mobile telephones. This generated pressure on subcontractors to increase supply, but their delivery times increased substantially, which caused Nokia problems in respecting its export commitments. This was on top of continuing quality problems with the subcontractors' output. As a result, it was forced to increase its own, in-house, production activity, in the face of a threat of longer-term market damage (Korhonen, 1999). This example demonstrates just how high the potential cost to a company can be if the quality and reliability of subcontractors are not assured. Box 6.2 below illustrates the extent of demands on quality assurance processes, and supervisory requirements to conform to the emerging codes of conduct regarding the use of foreign labour, in outsourcing arrangements in the clothing sector. In the case examined, the burden of quality assurance and code of conduct supervision is mainly shifted onto intermediaries and subcontractors further down the supply chain by the US retailer JC Penney. Contractors tend to maintain constant pressure on subcontractors to reduce prices, so the subcontractors are always seeking ways to reduce labour costs, including attempts to get around the codes of conduct.

LONG-TERM RELATIONSHIPS

The problems of assuring quality, reliability and efficiency of subcontractors have led many contractors to seek longer-term solutions, such as in the example of Toyota in Thailand noted above. This has resulted in a stronger emphasis on building long-term relationships between contractors and their subcontractors rather than short-term contractual arrangements. This has been occurring across the range of companies, in line with

BOX 6.2   RETAILERS AND SUPERVISION OF
           INTERNATIONAL SUBCONTRACTORS
           UNDER CODES OF CONDUCT: THE CASE
           OF JC PENNEY IN THE PHILIPPINES

The 'U.S. retailer JC Penney has "Foreign Sourcing Requirements" that apply to all of its suppliers. Among other provisions, the sourcing requirements state that "JC Penney will not knowingly allow the importation into the US of merchandise manufactured with illegal child labor." With regard to the Philippines:

1. JC Penney purchases infant and children's apparel from Renzo, a US-based importer. Pursuant to its sourcing requirements, JC Penney requires Renzo to certify that its imports are not made with child labor.
2. Renzo imports from its Philippines agent, Robillard Resources. Renzo communicates to Robillard the JC Penney sourcing requirements and its obligations and requires Robillard to sign a certificate that its products are not made with child labor.
3. Robillard purchases from a number of contractors in the Philippines, one of which is Castleberry. Robillard requires Castleberry to certify that its products are not made with child labor. The owner of Robillard visits Castleberry from time to time, monitoring for quality control, but also for compliance with the sourcing requirements. Occasionally, a representative of JC Penney also visits.
4. Castleberry does cutting, finishing and packing. It subcontracts sewing to about thirty plants.
5. The thirty or so subcontractors who do the sewing do not sign a certificate stating that no child labor has been used, but are supervised by Castleberry line supervisors, who are each responsible for several subcontractors. They spend almost their entire time with the subcontractors. It is apparent that their primary interest is quality control, but they also monitor compliance with other standards.
6. Homework contracts – piece work contracts are made with heads of households ... This is not monitored by any company' (US Department of Labor, 2003, Box III – 7).

the emphasis Japanese companies have long had in their approach to subcontracting relationships (Morris and Imrie, 1993). Long-term relationships provide a better basis for the transfer of methods and technology that improve the subcontractors' operations. While this approach appears to negate some of the advantages of short-term contractual arrangements, particularly the flexibility to move quickly from one supplier to another, perhaps in a new lower-cost location, it does enable a contractor to deal with some of the inevitable constraints on effective subcontractor performance. As noted in the list of outsourcing costs, often these relate to 'soft' aspects such as language dissimilarity and cultural differences in general. Switching from one supplier to another involves additional costs, including the search for and evaluation of new suppliers, and contractors have to implement quality assurance and supervision processes with respect to the new suppliers all over again. As Quinn and Hilmer (1994, 47–8) argue, 'outsourcing entails unique transaction costs – searching, contracting, controlling, and recontracting – that at times may exceed the transaction costs of having the activity directly under management's in-house control'. Again, this is where intermediaries (such as Li & Fung – see Box 6.1 above) have come into their own, but their service, of course, does come at a price.

The furniture multinational, IKEA, provides another example of a company that takes a more long-term approach to relationships with its subcontractors, as demonstrated by its activities in Vietnam. 'IKEA keeps its retail prices low by driving hard bargains with its suppliers, who generally make thinner profit margins on their sales to IKEA than they do to other foreign buyers. But, in turn, IKEA offers the prospect of forging long-term, high-volume business tie-ups for fledgling Vietnamese entrepreneurs, whom IKEA advises in detail on everything from sourcing raw materials to improving productivity and buying equipment' (Cohen, 2003, 56).

DIFFICULT FOR SMEs?

The experiences of a Japanese SME, AS'TY INC, currently with about 200 employees, which began international subcontracting in the late 1980s, are instructive regarding the potential pressures, risks and demands of effective international outsourcing for smaller firms that are new to the business, and the time it can take to sort out these issues. The company manufactures and sells a range of clothing and accessories such as handbags to major Japanese retailers. The catalyst for an interest in foreign sourcing was the growing price competition within its markets emerging from low-labour cost countries like South Korea at that time. It initially set up a trading department within the company as a base for its foreign activities. Recognizing its lack of internal knowledge and experience to take on the new task, it hired two staff from Japanese trading companies. While FDI to establish a foreign manufacturing base was considered as an option, it was rejected because of the perceived time, cost and financial stress that it would involve. In contrast, international outsourcing was regarded as involving low capital commitment, low risk and greater flexibility, and would be faster to implement. As a result, it opted for international outsourcing as its most appropriate initial mode path.

However, the early outcomes were very negative: there were many delays with deliveries, specifications were frequently not adhered to, and, in one case, rather than handbags, the boxes were merely filled with paper. To make matters worse, the subcontractors had convinced AS'TY to make payments in advance. Rather than withdrawing from outsourcing, the company viewed what happened as 'lessons' rather than 'mistakes'. Over a period of two to three years, the problems were sorted out, some suppliers were dropped, and longer-term relationships were built with acceptable performers in Hong Kong, China and South Korea. Even over the longer term, though, quality control remained an issue, given that visits and inspections by AS'TY staff were infrequent. Time and cost constraints prevented more consistent attention to quality control at the subcontractors' production sites. At times, contractors were found to have outsourced some of their work for AS'TY, in contravention of their contracts. Timely scheduling of deliveries remained a problem. In the end, AS'TY decided to set up its own production operation in Vietnam, in a new industrial zone set up in Haiphong to cater specifically for Japanese manufacturing companies. Nevertheless, this move also proved to be problematic, because the Zone did not attract Japanese companies, while there was a lack of local material supplies and trained workers, and the extra distance to Japan compared to East Asian suppliers added to costs.

On top of all these outsourcing frictions there is the ever-present threat of political action, which has been brought to the fore by the publicity surrounding the outsourcing of service jobs to India. This has led some US companies to outsource some of their work to Canada. As well, though, Canada has become a base for outsourcing some of this work on to India. As the managing director of the subsidiary of one US company in Canada commented: 'in some cases we use Canada as a front end to India . . . we find that this takes away the issues people have with India' – what we might call outsourcing of the political problem (Austen, 2004, 16).

CREATING A FUTURE COMPETITOR?

Clearly, the above analysis demonstrates that international subcontracting is neither costless nor riskless. However, perhaps the biggest risk of all is that of helping to create a future competitor that ultimately threatens the contractor's market position. International subcontracting is not just about lowering costs; whether considered or not, embarking on this path may have significant long-term strategic consequences for the contractor. There are many examples of subcontractors seeking to move up from that state to become competitive suppliers to contractors in their end-markets: it is an ever-present, almost natural threat. For instance, Taiwanese companies BenQ (mobile telephones) and Acer (personal computers) have been attempting to build global brand names for their products as part of an attempt to break free of their subcontracting role and achieve higher profit margins, with some success. BenQ makes about 35–40 per cent of its sales under its own brand name. However, this requires a major balancing act: Motorola, for example, is an important customer of BenQ, and is a major supplier of mobile telephones to the Taiwanese market. The conflict has been partially resolved by making models under the BenQ brand that have a different appearance from those supplied to contractors like Motorola (Miles, 2005). Still, Motorola has shifted orders elsewhere as BenQ's brand became more powerful (Dean, 2004). Similarly, Taiwan's Asustek started as a supplier of motherboards for PC makers, but has moved on to make notebook computers under its own brand name, Asus, constituting about half of its total sales. It is now in first place in the Taiwanese market and its sales in Europe and Asia have been growing rapidly, with very little advertising: it is wary of alienating its contract customers (Dean, 2004). Even Chinese clothing manufacturers 'are no longer content with doing processing jobs for foreign companies . . . "we need to develop internationally famous brands of our own. Name brands will be our teeth" . . . says Jiang Hengjie, vice-president of the China Garment Industry Association' (Ning, 2005, 5).

The fact that there is only a limited number of subcontractors to have successfully made the transition to operations under their own brand name – such as South Korea's Samsung – is indicative of the cost and difficulty of this step. For the subcontractor, there is always the threat that, once it starts to sell part of its output under its own brand name, the contractor will reduce or totally remove its purchases and move to another supplier (assuming one is available), thereby putting the subcontractor's business in jeopardy in the short run, whereas building a strong brand name is a long-term exercise. It is noteworthy that the Chinese computer maker, Lenovo, which purchased the PC operations of IBM in 2004 as part of an effort to build global recognition for its brand, still negotiated the right to use the IBM name for five years as part of the deal. Nevertheless, the case of the US bicycle producer Schwinn, presented in Box 6.3 below, provides a salutary lesson in the dangers of outsourcing, with Schwinn paying the ultimate price of not just being surpassed in global markets by two of its subcontractors, but ultimately being forced into bankruptcy.

BOX 6.3   HOW NOT TO USE OUTSOURCING: THE CASE OF
THE SCHWINN BICYCLE COMPANY

When it went into bankruptcy in 1992, Schwinn was a 97-year-old company with a strong brand name and reputation within the US market. It began sourcing from Japan in the 1970s with the objective of reducing the costs of getting its bicycles into the US market. In 1978, as Taiwanese bicycle producers were becoming more price competitive than their Japanese counterparts, Schwinn began importing from Taiwan's Giant Manufacturing, simply adding the Schwinn name to these bicycles. In 1981, as a result of a strike at Schwinn's main factory in the US, it went into a partnership arrangement with Giant, with no equity involved (Giant had refused to sell any), and transferred key technology to ensure that Giant would be able to replicate Schwinn's standards. By 1984, Giant was providing 700 000 bicycles a year to Schwinn, about 70 per cent of Schwinn's US sales. In the process, Schwinn had taught Giant a great deal, exposing it to the marketing and distribution demands of the US market from the inside.

Emboldened by its success and the improvements made in its operations, Giant began to market bicycles under its own brand name: in 1986 in Europe, and in 1987 in the US. It was able to use the Schwinn connection to help its initial foray into the US market, and even hired former Schwinn staff to assist with US marketing and distribution activities. It also pursued a policy of technological advancement based on heavy investment in research and development, improving on Schwinn's original technology, and becoming a leader in lightweight carbon fibre bicycle frames, and building strengths in mountain and racing bicycles. By 1993, Giant was the world's leading bicycle exporter, in value terms, with 70 per cent of its sales under the Giant brand name. In 1997, it opened a factory in the Netherlands to better serve European markets and to facilitate greater responsiveness to changing market tastes. It moved some of its production to China via a joint venture to take advantage of lower labour costs, and established a research and development facility in the US. By the mid-1990s it had built a powerful marketing machine, including the sponsorship of racing teams.

As bad as the Giant story was for Schwinn, worse was to come. In response to the moves by Giant, Schwinn established an alliance in 1987 with a newly emerging Chinese subcontractor, China Bicycles Company (CBC), that had been supplying some retailers in the US with low-priced, retailer-branded bicycles. As part of the alliance Schwinn took a 33 per cent stake in CBC, later diluted to 18 per cent when CBC listed on the new, local, stock market. Again, as a result of technology transfer from Schwinn, and exposure to the US market, CBC made rapid strides in improving its quality and overall performance, and its understanding of the demands of global markets. Thus, already in 1990, it bought a US importer and distributor (for $US17 million), and in the process acquired the Diamond Back brand name, through which it was able to begin competing directly with Schwinn in the US market. By 1993, CBC had become the world's largest bicycle exporter by volume, selling about 30 per cent of its bicycles under the Diamond Back label.

At the time of bankruptcy, Schwinn's US market share had fallen to 5 per cent, down from 25 per cent in the 1960s. It was only producing 10 000 bicycles in the US, relying on imports for the rest, including from Giant and CBC. In 2001, the US firm Pacific Cycle purchased the Schwinn brand name and began sales of bicycles under the resurrected name. In early 2004, Pacific Cycle was acquired by Dorel Industries of Canada. Through a combination of East Asian sourcing and the continuing strength of the Schwinn brand name, Schwinn bicycles have ridden back onto the world stage – albeit under new, and foreign, ownership. The ability to do so is a testament to the longevity and power of a well-established brand name (with 88 per cent awareness in the US market), combined with the potential of international subcontracting. In 2004, Pacific Cycle (including brands other than Schwinn), as part of Dorel, had achieved a 27 per cent share of total US bicycle sales.

Sources: Baum (1998), Edwards (2004), Marsh (1997a, 1997b), Tanzer (1993) and Dorel Industries web site, accessed 25/1/05.

OTHER STRATEGIC RISKS

Part of the rationale for outsourcing in general in the 1990s came out of the evolution of ideas around the concept of a company's core competence (Hamel and Prahalad, 1994). Although not necessarily as intended originally, focusing 'on the core has often been interpreted . . . as a call to eliminate the non-core, with scant regard to the complexities of competence' (Hendry, 1995, 195–6). From the idea of eliminating the non-core, it is a short, almost inevitable, step to outsourcing, given the prospect of cost reduction and other benefits, as noted above. However, Hendry (ibid., 196) warns of the risk in outsourcing of the potential loss of 'longer-term capability . . . [that] what is lost is not tangible . . . and it may not even be apparent in the short term'. He adds (197), 'as soon as you start breaking the organisation up you have to make the shared knowledge base explicit, in which case it becomes imitable . . . or to localise it in the core. In the latter case you not only lose the power to add value through the non-core functions, but could also, inadvertently, lose key aspects of the core competence itself'. These concerns were earlier alluded to in Quinn and Hilmer's (1994) outline of the strategic risks of outsourcing. They refer to the potential 'loss of critical skills or developing the wrong skills . . . loss of cross-functional skills . . . [and] loss of control over a supplier . . . many companies fear they may not be able to maintain sufficient knowledge internally to manage specialist suppliers' (52–4). In essence, there may be a trade-off between short-term efficiency and long-term learning, and between competitive advantage and strategic vulnerability.

CONCLUSION AND MANAGERIAL CONCERNS

The analysis of international subcontracting (or outsourcing) has revealed much of its potential power as a foreign operation mode, whether in outward- or inward-oriented form, and notwithstanding the definitional issues and overlap with foreign direct investment and importing/exporting. In its non-FDI form, it involves a relatively low commitment to establish an effective production base in a foreign market, and may deliver a substantial reduction in costs, while aiding flexibility with regard to market servicing and production levels, through the ability to add or delete subcontractors without investment. Further, the rise of subcontracting specialists such as Flextronics, with their global networks, and of intermediaries like Li and Fung, has provided an increasingly more amenable environment for the use of subcontracting, along with developments at the multilateral level that have resulted in reduced barriers to the trade in goods and services, and freer FDI flows. There is little doubt that there are fashion and demonstration effects in the current attitude to outsourcing, generating a perspective that could be summed up as: why not outsource? Increasingly this is being felt in the services sector where the boundaries of what services can be profitably outsourced are gradually being extended, and overall international outsourcing in this area has been experiencing very rapid growth, albeit from a low base compared to manufacturing. At the same time, though, the analysis exposed many of the additional practical demands, problems, unanticipated costs and strategic risks that companies may face as a result of using subcontracting in their international operations. For instance, the Schwinn case (Box 6.3) illustrated that, through stimulating and assisting the rise of a future competitor, a contractor could help to engineer its own downfall. A survey of 200 manufacturing companies in the Netherlands concluded that 'international outsourcing is a balancing act between lower production costs abroad and lower transaction costs locally' (Mol, van Tulder and Beije, 2005, 599).

Thus the seemingly simple and obvious benefits of engaging in international subcontracting have to be balanced against the evident risks, and action taken to minimize these as far as possible. Nike's continuing heavy investment in marketing, distribution (own store outlets), design, and research and development is an example of a company that makes it difficult for subcontractors to rise up in competition. Further, it stays very close to its subcontractor network, which has the added benefit of providing up-to-date intelligence on any untoward subcontractor moves. 'Nike expatriates become permanent personnel in each factory producing Nike footwear, functioning as liaisons with corporate R&D, headquarters, and worldwide quality assurance and product development efforts', binding each subcontractor more tightly to the Nike network and all that it represents (Quinn and Hilmer, 1994, 51).

While Nike might be seen as a special case in terms of the level of sophistication it has brought to its international subcontracting and marketing processes, it does demonstrate what may be required to ensure that an international subcontracting system operates effectively and its strategic risks are minimized, particularly when, as in Nike's case, all in-house production activity has ceased. While there is no investment in physical production facilities in foreign markets, there is still very substantial investment in areas such as technology, design and marketing across their global network. Nike's experience also would seem to indicate that there is much to learn in operating an effective subcontracting system, not only in honing the full range of activities involved, but in compensating for what is lost in withdrawing from manufacturing operations. Nike's systems incorporate the benefits of over two decades of learning how to play the international subcontracting game. For smaller companies, and particularly for those embarking on international outsourcing for the first time, the performance of subcontractors and of stretched-out logistics systems is important but demanding to assure. With limited resources to supervise and control outcomes along the supply chain, problems such as quality deficiencies and delivery unreliability can easily emerge. In many companies this is difficult to handle because of a lingering perception of purchasing as being a relatively low-skill and low-status section within the company (Korhonen, 1999; Quinn and Hilmer, 1994). A change in this perspective is needed, along with an upgrading of logistics and related IT systems that facilitate the links to and information flowing from the various parts of the international supply chain. To some extent, this involves a re-shaping of the company from within, and a re-ordering of resource use priorities. International subcontracting has wider implications than the effect on international operations, and these are not always anticipated at the outset.

There is also the difficult question of what parts of the company should be outsourced; or, put differently, how far can and should outsourcing go? One approach has been to examine outsourcing options first in areas considered to be 'non-core', although, as noted above, it is by no means clear what fits into this category given the subtle and often informal interconnections that exist between staff, and across functions and activities within companies. A frequent target for outsourcing operations is the IT department, as one study of European and US companies found: 'senior executives frequently view the entire IT function as a noncore activity and . . . consequently, many senior executives view IT as a necessary cost to be minimized' (Lacity et al., 1996, 13). The researchers 'found that companies engaging in total outsourcing [of the IT function] experienced significant difficulties a few years into their contracts' (14). As a result, companies in the study were moving toward 'selective sourcing', with the total IT role broken down into component parts, and a more careful selection of which parts were appropriate for outsourcing, generating improved outcomes. Of course, this is not a straightforward exercise, requiring a clear understanding of the external, and foreign, IT service market and what it can provide, as well as the internal IT situation. Lacity et al. (1996) were able to point to two important considerations in the choice: (a) 'outsourcing technically immature activities engenders significant risk' (22), because of a lack of knowledge to evaluate effectively vendor offerings, and (b) 'in cases in which technical integration with other business processes is high, the risks of outsourcing increase' (23), in line with other studies showing the problems of outsourcing when important interconnections to key areas inside a company exist.

In the face of the many uncertainties surrounding the choice of parts of the company to outsource, and of the additional uncertainties in the international context, a more pragmatic approach may be to start on a small basis, making limited commitments and short contracts, learning from these experiences, remaining adaptable, while gradually extending the amount and province of outsourcing operations, and range of market destinations that are served from outsourced foreign bases. It is easier to know what adjustments to make at first when subcontracted outcomes are fed back through a company's home market operations. In an overall sense companies will increasingly be required to come to terms with international subcontracting as others, including competitors and suppliers, embark on this path and pressure them to follow suit. For the foreseeable future, the outsourcing revolution seems set to continue unabated. It will require companies to become adept at its use, ensuring that it contributes to the most effective exploitation of international market possibilities.

REFERENCES

Abernathy, F., J. Dunlop, J. Hammond and D. Weil (1999), *A Stitch in Time: Lean Retailing and the Transformation of Manufacturing – Lessons from the Apparel and Textile Industries*, New York: Oxford University Press.

Austen, I. (2004), 'US firms look to Canada for outsourcing help', *International Herald Tribune*, 25 November, 16.

Australian (2004), 'Tax-free for outsourcers', 22 June, IT Business 2.

Australian (2005a), 'India gets a tick', April 26, 7.

Australian (2005b), 'Indian providers prosper from continuing outsourcing boom', 25 January, IT Business 3.

Baum, J. (1998), 'Riding high', *Far Eastern Economic Review*, 7 May, 58–9.

Benito, G.R.G. and L.S. Welch (1997), 'De-internationalization', *Management International Review*, **37**, special issue no. 2, 7–25.

Birou, L.M. and S.E. Fawcett (1993), 'International purchasing: benefits, requirements and challenges', *International Journal of Purchasing and Materials Management*, **29**(2), 28–37.

Business Central Europe (1995), 'Industry – textiles and clothing', *The Annual*, 61.

Cohen, M. (2003), 'Outsourcing: IKEA bets on Vietnam', *Far Eastern Economic Review*, 25 September, 56–8.

Czinkota, M.R. and I.A. Ronkainen (2005), 'A forecast of globalization, international business and trade: report from a Delphi study', *Journal of World Business*, **40**(2), 111–23.

Dean, J. (2004), 'Taiwan tech's snazzy new look', *Far Eastern Economic Review*, 2 September, 28–31.

Economist (1992), 'Why networks may fail', 10 October, 81.

Economist (1995), 'The outing of outsourcing', 25 November, 67–8.

Economist (1998), 'Globalisation – the strange life of low-tech America', 17 October, 85–6.

Economist (2000), 'American textiles – sweatshops to body scans', 29 April, 66–71.

Economist (2001), 'Li & Fung – link in the global chain', 2 June, 62–3.

Economist (2004a), 'Manufacturing in Japan', 10 April, 57–9.

Economist (2004b), 'Special report, mobile phones: battling for the palm of your hand', 1 May, 65–8.

Economist (2004c), 'The textile industry – the looming revolution', 13 November, 77–8.

Economist (2005a), 'Going Japanese – how Japan learned to fly', 25 June, 68.

Economist (2005b), 'The textile industry – the great stitch-up', 28 May, 61–2.

Economist (2005c), 'The rise of nearshoring', 3 December, 59–61.

Edwards, B. (2004), 'A world of work – a survey of outsourcing', Supplement, *Economist*, 13 November, 1–16.

Frear, C.R., L.E. Metcalf and M.S. Alguire (1992), 'Offshore sourcing: its nature and scope', *International Journal of Purchasing and Materials Management*, **28**(3), 2–11.

Hamel, G. and C.K. Prahalad (1994), *Competing for the Future*, Boston: Harvard University Press.

Hendry, J. (1995), 'Culture, community and networks: the hidden cost of outsourcing', *European Management Journal*, **13**(2), 193–200.

Hiebert, M. and J. Slater (2003), 'In search of a ready scapegoat', *Far Eastern Economic Review*, 13 November, 14–16.

Hiebert, M., D. Murphy and C. Vanderwolk (2004), 'One big winner, many small losers', *Far Eastern Economic Review*, 9 September, 30–32.

Korhonen, H. (1999), *Inward–Outward Internationalization of Small and Medium Enterprises*, Helsinki: Helsinki School of Economics and Business Administration.

Lacity, M.C., L.P. Wilcocks and D.F. Feeny (1996), 'The value of selective IT outsourcing', *Sloan Management Review*, **39**(3), 13–25.

Liu, H. and P.J. McGoldrick (1996), 'International retail sourcing: trend, nature, and process', *Journal of International Marketing*, **4**(4), 9–33.

Luostarinen, R.K. and L.S. Welch (1990), *International Business Operations*, Helsinki: Export Consulting KY.

Mackenzie, K. and T. Denton (2002), 'HP moves R&D to India', *Australian*, 27 August, 27.

Marsh, P. (1997a), 'Competitiveness propels cycle of expansion', *Financial Times*, Supplement on Taiwan, 7 October, IV.

Marsh, P. (1997b), 'Taiwanese bikes – made in the Netherlands, designed in the US', *Financial Times*, 24 October, 14.

Matterson, H. (2004), 'Mayne push to lead Indian drug trial', *Australian*, 21 May, 23.

Michalet, C.-A. (1980), 'International sub-contracting: a state-of-the-art', in D. Germidis (ed.), *International Subcontracting: A New Form of Investment*, Paris: OECD, pp. 37–70.

Miles, J. (2005), 'Dancing with the enemy – a survey of Taiwan', *Economist*, 15 January, 1–12.

Mills, K. (2005), 'Offshoring losing its lustre', *Australian*, 12 August, IT Business 2.

Min, H. and W.P. Galle (1991), 'International purchasing strategies of US firms', *International Journal of Purchasing and Materials Management*, **27**(3), 9–18.

Min, K.J. (2003), 'A new spring in its step', *Far Eastern Economic Review*, 13 February, 30–33.

Moffett, S. (1996), 'The road less travelled', *Far Eastern Economic Review*, 29 August, 63–4.

Mol, M.J., R.J.M. van Tulder and P.R. Beije (2005), 'Antecedents and performance consequences of international outsourcing', *International Business Review*, **14**(5), 599–617.

Morris, J. and R. Imrie (1993), 'Japanese style subcontracting – its impact on European industries', *Long Range Planning*, **26**(4), 53–8.

Munthe, G.N. and A.M. Hukom (1993), 'On the fast track', *Indonesia Business Weekly*, **1**(11), 4–10.

Nakamoto, M. (2004), 'Canon to increase automation', *Financial Times*, 23 November, 20.

Navaretti, G.B., A.M. Falzoni and A. Turrini (2001), 'The decision to invest in a low-wage country: evidence from Italian textiles and clothing multinationals', *Journal of International Trade and Economic Development*, **10**(4), 451–70.

Ning, X. (2005), 'Garment sector requires brands to win', *China Daily*, 7 April, 5.

Nordas, H.K. (2004), *The Global Textile and Clothing Industry post the Agreement on Textiles and Clothing*, Geneva: World Trade Organization.

Perman, S., L. Duvillier, N. David, J. Eden and S. Grumiau (2004), *Behind the Brand Names*, International Confederation of Free Trade Unions, 6 December.

Quinn, J.B. and F.G. Hilmer (1994), 'Strategic Outsourcing', *Sloan Management Review*, **35**(4), 43–55.

Sender, H. (1996), 'Sprinting to the forefront', *Far Eastern Economic Review*, 1 August, 50–51.

Sender, H. (1998), 'Against all odds', *Far Eastern Economic Review*, 30 April, 63–4.

Shameen, A. (2003), 'You want it, we'll make it', *Far Eastern Economic Review*, 20 March, 32–5.

Shankar, J. (2003), 'India lobbying against anti-outsourcing laws', *Australian*, 17 June, 34.

Sharpston, M. (1975), 'International sub-contracting', *Oxford Economic Papers*, **27**(1), 94–135.

Slater, J. (2003), 'GE reinvents itself in India', *Far Eastern Economic Review*, 27 March, 42–5.

Tanzer, A. (1993), 'The students who rose up and ate their teacher', *Business Review Weekly*, 12 February, 60–62.

Taylor, W. (1993), 'Message and muscle: an interview with Swatch titan Nicolas Hayek', *Harvard Business Review*, **71**(2), 98–110.

UNCTAD (2004), *World Investment Report 2004*, New York and Geneva: United Nations.

US Department of Labor (Bureau of International Labor Affairs) (2003), *Implementation Experiences of Codes of Conduct in the U.S. Apparel Industry*, 7 August, www.dol.gov/ilab.

Wattanapruttipaisan, T. (2002), 'SME subcontracting as a bridgehead to competitiveness: an assessment of supply-side capabilities and demand-side requirements', *Asia-Pacific Development Journal*, **9**(1), 65–8.

7. Project operations

INTRODUCTION

As a distinct form of international business operations, project operations are somewhat loose in scope and difficult to define with precision. They may involve a broad mix of activities and mode combinations. Indeed, major or large projects are a prime example of the need to view foreign operation activity as potentially involving complex mode packages. The project operations label represents a very broad umbrella of mode content. There may be elements of foreign direct investment (joint ventures common), contracts covering the transfer of technology (such as licensing), international financing arrangements, product, system and service exports/imports, including training, and international personnel transfers of varying duration. For major project contributors, typically the mix alters during the project cycle. The activities and content of project operations range across a varied mix of combinations of hardware and software, potentially including such aspects as the design and construction of facilities such as housing projects, factories, industrial complexes, mines, defence systems, roads, bridges and IT systems; and software components such as education and training, as part of technology transfer arrangements. The project operations umbrella appears to have been broadening of late, judging by the following comment about Nike's international business activity: 'Nike . . . does not make shoes any more; it manages footwear projects' (*Economist*, 2005, 60).

There is a wide range in the size of projects – from small projects, for example a community housing project, to the large and spectacular, and controversial sometimes, such as the Three Gorges dam project in China, the world's largest hydro-electric power project which is expected to have cost as much as US$29 billion on scheduled completion in 2008 (Callick, 2006; Chao, 2005). It has been estimated that total construction work in China was worth more than US$400 billion in 2002, making it the third largest market globally (Tuchman, 2003). The 2008 Beijing Olympics has sparked a wide range of major project developments (buildings, infrastructure) in and around the city, and these have been the focus of strong marketing efforts by international project suppliers. Taken overall, the global project sector is immense, although there is a lack of formal statistics on the international component of this business area.

According to data collected by *Engineering News Record* (ENR), the *foreign* component of construction project work by the top 225 international contractors amounted to US$139.82 billion in 2003 (source: ENR website – Top 225 International Contractors). This represents only part of the total international side of project work, and it is only a fraction of the global project business area: the bulk of project work is undertaken in companies' domestic market. Many companies undertaking project work carry out little or no international work: for example, the largest Japanese construction contractor in 2003 (US$13.39 billion), Shimizu, only undertook 6.9 per cent of its total work offshore. The largest Swedish contractor, Skanska, was unusual in that the bulk of its work was foreign, constituting 81.8 per cent of its total business (source: ENR website – Top 225 Global Contractors). The aggregate amount of foreign project work in the ENR list exhibits a high level of variability over time. Typically, major projects include contributions from both local and foreign businesses, whatever the location of the principal contractor.

While US, European and Japanese companies dominate the list of project companies engaged in international activity, there has been considerable internationalization of the list of project providers over the last two decades. Companies from diverse countries (such as Korea, Brazil and Egypt) have moved from subcontractor roles in their own countries to international operations, eventually achieving the position of lead contractor in various foreign locations. For Turkish contractors, the process of internationalization took place in an evolutionary manner over an extended period of time, with heavy involvement in the nearby region (Kaynak and Dalgic, 1992). There were 11 Turkish companies in the ENR list of top 225 construction companies in 2003 as measured by amount of international work. Even more spectacular has been the rapid international expansion of Chinese companies in more recent times. Since embarking on international operations, Chinese construction firms have undertaken projects in about 180 countries, with the value of foreign construction work reaching US$17.7 billion in 2003 (Murphy, 2004). In the ENR top 225 international contractors list in 2003 there were 44 Chinese companies. In general, the emergence of project companies from a widening array of countries onto the international arena has meant an increasingly competitive environment for all involved, including that within the different players' home markets. As Murphy (2004, 31) has noted, 'the Chinese have become increasingly formidable competitors for European, American and Japanese firms that have dominated the lucrative project-management end of the international market in places like the Middle East and Africa. And for the first time, American firms face the prospect of a Chinese challenge on home ground'. The US subsidiary of China State Construction Engineering

Corporation recently won the contract to build a US$190 million office, retail and hotel complex in New York.

DEFINITION

A project has been defined as a 'complex transaction covering a package of products, services and work, specifically designed to create capital assets that produce benefits for a buyer over an extended period of time' (Cova et al., 2002, 3). The creation of human assets (knowledge and skills) could be added as an important complementary goal in most projects. Cova et al. (2002) further stress four main characteristics that distinguish projects from other forms of international business operations.

Discontinuity

There is a definite start and finish date for projects, even though various extensions may be involved, via instruments like management contracts, encompassing management and training to facilitate the smooth running of the completed project. As well, under BOT (build operate transfer) (or BOOT (build own operate transfer) arrangements (see treatment later in chapter), there is a continuing involvement of the contractor in running the completed facility for an extended period of time (30 years or more not uncommon), with charges for utilization of the project facility ultimately paying for the project (such as a toll road).

Uniqueness

Projects involve a package of contributions that are, to a greater or lesser extent, specific to each buyer. The extent of customization for each individual project varies considerably: suppliers have a strong cost incentive to include as much of their inventory of standardized components, parts and subassemblies as possible, but there are always specific requirements related to buyer and government concerns, and physical location, that force suppliers to customize their offering in some way.

Complexity

The project mix is often highly complex, particularly when major projects are involved. As noted, there is the issue of customization, and the frequent demand for indigenization of activity and supplies as far as possible. The large scale of some projects can accentuate the extent, variety and technical demands of different contributions, and their organization. For example, it is estimated that 12 000 workers, spending 72 million hours, and using 150 000 tonnes of steel, will be required in the construction of a new petro-chemical complex in China, for BASF, the German chemical group (Ahmad, 2004, 9). Construction of the Chek Lap Kok airport in Hong Kong in the 1990s involved the awarding of 183 contracts, for which 59 joint ventures were created amongst suppliers, constituting 155 partner firms from 19 countries, generating an immense organizational and coordination task over nine years of construction (Hung et al., 2002). For large projects, financing is an important issue, and project bidders have had to become increasingly involved in organizing finance, sometimes through their own financing arms. Likewise large projects that have a substantial impact in the host country invariably require a range of government approvals, demand-ing political and lobbying activity on the part of contractors. Environmental impacts increasingly have had to be taken into account in most countries. Taken overall, the various issues surrounding, and inputs into, projects create a complex mix of technical, financial, political, social and environ-mental factors that project contractors have to deal with both preceding and during project implementation, and often in their aftermath as well.

Risk and Uncertainty

The uniqueness and complexity of projects, and the size and cost of large projects, tend to generate high levels of perceived risk and uncertainty for the various parties. This is further accentuated by the time scale involved with many projects. For example, construction of the Three Gorges Dam began in 1994 but it was not due to be completed until 2008 (Chao, 2005; Callick, 2006). Inevitably, the project is sold long before it is completed; in essence, it represents a promise about a future outcome, albeit defined by drawings and specifications within the terms of an agreed-upon contract. It cannot be bought off the shelf. Consequently, there is considerable risk and uncertainty for the various contributing organizations, and for the many individuals connected with planning approvals and implementation of a project; project failure can be a high-cost personal outcome for key individuals involved in the approval process. Substantial commitments by the buyer and the contractor have to be made well in advance of the project start, while there is a 'large potential for downside losses' for projects as a whole (Branconi and Loch, 2004, 119). These are in addition to what might be considered more normal political and technical risk factors, accentuated as they often are with large, high-profile and technically demanding pro-jects, with the intrusion of government in many situations, as well as being affected by cultural differences between the various parties, and within increasingly culturally diverse multinational project teams (Chevrier, 2003; Makilouko, 2004).

The risks may be further enhanced by having to deal with bribery and corruption at many levels. In an investigation of bribery amongst various business sectors internationally, Transparency International (2002) found that it was highest in public works and construction, as measured by a preparedness of senior public officials to demand or accept bribes. Despite the fight against corruption by World Bank officials, it has been estimated that anywhere between 5 per cent and 30 per cent of World Bank funding for projects in developing countries has been misused and/or diverted through corruption (Hiebert and McBeth, 2004). Further, project activity in some contexts can be so dangerous for all those involved, and projects liable to physical attack, such as in Iraq, that the viability of any project is always in question.

FORMS OF PROJECT CONTRIBUTION

Project contributors can take different supply positions with respect to the whole project: performing a design role in the pre-tender phase; acting as the principal contractor with overall responsibility for the project; acting as a major supplier, without overall responsibility, on a partial project basis; or making a smaller contribution as a subcontractor to a partial or principal contractor. The latter three forms are illustrated in Figure 7.1. The principal contractor, as the term implies, has overall charge of the project, although it is rare for this company to supply all parts of the total project. Instead, it is usual for the principal only to supply part of the whole project, with a range of other suppliers, sometimes providing key systems to the project, and some may even be specified by the buyer (Luostarinen and Welch, 1990). The principal contractor will frequently be a consortium formed specifically to bid for a given project. For large projects, it might include two or three major multinational project companies, and a local company that is in a position to assist in the localization of suppliers and with the penetration of local networks, particularly at the government level. Through the consortium arrangement the partners are able to strengthen the asset base (technical, financial, human) of the submission and to spread project risk. In China, as a result of restrictions on the establishment of wholly owned construction companies and of operations on a project-by-project basis, many contractors and consultants have established joint venture operations as a way of chasing project opportunities (Gale and Luo, 2004; Tuchman, 2003). As Figure 7.1 shows, for large projects, usually there will be many smaller subcontractors in the supply mix.

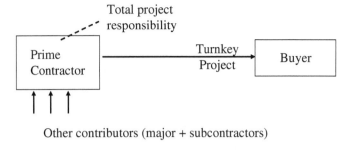

OR

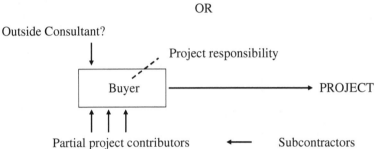

Source: Adapted from Luostarinen and Welch (1990, p. 127).

Figure 7.1   Project positions

In the form of a turnkey project, the principal is separate from the buyer, with the responsibility for delivering the completed project in start-up form. Effectively, in turnkey project situations, the buyer hands over the full task to an independent company or consortium, perhaps with a separate consultant used to advise on different aspects of the principal's submissions and work. The Centre on Transnational Corporations (1983, 6) has defined a turnkey project as existing when 'one party is responsible for setting up a plant and putting it into operation . . . [including], in general, the responsibility for supply and establishment of the works, plants and facilities on a turnkey basis, including:

- supply of technology and know-how,
- basic design and engineering,
- supply of complete plant and equipment,
- design and construction of civil works,
- complete erection of plant and equipment,
- and commissioning of the total plant facilities up to the stage of start-up'.

In contrast to the turnkey situation, the buyer might take over responsibility for the overall task of organizing, directing and integrating the
various contributions to a project, effectively assuming the principal contractor's position. For example, some government departments will have
considerable expertise in a particular field, such as water management
systems, and be in a position to manage a project within this area of
responsibility. In other cases, particularly with large projects that call
upon a wide range of expertise, experience and specific technical know-
how, the buyer is less likely to be equipped to drive a project and so will
usually call upon the assistance of outside consultants in the management
process (see Figure 7.1). The consultants will often be those with experience in acting as principal contractors in the global project business,
including the large multinational construction and engineering firms.
For example, Bechtel, the largest construction company in the US, acted
as the consultant to the Hong Kong government on the construction
of its new airport and related infrastructure development, advising on
planning, programming and design (Holberton, 1992). Either way, different parts of the total project have to be developed and fitted together,
and partial project contributors will often be responsible for a major sub-
area within the total project, and within this sub-area be acting like a
principal contractor, although having to coordinate and integrate with
other partial project contributors as part of total project development.
Construction of Taiwan's high-speed rail system was broken down into
nine component parts, each treated as a separate turnkey project and, as
one of the organizers noted, 'the challenge will really be on-site management and co-ordinating the interface between the different contractors'
(Tyson, 1998, 6).

The contribution of different subcontractors to a project varies in size
and importance. The subcontractor's overall economic role and supply cost
may be relatively small, but critical to the ultimate success of the project on
completion: for example, the communication system within a mine, or
other key technical functions within a large project. It is at the subcontractor level that local suppliers tend to play an important role, such as in civil
works (roads, for example) and the like, often those parts that are cheaper
to supply locally and that use local labour, and where it is easier to fulfil the
demands for a local role in response to pressure by the local government.
There is, of course, another level of supply to the more important players
in project development noted in Figure 7.1: suppliers of component parts,
raw materials and so on, screws, nails and the like, and services, the standardized inputs that are typically bought off the shelf, from foreign or local
sources. The suppliers in this group play no role in project development and
will not be analysed in this chapter.

PROJECT PLUS ARRANGEMENTS

As noted in the discussion on management contracts, project operations are frequently part of broader packages of connected involvement in the foreign market, sometimes including management contracts. Some of the forms of connected involvement are shown in Figure 7.2. Preceding a project, a company might win the right, in open competition by tender, to undertake the feasibility study that normally precedes a project, and then go on to win the bidding process for the ultimate project which it has played a major role in shaping. In some situations companies are prevented by bidding rules from undertaking both roles, such as with World Bank projects, because of the obvious ability directly or indirectly to influence the choice of project principal through the feasibility study process. At the least, there is an inevitable tendency to bias the design and specifications of a project in favour of the technical solutions that it knows and is best equipped to deliver. It can be argued further that, in undertaking the feasibility study, the ultimate project principal can ensure that the design is technically feasible and fits the environment and infrastructure demands.

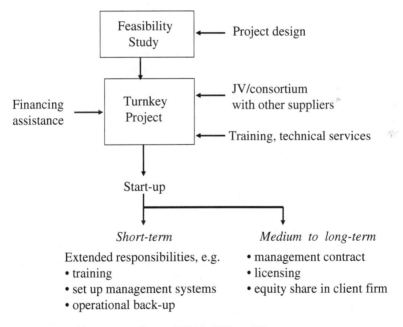

Source: Adapted from Luostarinen and Welch (1990, p. 130).

Figure 7.2   Project plus arrangements

As noted above and in Figure 7.2, preceding the submission of bids, project companies frequently form joint ventures or consortia with other potential suppliers, foreign and local. Associated with the project itself, often there is financing support provided to the buyer in a variety of forms: the major global project suppliers have had to become major financing agents as part of the effort to win project business, and in some cases have developed their own financing arms to provide the necessary finance to enable clients (particularly in debt-burdened developing countries) to go ahead with desired projects. In addition, the project principal might be called upon to provide a range of technical assistance and training services to different suppliers to the project, under the terms of separate contracts, thereby ensuring that these suppliers are able to meet the quality standards demanded by the principal and the project contract. This will mainly concern local subcontractors and suppliers with little or no international experience. The local government in the country in question tends to see this as an important benefit flowing from the project, facilitating the transfer of technology and skills to local companies.

After completion of the project, a wide variety of arrangements with the project buyer may be entered into, as shown in Figure 7.2, thereby extending the project principal's involvement. The example of Alfa Laval noted in the management contracts chapter exemplifies the longevity and complexity that such arrangements might assume, built upon, and around, the initial project. In such cases, the project could be viewed as a key stepping-stone strategy to deeper, long-term foreign market penetration. Upon completion of the project, to full start-up stage, it still may be necessary to provide short-term support services such as staff training, establishment of quality assurance and other management systems, and back-up during the initial running-in phases, to the client firm.

Over the medium to long term, the client firm may require ongoing assistance with managing and operating the new facility, incorporating new technological developments and expanding the reach of its marketing activities. In these circumstances it is not uncommon for the project principal to enter into different types of mode arrangements to cover the various forms of transfers and direct involvement in the client firm's operations. As noted above, management contracts are sometimes used as a convenient form to cover the transfer of managerial, technical and training staff and direct involvement in the running of the project facility for an extended period. Marketing services may be treated separately, as a recognized function that needs to be developed successfully if the new facility is to survive in the longer term where it has to operate in a free market environment, perhaps including the development of an international marketing capability. Where technology flows to the client firm take place, both initially and on a continuing basis, project builders will often seek to obtain additional returns, control the use of the technology and/or limit wider dissemination possibilities by the client firm through the establishment of a licensing agreement.

As in the Alfa Laval case noted in the management contracts chapter, project firms are sometimes pressured by the potential buyer or the local government to take a minority equity interest in the client firm. From the client firm's perspective, this has the twin benefits of opening up an additional source of finance to help pay for the project, as well as providing an additional long-term spur for the project builder to do an effective construction job in the first place and then to assist in ensuring a positive outcome from ongoing operations. In simple terms, it is a way of ensuring commitment to a successful outcome. However, with or without this pressure, project companies may seek such involvement as a way of generating additional returns in the long term from a completed project, as well as providing a voice at board level in decision making that affects the viability of the client firm in its use of the project facility. When connected with a management contract or other form of ongoing involvement, it can be used as part of a broader package aimed at delivering the type of outcome that allows the project firm to seek further project work, either with the same client firm or elsewhere in the same foreign market. A successfully functioning project facility can be used as a key *reference* point in marketing activity, apart from the benefit of an already developed local contact network, built through the various forms of local involvement, including links with government officials and various business contacts.

An important form of continuing involvement by project builders after completion that has emerged in the last two decades has been the co-called BOT (build operate transfer) or BOOT (build own operate transfer) contractual arrangements. Essentially they are another way by which client organizations, typically government or quasi-government entities, can finance major projects such as power stations or other social infrastructure developments. In such cases, financing of the project cost is usually organized by the project principal, contributing perhaps 20–40 per cent from its own funding sources, as part of a broader private sector funding group, with payment obtained over time as the completed project is used. For example, the revenue from a toll road over a period of time, perhaps as long as 30 years, pays for the cost of its construction and an adequate return, after which ownership and operation rights are transferred back to the government or other project instigator (Blanden, 1994; Tiong and Yeo, 1993).

Clearly, the mode package associated with a given project may be quite diverse, but this diversity often emerges after the formal completion of the project. As a result, the operation package is likely to undergo a number of changes over time, although based on the original project work. Effectively, the various activities associated with extended mode use are about ensuring the operational and market performance of the completed project.

PROJECT STAGES

In analysing the nature of projects it is useful to view them as a process: a series of steps or stages over time rather than a specific act. For the project principal, from initial recognition of a project opportunity to completion of the project facility, in the case of major infrastructure projects, it is not unusual for the whole process to take ten years or more. Thereafter, as noted in the previous section, the principal might continue to be involved in ongoing operations connected to the functioning project facility, which could lengthen the overall process for an extended period of five years or more. While there are many variations on the way the process will proceed in each individual case, we have attempted in Figure 7.3 to provide an overview of the project process, including major steps or phases that are

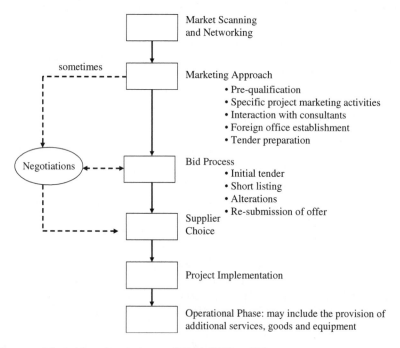

Source: Adapted from Luostarinen and Welch (1990, p. 137).

Figure 7.3   Project development: supplier's perspective

generally found to apply, from the earliest point to the post-construction stage. One or more stages could be by-passed, and the overall process compressed, when, for example, a project builder is approached to bid for a project, or part thereof, by the buyer, thereby dispensing with the need for scanning and marketing action. Likewise, in the Alfa Laval case, the client firm was satisfied with outcomes from the first project and Alfa Laval's subsequent management contribution so that, in the lead-up to the second project, it dispensed with the bulk of the normal open marketing and bid stages. The process overview presented in Figure 7.3 is from the perspective of the project principal and/or a major supplier to the project.

Market Scanning and Networking

Project companies typically become involved in the marketing process at a very early stage: they would argue the earlier the better! This is because they seek to bring to bear influence on the project decision makers and the framing of a project in a way that puts them in a positive light from the earliest possible point. The ideal would be to be able to suggest a project to a potential buyer, and this sometimes occurs, although it does entail preceding contact with the relevant parties in a particular market and an understanding of the likelihood of emerging needs for the client firm and the market context. Thus even the ideal requires preceding market scanning and in-depth networking at a personal level. An interviewee in an Australian study of project companies described his company's attempt to get involved as early as possible in the following terms: 'when they're [projects] in the pipeline, when they're not even advertised, we start tracking them. Otherwise we pick them up when they're advertised. But picking them up as early as possible is the preference. Because that way if you've got advance notice, then you're doing a country visit, you're already establishing relationships, you're already finding out information and planning your bid' (study details are in Welch, 2005a, 2005b).

Companies continually stress the importance of building and maintaining personal contact networks as a key part of their marketing investment. For example, a Swedish multinational, in attempting to track and influence project business with a large public organization in one of the ASEAN countries, maintained a high level of personal contact with relevant staff (see Figure 7.4). 'They are maintained at several organizational levels. Around 25 persons from the seller have contacts with about 10 persons at higher levels and 35 persons at lower levels of the organization. Various kinds of information can be obtained depending upon how close the contacts are. The competitors work in the same way' (Jansson, 1989, 272). Given the range of potential project opportunities, in the varied market

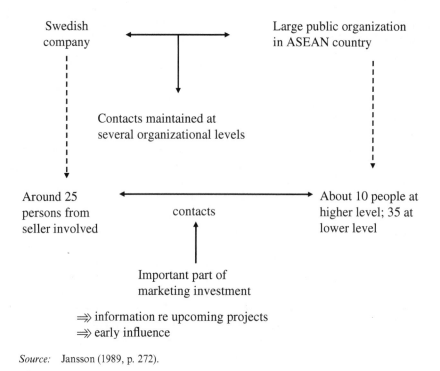

Source: Jansson (1989, p. 272).

Figure 7.4   Marketing through network investment

contexts of the global arena, this is a demanding activity, and companies inevitably have to make difficult choices about where and how they use their marketing resources. Few companies can afford to maintain offices in a wide range of foreign markets to act as 'listening posts' and to carry out networking and influence functions, so that these on-the-ground activities for most companies are of a more sporadic and disjointed nature, with infrequent visits to many markets, until more concrete opportunities emerge.

   Because of the role of multilateral institutions such as the World Bank and the Asian Development Bank in financing and overseeing a large amount of global project business, particularly in developing countries, many project companies maintain strong networks with key personnel, and a close watch on developments, within these institutions. This is a demanding activity, as Welch (2005a, 185) notes, requiring 'considerable knowledge about multilateral project cycles, tendering processes and policies – and, critically, personal familiarity and credibility with key decision-makers in the multilateral institution'. In addition, governments seek to have their own nationals appointed to advisory and consulting roles as a way of attempting to ensure that their own project companies win a share of the total project pool. Australian authorities took an active role in having an Australian placed on the World Bank's supervisory panel overseeing the large project aimed at modernizing the grain handling and storage facilities and systems in China, as a way of ensuring that the interests of Australian bidding companies were protected (Welch et al., 1996).

Marketing Approach

Thus, even with attempts to get involved early, companies seeking project business often end up becoming involved well after the initial development of a project from the buyer's perspective. In the China grain project referred to above, Australian companies became aware of the project about two years after their competitors from the northern hemisphere (Welch et al., 1996; see also Welch, 2005b). As well, many project companies in the earlier stages of international activity find out about foreign project opportunities through diverse routes, such as contacts in the domestic market or via government trade assistance agencies, that tend to come into play after the foreign project concept has been formulated and articulated publicly. However, whatever the starting point, more substantive marketing activity tends to occur when companies have a clearer idea of the project opportunity and their prospects of winning a share of the business. Depending on the size of the opportunity, this could be carried out through the establishment of an office in the market in question, and the sending of expatriate staff to prepare the ground for an eventual bid – holding seminars for key players, contacting key personnel within the government, the buying organization, potential suppliers and subcontractors, and in general to get a 'feel' for the project context and the likely bid process and bid factors, as well as seeking to bring to bear some influence on project specifications and the ultimate choice of contractors.

In a study of Australian companies involved in projects funded by multilateral agencies it was found that, as they became more international in their activities, they sought to build a more enduring presence in foreign markets through a 'web of local representatives, branches and subsidiaries'. One company had offices in over 40 countries, but establishing and maintaining this presence was a challenge: a sufficient level of work had to be generated to justify the investment, but having the presence was seen as the key to winning project business. One company representative interviewed in this study stressed the advantages of having local and expatriate staff operating from a local office: 'an almost unbeatable combination . . . because the two categories of people have access to two different sets of local networks. There are certain people who will see a visiting businessman from Australia, but would never see a local employee of a foreign company. But there are things which local bureaucrats or industry representatives will tell local people that they will never tell an Australian' (Welch, 2005a, 191).

As noted above, consultants to the project buyer often play an important role in project design and evaluation of project bids, even undertaking feasibility studies in some cases, and are, therefore, an important focus of marketing activities. After an examination of the marketing processes of a Swedish project company in Southeast Asia, Jansson (1989, 270) concluded: 'It is important to have good relations with the consultants when establishing a business in the area. The company's first order was won very much due to a consultant's recommendation. The next order received was for a project financed by the World Bank. The person in charge of the project at the bank and a Danish consultant worked out the tender specification. Thanks to good contacts with both these parties the specification was written largely with a bias toward the company's system. However, it was softened a little, which made it possible for a competitor to come in.' Project companies seek to develop and maintain relations with consultants long before projects emerge, although there is evidence that networks and relationships with consultants are biased by national, language and cultural connections – and this is reinforced by the efforts of governments and trade assistance agencies to insert their nationals into consulting roles at multilateral institutions (Welch et al., 1996).

The preparation of a project's design and specifications may be conducted by consultants or the buyer, but is often handled through the conduct of a feasibility study that is the subject of open, competitive bidding, particularly in the case of large projects (see Figure 7.5). When there are no restrictions on so doing, potential project suppliers with a perceived strong chance of winning a major part of the ultimate project tend to fight hard for the right to conduct the feasibility study, even though the value of the study is typically small, out of all proportion to the project's value and the marketing resources that project companies throw into the fight. In one case in Australia, as part of the attempt to win the feasibility study preceding a very large mining project (over US$ one billion), a large, multinational project company pursued a sophisticated sales and network strategy with respect to key personnel in the buyer company, even including two psychologists in the sales team to advise on relational connections, staffing and influence tactics. Project companies are prepared to go to such lengths in some cases because of the opportunity to bias the specifications in their favour, to build relationships with the buyer, consultants and local suppliers, and to build a deeper understanding of what the buyer is seeking to achieve through the project, as a prelude to bid preparation.

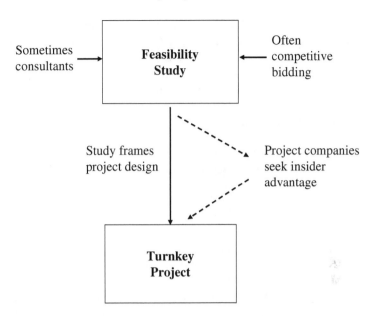

Figure 7.5   Importance of feasibility study

Preceding the bidding stage, companies may be required to undergo a pre-qualification process in some countries (see Figure 7.3). This is seen as a way of testing the eligibility of potential bidders, and governments in some countries build up a list of qualified contractors as a screening mechanism (Luqmani et al., 1988). For example, in inviting proposals for an upcoming number of hydropower projects in Pakistan, the government sought pre-qualification of potential bidders as the first step to a feasibility study and eventual choice of a constructor for each project, with the right to undertake both (advertised in *Economist*, 7/5/05, 37).

As well, where project companies are planning to undertake construction through a joint venture or consortium, the formation of this vehicle, a demanding exercise in itself, has to occur before a bid can be developed. When there is pressure to include relatively unknown local companies, knowledge and connections may have to be developed from a low base. A study of 160 Chinese/foreign construction joint ventures established in China found that '73.2% of partners in JVs . . . had no relationship with each other before negotiations began to form a JV' (Gale and Luo, 2004, 36). The average time taken for negotiations was about eight months. In chasing business connected to a World Bank-funded grain handling and storage project in China, some Australian companies entered into joint ventures with Chinese firms as a prelude to the bidding process. One company representative related the importance of relationship building in establishing the joint venture: 'It became fairly obvious fairly early on that the Chinese were going to give preference to manufacturers that had local content and after talking to [various people], the general consensus was that a joint venture was one of the possible ways to go. We indicated to Austrade (government's trade assistance agency) that we were interested and they hunted around and found a joint venture partner for us . . . The decision . . . was not one we had a good deal of say over. The Ministry of Railways chose . . . The relationship building stage took about a year to 18 months. It took that long to get to know each other' (Welch et al., 1996, 588).

Bid Process

When the project content and tender specifications have been settled by the buyer, the competitive bidding process can be opened, although sometimes buyers are prepared to go straight into negotiations with a preferred supplier, as shown in Figure 7.3. Apparently, this is more common in industrial projects, but less common for construction projects (Luostarinen and Welch, 1990). Size of project, previous work for the client and the nature of the client are all relevant factors. Government organizations, for example, tend to have rules requiring open, competitive bidding processes. Becoming involved in the bidding process, particularly for large projects, can be a very expensive process for project companies, tying up a substantial number of staff for what could be an extended period of time, with no certainty of outcome. If the likelihood of winning substantial work is low, potential bidders will normally pull out at this stage. The UK construction company Wimpey rated the chances of winning each project of interest, and used this as the key criterion on whether to bid or not. Its bidding response framework was as follows: less than 5 per cent chance, no bid; from 5 to 10 per cent chance, only submitted a bid if the preparation costs were low; 10 to 20 per cent chance, submitted a bid if there were no other projects [presumably more attractive] on the horizon; 20 to 30 per cent chance, submitted a bid; and with a greater than 33 per cent chance of success, it fought to the finish (Cova et al., 2002, 135). However, rating the chances of success was a difficult exercise, influenced by different and changing perspectives about prospects within the firm, although individual, somewhat subjective, perspectives were often decisive.

In preparing a bid, a company will have to interact with a range of potential suppliers and subcontractors. Some may have long-standing relationships with the company, providing well-known solutions, and can be easily fitted into an overall bid. Often, in foreign contexts, there will be strong government pressure to include major local contributions, as in the South Korean railway case noted below, which can be more demanding to assess and accommodate, particularly when there is little experience or knowledge of potential candidates. As well, there may be a requirement by the buyer that a particular subcontractor be used to supply a specific part of the project.

Project bidding is typically not a simple act of submitting a bid and awaiting a final outcome, but rather it is a process that may be stretched out over many years for large projects, potentially involving many steps, as shown in Figure 7.3, including short listing, various rounds of negotiations, alterations and re-submission of bids. The bidding process in the early 1990s for the high-speed rail project in South Korea, linking the city of Seoul in the north and the southern port of Pusan, provides an illustration of just how demanding this stage can be, accentuated in this case by the role of government and national interest concerns. The main competitors for the contract were French-based GEC Alsthom, a German consortium headed by Siemens, and Japan's Mitsubishi. The contract was seen to be important, not just in its own right, with a total project cost estimated to be around US$13 billion, but also because it was to be the first high-speed rail system on the Asian mainland, and therefore represented a critical reference project for expected similar projects in the future, such as in Taiwan. The bidding process took about four years to conclude, including seven rounds of negotiations. In June 1993, after five rounds, Mitsubishi was eliminated as a contender, while in September 1993, after six rounds, GEC Alsthom was publicly declared the 'winner' by the South Korean government, but in fact it had only won a priority right to negotiate the final contract. The Siemens consortium was asked to maintain its bid, as part of the pressure on GEC Alsthom to come up with further concessions in order to win the final contract. GEC Alsthom was announced as the final victor in April 1994, but it had made further concessions to win the deal: reducing its bid price by a further US$270 million, on top of the US$1.2 billion reduction which had already been agreed to, while increasing the proportion of local manufacturing from 44 per cent to 50 per cent. In the end, the contract price agreed to for the supply of locomotives and electrical equipment was about US$2.1 billion. The deal was financed by a consortium of French banks (Burton, 1993; Paisley, 1993; Ridding and Burton, 1994).

Financing is frequently an important part of the negotiation process. As always, interpersonal and cross-cultural issues in the international negotiations surrounding a major project can have a substantial impact on outcomes. Under the pressure of seeking to win projects, research indicates that there is a long-standing pattern of bidders tending to underestimate project costs and to be over-optimistic about likely project outcomes, particularly when there is perceived 'glory' associated with a 'prestige' project, as illustrated by the mounting losses for the Australian project builder Multiplex in constructing London's new Wembley Stadium (*Economist*, 2005, 59).

Project Implementation

The size and complexity of a project influence the nature and length of the implementation phase. The Three Gorges Dam project in China and the Korean high-speed rail project noted above demonstrate that project completion times of a decade or more are possible for certain types of project. The implementation phase is, of course, the crux of the project operation. If it has not already done so, for large projects the project principal and other key providers normally would set up a foreign office as close as possible to the construction site to organize and oversee project work, and to maintain links to company headquarters where much of the planning and technical development will be carried out. Company staff are usually transferred from various international locations to the new site and play a key role in managing the project work, acting as agents of technology transfer, undertaking training of local staff, developing and maintaining relationships with government officials and the range of local and foreign suppliers, ensuring the compatibility and appropriate timing of the different local and foreign project contributions, and providing a timely on-the-ground capacity to respond to emerging, unforeseen contingencies. Frequent adjustments, small and large, to project design and construction processes tend to be required as project work unfolds. Depending on the type of project, there will be a wide array of international transfers in order to carry out the project work – people, goods, services, machinery, equipment, and complete, functioning units – under various types of contractual arrangements. Alongside the local contribution, that may also be substantial and diverse, the result is a complex and changing mix of operations over the life cycle of the implementation stage of the project.

Operational Phase

After project completion and handing over, continued involvement in the running of the project and continuing supply of inputs, parts and replacement equipment may result in an extended project stage, again covered by different contractual and operation mode arrangements. For industrial projects, such as factory construction, a continuing relationship and follow-up sales can be particularly important and constitute a substantial long-term return from the original project work (Jansson, 1989).

CONTRACT CONTENT

As with the variability of projects there is a wide range in types of contractual arrangements covering projects and their content. For large projects, the contract can be mammoth in size, with detailed specification of its
content. At the heart of the contract, of course, are the engineering and
technical specifications of the project and the construction schedule. This
was almost 'down to the last screw' in many East–West projects in the past.
Nevertheless, it has been argued that contractual relations in the project
business 'comprise four main components: the relationship between the
parties; the responsibilities of each party within the transaction(s); the risk
apportionment of the contract for given actions and events; and the reim-
bursement structure' (Thompson et al., 1998, 34). The international federation of national associations of independent consulting engineers, FIDIC,
with membership from over 60 countries, has been instrumental in developing relatively standardized contract forms for various project situations
that are extensively used in the international project business. It claims to
represent the bulk of the private practice consulting engineers in the world
(see FIDIC website).

It has been argued that 'the culture of construction business is characterised by short-term financial considerations, reflected in uncooperative,
suspicious attitudes . . . and a focus on competitive tendering . . . focusing
on formal contracts . . . Most standard forms of contracts actively encourage non-collaborative behaviour, whereby actors develop their own objectives, goals, and value system without considering the impact on others or
on project performance . . . Standard contracts are tools to seek strict liabilities and attach blame' (Huemer, 2004, 191). This perspective stresses the
adversarial side of the project business, and the readiness to seek redress for
perceived non-compliance with the terms of the contract by both sides of
the final contract. A survey in the mid-1990s found that a 'quarter of the
UK's contracting firms earned between 10% and 15% of their turnovers
from contractual claims against clients or suppliers' (Thompson et al.,
1998, 33). This is not surprising given that cost overruns and deviations
from plans and schedules are endemic in the project business (Packendorff,
1995).

As a result, great emphasis is placed on the details set down in the contract regarding aspects such as method of payment, foreign exchange and
exchange rate fluctuations, treatment of unforeseen contingencies, guarantees, limitation of liabilities, penalties for non-performance, and dispute
resolution procedures. This contractual and adversarial emphasis is seemingly at odds with the investment in relational development on the part of
potential suppliers in the prelude to supplier and contract determination,

and a general recognition of the value of trust and good relationships. It is noteworthy that, in a survey of regular clients in the UK construction industry, it was found that '80% recognised that a good relationship is more likely to ensure good performance than anything written in the conditions of the contract' (Thompson et al., 1998, 36).

However, there are differences, in types or contracts, how they are applied and how conflict is handled in different cultural contexts. Kadefors (2004, 176) has noted that 'Swedish contractual arrangements have much in common with those in the UK and US, but an important difference is that contractual disputes are seldom resolved by any formal mechanism – by neither courts nor any kind of alternative dispute resolution mechanism. Instead, the parties handle most conflicts themselves, often at a low organisational level and without the involvement of lawyers.' Similarly, in a study of Danish architectural firms in Germany, Skaates et al. (2002a) found that, compared to German firms, Danish firms were more informal and frequently avoided using lawyers in contract negotiations. Overall, there was substantial difference in rules and norms in project business between Germany and Denmark: from the Danish perspective there was a high level of formalization in the German project context. In general, there was less disputation in Denmark than in Germany. It has been reported that the contract for a large construction project in Shanghai, involving restaurants and shops, valued at US$170 million, was only six pages long. The chairman of the Hong Kong company, Shui On Group, had built strong links with key decision makers in China and had a long history of successful projects there (*Economist*, 2004).

As to cost and payment terms, like all aspects of the contract, these will be determined in the negotiation process and depend on factors such as the nature and importance of the project to the buyer and bidder, the influence of the local government and the relative bargaining power of the parties. In negotiations for Korea's high-speed rail project noted above, the buyer was able to extract deep concessions on price and local involvement from the eventual supplier GEC Alsthom because of the latter's well known desire to have a functioning reference project in place in Asia to facilitate its marketing push into other, nearby, countries. The payment options are ranged between the extremes of the cost-plus contract and the fixed-price contract. In the former category, a percentage or fixed amount is paid over and above the costs incurred by the project builder in completing the project. The buyer incurs the full risk of a blow-out in costs, while the builder has an incentive to stretch out its activity and cost profile. It is relatively open-ended as to the buyer's commitment, although suspension of a project due to cost-overruns and financial difficulties for the buyer occurs in some cases. For the builder, it does reduce the need to cover all contingencies when estimating costs that may be well into the future, so that it provides a 'flexible basis for adapting in an uncertain situation' (Luostarinen and Welch, 1990, 139).

At the other extreme, the fixed price contract could be said to transfer the risk to the builder, although there is certainty as to the cost target for both sides. This approach, 'which may be superficially attractive to the owner/purchaser, can lead to improvident cost cutting by the contractor . . . Moreover, requiring a lump-sum contract may lengthen the time prior to start-up because of the more detailed design work necessary prior to arriving at a reasonable lump-sum figure (Centre on Transnational Corporations, 1983, 16). Huemer (2004) further argues that this method engenders a focus on penalty clauses, for example, consequent upon changes in design introduced by the buyer, or external exigencies, and produces a 'claims mentality'.

There are many variations between the two extremes as both parties to the project deal seek to develop a more amenable arrangement, such as the following:

'(a) A target price (covering costs plus a fee) is set, and any costs beyond this point are shared between the parties;
(b) Incentive contracts – a target cost of completion is set, but if the final cost is lower the savings are shared;
(c) A mixed lump sum/cost basis – costs during the construction phase are reimbursed, but [equipment, machinery and know-how are] supplied on a fixed price basis' (Luostarinen and Welch, 1990, 140; based on Centre on Transnational Corporations, 1983, 16).

In an evaluation of the contracts for 15 turnkey projects in various developing countries, the Centre on Transnational Corporations (1983, 30) found that all were on the fixed price or mixed fixed price/cost basis.

As to the timing of payments, there is a relatively consistent pattern, of initial down payment, intermediate payments as work proceeds, and the final payment on demonstrable completion. Branconi and Loch (2004, 122) maintain that 'contractors mostly receive a 5–15% down payment, allowing them to start the job. Intermediate payments allow equipment delivery . . . The final 5–10% payments are critical. They are frequently tied to mechanical and/or final completion and to passing performance tests and enable the client to exercise maximum pressure on the contractor. It can (and does) happen that the client, already successfully operating the facility, comes up with formal arguments or minor [problems] to keep the money'. For project companies, it is a demanding balancing act, managing the inflows from prepayments from new projects while ensuring that completion payments from old projects are not unduly delayed. The Anglo-French group Alstom faced cash outflow problems in 2001 as a number of major projects were nearing completion, and cash draining, relative to prepayment inflows. One power project, in Saudi Arabia, which was part of the near-completion mix, had been totally prepaid (*Economist*, 2001, 63).

DEALING WITH PERCEIVED RISK AND UNCERTAINTY

It has been noted above that basic characteristics of projects – a future promise, complexity, discontinuity and uniqueness – combined with the cost and time to completion for large projects, tend to generate a high level of perceived risk and uncertainty on the part of project buyers, a perception that can be accentuated by lack of experience of each other on the part of the buyer and supplier and a high level of cultural difference (see Figure 7.6). This is the reality that project companies face in seeking to win international project business, and, while the project package that a company offers is a crucial part of any bid, a key part of what it also has to accomplish is a reduction in the sense of risk and uncertainty on the part of the buyer. In essence, the appeal is 'trust us, we will deliver', but achieving this is not a straightforward exercise. Establishing the credibility of a potential

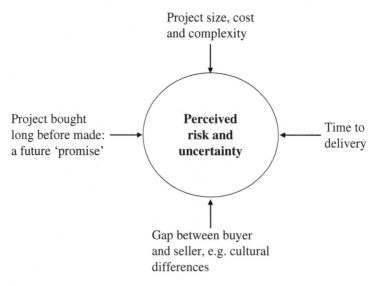

Source: Adapted from Luostarinen and Welch (1990, p. 143).

Figure 7.6   Perceived risk and uncertainty: buyer's perspective

project supplier is critical in building assurance. A record of having delivered the same or equivalent projects is at the core of this credibility, preferably in the market in question, but at least in similar locations elsewhere, and with success, representing reference projects that the buyer can go to and, in a sense, can feel and touch something of what they are aiming to buy, so that the future promise becomes more tangible.

Of course, the technical competence of the project buyer and its consultants in the field is a factor: the more competent, the greater the ability to ask more demanding questions of potential suppliers and influence project design, thereby reducing perceived uncertainty. Nevertheless, there are many issues beyond the technical details of any project solution. From a study of power plant construction projects, Lampel et al. (1996, 576) concluded that 'top management is likely to put considerable weight on such factors as reputation for reliability, innovativeness, previous experience with similar problems, and wherever pertinent, trust in these organizations which results from past relationships'.

Thus another approach to building confidence on the part of the buyer in the ability of the supplier to deliver as promised is through sustained personal contact and network development activity, what might be called the bidder's relational strategy. The quality of buyer–seller relationships has been shown to play an important contributory role in building trust between the parties and assurance about outcomes (Welch et al., 1996, 580). This has already been noted above, emphasizing the attempt by project companies to insert themselves as early as possible into the buyer's network in order to generate information about the project and the buyer's concerns, to transfer information to relevant parties in the buyer's organization, and to attempt to influence positively outcomes in the project development process, in terms of project design and choice of project builder. As one Australian project manager involved in international operations observed in an interview: 'I guess the important thing in any international [project] work is your ability to deliver . . . so your whole life exists on that ability . . . But the thing that does guarantee it is you have to understand what the client really wants. It gets back to putting in the bid . . . The most critical thing you can do . . . is to understand what they want' (from study outlined in Welch, 2005a, 2005b). And this means getting close to the client. Through personal interaction, it is possible to respond directly, on the spot, to particular client concerns. Project companies continually stress the importance of relational activity, and that it should be, as far as is feasible, a sustained activity through time, even when projects are not on the immediate horizon.

However, getting to the right people, those who actually have an influence on the project decision process, can be very demanding. Influencers are not always obvious to an outsider, and may have positions at various levels of a buying organization or government department (Cavusgil and Ghauri, 1990). The difficulty sometimes of discerning the key people in the buyer's network, and then seeking to build relationships with them at a personal level, was illustrated in the prelude to the large project in China in the 1990s to modernize grain handling and storage by moving to bulk transport and storage systems. There was a wide range of Chinese institutions involved in the project's development, as well as the World Bank which was funding a large part of the overall project. Australian companies made concerted efforts, both individually and collectively through coordinated action, supported by the Australian government's trade assistance agency, to win parts of the overall project. They appointed a Chinese marketing officer to assist in network development within the relevant Chinese organizations. Throughout the whole networking exercise, over an extended period, and involving considerable investment, there was a sense of never having fully 'cracked the network puzzle'. One of the major players on the Australian side spent two years building relations with a number of individuals in different Chinese organizations, with the assistance of two Hong Kong Chinese agents, only to find that the role of those contacted in project development was inconsequential and they had to start afresh with network establishment.

The networking and bid efforts were supported at the government-to-government level through visits by trade delegations both ways, including government and company representatives, focused on the project opportunity (Welch et al., 1996). This experience was similar to that found in a study of 24 Scandinavian companies in the Chinese market: 'Social relations were of high significance both in order to obtain important information and to influence Chinese decision makers. How to obtain information about possible customers and up-coming purchases was commonly viewed as a difficult task' (Björkman and Kock, 1995, 524). Social relationships were found to set the scene for business exchange.

Huemer (2004, 188) has argued that 'characteristics of international construction projects accentuate the challenge of trust as well as the comfort of predictability . . . [so that] construction work is often characterised by reliance on previous experience and established routines, where actors normally are keen to follow established patterns of behaviour'. This applies to network development and maintenance, to the point where it can sometimes be characterized as informal partnering, particularly with supplier companies, but can also apply to connections with client organizations. Companies prefer to do business with those firms where there is assurance or trust in what can be delivered, based on past experience; in part, this is about predictability of outcome, with a consequent lowering of perceived risk and uncertainty. As a result of this approach, it is not surprising to see long-standing connections between different suppliers and major project companies, with experience over many projects. Hadjikhani (1992, 149) concluded, from an investigation of the Swedish company ASEA prior to its bid for a major project in Brazil, that longer-term relations were part of the ability to respond to emerging opportunities: 'the project manager's strategy is to [use] earlier relationships as far as possible and avoid new relationships. Establishment of new relationships would increase the cost, time and uncertainty. In other words, the relationships have a much longer lifetime than the project itself'. For project suppliers, this can sometimes lead to complicated relationships with other suppliers. With some projects, they may be cooperating partners in the project bid and in construction, whereas, at other times, for other projects, they may be direct competitors, perhaps building their competitive capacity over time through cooperative activities and technical interaction.

Hadjikhani (1996, 323) applied a similar perspective in examining project buyer–seller relationships through time, observing that 'when a project is terminated it leaves a sediment of trust and interdependence originated from earlier relationships', developing the concept of 'sleeping relationships' as a way of characterizing the intermittent contact that may be maintained between buyer and seller between projects. Interconnections may be maintained because of financial, organizational or technical interdependencies – for example by providing continuing technical advice – and personal social ties could be re-established from time to time. Without refreshment in some form, and this requires an investment of scarce marketing resources relative to other, seemingly more current and obvious, opportunities, it is inevitable that the strength of any sleeping relationship will diminish over time. Nevertheless, the research on sleeping relationships does point to a number of conclusions that may be important in international project marketing: history matters, and can even be decisive in project design and supplier choices; project competition has a long-term perspective, it is not just about bidding and short-term negotiation tactics; each project might be unique but this does not necessarily apply to relationships; and relationship development and maintenance could be just as important after project completion as before.

It has been observed that 'project marketing firms all too often focus only upon the management of individual projects during the delivery process and on sporadic, last moment running after "promising" potential projects, rather than relationship management of all phases of the project cycle, especially in the post-completion stage' (Skaates et al., 2002b, 401). The maintenance of connections to a buyer after completion does not necessarily have to involve large resource commitments; it could be as simple as continuing personal contact through various means, including social interaction during

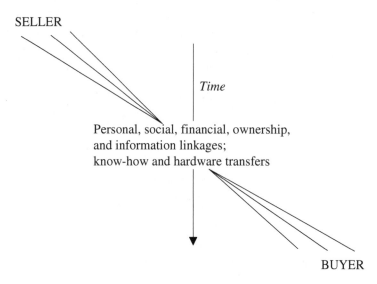

SELLER

Time

Personal, social, financial, ownership,
and information linkages;
know-how and hardware transfers

BUYER

Source: Adapted from Cavusgil and Ghauri (1990, p. 48).

Figure 7.7   Buyer–seller linkages

market visits for other purposes, sending of newsletters, updates on technical developments, and the like (Cova and Salle, 2000). However, it does require a deliberate, targeted and ongoing set of steps which ensure that the project completion is not the end of the relationship – presuming, of course, that this has not been ruptured by disagreements, conflict, or resort to legal action, and general dissatisfaction with the outcome and the process on the part of the buyer.

Figure 7.7 summarizes the range of linkages that is often involved in project buyer–seller relationships, also showing that these may be maintained through an extended period of time. They vary in intensity over the full project cycle, inevitably becoming broader and more concentrated in the construction stage.

FINANCING ISSUES

The global demand for projects is immense: it could even be said that there is a global lust for projects of all types. For example, China's continuing rapid economic growth has created a growing need for power developments to keep pace with the increased demand for energy: the investment in power projects required over the five-year period from 2004 to 2008 has been estimated to amount to US$108 billion (Song, 2003). In a global context, the demand for projects far exceeds the resources available to enable the wish list to be enacted. This is especially so for the bulk of developing countries. Inevitably, then, the availability of finance has become a critical issue in the project business as clients scramble to find ways of generating finance for their project needs. One avenue for developing countries is the multilateral development banks such as the World Bank and the Asian Development Bank as providers of aid and loans: the World Bank distributed US$20.5 billion in loans in the year to 30 June 2004 (Hiebert and McBeth, 2004). While significant, this is only a small proportion of global project financing needs. China's growing needs have placed heavy strain on the limited overall pool of finance, and then there is the pressing demand arising from the huge infrastructure backlog in India.

As a result, there is considerable pressure placed on those bidding for project business to assist in finding, or to provide directly, financial solutions for the project buyer so that projects can go ahead. This pressure has existed for some time. For example, one project company indicated in the early 1980s that 'up to 60% of the effort of selling a project is now financial rather than technical' (ENR, 1984, 31). A survey of local contractors and international bankers in Singapore concluded that project finance was 'the most important factor in winning overseas projects' (Tiong and Yeo, 1993, 83). In the early 1990s, a representative of Bechtel, the large US project company, commented that 'there are more projects than there is money available. If the firms can't contribute to bringing in the money, they won't get the work' (Reina and Setzer, 1992, 34). This demand developed alongside the trend in the 1990s of governments seeking to privatize a range of their functions, including infrastructure development and its financing, thereby reducing their need to call upon taxpayer-generated funding.

As a consequence, many of the large project companies, for example Bechtel and ABB, developed financing arms as a way of supporting what has come to be regarded as an essential side of the project business. This is apart from the pressure on project companies to contribute finance by taking an equity share in the client firm. BOT financing systems (see outline above) have been viewed by many as a convenient solution to the problem of lack of finance for major projects, and they fitted the attempt by governments to reduce their role in infrastructure financing. However, the problems encountered with extracting payment from operating the project facility over the long term, when prices are held down by external, government-imposed regulation, have cooled the interest in this form by finance providers and project companies, particularly in many parts of Asia. With power utilities there is always strong political pressure on governments to ensure that price rises are kept to a bare minimum. The major private commercial banks have been an important external source of finance, as in the case of the high-speed rail project in Korea.

Devising financing solutions can be a creative exercise, with countertrade part of the general mix. One of the more bizarre examples of the attempt to use countertrade as a way of financing projects emerged in the mid-1990s as many of the emerging economies of the former Soviet Union sought to fast track development and infrastructure projects. 'When the people of the Russian republic of Kalmikia decided that they wanted a new airport for their capital, Elista, they turned to the chairman of Alarko, a Turkish construction company . . . he told the authorities in Kalmikia that it would cost them US$105 million, and that he would require a 10% down-payment . . . [they replied] "that could be a problem; we don't have that sort of money". "What do you have then?" asked the flexible [Turkish chairman]. "Well", they replied, "we do have a lot of sheep" ' (Hindle, 1995, 37).

GOVERNMENT RELATIONS

Despite the general move by governments to reduce their role in financing projects, they still play an important role in project financing, in some cases pre-eminently so. In various other ways, too, governments may have a significant impact on the way individual projects are developed and shaped, and the parameters of a potential role for foreign project companies. For the Hong Kong airport project noted above, the government provided 71 per cent of the total budget for the airport's construction, amounting to HK$111 billion (Hung et al., 2002). Although utilizing consulting advice, the Hong Kong government, as the project buyer, including a range of departments and individuals, was a key player in decisions about the project during all phases. The Chinese government has been the major source of finance for the huge Three Gorges dam project (Chao, 2005).

For foreign companies seeking to win project work, relations with and influence on the government officials involved become critical to the marketing process (Jansson, 1989; Cavusgil and Ghauri, 1990). In other situations, while the government may not have been involved in direct financing, if a project is important in the country context, it will normally use the different tools at its disposal to influence project outcomes. While there have been growing attempts to free project markets to allow foreign competition, government pressure in support of a major contribution by local companies to host country projects is the reality that international project operators routinely face. This pressure can be applied in a variety of forms, from informal demands to formal regulatory requirements. For example, new regulations in China effectively prevent project companies from operating on a project-by-project basis, forcing them to set up a Chinese base, working through joint ventures with Chinese firms given the restriction on establishing wholly foreign-owned construction companies (Gale and Luo, 2004; Tuchman, 2003). One foreign consultant has commented: 'most doors into the [project] market are marked "Chinese only". Foreign companies are pretty much excluded from most of the work' (*China Economic Review*, 2005, 32).

In extreme cases, often politically based, governments may be prepared to abandon projects, withdraw funding or suspend bidding processes, in order to exclude certain foreign operators. As a way of retaliating against France's recognition of Armenian claims of genocide having been committed by Turks during World War I, a major road tender was cancelled by Turkey because both of the bidding consortiums included French companies (*International Herald Tribune*, 2001). After the change of government in the Philippines in 2001, the new government declared the contract regarding a new international airport terminal in Manila (entered into with the previous government) null and void on the grounds that the government's own foreign investment limit on infrastructure projects was illegally breached and that local officials had been bribed in the bidding process, forcing the German contractor, Fraport, to contemplate the potential loss of a US$327 million from completed work on the project (Hookway, 2003).

In general, governments play a key role in determining the setting for all aspects of the project cycle, not just in terms of the legal or regulatory framework. Governments have significant power in their local context, and how this is used provides an important signal to foreign project firms. European and American firms were major investors in power generation projects in China in the early 1990s. However, after problems surrounding long-term power purchasing arrangements with government bodies, resulting in investment failure in one high-profile case when the provincial government reneged on a 20-year purchase contract, these companies have been reluctant to become involved in similar power generation projects in recent times despite the many opportunities (Song, 2003). In Vietnam, the French water utility company, Suez, signed a BOT contract for the construction of a water treatment plant for Ho Chi Minh city in 1997, with the backing of the Asian Development Bank (ADB) and financing by a consortium of companies, including two French banks. Nevertheless, subsequent negotiations with the city authorities regarding the pricing of the water, and environmental and other issues, bogged down. With costs rising and uncertainty about the long-term financial outcome increasing, Suez withdrew from the project in 2003, having incurred about US$20 million in costs (Cohen, 2003).

The government's impact on the extent of corruption and bribery surrounding projects is critical: it is not merely a question of having laws in place but whether and how these are applied. In the early 1990s, government officials and politicians in Japan were shown to be condoning corrupt payments, in some cases to themselves, and bid rigging in the awarding of public works contracts, as well as maintaining various covert links with construction company managers (Thomson, 1993). When bid rigging was exposed, Japanese officials argued that their 'designated bidding system' prevented 'unhealthy competition'. The overall effect was to restrict access to the public works market by foreign contractors. Under pressure from the US government, the Japanese government introduced measures in 1994 to improve access to this market, for example by introducing measures to ensure an open and competitive bidding system (Nakamoto, 1994). However, in the run-up to the awarding of contracts for the new Nagoya airport some years later, examples of bid rigging emerged, and one commentator observed that the practice was 'still ubiquitous', despite continuing US pressure to stamp it out (Amaha, 1999).

Official graft in the distribution of World Bank funds for projects in various countries has been a continuing issue for the World Bank despite concerted efforts to stop it. 'Local government officials [sometimes] skim money off the top as they distribute funds and award contracts; business owners pay them bribes, win contracts, inflate project costs and pocket the difference' (Hiebert and McBeth, 2004, 14). The Asian Development Bank (ADB) has also experienced problems in preventing collusion and graft in projects that it finances. In a recent case involving a large water treatment facility in Thailand, an external investigation noted that 'Thai authorities later uncovered evidence of a complex web of collusion among officials and companies' (Gay, 2004, 19). The case led to a refinement of ADB lending procedures, but an admission that corruption was difficult to prevent. Government departments often play a key role as the executing agencies for local projects funded by the World Bank or Asian Development Bank. As the manager of one project company observed, 'the information you get from the ADB or World Bank website does not always correlate with the executing agency's concepts and ideas and wishes and desires' (Welch, 2005b, 299). In testimony before a congressional hearing in the US on 13 May 2004, an academic who specializes in South East Asia, Jeffrey Winters, estimated that the World Bank had lost US$100 billion owing to corruption since its lending operations began in the mid-1940s (Hiebert, 2004).

Governments not only affect the prospects of foreign firms seeking project work within the local context, they also have an impact on the attempts of local firms to win business in foreign markets. This may be at the level of broad encouragement and support, but it is often more concrete. For major, high-profile projects, government-to-government lobbying is sometimes used, in some cases at the highest level, involving prime ministers and the like, while royalty, where available, has also been called upon to play a contributory promotional role on occasions. Government and semi-government trade agencies often become involved in supporting the attempt to win foreign project business. For China's large grain storage and handling systems project, instead of disparate, individual efforts by individual companies, the Australian government's trade assistance agency organized and supported a combined promotional effort in an attempt to maximize marketing impact (Welch et al., 1996). As well, many countries have financing support arrangements to assist their companies in matching financial arrangements that may be available to competitive companies.

Further, government assistance for local firms in the international arena is often engineered by linking foreign aid and project work by firms from the country providing such aid. In their study of local contractors and international bankers, Tiong and Yeo (1993) found that government assistance was an important contributory factor in the ability to win overseas project work. Despite WTO, EU, OECD and some countries' efforts to limit the role of government financial assistance for project bidding in the international arena, and export subsidies generally, and to open up government procurement to international competition, it is a difficult area to institute consistent and transparent policies. Poor recipient countries are obviously happy to see competitive foreign government action (for example via the provision of cheap finance) that lowers the cost of project building activity in their jurisdictions. At the same time there is concern that developing countries will be locked into arrangements that will result in their paying for goods and services at inflated prices. In 2004, the OECD instituted a pilot programme among member countries to ensure that bidding for projects financed by untied aid would be subject to open competitive bidding (OECD news release, 8/11/2004).

Clearly, governments may play many, diverse, roles in the development and shape of international projects – across the full range of the project cycle. A government may act as a project buyer, financier, influencer, facilitator, evaluator, resource provider – and 'terminator'. It is not surprising, therefore, to find governments as important targets of project marketing campaigns and long-term relational development activities. But the government is not a unitary entity. Knowing which parts are important and the relevant officials, and reaching and influencing them, can be a major exercise in network investment, as the China Grain project noted above exemplifies (Welch et al., 1996).

THE PROJECT MIX: AN OVERVIEW OF KEY FACTORS

For project companies operating in the international arena, winning bids for projects, successfully completing them and maintaining long-term international activity require performance on many levels and the ability to deal with an array of demanding issues over extended periods of time. Within this context, mode choice and use decisions are difficult to separate from other pressing issues. The key factors in successful project operations have been summarized as (1) the package mix, (2) the relational mix, (3) the strategic mix, and (4) understanding of the project milieu (Welch, 2005b).

The Package Mix

This refers to the broad mix of elements that forms the eventual completed, operating project, including price; financing arrangements; hardware, software and service components; human skills and know-how; technology and operation mode combination (Cova and Holstius, 1993). Taken together, companies seek to offer a superior mix to competitors that is attractive to the buyer in an overall sense as a project solution, but also satisfies concerns on other critical dimensions that may vary from project to project. As the above analysis identified, price frequently comes to dominate project negotiations, as in the case of Korea's high-speed railway project, with buyers seeking to reduce a project's cost and limit its associated financing demands. This can generate an approach of designing down to a price, and of concentrating on the more concrete aspects of the package, like equipment and technical performance, rather than on less tangible, but important, areas such as skills transfers (Luostarinen and Welch, 1990). It is often adduced as a reason for projects failing to achieve expected performance levels. The 'softer' areas of project development activity are more difficult to determine with precision in advance and can be readily targeted under pressure to reduce costs. Along with the price of a project, the ability to organize what is perceived by the buyer as reasonable, low-cost financing can be decisive in choice of contractor, and therefore occupies a key place in project marketing by suppliers. However, in difficult construction situations or in new and technically advanced industrial projects, the ability to devise appropriate technological solutions tends to come to the fore among mix factors.

Given the uncertainty surrounding projects, an important part of the project mix is the intangible dimension represented by such elements as the buyer's assurance and trust in, and perceived credibility surrounding, the project supplier, requiring a development process and verifiable performance record on the part of the supplier that may take many years to put into place (Welch, 2005b). The mode package used to set up and deliver the project typically contains a broad spread of modes, often subject to the strictures and pressures of the project's local context, so that joint ventures may have to be formed with local companies; it is normal that local suppliers have to be used for many parts of the project rather than foreign imports of hardware, software and services; in the face of project risk, the prime contractor may seek to set up a consortium with other suppliers as a way of spreading risk; and contractual modes such as licensing might be employed to cover the varied know-how and technology transfers that accompany project construction.

The Relational Mix

A strong theme of this chapter, reflecting recent research on international project operations, is the important role of network relationship maintenance and development over all stages of the project cycle, and even between projects. In some respects, it is the relationships outside the formal project cycle that can provide the key marketing foundation for project companies. 'The firm needs a wide "contact net" of connections to scan effectively and obtain a "first-mover" advantage. These connections are often of an "extrabusiness" or social nature. They also include "non-business" or sociopolitical actors . . . with governments "ever present", particularly in developing countries' (Welch, 2005b, 291; see also Ahmed, 1993; Cova and Salle, 2000). Supplier networks also have to be developed and maintained as part of project marketing and performance, and the quality of the product mix. The problem for project companies, especially smaller ones, is the breadth and depth of relationships over time that is required in order to be effective, in a variety of foreign market locations, given the transience, irregularity and often unpredictability of foreign project opportunities. While there tends to be general recognition of the value of having an on-the-ground presence in foreign markets as a base for network development and maintenance, ensuring regular personalized contact, particularly on the social side, and as a listening post, cost limits the scale of such investments for many firms. As a result, project firms rely on visits and other forms of communication, with the Internet playing an increasingly important part. In an Australian study of project suppliers to multilateral organizations, they were found to have developed extensive in-country networks that included 'government departments and officials . . . local service providers, agents and community stakeholders' (Welch, 2005b, 299).

The Strategic Mix

The strategic mix refers to what have been called a company's 'anticipatory' and 'adaptive' capabilities with respect to projects (Bansard,
Cova and Salle, 1993; Cova, Crespin-Mazet and Salle, 1994). The anticipatory capabilities are those that could be regarded as at the core of a
project company's ability to operate in the international arena – from
project to project and from market to market. They include aspects such
as the development of standardized product and service components that
can be readily moved into varying project situations, in the manner of
general systems development and marketing (Luostarinen and Welch,
1990; see Chapter 6). Other important elements could be databases on
and links to potential foreign customers, consultants and supplier companies. In a study of Australian companies supplying multilaterally
funded projects, Welch (2005b) found that companies with a flow of
projects developed strong anticipatory capabilities through direct links
with multilateral organizations and systematic tracking of forthcoming
opportunities.

Adaptive capabilities are those enabling project companies to adjust their
offerings, their way of doing business and relating to customers, and dealing
with differing project contexts. They include technical abilities – being able
to adjust to varied technical specifications and problems; financial abilities
– being able to assist with creative financial solutions for project buyers; and
knowledge and contact systems – being able to activate and utilize local contacts and knowledge to support and adapt project marketing and implementation. In a study of Australian project companies, flexibility and
adaptability were found to be critical in responding to the twin masters of
multilateral institutions and local governments as executing agencies: 'On
the one hand, the formalised, rigid requirements and detailed procedures
specified by multilateral organisations . . . are an important influence on the
internal [anticipatory] capabilities and external relationships that suppliers
develop . . . Yet, at the same time, since much procurement is decided at the
national level, the highly standardised procedures and rules that operate at
the multilateral level are not consistently applied by executing agencies. As
a result, the project context for suppliers is characterised by a high degree of
regularity yet simultaneously a high degree of variability' (Welch, 2005b,
303). This is apart from the normal demands of dealing with multiple suppliers, clients and officials in different cultures and countries, requiring
different approaches, and placing a premium on adaptability.

Understanding of the Milieu

The performance of project companies in the previous three elements of the project mix depends heavily on companies' understanding of, and ability to respond to, the local project context, political, social, cultural and business: what has been referred to as the project milieu (Cova et al., 1996). This is in recognition of the various ways in which the local context can influence a project, at all stages. As noted throughout this chapter, the project is not just a technical solution arrived at in a vacuum: there are multiple ways that local factors may affect project operations; for example, local governments are important; local pressure groups, such as environmental groups, may have an impact; and there may be unique country risk factors, including political turmoil, wars and economic instability.

CONCLUSION

Considered in foreign operation mode terms, there is no doubt that project operations are 'messy and awkward'. They usually cannot be regarded as a direct alternative to other mode forms: the option presented is normally only for a project or set of projects, so that direct alternative modes, such as direct foreign investment, by interested companies are not a consideration. While project operations have distinctive features, they defy easy categorization. They fit the idea of modes in a package or combination sense. As noted above, it is common for all main groups of modes to be represented in project activity (exporting, contractual and investment) but there may be considerable variation in the extent and way that they are employed over time, preceding, during and after construction (see Figure 7.2). Governments, both home and host, and other external influences, tend to have a major impact on the content of the project-related mode package, the character and pattern of the project cycle and the ultimate project form. While the set-up of a company for delivering a project or part thereof, especially in the implementation phase, has many of the features of a temporary organization, it often fits into a more long-term networked system of relationships and links between suppliers, and between governments, buyers and suppliers, at times, as part of so-called 'sleeping relationships'.

Companies undertaking projects are not only those concentrating on this area of business, but include those from areas that are important to particular project types – for example, as suppliers of major equipment. Thus some companies move in and out of project involvement as opportunities sporadically appear and fade. The variability of the international project market, particularly on a country-by-country basis, makes it difficult for project companies to maintain consistent forms of foreign market involvement, but at the same time it creates a strong need for these companies, and their staff, to be flexible and responsive to changing market circumstances. The concept of commitment conceptualized in the internationalization literature emerges in diverse forms for project companies in their international activity. It exists, but not necessarily in simple 'establishment chain' terms; rather it is seen in aspects such as network and relationship development; and in human resource, behavioural and financial commitments (Welch, 2005b).

REFERENCES

Ahmad, S. (2004), 'A survey of China', *Economist*, 20 March, 1–18.

Ahmed, M.M. (1993), *International Marketing and Purchasing of Projects – Interactions and Paradoxes: A Study of Finnish Project Exports to the Arab Countries*, Helsinki: Swedish School of Economics and Business Administration.

Amaha, E. (1999), 'Trade – building hope', *Far Eastern Economic Review*, 15 April, 83.

Bansard, D., B. Cova and R. Salle (1993), 'Project marketing: beyond competitive bidding strategies', *International Business Review*, **2**(2), 125–41.

Björkman, I. and S. Kock (1995), 'Social relationships and business networks: the case of Western companies in China', *International Business Review*, **4**(4), 519–35.

Blanden, M. (1994), 'Project finance: make them pay', *The Banker*, **144**(1), 66–8.

Branconi, C.V. and C.H. Loch (2004), 'Contracting for major projects: eight business levers for top management', *International Journal of Project Management*, **22**(2), 119–30.

Burton, J. (1993), 'S Korea bargains hard to take the fast train', *Financial Times*, 23 August, 4.

Callick, R. (2006), 'Mao's lake finally appears as dam nears completion', *Australian*, 19 May, 10.

Cavusgil, S.T. and P.N. Ghauri (1990), *Doing Business in Developing Countries*, London: Routledge.

Centre on Transnational Corporations (1983), *Features and Issues in Turnkey Contracts in Developing Countries: A Technical Paper*, New York: United Nations, ST/CTC/28.

Chao, L. (2005), 'Dam emerges despite funds scandal', *China Daily*, 29 March, 5.

Chevrier, S. (2003), 'Cross-cultural management in multinational project groups', *Journal of World Business*, **38**(2), 141–9.

China Economic Review (2005), 'Under construction', **15**(3), 28–33.

Cohen, M. (2003), 'A lesson from Vietnam for water-project financing', *Far Eastern Economic Review*, 15 May, 28.

Cova, B. and K. Holstius (1993), 'How to create competitive advantage in project business', *Journal of Marketing Management*, **9**, 105–21.

Cova, B. and R. Salle (2000), 'Rituals in managing extrabusiness relationships in international project marketing: a conceptual framework', *International Business Review*, **9**, 669–85.

Cova, B., F. Crespin-Mazet and R. Salle (1994), 'From competitive tendering to strategic marketing: an inductive approach for theory-building', *Journal of Strategic Marketing*, **2**, 29–47.

Cova, B., P. Ghauri and R. Salle (2002), *Project Marketing: Beyond Competitive Bidding*, Chichester: John Wiley & Sons.

Cova, B., F. Mazet and R. Salle (1996), 'Milieu as a pertinent unit of analysis in project marketing', *International Business Review*, **5**(6), 647–64.

Economist (2001), 'Alstom – nasty numbers', 8 December, 63.

Economist (2004), 'Face value – the king of guanxi', 25 September, 76.

Economist (2005), 'Project management – overdue and over budget, over and over again', 11 June, 59–60.

Engineering News Record (1984), 'Financial engineering wins jobs', 2 August, 31.

Gale, A. and J. Luo (2004), 'Factors affecting construction joint ventures in China', *International Journal of Project Management*, **22**(1), 33–42.

Gay, C. (2004), 'Thai project yields graft and new policies', *Far Eastern Economic Review*, 29 July, 18–19.

Hadjikhani, A. (1992), 'Managing international package deals projects', in M. Forsgren and J. Johanson (eds), *Managing Networks in International Business*, Philadelphia: Gordon & Breach, pp. 138–50.

Hadjikhani, A. (1996), 'Project marketing and the management of discontinuity', *International Business Review*, **5**(3), 319–36.

Hiebert, M. (2004), 'What was stolen? A $100 billion debate', *Far Eastern Economic Review*, 29 July, 20.

Hiebert, M. and J. McBeth (2004), 'Corruption – stealing from the poor', *Far Eastern Economic Review*, 29 July, 14–20.

Hindle, T. (1995), 'Master builders on the wild frontier', *EuroBusiness*, October, 37–9.

Holberton, S. (1992), 'Bechtel signs HK deal', *Financial Times*, 1/2 February, 2.

Hookway, J. (2003), 'Philippines – grounded investment', *Far Eastern Economic Review*, 11 December, 49–51.

Huemer, L. (2004), 'Activating trust: the redefinition of roles and relationships in an international construction project', *International Marketing Review*, **21**(2), 187–201.

Hung, A.L.W., G.M. Naidu, S.T. Cavusgil and R.S. Yam (2002), 'An exploratory study of project based international joint ventures: the case of Chek Lap Kok Airport in Hong Kong', *International Business Review*, **11**(5), 505–22.

International Herald Tribune (2001), 'French role dooms Turkish road contract', 2 February, 16.

Jansson, H. (1989), 'Marketing to projects in Southeast Asia', *Advances in International Marketing*, **3**, 259–76.

Kadefors, A. (2004), 'Trust in project relationships – inside the black box', *International Journal of Project Management*, **22**(3), 175–82.

Kaynak, E. and T. Dalgic (1992), 'Internationalization of Turkish construction companies: a lesson for Third World countries', *Columbia Journal of World Business*, **26**(4), 60–75.

Lampel, J., R. Miller and S. Floricel (1996), 'Impact of owner involvement on innovation in large projects: lessons from power plants construction', *International Business Review*, **5**(6), 561–78.

Luostarinen, R. and L. Welch (1990), *International Business Operations*, Helsinki: Kyriri Oy.

Luqmani, M., G.M. Habib and S. Kassem (1988), 'Marketing to LDC governments', *International Marketing Review*, **5**(1), 56–67.

Makilouko, M. (2004), 'Coping with multicultural projects: the leadership styles of Finnish project managers', *International Journal of Project Management*, **22**(5), 387–96.

Murphy, D. (2004), 'Construction industry – Chinese builders go global', *Far Eastern Economic Review*, 13 May, 30–33.

Nakamoto, M. (1994), 'Japan to open up bidding system for building works', *Financial Times*, 19 January, 12.

Packendorff, J. (1995), 'Inquiring into the temporary organization: new directions for project management research', *Scandinavian Journal of Management*, **11**(4), 319–33.

Paisley, E. (1993), 'Tender tactics', *Far Eastern Economic Review*, 2 September, 63.

Reina, P. and S.W. Setzer (1992), 'The top international contractor firms set sail for hot markets', *Engineering News Record*, **229**(8), 34.

Ridding, J. and J. Burton (1994), 'GEC Alsthom clinches $2bn S Korean deal', *Financial Times*, 19 April, 16.

Skaates, M.A., H. Tikkanen and K. Alajoutsijärvi (2002a), 'Social and cultural capital in project marketing service firms: Danish architectural firms on the German market', *Scandinavian Journal of Management*, **18**(4), 589–609.

Skaates, M.A., H. Tikkanen and J. Lindblom (2002b), 'Relationships and project marketing success', *Journal of Business and Industrial Marketing*, **17**(5), 389–406.

Song, K. (2003), 'Power – China's huge appetite', *Far Eastern Economic Review*, 18 December, 42–4.

Thompson, I., A. Cox and L. Anderson (1998), 'Contracting strategies for the project environment', *European Journal of Purchasing and Supply Management*, **4**, 31–41.

Thomson, R. (1993), 'Japanese bid-rigging helps US case', *Financial Times*, 25 March, 4.

Tiong, R. and K.T. Yeo (1993), 'Project financing as a competitive strategy in winning overseas jobs', *International Journal of Project Management*, **11**(2), 79–86.

Transparency International (2002), Press Release: Bribe Payers Index 2002, 14 May, Organisation's web site, accessed 3/5/05.

Tuchman, J. (2003), 'Business rules are changing for contracting in China', *Engineering News Record*, **251**(25), 14.

Tyson, L. (1998), 'Taiwan's high-speed rail project right on track', *Financial Times*, 18 March, 6.

Welch, C. (2005a), 'International consulting providers and multilateral institutions: networks and internationalization', *Advances in International Marketing*, **15**, 175–97.

Welch, C. (2005b), 'Multilateral organisations and international project marketing', *International Business Review*, **14**(3), 289–305.

Welch, D., L. Welch, I. Wilkinson and L. Young (1996), 'Network development in international project marketing and the development of external facilitation', *International Business Review*, **5**(6), 579–602.

8. Exporting

THE NATURE AND IMPORTANCE OF EXPORTING

Exporting represents one of the three main groups of modes that we will be treating in this book: it is a major mode option used by companies to achieve international market penetration. It has long been a focus of attention in national economic deliberations and policy, and of supranational organizations such as the World Trade Organization (WTO). The encouragement of international trade by various means, including the removal of the many obstacles to free trade that have been erected over time by governments, has been a policy objective at the supranational level for many decades that has produced a continuing reduction in tariff and non-tariff barriers across a wide range of industries and sectors, and provides continuing impetus to extension of the process in hitherto difficult areas, notably agriculture. In a broad sense, the global policy context has been gradually moving in favour of the use of exporting in international business activity. Because of their physicality, and government revenue, economic policy and customs considerations, international trade statistics have long been closely recorded and strongly represented in national governments' balance of payments accounts under the balance of trade or balance on current account section, and subject to considerable public and media attention and commentary. The growth of a country's exports tends to be viewed as a positive, in contrast to that for imports, and is generally encouraged by national governments, with potential benefits for companies seeking to develop international operations via exporting activity.

Under the umbrella of the term 'exporting' a wide range of activities and forms can be identified. While the term was used originally with respect to foreign sales of physical goods, it has come to be used also as applying to services. For the purposes of this chapter we will follow this broadened approach: 'exports' refers to exports of both goods and services. Of course, the goods/services distinction is frequently blurred by the reality that exports tend to involve a package of goods and services, with the one linked to and depending on the other (Czinkota and Ronkainen, 2001). From a global perspective, measured exports of physical merchandise in total exceed those of services by about 4:1, despite the sustained rise in trade in international services over the last three decades (WTO, 2005). This situation is explained in part by the dominance of services in overall foreign direct investment activity relative to the manufacturing, mining and primary sectors. While investment in services constituted only about a quarter of FDI stock in the 1970s, this had risen to about 47 per cent by 1990 and in 2002 had reached about 67 per cent of total outward FDI stock (UNCTAD, 2004). In 2004, 63 per cent of cross-border M&As and about 60 per cent of greenfield projects were in the services sector (UNCTAD, 2005). In total, sales of the foreign subsidiaries of internationally active companies were far in excess of global exports of goods and services (UNCTAD, 2005).

In this chapter we will focus on the choice and use of exporting as a mode of international operations – in its own right, as well as in combination with other modes. The general topic of exporting tends to be well covered in international marketing textbooks (see, for example, Hollensen, 2001; Albaum et al., 2002), particularly when compared to the treatment of contractual modes. In this respect, the coverage of distribution questions in traditional international marketing textbooks is particularly pertinent. Of course, a high proportion of global trade (in goods, and increasingly in services too) is represented by MNC internal flows so that exporting decisions in different global locations are part of, and subject to, a far broader operations and company landscape (UNCTAD, 2005).

Exporting, as a part of international merchandise trade, was a concern of early theory development that led to the Law of Comparative Advantage, as part of the argument for free trade between countries. It was some time before research and theory development acknowledged company issues, and other mode forms, with exporting placed in this broader context. The interaction aspects of exporting with other operation modes have yet to be fully explored, but we will seek to expose this context as it applies to exporting, while stressing key features that make exporting, in its many forms, an important mode category in its own right. Chapter 6 illustrates how exporting and importing activities are often closely entangled with other ways of operating. The growing global interest in the possibilities of subcontracting or outsourcing, particularly with regard to services recently, has been important in driving the growing connected trade in goods and services (WTO, 2005).

As noted above, exporting performance is still regarded as a key, positive economic indicator by governments, and it represents an area subject to a variety of schemes in different countries, to encourage companies into exporting and to expand activities, in ways, and to an extent, not found for other forms of outward mode expansion; for example, with regard to outward direct foreign investment and international outsourcing. Many governments have set up trade assistance agencies with a foreign infrastructure to support exporting attempts by companies, punctuated by broad campaigns from time to time extolling the opportunities and national benefits of exporting, although there seems to have been a move away from broad-based campaigns toward more selective approaches such as networking and export grouping schemes (Welch et al., 1998). Ultimately, such schemes have the capacity to influence whether and how exporting is used in companies' approaches to international expansion.

A range of studies has shown that exporting tends to be one of the most commonly used modes in the early stages of companies' internationalization patterns, particularly for manufacturers, and those in the agricultural and mining sectors. For example, in a large study of Finnish manufacturing SMEs, it was found that almost 96 per cent began outward international operations via so-called 'non-investment marketing operations', which basically meant exporting (Luostarinen et al., 1994). A study of 246 UK high-technology firms found that about 92 per cent first entered foreign markets via various exporting modes (Burgel and Murray, 2000). A similar pattern emerged in an Australian study of SMEs, which was in line with a broad result for SMEs in the various country studies under the programme of research instituted by the OECD in the mid-1990s (Dept. of Foreign Affairs and Trade, 1995).

Exporting is often viewed as the only mode option, with no consideration of alternatives, by those embarking on international activity. Of course, it may well have been preceded by inward operations: in the Finnish study mentioned above, more than half of the manufacturing SMEs began their international activity with inward operations, which meant product imports for the bulk of companies in the study (Korhonen et al., 1996). As noted in Chapter 2, the choice and form of exporting used by a company in initiating outward international activity may be explained by these preceding activities, perhaps generating considerable learning, and delivering relevant networks, that facilitate exporting. Such inward–outward connected processes were found also in licensing and franchising by Australian companies (Welch and Luostarinen, 1993). For companies developing new technology that is incorporated in products or processes, licensing sometimes comes into consideration as a mode of internationalization. A study of foreign licensing activity by Australian companies at different stages of internationalization at the time of the study found that licensing was the first step into the relevant foreign market in about 57 per cent of the cases while in over 18 per cent of cases it had been preceded by exporting. In some cases, though, licensing acted as a 'Trojan horse' for exporting, opening up linked export sales such as equipment, machinery and raw materials. As well, licensing was sometimes used as a 'stepping stone' to other, replacement, ways of operating, including exporting (Carstairs and Welch, 1982).

Exports of services, especially pure services, and in the initial stages of foreign expansion, tend to be much more difficult to accomplish than product exports, and pose far more difficult delivery questions to the extent that it might be expected for other modes, such as alliances, to come into play whatever the stage of internationalization, as shown in many studies of service exporters (LEK Partnership, 1994). In an Australian study of internationalizing SMEs (ISMEs) it was concluded that, 'relative to manufacturing ISMEs, service sector ISMEs are much less likely than average to establish their own operations overseas, and also less likely to use agents, but they are more likely to use networks and alliances (Dept. of Foreign Affairs and Trade, 1995, 27). An illustration is the provision of legal services in a foreign market, with a different legal system and language: for example, in the case of an Australian firm providing legal advice for customers in Norway. There are many examples in the services sector where the foreign customer moves to where the service is provided rather than the service being provided in the foreign location, such as in education and health. In essence, these still represent service exports, involving the delivery of a service to foreign customers, and solving the service delivery question. Thus a distinction is sometimes made between 'inbound services', like tourism and health, provided in the home country to foreign customers, and 'outbound services', provided to customers located in foreign markets (LEK Partnership, 1994, 20).

When comparing the three main groups of mode options, it is not surprising that exporting is often preferred as the starting route to international involvement. It tends to be viewed as a relatively easy, low-cost way of getting started, particularly in cases where foreign customers initiate the exchange, which is a common occurrence for both manufacturing and service sectors. Australian research found that about one-third of service exporters began exporting as a result of unsolicited external inquiries (LEK Partnership, 1994). While fortuitous or unsolicited approaches are common also for other modes (for example, see Chapter 3), responding to a fortuitous export order may require little if any additional work on the part of the supplier beyond that required for domestic sales, especially if, for instance, documentation, shipping and other practical exporting demands are outsourced to external organizations like freight forwarders. Exporting may be a relatively simple extension of what they are already doing in the domestic market, whereas other mode forms tend to involve a more substantial shift in the way of thinking about, and undertaking, business. Some companies have even referred to domestic operations over large distances as akin to 'exporting at home', acting as a preparatory step to the international move (Welch and Wiedersheim-Paul, 1980b). In contrast, the demands of setting up overseas facilities, entering into joint ventures, or establishing extended contractual arrangements with foreign parties tend to be viewed as substantial steps in the early stages of international activity, with perhaps licensing as an exception. For example, the move into franchising as a first outward international step for a manufacturer without any previous experience of using this mode is such a major departure from normal operations that it is rarely even contemplated (see Chapter 3).

So-called parallel exports represent an unintended path into exporting for some firms, and one which companies will often go to considerable lengths to shut down. In a study of 27 US companies across a wide range of industries, parallel exports were found to be a common 'problem' which they 'preferred to curtail' in the interests of ensuring control over their international marketing activities and pricing (Michael, 1998, 31). For about half of the firms in the study it was their authorized domestic distributors who were undertaking the exporting activity via unauthorized foreign intermediaries. For 22 per cent of the firms it was large retail chains who were undertaking the exporting, after buying directly from the manufacturer. Another path used by 22 per cent of firms was found when an authorized foreign distributor re-exported supplies to other foreign markets via unauthorized intermediaries in these other markets. In these cases, the operation mode choice is effectively taken out of the hands of the manufacturer, even though the end result may well have been the same with the manufacturer being in a position to choose.

Nevertheless, parallel exports could set a path for the pattern of international activity by some companies, whether viewed as generating positive or negative outcomes, and influence their foreign operation mode constructions and management processes. While parallel exports are a widespread phenomenon in world markets, particularly amongst European Union (EU) countries where it is legally difficult to prevent, there are no reliable statistics regarding their extent and size, so it is difficult to evaluate their overall impact on mode decision making. In the mid-1990s, a study of the EU's pharmaceutical industry indicated quite rapid growth in parallel exports, which some governments were supporting as a way of reducing costs in their health systems. In general, judicial interpretations of EU law supported this trade: they 'have sharply limited the right of a manufacturer to control the distribution of its product once it has been introduced into one Member State within the EU' (Chaudhry and Walsh, 1995, 15). It was estimated that the market for parallel exports of drugs to the UK from elsewhere in Europe was worth about £700 million annually (Freeman, 2001).

It could be argued that, with greater international price transparency as a result of the Internet, price differentials between countries will be reduced, thereby minimizing a major driving force behind parallel exporting. Recent examples, though, raise questions about the likelihood of this occurring. In some Asian countries, notably Thailand and Malaysia, Microsoft has introduced modified versions of its software which it is selling at lower prices than in the rest of its global operations, in part as an attempt to reduce the extent of piracy of its software within these markets, as well as in response to government pressure. Inevitably, this action opens up the prospect of parallel exports back into markets where Microsoft's higher prices apply, although in the above cases there was protection through the use of local language versions of the software (*Australian*, 2004). Microsoft is planning to extend this approach of offering lower-price versions of its software into the Indian market (*Australian*, 2005). Pfizer and other pharmaceutical companies have been battling to prevent parallel exporting by Canadian wholesalers back into the higher priced US market (Bowe, 2004).

THE EXPORTING MODE DECISION

The choice of exporting as a mode of foreign operations, and the choice of a particular form in which this will be enacted in the foreign market, do not necessarily occur in an orderly, systematic and sequential pattern. The preceding discussion makes that abundantly clear. Long-standing empirical investigations demonstrate that there may be diverse paths, in some cases over extended periods of time, to the final act of exporting to a foreign market through a specific form, such as an independent foreign intermediary. Figure 8.1 shows the range of influences and processes that typically precede the move into exporting in some form. The process leading into the idea of international operations, in whatever mode form, tends to play a critical, though not necessarily decisive, role in subsequent steps. The processes leading to international decision making may be as much about the preceding experience of key individuals and their background as about what transpires within the company in question. The idea about exporting may be embedded in particular individuals, and their influence within the company could explain the exporting path (McGaughey et al., 1997).

In their study of UK firms, Burgel and Murray (2000) examined the impact of management's international experience on foreign mode choice. They found that the impact was significant, but not in the manner expected: having international experience meant that managers were more likely to bypass the use of intermediaries in international operations. A similar result was obtained in another UK study of high-technology firms, an in-depth investigation of ten companies. In four of the firms, the process of foreign market entry was based primarily on the past experience (previous employment) of the relevant managers, and the networks this had generated (Crick

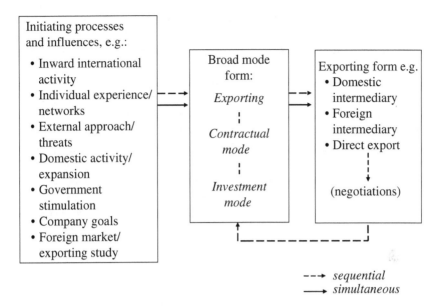

Figure 8.1   Path to choice of exporting form

and Jones, 2000). Background research also reveals the importance of preceding experiences within the domestic market in explaining the process of international entry and its form (Wiedersheim-Paul et al., 1978). Burgel and Murray (2000, 54) found that the 'strongest predictor of the chosen foreign entry mode was the existing, domestic sales mode of the firm ... the explanatory effect of this variable is arguably due to the presence of embedded routines and experiences with the domestic sales mode'. In the various country studies of the internationalization of SMEs that were part of the overall OECD programme, the bulk of SMEs were found to have first established themselves in their domestic markets (Dept. of Foreign Affairs and Trade, 1995).

In other cases the path may be externally driven, coming in almost a complete package: for example, when a company is approached by a foreign agent or distributor seeking to represent the product or service within a specific foreign market. Because of the manner in which the approach is made, effectively the company is making the overall mode decision (exporting versus other main modes) and its specific form, as well as the foreign partner and market decisions in one package (in Figure 8.1, this is shown as simultaneous decision making). This could, of course, be an outcome of preceding international inward operations, exposing exporting options and contacts, representing another potentially important stage, and elongation in the path to exporting (Welch and Luostarinen, 1993). The Internet and the international exposure that it brings for all companies has the potential to pitch many companies rapidly into exporting before the step has been evaluated and planned. The government sometimes acts as an external change agent, stimulating domestic companies to consider exporting possibilities, through incentive schemes, publicity campaigns, and the like, or via direct approach – perhaps to encourage a company to join a particular exporting programme, as in exporting groups – before any exporting plans have been made (Welch et al., 1998).

While the empirical evidence indicates that many companies start to export through external approaches or stimulation, this is not always the case, with many companies going through a more orderly and systematic path of considering whether to 'go international', perhaps favouring exporting, but undertaking foreign market investigations, seeking advice from internationalized companies and individuals with relevant experience in their network, or utilizing assistance from government trade promotion agencies, banks and other relevant players in the international field. In a large Australian study of new exporters, 25 per cent were classified as 'successful intenders', whereas 50 per cent were defined as 'accidentals' that become exporters without original intention, for example as an unexpected opportunity emerged (Austrade, 2001, 33). Out of this process will come a range of information, often with mode bias, which, when combined with the perspective of key decision makers within a company, will determine whether exporting will occur, and, if so, its likely form. In some instances the feedback from the investigation will be so negative as to encourage a decision not to go ahead with the international move at all (Wiedersheim-Paul et al., 1978).

As already noted, the decision to go ahead with exporting, and then in a specific form, could be part of a package, that is, occurring simultaneously (see Figure 8.1). This is most likely to take place in situations where a potential intermediary approaches the manufacturer, offering to represent the company in a specific foreign market. For example, the Australian yacht fittings company, Ronstan, began exporting operations through an initial, fortuitous on-site visit by a Canadian pilot with an interest in yachting, who established an agency in Canada and began importing Ronstan products. Approaches by potential intermediaries are common for companies participating in international trade fairs which bring together sellers, purchasers, suppliers and intermediaries looking for new prospects (Rosson and Seringhaus, 1995, 1996). For example, in a study of emerging high-technology firms in the US, unsolicited approaches by potential European distributors were an important trigger for internationalization. Much of the contact occurred at US trade fairs attended by European distributors

specifically searching for interesting new products that they could potentially handle (Roberts and Senturia, 1996). Of course, many companies
involve themselves in trade fairs in a deliberate way to find potential intermediaries: the decision to export and the particular form having already
been determined. An example is the Australian company Data Electronics
which, in the early 1990s, used trade fairs as a venue to seek interest from
potential distributors in a wide range of foreign markets. It was after the
fair and initial contact with interested parties that it undertook investigation and evaluation of the potential distributors, with the help of the
Australian government's trade promotion agency (Yeow, 1993).

Trade fairs operate as concentrated networking venues that play an
important part in international marketing, and have a long history in
the European context. That so many deals follow from this environment
demonstrates the convenience factor for companies seeking to start or
expand international activity. The key questions for international marketers of which market to enter, what specific operation mode to employ,
which foreign representative to partner with, and what part of a company's
product and service range to emphasize in foreign markets, may be dealt
with effectively in one decision-making step, driven by the intervention of
an interested external party that presents them in packaged form. In other
cases, however, the issues do not necessarily present themselves in such a
neat package. They are often disconnected, and dealt with in no particular
order. The interests and bias of key players tend to drive how these questions are considered and actioned: it is not uncommon for individuals to
start the process with a specific country bias. Empirical research shows that,
not surprisingly, migrants often go back to their country of origin as the
first step in international expansion when they are in a position to determine this decision, while, more generally, international experience with
specific markets has been shown to have an impact on decision making in
various ways, including the choice of countries of interest (Fletcher and
Bohn, 1998; Simmonds and Smith, 1968). Networks back to a former
country are often maintained, providing a ready-made basis for the development of international operations. Such networks can evolve into broader
multi-country connections, as in the overseas Chinese network, facilitating
international trade (Rauch, 2001).

Thus the exporting form decision is inter-mixed with, and sometimes
influenced by, the way these other key questions are handled, concomi-
tantly or sequentially, and their outcomes. To begin with a focus on a particular market as a starting point necessarily imposes constraints on other,
subsequent questions, such as intermediary options in the foreign market.
Research evidence does not show any firm order of these key decisions or
the level of importance of the mode (exporting) form decision relative to

others. The impact of the Internet is a further complicating factor: it is not clear that companies have a definitive idea at the outset of how to handle the exporting and distribution demands of responding to often unantici-pated international orders via the Internet. Some products and services are amenable to electronic delivery in an international context, but they are limited in scope at this stage (Petersen and Welch, 2003). While this chapter concentrates on the exporting form decision, we nevertheless recognize the broader context of this decision and its potential impact.

Figure 8.1 shows further that the exporting form decision is linked to negotiations activity with potential foreign market representatives. While a potential exporter may have deemed a specific exporting form as being most appropriate to its circumstances, and found a seemingly suitable partner, there is necessarily a round of negotiations to be traversed before a settled arrangement is achieved. There is no certainty about the outcome of this process, even in cases where the initial approach has been made by, for example, the foreign intermediary. Negotiations can develop a life of their own, and it is not uncommon for the parties to go their separate ways because of differences that emerge.

A well-established foreign distributor is likely to have relatively settled ways of doing business and, even though initiating contact, will try to ensure accommodation to that pattern by the exporter that has been the target. Negotiations might encompass those changes which the potential intermediary regards as necessary for the foreign market in question, reflecting differences in the cultural and business context. The potential intermediary could seek various changes in the exporter's product and/or service package, promotional support, extended credit terms, and the like, all of which add to the costs of the exporting activity, perhaps unaccept-ably so. The stronger and better established a foreign market representative, the more likely it is that the exporter will be pushed to make such conces-sions. In some foreign markets there may be a limited choice of on-the-ground foreign representatives, so that the exporter could be called upon to 'sell' a case to be taken on board, including 'sweetening' the deal through extended support and other incentives and gifts. Finding appropriate foreign intermediaries and negotiating acceptable arrangements can be a demanding exercise in certain markets (the Japanese market is often mentioned in this respect) so that some companies see themselves as effectively being forced to look for alternative servicing forms (Czinkota and Ronkainen, 2001). Thus, in Figure 8.1, the exporting form decision and negotiation processes are shown as potentially leading back to a reconsid-eration of the overall mode for the market/s in question.

In situations where exporting is part of a broader mode package, such as when connected to international franchising or outward foreign direct

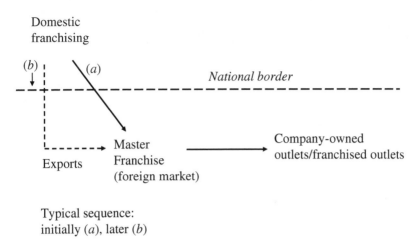

Typical sequence:
initially (*a*), later (*b*)

Figure 8.2   Exporting as second-line choice

investment, the process and choice of exporting form may be governed by decision making with respect to the primary mode, with exporting fitting within the broader context. For example, as illustrated in Figure 8.2, the initiating processes and influences with respect to international operations might lead to a decision to franchise, with exporting added at a later stage as operations in the foreign market unfold, in a support role.

EXPORTING MODE FORM

Once exporting has been chosen, or adopted, by a company as the method of servicing a foreign market, it has a number of options or mode forms available to it in achieving foreign market penetration, although, as noted above, this may be part of a complete package solution. The broad options available to companies are shown in Figure 8.3, excluding the establishment of an owned sales facility in the form of a sales subsidiary or sales office to handle the exporting activity within the foreign market. Because it involves direct investment it will be treated within that section (Chapter 10), even though it may be set up specifically for the purpose of supporting the company's exporting operations. There are cases where a foreign distributor is used alongside a company's sales subsidiary within the foreign market, although the sales subsidiary tends to be established at some time after the initial distributor set-up. In some instances, however, a company may have an eye to such an arrangement when the entry process is occurring (Petersen et al., 2001). Also there are many examples of companies

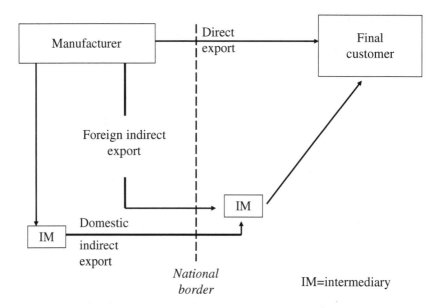

Figure 8.3   Export operations

using more than one distributor in some foreign markets – the US is often geographically split up for distribution purposes – and these may be supported through the establishment of a warehouse or other storage facility, perhaps set up within a free trade zone (see Chapter 6; McNaughton, 2002; Petersen and Welch, 2002).

DOMESTIC INDIRECT EXPORT

As Figure 8.3 indicates, one important exporting path, particularly in the initial stages of internationalization, involves the use of intermediaries located within a company's domestic market: so-called 'domestic indirect export'. For a sample of Greek SMEs, in 6.1 per cent of cases, foreign operation mode use involved indirect domestic export (Dimitratos and Lioukas, 2004, 463). A study of Finnish industrial SMEs found that 35.3 per cent of companies began their exporting activities through domestic-based intermediaries (Luostarinen et al., 1994, 228). Trading companies represent a major component of this diverse group. They have long played a key role in the internationalization of Japanese companies, still handling a high proportion of Japan's total foreign trade, including both imports and exports, as well as increasing involvement in the service sector, including franchising

(Shao and Herbig, 1993). The convenience of using trading companies that operate in the domestic market, from the perspective of potential exporters, is obvious: such activity may amount to little more than a normal domestic transaction. The exporting 'work' is carried out by the trading company. In some cases the resulting exporting activity may be viewed in almost abstract terms by the producer. A major consideration for the potential exporter is the ability to tap into the global distribution and information networks of the trading companies and their understanding of the requirements of different foreign markets – an attractive prospect for a company with no international experience. The trading company route to exporting tends to be seen as a relatively low-commitment, low-risk way of getting started in foreign markets, of testing foreign market receptivity to what a company has to offer. In this sense it does represent a mental start to exporting activity. Even in this limited form, it brings a foreign focus, and may set in motion changes within the company that reflect the new involvement, particularly if the trading company requests a number of changes for the foreign market, such as to a product's features or packaging.

While trading companies offer a range of potential advantages for exporters, these do not apply to all firms, and they can act in the longer term to retard internationalization of the producer. The large trading companies might carry competing lines, thereby making them less attractive as intermediaries. For small firms starting out, there is a concern about becoming 'lost' in the trading companies' long list of clients. While the breadth of coverage of products and services by some of the trading companies is very extensive, this can never extend to all areas, especially where sophisticated and fast-moving technology is concerned, requiring unique or highly specialized knowledge and skills for marketing and servicing. It is noteworthy that, in a study of foreign mode use by 246 high-technology UK companies, trading companies appeared not to be used at all in the main foreign market, initially or subsequently (Burgel and Murray, 2000). Without close foreign market contact, the producer may be unaware of the limitations of a trading company in selling its product or service. In the longer term, because the producer is removed from involvement in the ultimate market, there is an information and control gap. Without direct involvement in the foreign marketing process, there is a lack of learning about the foreign market and exporting in general, as well as the development of key networks, important aspects of the ability to deepen and extend international operations.

A Japanese government official has expressed concern about the potential constraining effect of trading companies on Japanese companies' internationalization: 'the flexibility of the shosha (trading companies) is so extensive that it may be retarding the maturing of the rest of Japan Inc. "If there is a bad side to the trading companies, it's that they are so good at this that the manufacturers never develop their own international abilities", says a Miti official. "They rely too much on the trading companies"' (Sender, 1996, 50). In a study of food exports by US companies it was found that foreign buyers preferred to deal directly with the source of supply rather than a trading company, and that direct lines of communication between buyer and processor were favoured when problems arose or product modifications needed to be made (Vantreese, 1992; Durham and Lyon, 1997). An Australian food industry consultant, advising Australian companies seeking to penetrate the Japanese market has argued: 'It's OK to start with a trading company, but it is essential to get to know your customers . . . The lesson for Australian export managers is that they must NOT leave things totally in the hands of the big trading companies. They won't like it, but you must insist that they take you to visit your customers. You must establish a relationship with them, and you can then move on to opening a representative office and do it yourself' (Davis, 1993, 77). Given the list of advantages typically ascribed to trading companies, it is of note that some US studies reveal small firms questioning trading companies' usefulness in 'initiating or promoting export endeavours' (Castaldi et al., 1992, 23).

Trading companies are not the only form of domestic intermediary that companies use to create foreign sales. In the US, export management companies (EMCs) are an important form. Unlike trading companies they often do not act as customers for the exporter, effectively managing the exporting activity on behalf of the exporter. They could be likened to an outsourced export department for the exporter performing a wide range of exporting services, perhaps including market research, selling activities, financing, documentation and negotiations (Albaum et al., 2002; Castaldi et al., 1992). While many EMCs still operate on a commission basis (perhaps with a retainer), others have become more like trading companies, and increasingly so according to one study, operating on their own account, assuming title to the exported products they handle (Perry, 1992). Export houses are heavily used by exporters in the UK to achieve export sales. While offering many services to exporters, their main role is similar to that of trading companies: buying the goods off the UK exporter and fully undertaking the foreign distribution and selling function (Young et al., 1989). There are different types of export agents that operate in companies' domestic markets, offering a range of exporting services: from limited consulting services up to the full range, as noted above with EMCs, on a commission or fee for service basis.

In some cases, buying offices in a country, acting on behalf of foreign importers or on their own behalf, for example as part of large foreign retailers, purchase local products and undertake the exporting process in a similar manner to that by the trading companies. The literature notes many examples of exporters being assisted in penetrating foreign markets through cooperative arrangements with other exporters within the same market. In so-called 'piggyback' arrangements, one company uses the facilities of another, including foreign distribution networks, to handle their exporting activity, typically in situations where products are complementary as viewed by foreign customers (Albaum et al., 2002; Young et al., 1989). Sometimes formal cooperative marketing institutions or groups, common in the agricultural sector, are set up to handle the exporting function for domestic producers, often facilitated by government support or operating in a government-mandated monopoly foreign selling role (Welch, 1992; Welch et al., 1998). For example, Colombia's National Federation of Coffee Growers has acted for a long time as 'buyer, marketer, technical adviser and banker to Colombia's 560,000 coffee growers', with global activities under the Juan Valdez brand name, including a move into franchised retail operations (*Economist*, 2005, 37). Clearly, there are many export intermediary options that may be accessible by a company within its domestic environment – all of them attractive to a greater or lesser extent because of their ease of access for the would-be exporter and lower cost, risk and commitment that typically has to be taken on. On the whole, though, most exporters do not use this path, pointing to the greater exposure to and perceived attractiveness of other routes which we shall now examine.

FOREIGN INDIRECT EXPORT

As Figure 8.3 illustrates, exporting via foreign intermediaries is a second major path which companies may use in servicing foreign markets. In a study of Finnish industrial SMEs, 32.9 per cent of companies began exporting through foreign intermediaries (Luostarinen et al., 1994, 228). An investigation of the foreign operation mode used by a sample of Greek SMEs in established and emerging foreign markets found that, in 57 per cent of cases, exporting via foreign intermediaries was the mode used (Dimitratos and Lioukas, 2004, 463). This was similar to an Australian study of small exporters in which 60 per cent of firms reported utilizing foreign intermediaries in their exporting activity (*Business Review Weekly*, 1996). A UK foreign mode use study of 246 high technology companies (average size 20 employees), focused on the companies' most important foreign market, found that, on entry, in 48 per cent of cases, exporting via foreign intermediaries had been used, and this had risen to 53 per cent at the time of the study (Burgel and Murray, 2000, 47). Clearly, exporting through foreign intermediaries is an important path of foreign market exploitation. Research shows that companies tend to use more than one channel in their overall exporting operations, in responding to the circumstances encountered in different foreign markets (Munro and Beamish, 1987). In a large Australian study of SMEs' internationalization patterns and processes (532 companies), it was found that 'about 65 per cent of the ISMEs [internationalizing SMEs] used more than one strategic option for internationalisation, and over 70 different "patterns" of combinations were evident' (Dept. of Foreign Affairs and Trade, 1995, 26). In the services sector, a large study of foreign operation mode choice by US firms revealed a quite varied pattern of usage of intermediaries among different industries: from a high of 38.4 per cent in computer services to zero in advertising and accounting (Erramilli, 1990).

Taken overall, there are many reasons for foreign intermediary use by exporters. The seemingly lower cost and financial risk associated with intermediaries compared to the attempt to carry out equivalent activities through one's own staff or by setting up a selling operation in the foreign market are important considerations, particularly when there is uncertainty about the size and viability of the market. As a perceived lower-cost method, using foreign intermediaries is often viewed as a way of expanding to a wider range of foreign markets. In some cases, intermediaries have international operations themselves, so that an exporter can expand to new foreign markets with the same intermediary with minimal effort. The intermediary's local market knowledge and marketing infrastructure are a major advantage for a potential exporter with limited experience or knowledge of the market in question. Being a local, the intermediary is usually better equipped to deal with cross-cultural issues, including differences in language and ways of doing business, and government relations. These were important considerations for the Chinese multinational, Haier Group, which has widespread international operations and has become one of the world's largest producers of home appliances. Haier has relied heavily on distributors in its foreign markets rather than setting up its own marketing operations to overcome the disadvantages of foreignness in so many new markets while undertaking rapid and diverse international expansion (Liu and Li, 2002).

However, utilizing a local intermediary does not always deliver advantageous local knowledge and connections. A large US multinational (confidentiality restriction on identity) had an explicit policy in the early 1990s of using foreign intermediaries in culturally and physically distant markets because of aspects such as low cost of market entry; obtaining local cultural familiarity; accessing local business networks; obtaining feedback from the relevant market; and receiving advice on product and promotional adaptation. However, this did not work in the Korean market because the lower status of the Korean distributor meant that it had thinly developed networks with, and therefore access to, key customers within the large Korean conglomerates. After about two years without success, the multinational changed its mode – to a joint venture – and involved a senior vice president in the marketing process, ensuring that the company could achieve access at the highest levels in the conglomerates. Similarly, a recent study of Australian project operators found that locals and visiting Australian businessmen had access to different sets of networks in some Asian markets, and different information and influence as a result (Welch, 2005).

Despite the heavy use of foreign intermediaries in companies' international operations, many studies show that they are a, if not the, major cause of problems for exporters. Early research on internationalization revealed that, as foreign market penetration proceeded, companies frequently switched modes, moving on to the establishment of some form of owned sales operations (Johanson and Wiedersheim-Paul, 1975). Other research indicated problems with using intermediaries at several levels, notably in finding, selecting, negotiating with, and signing up appropriate intermediaries, and in maintaining effective relationships over time (Howard and Borgia, 1990; Samiee and Walters, 1990). In some respects there is a certain inevitability about the evolution of tension in relationships between intermediaries and exporters as operations develop: initially the exporter may be highly dependent on the intermediary, given a lack of networks and experience in, and knowledge of, the foreign market. This is bound to change with foreign market involvement, such as via market visits and on-the-ground contact with foreign customers, resulting in a stronger ability and desire to control developments in the foreign market, particularly if sales increase and show even greater promise. The approach to achieving greater control over a foreign intermediary was expressed by the head of a Danish company's Asian operations in the following terms: 'when I am out here it is easier to kick them. The intermediaries have more than one product line, so they often prefer the ones where money comes in the easiest. The chances of them doing something with your product are greater if you breathe [down their] neck all the time' (Nielsen, 1998, 52).

Another Danish company's regional Asian head commented: 'The agents don't tell you who they sell to. It is their way of putting pressure on you. Therefore, you visit the agent and go along for customer visits to keep up-to-date with the markets' (ibid., 36). The problem of parallel exports noted earlier is an illustration of the difficulties of, and consequences of not, maintaining control over the activities of intermediaries, particularly distributors, of even knowing what they are doing in the assigned, or other, foreign markets. A quantitative investigation of foreign intermediary replacements and switches to in-house operations by Danish companies found that control difficulties were a common trigger for both types of shifts, although the exporter's accumulation of market knowledge only appeared as a factor in replacements (Benito et al., 2005).

The concern about control, and of not being locked into reliance on just one intermediary in a given foreign market, leads some firms to seek non-exclusive intermediary arrangements, opening up the option of the appointment of another intermediary if problems arise with an existing appointee. Not surprisingly, foreign intermediaries typically look for exclusive arrangements, although this is partly related to the size of market and extent of an intermediary's marketing infrastructure. An alternative approach used by some exporters is to appoint exclusive intermediaries, but only within restricted regions in a foreign market. By appointing, for example, four exclusive intermediaries in one market, the exporter limits the potential market damage created by problems associated with any one intermediary, helping to ensure the maintenance of viable overall activity in the market in question. A variant, used by an Australian company, was described as 'Sometimes we appoint, say, five agents for the first year and then select the best and most reliable' (Price Waterhouse Associates, 1982, 35).

The control concern tends to be heightened in legal jurisdictions, such as in European code law-based countries, that provide substantial protection for intermediaries in situations where exporters seek termination of arrangements: overriding any contractual agreements that might have been entered into between the parties. In common-law countries, such as the UK, Australia and the US, legal rights are determined by the terms of a contract signed by both parties. As a result, some exporters have different intermediary policies for common-law and code-law countries, or other countries where it is difficult to dispense with intermediaries, for seemingly justifiable reasons such as non-performance: for instance, undertaking far more detailed search and evaluation of potential intermediaries in code-law countries. Others have adopted the approach of only entering into relatively short-term agreements with their foreign intermediaries, even as little as one year, as a way of attempting to build in greater flexibility. In addition, there are examples of exporters entering into verbal agreements with distributors, again as a way of enhancing flexibility and perceived control. A Danish company in Asia, in order to avoid the problem of severance payments to intermediaries on termination and to make it easier to get out of existing arrangements, adopted a policy of not having written contracts with their intermediaries (Nielsen, 1998). Of course, such approaches have to be negotiated, with many potential intermediaries wary of limited-term, insecure arrangements, so that the number, and even possibility, of potential intermediaries may be very limited.

AGENTS VERSUS DISTRIBUTORS

While there are many variations in the precise form and structure of intermediary arrangements, two main forms can be identified – agents and distributors – with significant legal and other differences in market servicing characteristics. The terms 'foreign agent' and 'distributor' are often used loosely and interchangeably, and each sometimes in a generic way as an equivalent of the term 'intermediary', but the distinction is important from a company perspective when seeking the most appropriate intermediary form for exports. In simple terms, an agent operates on behalf of the exporter in the foreign market, performing a range of functions in seeking to facilitate sales of the exporter's products and/or services, taking orders, usually on a commission/retainer basis, but does not purchase and take title to the product/s. In contrast, a distributor does purchase the exporter's product, thus not only representing the exporter in the foreign market, but acting as its direct customer, and operates independently from the exporter. Also there are important legal differences in this distinction: by purchasing the product and taking title, the distributor takes on a higher level of legal responsibility for the performance of the product in the relevant foreign market, compared to the agent. Local warranties apply to a distributor but not an agent. In general, there is a higher degree of control in agency relationships, particularly over marketing activities, than in distributor arrangements, but higher financial risk in the sense that the cost of a customer's non-payment or slow payment is borne by the exporter rather than the agent.

The problem of parallel exports noted earlier is indicative of control problems that can arise in distributor arrangements that stem from the acquisition of title to the exporter's products, introducing a range of rights that are protected in various ways under local laws, particularly within the EU (Gourlay, 1994). In a study of the channel relationships of 120 Norwegian firms, Solberg and Nes (2002) found that perceived marketing control by exporters was greater under foreign agency than under distributor arrangements. An earlier investigation of US exporters concluded that agents operated as a 'quasi-integration mode' (Bello and Lohtia, 1995). The situation in the foreign market can become even more complex when an agent organizes distribution through an established distributor in that market.

Agents tend to be favoured over distributors in situations where market volume is likely to be limited and the exporter is seeking to limit the cost of market development. For slow-moving, expensive products, distributors are likely to be less prepared to become involved because of the cost of holding inventories, so that agents may be the more feasible path. For products requiring spare parts and servicing support, such as with machinery and equipment, distributors tend to be the favoured route (Gourlay, 1994). The demands of technical representation may restrict both agent and distributor forms. The Australian company, Autoscan Systems, marketed a technologically advanced product to laboratories, mainly at universities, that required considerable direct contact and technical discussions, and only when this had been settled, and funds applied for by the university, did an agent come into play, hired by the university to handle the commercial negotiations and arrange importation (Yeung, 1993).

The choice of agent versus distributor, apart from the type of broad considerations noted above, is undoubtedly affected by company-specific concerns, the nature of its preceding international experience, including commitments entered into and outcomes from past activity, and approaches it has received. As an illustration, in the early 1990s an Australian company in the metals business, Pasminco, despite the attempt to undertake more direct business with foreign customers, still relied heavily on sales agents in many foreign markets. The stated reasons for continuing to use agents were the experience and continuity that the agents provided in certain foreign markets – a consistent Pasminco face – for example, in Taiwan and India, the same agents had been used for over 20 years; because of fluctuating demand for metals, there was not an assured basis for establishment of local sales offices with permanent sales staff, whereas their agents represented exporters in other areas that tended to balance activity over time; the agents provided considerable market intelligence and filtered much of the administrative workload associated with a diverse customer base; the agents provided local knowledge and eased the language burden, and undertook credit checks and assisted with the importing process, such as dealing with customs, for inexperienced customers (Horneman, 1993).

As to the preference for distributors, it is often the perceived lower costs relative to a staffed sales office/subsidiary that are stressed, rather than differences relative to agency arrangements. Compared to agencies, though, the general characteristic influencing choice that appears to be important is the up-front commitment that distributors are required to make in purchasing the goods in question. This tends to be seen as creating a stronger incentive to achieve satisfactory sales outcomes. In addition, the fact that distributors have to shoulder a range of other responsibilities because of their greater liability under local laws, compared to agents, is often viewed by exporters as reducing their own liability in foreign markets, for example, with regard to local warranties applying to goods sold, that become the responsibility of distributors. Nevertheless, numerous studies demonstrate that exporters' expectations are frequently not met by their appointed distributors, for a variety of reasons, including lack of market response to the goods or services in question. Even worse, there have been examples of distributors deliberately playing down some exporters' products or, in the case of a small Australian biotechnology company (confidentiality restriction on name), in its early internationalization having one of its products 'locked up' by distributors both in Japan and in the US as a way of stopping its appearance in the marketplace. Orders were made by the distributors, and paid for, but the stock simply remained in the warehouse, as the exporter eventually discovered.

SELECTION OF INTERMEDIARIES

Given the importance of intermediaries to the success of exporters, and the extent of problems exporters claim to encounter with their intermediaries, the selection process would appear to be a critical step in using them as the path to exporting. Nevertheless, many exporters, especially in the earlier stages of export development, make rushed decisions when choosing intermediaries, with limited search and evaluation of alternatives. This may be because of the perception of limited time and resources to conduct a thorough investigation, perhaps because of the pressure to respond to an unsolicited foreign inquiry or order, as commonly occurs, or because of an approach by an intermediary to represent the exporter in a foreign market, for example, as noted above, as a result of participation at a trade fair, even if the exposure of intermediary interest is a deliberate activity. Future problems can be avoided, or created, during the selection process, and experienced exporters frequently indicate how much more care they take with the process compared to earlier decisions. Managerial guidelines for evaluation and selection of intermediaries are readily available, and government services are frequently employed in generating candidates (see Albaum et al., 2002).

INTERMEDIARY RELATIONSHIPS, PERFORMANCE AND SWITCHES

The above analysis indicates that finding a suitable foreign intermediary, in whatever form, and negotiating an acceptable arrangement can be a demanding exercise for the exporter. In the long run, however, much of the foreign market success in using intermediaries depends on the way in which the relationship between the parties evolves. For example, in a recent study of 290 US manufacturers using foreign distributors, it was concluded that 'Distributors are shown to accomplish the sales and profit goals of their manufacturer principals to a greater extent when the ties that bind the partners are close . . . Conversely, trading partners whose weak ties limit information flows, adaptiveness, and collaborative spirit appear to suffer a performance penalty' (Bello et al., 2003, 10, 11). This research also indicated that, not surprisingly, resource adequacy was a factor in the development of close ties: the establishment and maintenance of positive relationships with intermediaries is a resource-demanding exercise. Despite their importance, however, for various reasons, it is common for exporter–intermediary relationships to become troubled or to break down to the point where exporters seek to terminate the arrangement and seek a replacement or to change mode altogether. Where sales prospects in the market concerned are deemed to be very positive, there is a strong incentive to take action. Even when the intermediary is demonstrating adequate performance, as noted above, the incentive to take over control of the foreign activity can be a powerful change factor.

Contrarily, research also indicates that a certain comfort level on the part of the exporter often develops with acceptable intermediary performance and a positive relationship between the parties. Early empirical research on the reasons for shifting to establishment of a sales subsidiary in the foreign market showed that the conditions supporting the move had existed for some time (the level of foreign business was the main quantifiable factor) and it needed a trigger to start the push for action to be taken. Examples of change stimuli were approach by a foreign party, change in foreign competition, and a new export manager; but mainly it was an emerging problem with the foreign intermediary (Ford et al., 1981). Even if it is relatively straightforward to drop an intermediary, this may be difficult because of the depth and breadth of the business enacted through the intermediary. To the extent that the product range handled by a given intermediary expands over time, along with sales and marketing network development, it becomes more difficult to contemplate, let alone accomplish, removal of the intermediary and building up an alternative operation.

Exporters often stress the fact that it is the foreign intermediary that builds relationships with foreign customers, and, to the extent that these are close and highly personalized, exporters run the risk of having their customers move with the intermediary in replacement situations. This concern was expressed by the head of a Danish company's Asian regional operation in the following terms: 'The loyalty is often towards the intermediary. If he drops us and takes on another brand he will be able to continue with many of his customers. The personal relationship will control which product the customer will buy' (Nielsen, 1998, 71; see also the case of Nilfisk in Spain, in Petersen et al., 2000). In some foreign contexts, certain distributors are known to actively discourage contact between the exporter and customers in the foreign market, as a way of maintaining control of operations, generating dependence and ensuring their position as distributors within that market. As these examples illustrate, the intermediary inevitably builds a position of some strength in the local context, and may well have the option of representing other foreign companies. This is apart from the legal and cultural constraints in many foreign contexts on removing intermediaries, as noted above.

The reality of many intermediary–exporter relationships is that the exporter is effectively the 'junior partner', with local information, knowledge and networks providing a considerable power base for the intermediary, and an ability to influence marketing processes and policies by the exporter – even having the dominant voice in some situations (Lye and Hamilton, 2001; Leonidou, 1989). Two studies of Norwegian exporters found that they rated foreign intermediaries as one of the most important sources of information relevant to their exporting operations, both preceding appointment and as the activity unfolded (Benito et al., 1993; Walters, 1996). It may take considerable effort and cost for the exporter to develop additional sources of information in the foreign market that are independent of the intermediary, with some risk of generating distrust on the part of the intermediary. Nevertheless, another study of Norwegian exporters concluded that exporters collecting information in foreign markets beyond that supplied by their intermediaries performed better than exporters relying only on information from intermediaries (Gripsrud et al., 2000). Exporters often point to the need to develop independent sources of information in the foreign market to enhance control and provide a more assured basis for decision making about the form of future involvement.

The problems associated with terminating foreign intermediaries have led some exporters to develop approaches which build greater flexibility into intermediary arrangements and processes to make it easier to enact foreign market servicing changes. Lego, the Danish toy producer, discussed future integration with some of its Asian distributors. Likewise, Scanbech, the Danish producer of packaging materials for pharmaceuticals, when it set up four new agents in Germany, advised them that they should consider the arrangement as temporary as it was likely to set up a sales subsidiary in the future (Petersen et al., 2000). Another Danish company has a set of deliberate policies surrounding switches from intermediary to sales subsidiary establishment, often by acquisition, that are initiated sometimes

years in advance of the actual step. The process tends to be initiated when
sales potential reaches about $US5–6 million. Marketing staff are often sta-
tioned with the intermediary to 'help' with marketing. However, in cases
where it wants to phase out the intermediary, the company is prepared to
use transfer pricing policies or reduced sales support to make the operation
less viable for the intermediary. The concern is that, if the business grows
successfully in the foreign market, the intermediary will have greater leverage and reason to fight removal, with potentially damaging consequences
(Nielsen, 1998). As exporters anticipate the likelihood that problems with
their foreign intermediaries might occur, or if market and mode strategy
changes by the exporter are to be instituted that entail a move away from
the use of intermediaries, there is an inevitable concern about the ability
and cost of undertaking intermediary replacement. This seems to be
increasingly leading to a variety of approaches to ease the switching cause,
including the development of built-in arrangements that are sometimes
negotiated up-front, as in the above Lego and Scanbech cases (Petersen
et al., 2000).

MANAGEMENT OF INTERMEDIARY RELATIONSHIPS

Preceding analysis has stressed the fact that exporting activity often starts
in a relatively unplanned fashion, and that form 'choice' tends to be part of
this picture. In many cases the path is driven by intermediary approaches
which define the exporting form. Research indicates a relatively high drop-
out rate among early exporters and, inevitably, this applies to intermediary
connections (Welch and Wiedersheim-Paul, 1980a). The preceding section
provides evidence of the often fraught relationships between exporters and
their foreign intermediaries, the performance implications of relationship
quality, and dissatisfaction on the part of exporters frequently leading to
attempts to switch intermediary or mode. A study of the UK intermediary
relationships of 21 Canadian manufacturing exporters over a seven-year
period provides some indication of the chequered history that is sometimes
associated with this exporting form (Rosson, 1987). Of the 21 relationships,
only one was growing successfully after the seven years; 11 had ended and
nine were described as static or inert. The driving forces behind outcomes
were changed interaction between the parties, such as an altered role for the
distributor; changes within the manufacturer, leading, for example, to the
UK market being given lower priority in two cases; environmental changes;
and five cases where there was little overall change. Where relationships were terminated, in four cases there was no replacement, because of

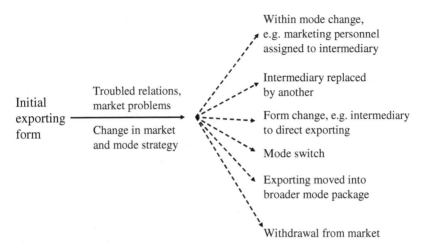

Figure 8.4   Exporting form and mode changes

company closure and market withdrawal. The replacement forms were quite diverse: use of a different distributor; switch to an agency form; move to direct exporting; and establishment of the exporter's own sales network in the UK. Some of the changes that exporters institute in response to the perceived need to alter an existing exporting arrangement are shown in Figure 8.4.

Clearly, the success or otherwise of indirect exports via foreign intermediaries is heavily dependent on the initial choice of intermediary in a foreign market, and then management of the resulting intermediary relationship. There is a considerable body of research and managerially oriented literature addressing the issue of intermediary management, with many 'how-to' publications, and advisory and information support mechanisms associated with the trade assistance bodies that governments maintain in various forms. The research and managerially oriented literature are aligned in stressing the importance for the exporter of developing a positive relationship with the intermediary, of building trust. Cavusgil et al. (2004, 7) argue that 'trust makes the relationship function'. Relationship building covers many aspects, including adequate margins and credit terms; delivery reliability; exporter visits and responsive communication; support provided by the exporter in the form of appropriate product information and promotion assistance; training; and technical and service back-up. There appears to be limited faith on the part of exporters in the ability of formal contracts to ensure positive performance by foreign intermediaries, and in their ability to protect the rights of the exporter. Enforceability of the contract is viewed as a problem in the legal environment of many countries, particularly for small firms.

As a result, it is not surprising that so many exporters stress effective relationship management as the only viable long-term strategy to ensure positive outcomes from intermediary use, that the only way to ensure a reasonable degree of control and effective performance is through the development of a positive, committed and active relationship with the foreign intermediary. From a study of Canadian exporters, Munro and Beamish (1987, 328), found that 'the large majority of those sampled tended to believe that good performance from the intermediary could *not* be attained through increased compensation or threats of losing the exporter's business. Rather, the more positive approach of providing increased support was viewed as the means for improving performance. Almost 80 per cent of those sampled reported that this approach had contributed to improvements in their intermediaries' performance over time'. The Danish toy producer, Lego, has used independent distributors extensively in the ASEAN region. However, as a way of enhancing control and improving performance it placed a marketing officer with the distributors in Malaysia and Thailand, which might be considered a half-step toward direct export or sales subsidiary establishment (Petersen et al., 2001).

However, active management of, and relationship building with, intermediaries is resource demanding, particularly on staff, so it is not surprising that exporters with many intermediaries in a range of countries find that they have to limit the extent of foreign visits and interaction. This is despite the recognition of the potential problems this may produce. The sales manager at a Danish manufacturer has commented: 'It is hard to know what is going on out here [SE Asia] when you are only visiting for one day. The intermediary can make a one day set-up with showroom display of your products, and no limit to the plans they have for your products, but it is hard to evaluate the potential. You can visit a customer, but it doesn't give you a realistic picture of actual market potential' (Nielsen, 1998, 51). The manager visited intermediaries over a three-week period twice a year, but stressed that it was necessary to be in daily contact with intermediaries to gain a 'realistic' picture of what was happening in each market. Exporters often refer to the erratic pattern of foreign sales that can arise from infrequent visits to intermediaries and irregular direct contact. There is a tendency for sales to rise after a visit and the flurry of activity associated with it – including additional promotion and customer interaction, involving both exporter and intermediary (see Figure 8.5). The extent of fluctuation of sales is partly dependent on the amount of time between visits: the longer the gap the greater the impact on sales of each visit.

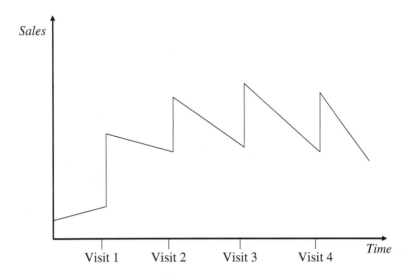

Figure 8.5   Effect of visits by exporter's staff on sales

Interaction with, and active oversight of, the intermediary are being facilitated by the growing use of the Internet and associated relationship software developments. Nevertheless, the relationship management literature indicates that, particularly at the international level, personal and social interactions remain important parts of the effective management of intermediary relationships.

The position of intermediaries, and their approach to the business enacted on behalf of the exporter, are important considerations for exporters, limiting what is feasible in the foreign market. Intermediaries will often serve more than one exporter, and exporters sometimes have unrealistic expectations about the extent of intermediary effort relative to the level of business likely to be generated. Intermediaries are, of course, concerned about the security of the exporter's business, and their own position. The foreign distributor's position has been likened to that of a circus performer engaging in a balancing act. On the one hand, if the distributor achieves strong sales growth, that may become an incentive for the exporter to replace the distributor with a sales subsidiary. On the other hand, if the distributor is perceived as performing too poorly, it risks termination and replacement. For the intermediary, this tends to be the reality that frames the relationship with the exporter, even if good relations evolve. As a result, intermediaries will often have a vested interest in limiting information disclosure, and, in general, operating in a way which maintains a sense of dependence on them by the exporter.

DIRECT EXPORT

The third major form of exporting shown in Figure 8.3 is that of direct or own export, whereby the exporter does not operate through independent intermediaries, in home or foreign markets, but undertakes the activity itself, dealing directly with foreign customers. In the Finnish research, 31.8 per cent of SMEs began with own exporting operations (Luostarinen et al., 1994, 228). For Greek SMEs, direct exports constituted 28.5 per cent of total mode use, whereas the equivalent for UK high-technology firms at entry was 44 per cent, declining to 36 per cent over time (Dimitratos and Lioukas, 2004, 463; Burgel and Murray, 2000, 47). In an earlier Australian study of 'successful exporters', 12 per cent of companies had used only 'direct to customer' in their exporting operations, while 37 per cent used both direct and indirect methods, the choice being dictated by the circumstances of individual markets (Price Waterhouse Associates, 1982). A study of foreign mode choice in the services sector by US firms found substantial variation in the extent of direct service exports between different industries. For engineering and architecture it reached 46.1 per cent, dropping to 25 per cent for management consulting, 23.3 per cent for computer services, and a low of 1.7 per cent for consumer services (Erramilli, 1990). This study indicated that exporting, whether through intermediaries or directly, was more feasible in the case of so-called 'hard services', when production and consumption could be disconnected, as in the case of packaged software and engineering design. A study of Australian companies selling packaged software overseas found that the most frequently employed foreign marketing channel was distributors, used by 41 per cent of companies, followed by direct selling, used by 39 per cent of firms (Gallagher, 1989). Exporting is less common for 'soft services', such as fast food and health care, where disconnection of production and consumption is severely constrained. In general, the direct exporting path is heavily used by firms at all stages of internationalization.

While it is difficult to comment on the exact extent of effect, it can be expected that the increasing development of international E-commerce and extended use of the Internet in all aspects of global commerce will accentuate the use of direct exporting operations. The growing role of the Internet is part of the broad development of international direct marketing activities, and in many cases Internet-based strategies have been developed on the back of other direct marketing forms, and remain in productive co-existence. This includes the more established, but still growing, international operations of direct mail companies, and telemarketing, with direct exporting to foreign customers often linked to these processes.

Even though some Internet-driven companies may be forced ultimately to set up foreign facilities to better service their foreign customers, much of the drive and argument for E-commerce in internationalization is the ability to refrain from any form of direct foreign set-up for extended periods, providing products to foreign customers through direct export. This is likely to be facilitated by the growing digitization of products, allowing delivery directly to foreign customers via the Internet (Petersen and Welch, 2003). Ekeledo and Sivakumar (2004) note that there are many areas of services where exports through electronic networks are common, including design and engineering services, accounting services and data processing. Much of this activity has been associated with the growth of business process outsourcing, with a considerable level of activity being undertaken in India. Technological change is important: digitization has not only widened the array of goods and services that can be provided directly to foreign customers, but it has also provided a wider range of options in terms of foreign market servicing. Intellectual property issues also are a factor, restricting the preparedness to enter into direct exporting arrangements via the Internet, particularly for purely digitized products or services. Some companies have attempted to protect their intellectual property in direct service exporting situations by associating the activity with licensing (Ekeledo and Sivakumar, 2004).

One of the important roles typically performed by a foreign intermediary, the provision of after-sales service in the foreign market, is being replaced in part by the Internet, via websites. Many companies have set up their websites to provide global support for customers – in some cases the bulk of after-sales service is provided through this means (Petersen and Welch, 2003). Of course, much depends on the type of product: some products, such as various types of equipment and machinery, require on-the-ground physical service facilities and staff. This is one of the problems for companies seeking to shift to direct exporting operations: foreign customers become concerned about the ability of the supplier to provide effective maintenance and service of products like machinery when required. A local intermediary is a tangible sign of commitment to this need – better still if this is a subsidiary operation established by the exporter in the local market. There has been considerable debate about the extent to which intermediaries will be by-passed as companies set up direct-to-customer lines via the Internet, using direct exports in the provision of the product and/or service. One study of 50 manufacturers found that the biggest issue facing them in selling online was channel conflict, and there have been many high-profile examples of manufacturers becoming embroiled in damaging conflict with their intermediaries as a result of setting up competitive, Internet-based direct sale lines (Allen, 2000; Petersen and Welch, 2003). However, in a large study of British exporters' use of the Internet as a sales channel in exporting, the use of intermediaries did not appear to conflict with successful use of the direct Internet channel into the foreign market. An interesting conclusion from the study was the importance of the role of a complementary direct export sales force in ensuring success of the 'virtual export channel'. Having a direct sales force substantially increased the chances of success of the virtual channel (Morgan-Thomas and Bridgewater, 2004).

While it is often assumed that the manufacturer has the stronger position when dealing with an intermediary – even dispensing with, or reducing, the intermediary role – when it has the option of Internet-based market servicing, the reverse is also possible. An intermediary that has well established, sophisticated Internet-based connections with its clients in the foreign market, along with physical distribution and servicing facilities, may be in an enhanced position in dealings with the exporter (Petersen and Welch, 2003). Indeed, it has been argued that 'contrary to existing wisdom, intermediaries will play a key role in electronic markets . . . a more likely outcome is the emergence of a class of commercial service providers which we term cybermediaries . . . to facilitate exchanges' (Sarkar et al., 1998).

Something of the thinking behind the adoption of the direct exporting path is revealed in the experience of the large multinational mining company, BHP Billiton, which has recently embarked on a process of replacing agents that have traditionally been used to handle much of its selling activity in many of its foreign markets. Instead, the company will be dealing directly with its foreign customers from two hubs (in Singapore and The Hague) and ten regional offices. Under the new regime, agents are viewed as standing between the company and its customers. According to a company spokesman, 'dealing directly with customers . . . allows BHP Billiton to "know what's going on . . . know where we can push and where we have to back off"' (Bachelard, 2002). Outside the 12 markets that have an on-the-ground operation, the company will be engaged in direct exporting activity.

For BHP Billiton, the resulting direct relationship with its customers was a powerful argument for the move to direct or own exporting, as is the case for many other exporters. This is a particular concern for companies selling technologically sophisticated and complex products, requiring a high level of technical interaction and communication between the exporter and foreign customer. The head of the Danish company Jensen's Asian subsidiary, a provider of equipment for the laundry industry, has commented: 'We provide a lot of support. When you sell such machines, you don't just sell the machine, but also confidence. If the customer has a problem, we must be able to help him. Furthermore, it is a complex product, so you need a lot of technical knowledge in the sale' (Nielsen, 1998, 39–40). Agents or distributors are often viewed as lacking the technical competence to be able to handle such products effectively. From another perspective, many exporters regard customer relationships as being critical to market control, so critical that they cannot be left to independent organizations to manage.

In general, direct exporting tends to be regarded as delivering a far higher level of control of the exporting operation than with indirect exporting – domestic or foreign. This applies to all aspects of exporting, negotiations, customer contact, technical interaction and marketing policies, such as pricing. The lack of control of pricing by the exporter over its distributor is a common cause of disagreements between the parties: the main cause in one Canadian study (Munro and Beamish, 1987). Research indicates that 'unsatisfactory experiences' with intermediaries is one of the reasons for the decision to switch to use of direct exporting, or to the establishment of a sales subsidiary (Price Waterhouse Associates, 1982). By direct involvement in the marketing process in the foreign market, the exporter can ensure that more complete, or unfiltered, market information is obtained. At the same time, through direct involvement, the exporter is able to build an in-house knowledge and skills base, potentially forming a springboard to the establishment of an on-the-ground presence if sales grow sufficiently.

However, these attractions are purchased at a price. A high demand is placed on the use of travelling sales staff, at considerable cost if frequent foreign visits and direct interaction are deemed necessary in a wide range of foreign markets. The exporter faces all the demands of cross-cultural adaptation, rather than working through a local, with all the potential for conflict, misinterpretation and error as a consequence. An Australian electrical engineering company that switched back from direct exporting to using agents commented: 'We used to deal direct but are using agents more and more because they're locals who can deal with the local red tape much better than we could. We get too frustrated' (Price Waterhouse Associates, 1982, 37). The international marketing literature has long stressed the importance of cultural sensitivity in operating in foreign environments (LaBahn and Harich, 1997). As it is, direct exporters frequently have to call on assistance from various local service suppliers, for example to provide marketing and promotion assistance, and perhaps translation and interpreter services. In contrast, many, if not all, of these purchased services would have been provided through an intermediary. At some point, if sales are growing, the difficulties of managing operations from a distance provide an incentive for the establishment of an on-the-ground sales facility. This has to be done from scratch, though, without the possibility of integrating one's intermediary and its existing operation, or its staff, as many exporters have done as the path to increased foreign market involvement, but also without the need to undergo the potential trauma of dismissing an ensconced intermediary (Benito et al., 2005).

CONCLUSION

The evidence presented in this chapter confirms the importance of exporting as a broad foreign operation mode used by companies in international
business expansion. Exporting is employed by large and small companies,
in primary, manufacturing and service sectors, at all stages of internationalization – on its own, but frequently in combination with other modes. For
many internationalizing companies, exporting is a first step into international operations, and frequently it is seen as a relatively simple, even
obvious, way to go, to the extent that other mode options tend not even to
be considered. Fortuitous approaches by interested foreign parties, including potential local or foreign intermediaries, are common, and partly
explain the heavy resort to exporting. However, the adoption of exporting
is only a first phase in its adoption as a foreign operation mode. The exporting form is a critical decision, although this might be part of a package if
an interested intermediary is the trigger for exporting adoption.

The exporting form options that may be available to the exporter cover a
wide range, from the simple, convenient step of utilizing a home market-
based intermediary, such as a trading company, through to undertaking a
large part of the exporting process on its own, so-called 'direct' or 'own'
exporting, short of the establishment of a sales subsidiary within the foreign
market. Foreign-based intermediaries remain a key component of exporting
activity – the principal form judging by diverse empirical studies. Although
the distinction, broadly speaking, between agents and distributors is important in legal and marketing terms, both forms offer exporters the ability to
access on-the-ground representation in foreign markets, and local contextual
knowledge, networks and cultural sensitivity, without having to commit
themselves to the establishment of facilities, supporting a more widespread
process of foreign market expansion. These characteristics are particularly
significant for firms in the early stages of international market penetration.

Despite the obvious advantages and extent of use of both domestic
and foreign intermediaries in exporting, a consistent message of empirical
research on exporters is that intermediaries are a major problem area.
Inappropriate activity by intermediaries, including parallel exports, disputation, poor relationships and lack of adherence to exporters' marketing and
pricing policies, is one of the issues that places a premium on effective relationship management, but often leads to moves by exporters to change either
the intermediary or the means of servicing a foreign market. Direct exporting may become part of the picture in that it involves taking charge of the
exporting activity in the foreign market, thus ensuring control over policy
implementation without having to work through an independent organization. Particularly for complex, high-technology products, with high technical

communication demands, this may be a powerful argument for using a direct exporting regime from the outset. However, appropriately supporting a direct exporting approach is demanding at a number of levels, including the availability and utilization of technical and sales staff in foreign markets. As a result, at some stage, if sales grow and prospects are good, the move to establishment of a sales subsidiary tends to become attractive, and the decision is not constrained by having to get out of an intermediary commitment. In general, whatever the starting form, exporting is often a stepping-stone to the use of another foreign operation mode, or modes, because of problems, or market growth that is seen to warrant a change in foreign market and mode strategy (see Figure 8.4). Rather than a complete switch of modes, though, exporting is frequently carried forward into a broader mode package, sometimes remaining the prime component of foreign market servicing, but in other situations performing a more supplementary role.

REFERENCES

Albaum, G., J. Strandskov and E. Duerr (2002), *International Marketing and Export Management*, 4th edn, Harlow, UK: Pearson Education.
Allen, L. (2000), 'Channel conflict crumbles', *The Forrester Report*, March (www.forrester.com), 1–16.
Austrade (2001), *Knowing & Growing the Exporter Community*, Sydney: Austrade.
Australian (2004), 'Microsoft goes local in Asia', 22 June, IT Business 7.
Australian (2005), 'Microsoft cuts price to reduce copying', 4 October, 31.
Bachelard, M. (2002), 'Heavy mettle', *Australian*, 19 July, 30.
Bello, D.C., C. Chelariu and L. Zhang (2003), 'The antecedents and performance consequences of relationism in export distribution channels', *Journal of Business Research*, **56**(1–16).
Bello, D.C. and R. Lohtia (1995), 'Export channel design: the use of foreign distributors and agents', *Journal of the Academy of Marketing Science*, **23**(5), 83–93.
Benito, G.R.G., T. Pedersen and B. Petersen (2005), 'Export channel dynamics: an empirical investigation', *Managerial and Decision Economics*, **26**, 159–73.
Benito, G.R.G., C.A. Solberg and L.S. Welch (1993), 'An exploration of the information behaviour of Norwegian exporters', *International Journal of Information Management*, **13**(4), 274–86.
Bowe, C. (2004), 'Pfizer cuts drug supplies to Britain', *Australian*, 7 September, 28.
Burgel, O. and G.C. Murray (2000), 'The international market entry choices of start-up companies in high-technology industries', *Journal of International Marketing*, **8**(2), 33–62.
Business Review Weekly (1996), 'Exporters leave it to the locals', 10 June, 69.
Carstairs, R. and L.S. Welch (1982), 'Licensing and the internationalisation of smaller companies: some Australian evidence', *Management International Review*, **22**(3), 33–44.
Castaldi, R.M., A.F. De Noble and J. Kantor (1992), 'The intermediary service requirements of Canadian and American exporters', *International Marketing Review*, **9**(2), 21–40.

Cavusgil, S.T., S. Deligonul and C. Zhang (2004), 'Curbing foreign distributor opportunism: an examination of trust, contracts, and the legal environment in international channel relationships', *Journal of International Marketing*, **12**(2), 7–27.

Chaudhry, P.E. and M.G. Walsh (1995), 'Managing the gray market in the European Union: the case of the pharmaceutical industry', *Journal of International Marketing*, **3**(3), 11–33.

Crick, D. and M.V. Jones (2000), 'Small high-technology firms and international high-technology markets', *Journal of International Marketing*, **8**(2), 63–85.

Czinkota, M.R. and I.A. Ronkainen (2001), *International Marketing*, 6th edn, Fort Worth: Harcourt College Publishers.

Davis, M. (1993), 'Get to know your customers', *Business Review Weekly*, 30 July, 77.

Dept. of Foreign Affairs and Trade (1995), *Winning Enterprises*, Canberra: Australian Government Publishing Service.

Dimitratos, P. and S. Lioukas (2004), 'Greek perspectives of international entrepreneurship', in L.-P. Dana (ed.), *Handbook of Research on International Entrepreneurship*, Cheltenham, UK and Northampton, MA, USA: Edward Elgar, pp. 455–80.

Durham, C.A. and J.D. Lyon (1997), 'Manufacturer versus trading company export behaviour: the US processed fruit industries', *Agribusiness*, **13**(1), 59–71.

Economist (2005), 'Colombia – carrying coffee to Seattle', 1 October, 37.

Ekeledo, I. and K. Sivakumar (2004), 'The impact of E-commerce on entry-mode strategies of service firms: a conceptual framework and research propositions', *Journal of International Marketing*, **12**(4), 46–70.

Erramilli, M.K. (1990), 'Entry mode choice in service industries', *International Marketing Review*, **7**(5), 50–62.

Fletcher, R. and J. Bohn (1998), 'The impact of psychic distance on the internationalisation of the Australian firm', *Journal of Global Marketing*, **12**(2), 47–68.

Ford, D., A. Lawson and J.R. Nichols (1981), 'Developing international marketing through overseas sales subsidiaries', paper presented at the International Symposium on Exporting, Washington, D.C., 31 May–3 June.

Freeman, A. (2001), 'A survey of European business and the Euro', *Economist*, 1 December, 1–16.

Gallagher, M. (1989), *Selling Packaged Software Overseas: The Successful Channels*, Canberra: Australian Government Publishing Service.

Gourlay, R. (1994), 'Exporting – representative selection', *Financial Times*, 5 April, 9.

Gripsrud, G., C.A. Solberg and A.M. Ulvnes (2000), 'The role of trust in shaping information collection behavior of exporters', in Proceedings of the 26th EIBA Conference, Maastricht, 10–12 December (on CD-Rom).

Hollensen, S. (2001), *Global Marketing*, 2nd edn, Harlow, UK: Pearson Education.

Horneman, M. (1993), 'Pasminco Limited', MBA assignment, Monash University, Australia.

Howard, D.G. and D. Borgia (1990), 'Exporting and firm size: do small exporters have special needs?', *Journal of Global Marketing*, **4**(1), 79–97.

Johanson, J. and F. Wiedersheim-Paul (1975), 'The internationalization of the firm: four Swedish cases', *Journal of Management Studies*, **12**(3), 305–22.

Korhonen, H., R. Luostarinen and L. Welch (1996), 'Internationalization of SMEs: inward–outward patterns and government policy', *Management International Review*, **36**(4), 315–29.

LaBahn, D.W. and K.R. Harich (1997), 'Sensitivity to national culture: effects on U.S.–Mexican channel relationship performance', *Journal of International Marketing*, **5**(4), 29–51.

LEK Partnership (1994), *Intelligent Exports and the Silent Revolution in Services*, Sydney: Australian Trade Commission.

Leonidou, L.C. (1989), 'Behavioural aspects of the exporter–importer relationship: the case of Cypriot exporters and British importers', *European Journal of Marketing*, **23**(7), 17–33.

Liu, H. and K. Li (2002), 'Strategic implications of emerging Chinese multinationals: the Haier case study', *European Management Journal*, **20**(6), 699–706.

Luostarinen, R., H. Korhonen, J. Jokinen and T. Peltonen (1994), *Globalisation and SME*, Ministry of Trade and Industry, Finland, Studies and Reports 59/1994.

Lye, A. and R.T. Hamilton (2001), 'Importer perspectives on international exchange relationships', *International Business Review*, **10**, 109–28.

McGaughey, S., D. Welch and L. Welch (1997), 'Managerial influences and SME internationalization', in I. Bjorkman and M. Forsgren (eds), *The Nature of the International Firm*, Copenhagen: Copenhagen Business School Press, pp. 165–88.

McNaughton, R.B. (2002), 'The use of multiple export channels by small knowledge-intensive firms', *International Marketing Review*, **19**(2/3), 190–203.

Michael, J. (1998), 'A supplemental distribution channel?: the case of U.S. parallel export channels', *Multinational Business Review*, **6**(1), 24–35.

Morgan-Thomas, A. and S. Bridgewater (2004), 'Internet and exporting: determinants of success in virtual export channels', *International Marketing Review*, **21**(4/5), 393–408.

Munro, H.J. and P.W. Beamish (1987), 'Distribution methods and export performance', in P. Rosson and S. Reid (eds), *Managing Export Entry and Expansion: Concepts and Practice*, New York: Praeger, pp. 54–70.

Nielsen, K.V. (1998), 'The forward integration of Danish companies into ASEAN Markets', MSc thesis, Copenhagen Business School.

Perry, A.C. (1992), 'US international trade intermediaries: a field study investigation', *International Marketing Review*, **9**(2), 7–20.

Petersen, B., D.E. Welch and L.S. Welch (2000), 'Creating meaningful switching options in international operations', *Long Range Planning*, **33**(5), 688–705.

Petersen, B. and L.S. Welch (2002), 'Foreign operation mode combinations and internationalization', *Journal of Business Research*, **55**(2), 157–62.

Petersen, B. and L.S. Welch (2003), 'International business development and the Internet, post-hype', *Management International Review*, **43** (special issue 1), 7–29.

Petersen, B., L.S. Welch and K.V. Nielsen (2001), 'Resource commitment to foreign markets: the establishment patterns of Danish firms in South-East Asian markets', in S. Gray, S.L. McGaughey and W.R. Purcell (eds), *Asia-Pacific Issues in International Business*, Cheltenham, UK and Northampton, MA, USA: Edward Elgar, pp. 7–27.

Price Waterhouse Associates (1982), *Successful Exporting*, Canberra: Australian Government Publishing Service.

Rauch, J.E. (2001), 'Business and social networks in international trade', *Journal of Economic Literature*, **34**, 1177–203.

Roberts, E.R. and T.A. Senturia (1996), 'Globalizing the emerging high-technology company', *Industrial Marketing Management*, **25**, 491–506.

Rosson, P.J. (1987), 'The overseas distributor method: performance and change in a harsh environment', in P. Rosson and S. Reid (eds), *Managing Export Entry and Expansion: Concepts and Practice*, New York: Praeger, pp. 54–70.

Rosson, P.J. and F.H. Seringhaus (1995), 'Visitor and exhibitor interaction at industrial trade fairs', *Journal of Business Research*, **32**(1), 81–90.

Rosson, P.J. and F.H. Seringhaus (1996), 'Trade fairs as international marketing venues', in H.G. Gemünden, T. Ritter and A. Walter (eds), *Proceedings of the 12th IMP Conference*, Karlsruhe, Germany, 5–7 September, pp. 1177–97.

Samiee, S. and P.G.P. Walters (1990), 'Rectifying strategic gaps in export management', *Journal of Global Marketing*, **4**(1), 7–37.

Sarkar, M., B. Butler and C. Steinfeld (1998), 'Cybermediaries in electronic marketspace: toward theory building', *Journal of Business Research*, **41**, 215–21.

Sender, H. (1996), 'That's the spirit', *Far Eastern Economic Review*, 1 February, 50–51.

Shao, A.T. and P. Herbig (1993), 'The future of sogo shosha in a global economy', *International Marketing Review*, **10**(5), 37–55.

Simmonds, K. and H. Smith (1968), 'The first export order: a marketing innovation', *British Journal of Marketing*, **2**, 93–100.

Solberg, C.A. and E.B. Nes (2002), 'Exporter trust, commitment and marketing control in integrated and independent export channels', *International Business Review*, **11**(4), 385–405.

UNCTAD (2004, 2005), *World Investment Report 2004 and 2005*, New York and Geneva: United Nations.

Vantreese, V. (1992), 'Distribution systems and market entry strategies', OP-18, Center for Agricultural Export Development, University of Kentucky, Lexington.

Walters, P.G.P. (1996), 'International market information infusion: data acquisition behaviour in Norwegian exporters', *International Journal of Information Management*, **16**(6), 437–44.

Welch, C. (2005), 'International consulting providers and multilateral institutions: networks and internationalization', *Advances in International Marketing*, **15**, 175–97.

Welch, D., L. Welch, I. Wilkinson and L. Young (1998), 'The importance of networks in export promotion: policy issues', *Journal of International Marketing*, **6**(4), 66–82.

Welch, L.S. (1992), 'The use of alliances by small firms in achieving internationalization', *Scandinavian International Business Review*, **1**(2), 21–37.

Welch, L.S. and R.K. Luostarinen (1993), 'Inward–Outward connections in internationalization', *Journal of International Marketing*, **1**(1), 44–56.

Welch, L.S. and F. Wiedersheim-Paul (1980a), 'Initial exports – a marketing failure?', *Journal of Management Studies*, **17**(3), 333–44.

Welch, L.S. and F. Wiedersheim-Paul (1980b), 'Domestic expansion – internationalization at home', *Essays in International Business*, **2**, 1–31.

Wiedersheim-Paul, F., H.C. Olson and L.S. Welch (1978), 'Pre-export activity: the first step in internationalization', *Journal of International Business Studies*, **9**(1), 47–58.

WTO (2005), *World Trade Report*, WTO website accessed 29/8/05.

Yeow, M.I. (1993), 'Data Electronics', MBA assignment, Monash University, Australia.

Yeung, E. (1993), 'Autoscan Systems', MBA assignment, Monash University, Australia.

Young, S., J. Hamill, C. Wheeler and J.R. Davies (1989), *International Market Entry and Development*, Hemel Hempstead: Harvester Wheatsheaf.

9. Alliances

INTRODUCTION

Alliances represent an important foreign operation mode option for internationalizing companies, extensively used but difficult to operate, and coming in diverse forms. The only limit to alliance forms seems to be the creativity of partners in devising what are seen as acceptable arrangements that achieve the international goals of the partners. Alliances in the international arena may vary from informal, agreed cooperation in a given activity in one or more foreign markets, for example in joint promotion of two companies' products and information sharing, to formal, legally structured agreements, perhaps including shared equity in a foreign enterprise, in the form of a joint venture, thereby generating a flow of foreign direct investment (FDI). It is not surprising that there is little agreement in the literature regarding what constitutes an alliance. Some researchers include licensing and franchising as alliance forms given the high level of cooperative activity that these mode forms require. Terms such as 'collaboration' or 'cooperation' agreements are sometimes used to describe or define alliances, as these aspects are assumed to be the essence of what alliances are about, while the term 'strategic alliances' is often employed to denote serious intent with regard to the achievement of specific international goals (Auster, 1987; Glaister and Buckley, 1996). One commentator has wryly observed that 'the alliance . . . is almost always called "strategic" in order to make it appear long-lasting, serious and vital. Nobody ever calls its alliances "tactical"' (Emmott, 1993, 16). The term 'consortium' tends to be applied to an alliance, equity-based or otherwise, that includes a multiplicity of partners, for example when several firms form a group to bid for a major project.

As with other mode forms, alliances are frequently embedded in, or enfold, broader mode combination packages that may include diverse mode use, and they may play a supportive role to the primary mode in the package, for example as a marketing alliance that supports exporting activity (Petersen and Welch, 2002). Some of the varied alliance links to other modes are shown in Figure 9.1. An example is the 'strategic alliance' (term used by Kone) that has evolved between Kone of Finland and Toshiba of Japan in the elevator and escalator business. It developed over time to include an equity swap, exports, cooperation on technical development,

Figure 9.1   Possible alliance mode links

sourcing and marketing, and cross-licensing (see Chapter 12; Petersen and
Welch, 2003; *Kone News & Views*, 2004: see Box 12.5). In whatever form,
though, alliances represent another way that companies can operate in
foreign markets, utilizing the varied contributions of a partner or partner
firms, rather than seeking to undertake the enterprise by themselves.
Because of the widespread types of assistance that an alliance partner
might provide, and the cost, uncertainty and risk associated with foreign
ventures, it is not surprising that alliances should be one of the alternatives
frequently emerging in mode evaluation and choice situations. One of the
influential management thinkers of the 1980s, Kenichi Ohmae (1989,
143), even concluded that 'globalization mandates alliances, makes them
absolutely necessary to strategy'. However, given the diversity of alliance
forms and combination possibilities, it is difficult to generalize about the
nature of alliances as a method of foreign operation and their potential role
in companies' internationalization (Welch, 1992).

International alliances have been the subject of extensive research, often with a focus on joint ventures, in many different country-contexts, as well as on a cross-country basis, providing divergent theoretical perspectives and a wealth of empirical data and company cases regarding this mode form. In a recent review of the literature, Parkhe (2004, 212) found that 'to date hundreds of books and more than eleven thousand articles have been published on alliances, the majority of them within the past decade'. While there is considerable year-to-year variation in the extent of international alliance formation on a global basis, overall there has been substantial growth in alliances from the 1980s through to the early 2000s, whatever the database or definition employed (Contractor and Lorange, 2002; Kang and Sakai, 2000). Alliances provide a large portion of revenues and research output for many large multinationals, for example contributing over one-third of revenues for IBM (Parise and Casher, 2003). The bulk of alliances in the 1990s were international in scope, with almost half being in the form of joint ventures, although this declined somewhat after the mid-1990s. Alliance growth has occurred in all sectors of business, with increasing involvement of service firms. Likewise, alliance use has spread across the full range of countries, although growth has been particularly strong in Asian countries (Kang and Sakai, 2000). The surge in international acquisition activity during the last two decades has been a factor in fuelling the global growth of alliances. Joint ventures are often created as a result of part rather than full acquisition of an existing foreign enterprise. Official records and empirical surveys of alliance activity probably understate their extent, and overstate the relative importance of equity JVs, because many of the non-equity examples, especially informal arrangements, tend to go unrecorded.

Many studies show a high drop-out rate from alliances, and that, despite the many obvious attractions of using alliances in foreign operations, it is difficult to make them work in practice, particularly in some countries, with the additional demands of cross-cultural interaction. As a result, there appears to have been an overall relative lessening of enthusiasm about the use of at least joint ventures, as indicated in a study of more than 3000 US MNCs for the period 1982 to 1997, showing a fall in the percentage of these companies' foreign affiliates with minority shareholdings from 17.9 per cent to 10.6 per cent, compared to a rise in wholly-owned operations from 72.3 per cent to 80.4 per cent of the total (Desai et al., 2004). This is also reflected in a shift away from the use of joint ventures (JVs) in China towards wholly-owned enterprises since the early 1990s: from 27 per cent (by value) of inward FDI in 1992, investment in wholly-owned enterprises had reached about 57 per cent by 2000 (Deng, 2001). This is confirmed in a recent study of 130 foreign-based MNCs operating in the consumer products sector in

China, showing that, while 36 per cent were using the JV form, this was the preferred form for only 19 per cent of companies – as against 79 per cent for wholly-owned investments (O'Neill, 2004).

Despite the high drop-out rate from alliances, the research demonstrates that, as in the use of other modes of operation, many companies have been able to use alliances effectively as building blocks in foreign market penetration. Alliances are often a stepping stone to deeper commitment: it is not uncommon for one alliance partner to take over the other's share in a foreign venture (Hennart et al., 1998; Reuer, 1998). Alliances have also been of considerable interest to government authorities engaged in the business of encouraging and supporting the internationalization of companies from their home base. There are many examples of governments initiating and directly and indirectly assisting the creation of alliances of local firms, and of local and foreign firms, and helping the resulting arrangement of companies into foreign markets, with mixed success (Welch et al., 1998). In some cases, on the grounds of 'national interest' or as a counter-weight to the perceived power of a large foreign multinational, governments in some countries have become directly involved in the ownership and management of joint ventures.

In this chapter we analyse the different types of alliances and their characteristics, and their potential contribution, as well as drawbacks, as a means of achieving foreign market penetration, solely or in combination with other forms of operation. However, detailed analysis of the choice between joint ventures and wholly-owned subsidiaries is presented in the following chapter dealing with foreign direct investment activity. Emphasis is placed on the dynamics of alliance activity: alliances are viewed, not as a single step, but as a process over time, with relatively early disbandment common, and the aftermath of which is important for companies' continued international expansion.

DEFINITION/TYPES

There is considerable diversity of alliance forms, and divergent perspectives about what constitutes an alliance, and what types of business arrangements can be appropriately included under the umbrella concept. The problem in defining alliances is that the essence of alliances is cooperation in order to achieve common goals, yet some aspect of this characteristic is present in the bulk foreign operation mode arrangements: for example, with exporting, cooperation with distributors may be critical to export success, while cooperation with franchisees has been shown to be a key element of franchising effectiveness. Alliances have been defined as 'inter-firm collaboration over a given economic space for the attainment of mutually defined goals'

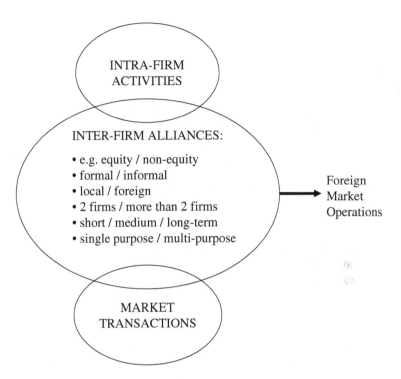

Source: Adapted from Scott-Kemmis et al. (1990, p. 12).

Figure 9.2   Alliances of foreign operations

(Buckley, 1992, 91). For our purposes, with the book's foreign operation mode focus, alliances are defined as arrangements where two or more companies engage in collaborative activity, while remaining as independent organizations, and result in foreign market operations. The companies may pool, exchange and/or integrate resources in the process of setting up and operating an alliance. The alliance activity, in whatever form, represents a springboard to foreign market activity, although this may be undertaken in association with other modes of operation in the foreign market, as shown above in Figure 9.1 (Auster, 1987; Buchel et al., 1998; Business International, 1990; Welch, 1992).

Another approach to the definition of alliances is to examine various types through consideration of a range of possible characteristics and component parts, ultimately building a broad picture of the nature of alliances. Some of these characteristics are illustrated in Figures 9.2 and 9.3. Figure 9.2 presents a summary of different key characteristics within the boundaries of intra-firm activities and market transactions (following

Scott-Kemmis et al., 1990, 12; see also Contractor and Lorange, 2002). Of course, long-standing research on inter-company buyer–seller relationships has shown that market-based connections may evolve over time, with relational bonding, to the point where they become cooperative and involve joint problem solving across different dimensions (Ford, 1990). However, the question is, can such bondings and resulting, often informal, joint activity be regarded as being of sufficient weight to constitute a method or part-method of operating in or servicing foreign markets? There is not an easy or precise answer to this question, and, to some extent, it is likely to be determined at the international operational level within the company and by managers' perceptions. At the other extreme are intra-firm joint activities, perhaps involving units within a multinational that are almost as independent from each other as if they were unrelated companies, but they are nevertheless excluded from consideration because of the common company umbrella with its potentially distorting effects on decision-making and implementation processes.

Within these extremes, a wide range of alliance types and characteristics is evident, depending on such elements as the following:

- number of partners;
- industry characteristics of partners – they may be in the same industry and competitive, or in complementary or unrelated industries;
- size of partners – they may be of the same size or of divergent size, e.g. small and large;
- nationality of partners – they may be local and/or foreign;
- formality of alliance – the arrangement may be informal or formal;
- equity/non-equity – an alliance could be based on legal incorporation and the partners sharing equity (varied arrangements), or based on a form of agreement, without equity, as to what the alliance will cover, perhaps involving a formal contract;
- nature and extent of commitment of parties to an alliance;
- length of association – the alliance might be short-term, for a specific project, or long-term;
- number of foreign markets where joint activity occurs;
- initiating source – this could be from inside the alliance, by one or more of the partners, or from outside, e.g. emanating from government intervention;
- importance of alliance to partners – alliance activity might be a minor or significant part of business to the different alliance partners;
- nature of alliance goals – there may be quite varied goals for an alliance, e.g. technological, market entry/expansion, competition, and access to resources.

Array of Options

Mixing up these different alliance characteristics generates an almost bewildering array of alliance options that companies potentially can utilize in
foreign operation mode choice situations, and we will only cover a limited
range of these in the process of exposing key alliance characteristics and
issues. Equity JVs are an important alliance form, and some of the options
in joint venture situations are shown in Figure 9.3. In the first case, the joint
venture between companies A and B is created in the source country X as
a prelude to the establishment of a fully-owned company within foreign
country Y. However, this example would typically not appear as an international alliance in country Y's or globally-based FDI records. The foreign

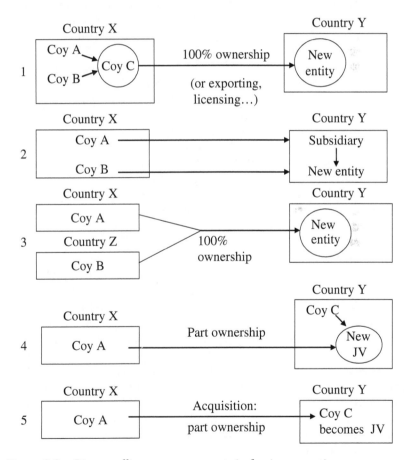

Figure 9.3   Diverse alliance arrangements in foreign operations

operation method is a wholly-owned subsidiary, but it is based in a domestic joint venture. Other forms of domestic groupings are feasible, such as export groups, and they may use a company structure as a basis for carrying out international activity on behalf of the participants (see, for example, Welch et al., 2000). This may involve exporting or licensing, or other non-alliance forms of foreign operation, but they are essentially alliance-based, although the alliance itself does not straddle countries, nor lead to a joint venture in the foreign location.

A variation on case 1 is when two or more companies from the same country (A and B) form a new joint venture in a foreign market (Y): case 2 in Figure 9.3. This may be an outcome of company B's attempt to penetrate the target market, seeking to use the existing operational experience, knowledge and networks of company A within the market, formed as a result of A's preceding direct investment. Japanese firms often link with other Japanese firms in foreign markets, via JVs, sometimes involving Japanese trading companies. Indeed, Japanese firms in China were found to regard the knowledge flowing from Japanese partners with experience in China to be far superior to that flowing from local partners (Lu and Beamish, 2004). In case 3, the alliance is formed between firms from different countries, for the purposes of operation in a third country via the establishment of a jointly owned foreign entity. Inevitably, such arrangements introduce at least three cultures into the operation of the joint venture in country Y: those of the two foreign partners and local staff. This form is sometimes used in project bidding and implementation situations. The joint venture is set up for a specific purpose, the project, in a given country, and is disbanded on completion.

Case 4, as shown in Figure 9.3, involves the establishment of an equity joint venture in country Y between a local firm and a foreign partner (or partners). An example is Huawei Technologies of China, a producer of telecommunications equipment, which recently entered into a joint venture with Canadian-based Nortel Networks, with Nortel having majority ownership. The JV will be headquartered in Ottawa, Canada. It will produce high-speed Internet equipment and will be involved in developing products for this area, although it will sell existing Huawei products from the outset (*Australian*, 2006). From Huawei's perspective, the JV is clearly aimed at achieving both product development and foreign market penetration objectives. This type of joint venture is often favoured by host governments in situations where desired technology transfer and significant financing are involved, and because it does not involve full foreign ownership. For the foreign partner, though, there may be opportunities to reduce the monetary cost of the investment by effectively purchasing equity in the new venture as compensation for various transfers such as equipment and machinery for production purposes that are being replaced at other locations within the company's network, technology and know-how, and the right to use trademarks. There are cases where companies have been able to finance as much as 50 per cent equity in the foreign JV through various non-monetary transfers. However, the Chinese government has sought to limit such capitalizations of technology to a level of 20 per cent in an attempt to prevent underfinancing of JVs (Chen, 1995).

Of course, there may be more than one foreign partner, from more than one foreign country, participating in the establishment of a new JV in a third country with a local partner. In order to assure long-term security of supply, in 2004 the four largest Chinese steel mills took a 40 per cent stake in an Australian iron ore mine; BHP Billiton of Australia retained 51 per cent equity, while two Japanese companies took interests of 4.8 per cent and 1.2 per cent. Linked to the deal was a long-term contract, worth US$9 billion, to supply iron ore to the Chinese steel mills (Chessell, 2004). In this case, the local partner (BHP Billiton) provided the valued asset (access to a local iron ore mine), and in return it gained a valuable long-term export contract.

Case 5 in Figure 9.3 is the equivalent of case 4 in terms of the final outcome, except that it involves acquisition of an equity share in an existing local company by a foreign partner. As a result, the foreign partner does not have to participate in the establishment of a new operation from scratch, although it may initiate and carry through restructuring and other changes as it undertakes a range of transfers to, and implants them in, the existing entity. A variation on case 5 occurs when the foreign party buys into a local operation that already operates as a JV with another foreign shareholder. A recent example is Vodafone's purchase of a 10 per cent share of India's Bharti Tele-Ventures, a large mobile telephone operator (14 million mobile customers), for about US$1.5 billion. Bharti was already 31 per cent part-owned by SingTel, the Singapore-based telecommunications company. Vodafone indicated that it would seek to increase its shareholding if the venture proved successful (Griggs, 2005). There are many examples of more complex JV structures that do not readily fit into any of the above five cases. However, in a study of the equity joint ventures of a sample of Japanese firms in China, it was found that the three most commonly used forms were a JV with a local firm or firms, a JV with a Japanese trading company (sogo shosha) or a JV with other Japanese firms (Lu and Beamish, 2004).

Equity Level

In all equity joint venture situations, a critical question is the level of equity held by the different parties. This is typically seen as a deciding factor in who has control of the JV operation. For many investors, 51 per cent equity means control, whereas 50:50 or minority equity situations do not. Tony O'Reilly, the former head of Heinz, the US food multinational, described how the company embarked on a strategy to become a major player in Third World countries through the use of joint ventures, set up with existing local producers, perhaps through part-takeover. However, the primary choice criterion was the need to achieve at least 51 per cent equity in each joint venture. The issue came to a head in Zimbabwe, where a suitable local firm was amenable to Heinz taking a controlling interest, but the Zimbabwean government insisted that only 49 per cent was permissible. It took two years of negotiation, and the personal intervention of Tony O'Reilly in the negotiation process, for the 51 per cent level to be agreed to, although, as a form of compensation, the government became a partner in the JV operation (O'Reilly, 1988). However, the equity level is not always such an overriding concern in JV involvement. As noted above, many companies have readily compensated for the lack of equity control in minority JV situations by using other modes such as licensing agreements and management contracts, which may provide added legal, intellectual property, marketing and managerial control. The growth, extent and variety of non-equity alliances are indicative of the fact that, rather than just equity and related control concerns, companies are frequently focused instead on the way alliance arrangements can deliver a range of foreign market penetration benefits. Ohmae (1989) has even argued that a preoccupation with control via equity is potentially poisonous to the development of positive alliance relationships.

Non-Equity Alliances

Joint ventures have been the subject of considerable research attention as a form of alliance, in part because the equity shares and legal arrangement give them a more public face, concrete shape and accessible records, thereby making them more amenable to empirical investigation. In contrast, many examples of non-equity alliance forms tend to be more 'messy', often with far looser shape, and in many cases lacking even a formal, signed agreement between the parties, so that they are less obvious and less open to external examination. A notable example was that between Coca-Cola and McDonald's, involving 'no piece of paper to fall back on – just a "common vision and a lot of trust"' (*Economist*, 1998, 73). In spite of this, the alliance has been long-standing (the relationship began in the 1950s) and has become extensive, covering areas such as marketing and equipment design. Obviously, such informal alliances are not maintained, or extended, unless they are delivering discernible benefits to the partners. One of the attractions of this form is that it can be more readily curtailed as circumstances change than formal arrangements involving tightly structured, contractual commitments.

Under the general heading of 'non-equity alliances' there are many types, ranging from loose, informal cooperation to tight, contractually driven association. In many respects, though, they mirror the JV examples noted above in Figure 9.3, in that there are possibilities of association within the home country or across countries as a prelude to operation in a specific foreign market, and/or with firms in target markets. Association and cooperation might be organized directly between the alliance partners, or through a third party – perhaps an industry association or a government body. Government trade organizations frequently attempt to broker co-operative links between domestic firms to support international operations by one or more of the companies concerned, particularly in situations where companies are attempting initial international entry, or seeking to penetrate a specific target market. Informal alliances often grow out of market interaction between the partners, perhaps in buyer–seller situations, where the parties come to recognize that there are opportunities for cooperation, and willingness based on positive interaction experience and recognition of compatibility. These may evolve further into more formal arrangements (Scott-Kemmis et al., 1990). For example, Coca-Cola entered into a formal, ten-year alliance with Disney in 1997, but this had been preceded by a supplier relationship since 1955, and a marketing alliance since 1985 (*Economist*, 1998). Information technology (IT) multinationals HP of the US and NEC of Japan have been involved in an escalating alliance since 1995, starting with a manufacturing agreement, followed by a joint product development arrangement for large clients, and then an alliance to jointly offer IT outsourcing services to customers in 2002, using a joint sales force (Grayson, 2002).

The evolutionary character of many alliances is one of the reasons for alliances sometimes being referred to as a process rather than an event or act. Evolution applies to developments preceding the start of an alliance as well as subsequent events (Baughn et al., 1997; Doz, 1996). Non-equity alliances are sometimes a prelude to, and testing ground for, a joint venture arrangement (Kang and Sakai, 2000). Negotiation of an alliance arrangement can be a demanding and lengthy process in itself, taking as long as four years, as some Norwegian companies noted in their experience of penetrating the Indian market via joint ventures (Tomassen et al., 1998).

At one extreme in the range of non-equity alliances is the contractual joint venture. As the name implies, rather than being governed by equity shares, the JV operates under the terms of an agreed contract between the partners, often for a specific term. The terms of the contract may impose tight restrictions on management as to strategy and operations of the JV.

Contractual JVs were common in the 1980s in China as a result of government direction, but have since declined with further liberalization of the
Chinese economy, with foreign companies favouring equity-based arrangements (Deng, 2001).

Marketing Alliances

Marketing alliances are a popular form of non-equity alliance, focused as
they are on what is usually regarded as a key area of foreign operation
success – marketing considerations. Some alliances concentrate on particular parts of the marketing process, for example physical distribution, while
others are more comprehensive in character, covering the bulk of the
foreign marketing role. Marketing alliances often focus on joint promotion
activity, which might include co-branding of products, joint advertising,
combined offers to customers or joint in-store promotions. The tourism
sector exhibits many examples of informal marketing alliances, such as
when tourism resorts cooperate to provide an extended offering to international tourists, as in the case of cooperation between some ski resorts in
northern Norway and Finland.

Marketing alliances may involve a link between small firms and multinationals, as illustrated in Figure 9.4, in which the small firm seeks to utilize
the multinational's multi-country network to assist in penetrating foreign
markets. In a study of Australian packaged software exporters, it was found
that 28 per cent had used marketing alliances to help sell and distribute their
products in foreign markets – 18 per cent with foreign multinationals (Bureau
of Industry Economics, 1989). Forms of assistance provided by the multinationals included 'sales catalogue listing, preferred supplier status, cooperative advertising and press support, joint selling, contact and liaison with
the multinational vendor's customers, market research information, [and]
assistance in distribution' (ibid., 70–71). Nevertheless, only 5 per cent of companies in the study relied exclusively on these marketing alliances for foreign
market penetration. For the multinationals, the attractions of such arrangements were the prompt expansion of their product range and their enhanced
ability to provide a more complete service to customers in varied foreign
markets. The Australian federal government attempted to 'persuade' foreign
multinationals into such arrangements through a scheme under which cooperation and definable export outcomes were rewarded with government
benefits, such as better access terms in bidding for government contracts and
reduced offset requirements in a government-mandated countertrade scheme
(Bureau of Industry Economics, 1989). In another Australian scheme, a state
government went further and sought to bring foreign and Australian firms
that produced complementary products together, so that each would market

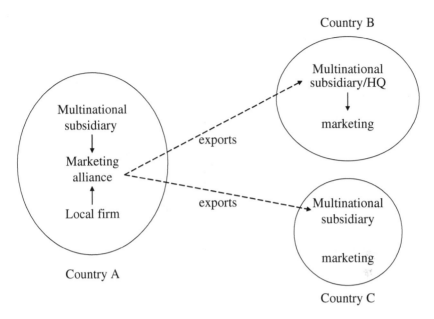

Figure 9.4   Alliances of small firms and multinationals

the other's product in the different markets, as shown in Figure 9.5 (Welch, 1992). In this scheme, as with the many forms of export grouping and marketing arrangements, the alliance is about facilitating exporting activity, and thereby generates a type of mode combination.

The examples of the government-supported alliance schemes noted illustrate the motivation of some companies engaging in alliances, and the differing perspectives of small, internationally inexperienced firms and those of well-established multinationals. There is a marked difference in the importance of the alliance to the respective firms: for some small firms it is almost about their survival; for those in narrow market niches, with limited domestic market opportunities, internationalization is critical, but small firms often lack the resources on their own to pursue international markets with any vigour. This concern was expressed by a representative of Cellabs, a small producer of medical diagnostic products, with heavy research and development costs, in the following terms: 'It has become blindingly obvious to companies in our industry that the problem is how to get their products into international markets. It is obvious to all of us now that none of us has the critical mass individually to get out there and make a dent in the world market' (Lyons, 1990, 6). Not surprisingly, the company was keenly interested in the prospect of an alliance to alleviate the internationalization

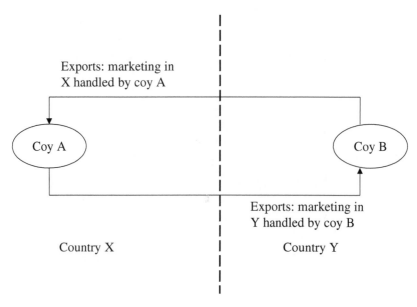

Figure 9.5   Cross-country marketing alliance

burden – in this case, with other firms in the same industry facing a similar situation. Joining with a multinational is another option, and multinationals typically maintain a large stable of alliances with small firms in different countries. However, there is a considerable difference in the importance of these alliances to the parties: often critical to the small firm but typically of minor or miniscule importance to the multinational. Inevitably, this disparity raises the issue of commitment by the multinational to the alliance. In the study of alliances used by Australian packaged software exporters, it was evident that many of the exporters felt that they could not rely on the commitment of their multinational partners to the various alliances and so engaged in additional marketing activity on their own behalf (Bureau of Industry Economics, 1989).

While marketing alliances tend to be the main form of non-equity alliance, there are many other types of cooperative arrangements that focus on other aspects of companies' international operations. These might involve joint or cooperative research and development, technology sharing, information sharing, co-production and shared output, cooperative supply arrangements, joint exploration activity in the mining sector, and joint use of personnel in international locations. These forms of cooperation will be typically linked to other forms of foreign operation, such as importing and exporting, projects and international subcontracting.

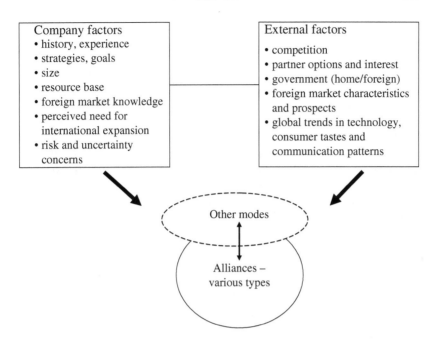

Figure 9.6   Determinants of alliance use in foreign operations

There may be considerable variation in the nature and extent of transfers between the alliance partners and the resulting foreign venture, depending on the type of alliance arrangement. In some arrangements, there is little or no joint activity and minimal transfers, for example in reciprocal foreign marketing alliances between two firms – using each other's local marketing and distribution capacity to facilitate the foreign sales of both parties. The whole point of the alliance is to minimize the level of direct foreign activity and cost. At the other extreme are joint ventures that require a heavy, continuing flow of resources from the foreign part-owner/s, for example staff, technology, equipment and finance, along with decision-making influence on policy and strategy.

WHY ALLIANCES?

As with the range in types of alliances, there is a multitude of factors that may be involved in companies' decisions to use alliances as a form of foreign operation. The various influences are summarized in Figure 9.6, under the general groupings of internal company factors and external factors. Amongst external influences, for instance, governments, home and foreign, have various direct and indirect impacts, creating pressures and inducements for the development of alliances (see Welch et al., 1998). However, many of the influences noted in Figure 9.6, such as strong market growth prospects, do not necessarily apply to alliances alone. They could as well be applied to the adoption of other modes. In a study of Norwegian companies that had entered the Indian market, with similar external influences applying to the companies, while joint ventures were the main mode used, licensing also was an important mode utilized by the entrant firms (Tomassen et al., 1998). For Vodafone, the perceived need to participate in the rapidly growing Indian telecommunications market did lead to a joint venture, but via a small stake (10 per cent) in an established joint venture company (Griggs, 2005). Factors affecting, and links to, other modes in combined operations in foreign markets also may be important in determining whether alliances are used, and their nature and structure. The ability to use a specific type of alliance itself is often critical in the preparedness of companies to entertain an alliance strategy.

As noted above, alliances sometimes evolve from other market relationships almost unnoticed, in the nature of an emergent strategy (Mintzberg and Waters, 1985). In addition, they may serve as transitory arrangements on the way to another form of operation. This is sometimes intended, but often not, arising from alliance problems or as alliance experience opens up new opportunities. An example of background thinking is outlined by a German interviewee in a study of the acquisition–alliance choice: 'in this case there are two alternatives: either you buy something – but in this case you tend to have a problem, because you must be able to run this business and cannot actually do so properly, since you do not have the experience . . . or you try to create a work platform by setting up strategic alliances with partners that already have these adjacent skills and know-how. And then once you are somewhat established in this market segment or the entire market, you talk with your partner about an acquisition' (Hoffmann and Schaper-Rinkel, 2001, 144).

It is not difficult to mount a strong, rational argument for the use of alliances in international operations given the nature and extent of potential contributions that a partner might be able and prepared to bring to the alliance. As shown in Figure 9.7, through an alliance it may be possible for a company to tap into various strengths of a foreign partner, such as its market share, brands, distribution system, technology, networks, staff skills, information system and cultural and market knowledge, which could assist in penetrating the partner's local market and other foreign markets. At the same time, though, the well known problems and failures

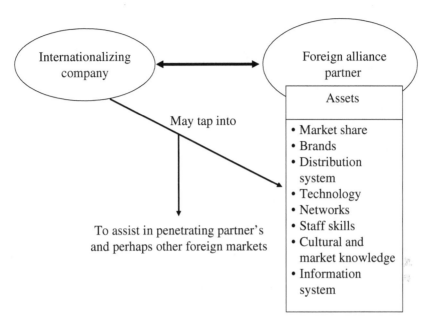

Figure 9.7   Accessing alliance partner's assets

of alliances can generate an approach-avoidance perspective by companies. On the basis of varied research, some have argued that alliances run counter to organizations' basic drive for independence. For example, Van de Ven (1976, 28) has noted that 'organizations do not coordinate for coordination's sake. Instead, organizations strain to maintain their autonomy'. Further, Macdonald (1992, 53) has stressed that 'the costs of collaboration are sufficiently large so that no firm would choose to collaborate if it could achieve the same objectives independently. Collaboration is very much a second-best solution'. The patchy performance of government-supported alliance schemes has raised questions about this route as well. A report to the Australian government concluded that 'unless Australian companies really want to join forces to increase their combined chances of export success . . . then no amount of incentives or government support will succeed' (Ferris et al., 1985, 60). Notwithstanding these basic issues, alliances still appear to be growing in international use, and large and small companies continue to assign them an important role in their internationalization, so that reasons for their adoption, and chosen roles, deserve closer examination.

In the widespread empirical research on alliances, particularly on joint ventures, many reasons for companies entering into alliances with an

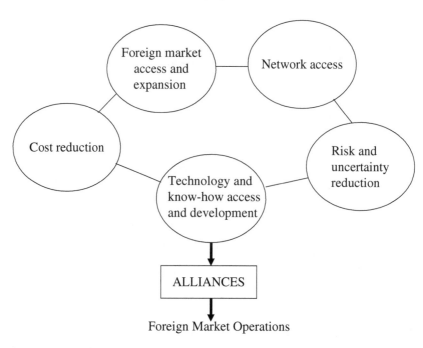

Figure 9.8   Alliance drivers

international focus have been exposed, although these reasons could
be distilled into five main areas, focused on what companies are seeking
to achieve through alliance involvement (see Figure 9.8): cost reduction,
risk and uncertainty reduction, technology and know-how access and
development, network access, and foreign market access and expansion,
which may be driven by offensive or defensive considerations (Buchel
et al., 1998; Glaister and Buckley, 1996; Harrigan, 1986; Hennart, 1988;
Narula, 2003). In general, companies are seeking to obtain contributions from alliance partners that would be difficult or costly to provide by
themselves, in the achievement of particular international and company
goals.

Widespread research reports that marketing considerations are a major
driver of the formation of alliances that operate in the international arena
(Kang and Sakai, 2000). In a study of the strategic motives driving international alliance formation by UK firms, the five most important motives
by order of importance were marketing-oriented (Glaister and Buckley,
1996, 315): (a) gain presence in new market, (b) faster entry to market, (c)
facilitate international expansion, (d) compete against a competitor and (e)
maintain market position.

Facilitate Foreign Market Penetration

Foreign market penetration concerns, such as those noted, link with other factors, as illustrated in Figures 9.6, 9.7 and 9.8, in pushing firms to contemplate the use of alliances. For example, lack of experience in, knowledge of and cultural compatibility with a given foreign market tend to accentuate the sense of risk and uncertainty about market entry, even though there might be a strong perception of market growth prospects. This was evident in the approach of Norwegian companies to the Indian market. An investigation revealed that joint ventures were the main operation mode used. The reasoning was explained by one interviewee in the study in the following terms: 'a wholly owned operation would have been too risky – we didn't know the market and we had no serious business in the country beforehand. The Indian market is difficult and complex. It is good to have a partner who knows the business and the bureaucracy, a partner who has the right connections' (Tomassen et al., 1998, 11). Exporting was ruled out because of very high import barriers. This perspective reflected that of other Norwegian companies in the study, as noted by the CEO of Jordan, the Norwegian dental products multinational: 'preliminary market studies . . . confirmed a perception . . . of "bureaucracy, corruption and tariff barriers and the importance of having a partner who knew the complexity of the market"' (ibid., 13–14).

Given the combination of factors noted in these cases, it was almost inevitable that many of the Norwegian companies would seriously pursue alliance options as a way of penetrating the market – in some cases in spite of the difficult negotiation process involved. The Norwegian cases also draw attention to the potential importance of the foreign partner's network in creating links to business, government and the bureaucracy, thereby supporting foreign market access. Network connections to the local community similarly were found to be a critical factor for German companies entering into technical collaborations with Indian firms (Kumar, 1995; see also Tatoglu and Glaister, 2000). The factors emerging in the Norwegian cases may be linked to other company influences, such as those noted in Figure 9.6, notably size and resource base, which further accentuate the attraction of alliances.

Small firms particularly tend to suffer from a lack of financial resources, available staff and foreign marketing skills to carry out extensive international marketing on their own, so that frequently they are drawn to the idea of various types of alliance arrangements as a way of compensating for their resource constraints. In addition, any help through the alliance which can alleviate the concern about failure in the marketplace is valued: for the small firm, the foreign operation may be of such significance as to call into question its overall viability. Nevertheless, small Australian software exporters did not rely solely on the marketing alliances formed with multinational companies for achieving foreign market penetration: there was a clear recognition of the limitations of these alliances in solving their foreign marketing needs and demands (Bureau of Industry Economics, 1989).

While large firms may not have the same sense of resource constraints as small firms in driving an interest in alliances, there are limits on the preparedness to commit resources, even for large firms, in unfamiliar, uncertain environments, along with recognition in many instances of the range of contributions that alliances can make to their foreign market objectives. For example, the head of Norsk Hydro Electrolysers (a division of Norsk Hydro, Norway's largest company), in explaining the company's joint venture choice as the basis for its foray into the Indian market, commented: 'it was not our plan to start some sort of production by ourselves down there. A wholly owned subsidiary was totally out of the question not only due to the limited capital we wanted to invest, but also to the risk of changing behaviour from the government' (Tomassen et al., 1998, 14). With slowing growth in the mobile telephone business in Western markets, penetration of rapidly expanding emerging markets such as India had become an important part of Vodafone's global strategy. Earlier, Vodafone had entered into an alliance through the purchase of an equity stake (about 20 per cent) in a regional operator, which it sold in 2003 when it became clear that the company would not achieve Vodafone's India-wide ambitions. In spite of this negative experience, it went down the same alliance route just two years later: it bought a 10 per cent share in a company (Bharti Tele-Ventures) that was India's largest mobile operator, having India-wide activities and with fast-growing revenues (Griggs, 2005). Even for such a large company as Vodafone is in the global mobile telephone business, to have entered the Indian market substantially on its own would have posed significant regulatory difficulties; even though the FDI limit has recently been increased to 74 per cent, it would have taken some time to build market share and the exercise would have incurred substantial costs. The risks of this path were considerable, with substantial uncertainty about the outcome. Against this alternative, the alliance path, with an assured market via the alliance partner, was clearly attractive, despite the up-front cost, and it was not without its own set of risks, including alliance stability and technology security.

In the list of strategic motives for international alliances in the study by Glaister and Buckley (1996, 315), which in general cover the main alliance factors mentioned in other studies, marketing factors lead, with technology, cost and risk considerations stressed thereafter, while response to government policy is assessed as the least important motive (see also Parkhe,

2004). The remainder of the list is as follows: (a) exchange of complementary technology, (b) economies of scale, (c) product diversification, (d) faster payback on investment, (e) concentrate on higher margin business, (f) share R&D costs, (g) spread risk of large projects, (h) reduce competition, (i) produce at lower cost location, (j) exchange of patents/territories, (k) conform to foreign government policy.

Technology

Technology is undoubtedly an important factor in alliance formation, as shown in a multitude of empirical studies (see, for example, Narula, 2003), although an alliance based on access to a foreign partner's technology or know-how, perhaps on an exchange basis as is increasingly the case in international alliances, may not directly involve operations in the foreign market; that is, the outcome may not lead to an alliance that could be regarded as a foreign operation method in the market in question: it is not a vehicle for direct foreign market penetration. Technological cooperation might be undertaken primarily at the R&D unit within headquarters, necessitating the movement of personnel from the foreign partner to the R&D unit. Typically, though, technological considerations in alliances do not operate in isolation, as in the Kone–Toshiba and Nortel–Huawei examples noted above. The Kone–Toshiba link started as exporting by Kone to Toshiba, with technical cooperation to adapt the product to Toshiba's requirements. Over time, technological cooperation extended, with two-way flows, but it was driven by a strong marketing focus. In the first instance, the alliance has allowed Kone a means of accessing the Japanese market, and the cooperation has been extended into the Chinese market.

Share Costs and Risks

The ability to share costs and risks through alliances in the process of penetrating foreign markets can be an important factor in their use in diverse situations. This is the case for many new ventures that involve significant set-up costs – perhaps the construction of expensive facilities in the foreign market, such as factories, mines or infrastructure. In the global mining industry, alliances of partners from different countries are commonly used as a way of spreading the costs and high risks in exploration and development. Business and political risk can be shared and alleviated by an alliance with a foreign partner in the partner's local market, utilizing the partner's local knowledge and connections, and the alliance ensures that there is a local face to the operation. In large, costly infrastructure projects, with a long time span to completion, it is common for the bidding companies to seek partner firms to share the costs and risks of the work. The low rating of the impact of government policy in the list is in contrast to the results of a similar study of motives in international JV formation between Ghanaian firms and partners from Western Europe, North America and Asia. The motive 'to overcome government-mandated barriers' emerged as a major consideration for the foreign partners (Boateng and Glaister, 2003). In an equivalent study of Western firms' motives for setting up in Turkey via joint ventures with local Turkish firms, conforming to government policy was eighth on the list, far less important than market access and risk-sharing motives (Tatoglu and Glaister, 2000). This is suggestive of variation in the importance of the different reasons for alliance use depending on the country context, particularly when developing countries are involved.

A PROCESS PERSPECTIVE ON ALLIANCES

So far, the analysis of reasons for companies using alliances has been within a relatively static context, as is much of the literature on alliances: typically via broad cross-sectional studies, companies are asked to outline the reasons why they chose alliances in foreign operations in a post-decision environment. The implication is that there is a consistent set of reasons over time for the companies concerned. As Glaister and Buckley (1996, 329) conclude, 'the dynamics of alliance formation are vital. Analytical techniques which only capture static benefits are unlikely to convey the full picture of strategic alliances'. In reality, the arguments for alliances are likely to change through time, reflecting the fact that alliance adoption and use in foreign operations is a process often stretched out over a considerable period of time, and managerial perception of the range of influences is bound to alter at different stages of the overall process, as well as the way in which an alliance is used in foreign market penetration (Kogut, 1988). In the following sections we analyse alliance adoption, use and disbandment from a process perspective, viewing this as an appropriate context for understanding how and why alliances are employed in international business operations.

Pre-Agreement Dynamics

The initial triggers for an interest in using alliances may differ substantially from the reasons for eventual adoption: the arguments are likely to evolve as market research and partner research are undertaken, and interaction and negotiation with a potential partner occur. In other words, reasoning is responsive to the process and its output. In a series of studies of alliances,

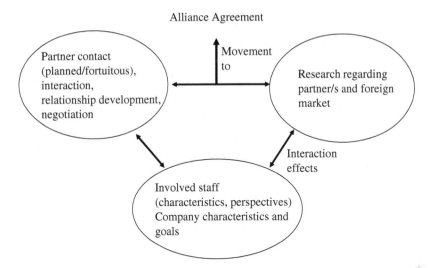

Alliance Agreement

Figure 9.9   Pre-agreement dynamics

Osborn (2003, 38) found that fortuitous approaches to form an alliance were common: 'Most senior executives did not initiate an alliance idea – most seem to remember that the other firm came to them.' As a result, there is something of a scramble within the company to develop a position on the fortuitous approach, but this is likely to alter as more thorough investigation is undertaken and if negotiations proceed (see Figure 9.9). Outside change agents such as brokers, consultants, government officials and lawyers also play a part in the process, and influence the development of ideas about, and attitudes toward, alliances, particularly in the pre-agreement phase.

Despite the importance of partner selection to the ultimate success of an alliance, research in the field indicates that often partner selection and evaluation processes are poorly handled (Osborn, 2003; Parkhe, 2004). Of course, this is not such an important issue for alliances, both formal and informal, that grow out of pre-existing, often market-based relationships, through which the partners have ample opportunity to test and assess potential partners for a more substantial connection. In a study of Sino–Hong Kong JVs based in southern China, potential partners were 'identified primarily on the basis of existing social networks which were defined in terms of business, familial and friendship ties . . . strong ties, where they existed, expedited the search process and provided a more robust basis for final selection and subsequent inter-partner cooperation' (Wong and Ellis, 2002). Loose, informal alliances that evolve over time typically do not have formal negotiations or a final comprehensive

agreement, but simply involve a relationship that responds to changing circumstances and the interests of the parties, as in the McDonald's–Disney
arrangement noted above. In such cases, the alliance is in a constant state
of evolution, with altering perspectives about the alliance and its role on
behalf of the parties to it.

In the pre-agreement stage, personal interaction between individuals
from both sides can introduce an array of additional unforeseen considerations. As well, changes in managerial personnel on either side of those
involved in developing, negotiating or executing an alliance arrangement
can result in changes in personal interaction dynamics and attitudes
towards the alliance. Relationship development, between the prospective partners and relevant individual staff, is a critical aspect of the pre-
agreement stage of alliances. One of the US-based consultancies in this
field even recommends that companies entertaining alliances should undertake a so-called 'relationship due diligence' with regard to potential partners, to assess whether there is a basis for a positive relationship between
the parties (*Economist*, 2000). Negotiations over the form of an alliance
and the content of the agreement can become a major sub-process, of some
duration, as many companies have found in the Indian market. The
Norwegian company Nera, a maker of microwave radio link systems, took
four years developing and negotiating a JV arrangement with an Indian
partner, the final form of which was described as 'in essence a compromise
between our ideal wishes and the Indian reality' (Tomassen et al., 1998, 11).

Many argue that much can be achieved in the pre-agreement stage in
developing understanding between the parties and heading off potential
problems that could arise once the alliance is operating (Buchel et al.,
1998). As Osborn (2003, 39) found, 'apparent incompatibilities can often
be reconciled with extensive discussions prior to the operation of the
alliance. After starting the alliance, however, undiscussed incompatibilities
are very difficult to resolve'. Rather than going into negotiations with a relatively fixed idea of the form and goals of alliances, based on extensive
global experience, MasterCard has adopted a more flexible approach,
and enters into alliances that are more fluid in content and operation
(*Economist*, 2000).

Agreement

Given the diversity of alliance forms, it is difficult to describe the content
of a typical alliance agreement and, as noted, in some cases the approach
of the parties is flexible, with a preparedness to adjust to changing circumstances, internal and external to the firm. Indeed, there is an expectation
from companies coming from some cultural contexts that it is reasonable

to revisit the terms of an alliance contract if its functioning is affected by a major change in external conditions. This is more likely if the company is from a so-called 'high-context' culture (such as Japan), whereas companies from a low-context culture are likely to stress adherence to the formal terms of an agreement (for example, Germany) (Hall, 1977). However, a formal agreement (including JV) is likely to cover such elements as the following:

- the alliance's purpose and scope of activity,
- contributions, rights and responsibilities of each partner (e.g. equity shares in JV),
- financial arrangements, profit sharing,
- management structures and processes,
- treatment of intellectual property,
- dispute settlement procedures and arbitration,
- termination and exit clauses (Buchel et al., 1998; Mockler, 1999).

Figure 9.10 presents an overview of alliances from a process perspective, from initial interaction to disbandment and replacement in some form. As Figure 9.10 illustrates, in the pre-agreement phase, one or all of the negotiating parties might withdraw from discussions, bringing an end to the process at that point. The strategy consultants Bain & Co have claimed that 'out of every 100 negotiations about forming an alliance, 90 fail to produce an agreement' (Gant, 1995, 73). Given the range of issues on which the parties typically have to reach agreement in a substantial alliance arrangement – including control, strategy and staffing – as well as the potential for negative dynamics in interaction processes, as shown in Figure 9.9, it is not surprising that so many alliances struggle to reach the starting line. In addition, the complexity and demands involved in reaching agreement tend to multiply with increases in the number of parties to alliances. Studies of export grouping schemes show that it is very difficult to form such groups in the first place, to reach agreement on goals and establish a basis of cooperation (Welch et al., 2000). While small firms are often a focus of such schemes from a government export promotion perspective, the owner/managers of such firms typically find it hard to accept the necessary compromises and subversion of individuality involved in grouping arrangements.

Alliance Establishment and Transfers

The nature and extent of post-agreement transfers depend on the type of alliance. For new joint ventures the set-up demands may be substantial, for example when a new manufacturing facility has to be built, requiring diverse transfers (finance, technology, staff, equipment and the like) to the

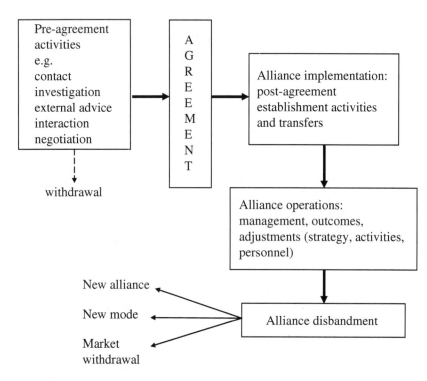

Figure 9.10   Alliances from a process perspective

foreign location. This is apart from the activities and costs associated with
on-site establishment of the new entity, including aspects such as legal
incorporation, ensuring intellectual property protection measures are in
place, obtaining various government approvals, selection and training of
staff, setting up of supply lines and distribution systems, and the creation
of joint management systems. A study of JVs involving British firms found
that they took longer than expected to set up (more than a year in most
cases), and were more difficult than takeovers to establish (Hyman, 1998).
When the alliance is an outcome of the acquisition of a part-share of an
existing enterprise, there may be limited initial direct involvement in the
alliance by the acquiring party, and limited transfers required. However, in
many cases involving acquisition, especially when the acquiring party is
seeking to take advantage of superior capabilities and technology, successful foreign market penetration is dependent on successful transfer of the
relevant strategic assets and implantation in the part-acquired firm. In
more informal alliances, with no concrete agreement form and perhaps no
specific date for the start of alliance–oriented activities, any transfers are

likely to be more spread out over the functioning process of the relationship, in line with the evolutionary character of many informal alliances.

Alliance Functioning

Research shows that alliances are inherently awkward to manage, in essence because they bring together two parties or more, often with different perspectives and goals, with a common but irreconcilable desire to control the alliance and what it does. In alliances such as JVs, where an independent corporate entity is created, inevitably there are two or more parent firms needing to cooperate and share so that the operation functions successfully, but both seeking a fit back to a broader parent context. In situations where one of the alliance 'parents' is a multinational with a strong corporate culture and set of global objectives, compromise with the divergent demands of another party may be difficult to accept and accommodate within tight global control protocols, setting the scene for conflict on a range of issues. Alliances are as much about building and managing relationships as about strategic direction and operations. Yoshino and Rangan (1995, 106) have observed that 'interfirm collaborations are plagued by ambiguities in relationships; tensions associated with the need to balance cooperation and competition; managerial mindsets acquainted with and often suspicious of inter-organisational links; myriad details that need to be managed; and lack of recognition of the complex linkages among the strategies, structures, and systems of both the participating firms and the alliance'.

Conflict between alliance partners may emerge in many areas and over a multitude of issues, including the following:

- Language and cultural differences between the partners in international alliances can generate problems in many areas, for example in communication styles and even the way of handling conflict, constraining the development of inter-personal relationships and trust. Cultural problems were an important background to the breakdown of the alliance between Volvo and Renault in 1994. At issue were aspects such as language, with the greater competence in, and preference to use, English by the Swedes, whereas the French would revert to French at times of conflict. There were differences in conflict-handling styles, and the French stressed styling and cost containment, whereas the Swedes emphasized engineering and safety (Bruner and Spekman, 1998).
- Staff appointments to the alliance (Peterson and Schwind, 1977; Robson et al., 2003).

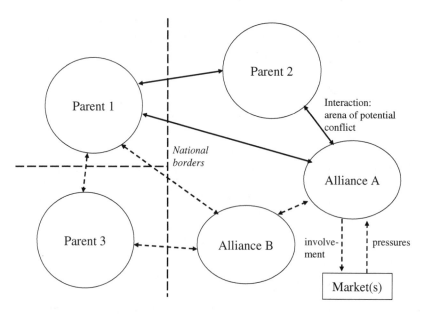

Figure 9.11   Alliance conflict

- Disagreements over alliance autonomy (control), strategy and policy, and a host of operational aspects such as product and service differentiation; pricing; distribution techniques; management methods, systems and processes; and approaches to sourcing and financing.
- When one of the alliance's parents attempts to use transfer pricing techniques and profit remittances in a way that is seen by the other as damaging to the performance of the alliance.
- The utilization and security of technology and intellectual property transferred to the alliance by one or more of the participating partners.
- As identified in Figure 9.11, conflict over the running of the alliance may emerge not only between the partners, but also between the alliance and either or both of its 'parents'. There is an inevitable tendency for the alliance operation to become more independent over time, as it acquires unique knowledge about and networks within the local market that allow it to distance itself from parental control. There may be times when managers of the alliance venture act in ways that are contrary to the declared wishes of one or more of its parents, in order to ensure operational success (Buchel et al., 1998). Alliance management requires a balancing act: between the goals and demands of the alliance's creators and drivers, the owners in JV

situations, and the need to be responsive to the demands of the relevant market(s) where it is involved, such as in dealing with competitive pressures. In addition, as companies expand the number and spread of alliances entered into, the potential for inter-alliance conflict arises, either directly or via their parents, sometimes within the same foreign market, with diverse national parentage and interests involved, for example, as shown in Figure 9.11, between alliances A and B.

Some of these issues will be settled beforehand as part of the negotiation process and will be incorporated in the final agreement, as part of a formal contract, but many of the expectations and objectives remain unexpressed or are vague, and are worked out as the alliance's operations unfold. Buchel et al. (1998, 70–71) refer to the case of Maxwell Electric, a multi-owner, foreign-Thai JV, established in Thailand, where there was a clear expectation of renegotiation of the JV in response to evolving conditions, and this was considered at an annual meeting of the parties. Whether planned or not, changes in the environment frequently put pressure on the parties to an alliance in ways that can never be anticipated in a formal agreement document. In rapidly changing conditions, a tight legal document can become a straitjacket, constraining the ability of the parties to respond to emerging pressures on the alliance.

As companies expand their international operations and the number and range of alliances, and alliance partners, inevitably there is an increase in the complexity and demands of managing a network of alliances and, as noted above, the various interactive effects within the network. The problem for many companies is that the set of alliances evolve with growing internationalization, often in a relatively haphazard way as more are added in response to emerging pressures and opportunities within a global context. The result is 'a tangled web of interdependent alliances' (Parise and Casher, 2003, 26). Using a study which involved multiple alliance personnel in a range of firms, Parise and Casher (2003, 25) concluded that 'most companies approach the design and management of their business partnerships by focusing on optimizing each individual alliance . . . and allocating resources based on the strategic importance of each partner'. Instead, they recommend a portfolio approach to each company's alliance network, viewing the network as a whole, assessing each alliance individually, as well as according to its part in the whole, taking account of the various interdependency effects. They add (36) that 'in roughly half the companies we studied, we are starting to see an alliance director emerge', as an organizational response to the concern about maintaining control over the growing portfolio.

Trust

Recent research has emphasized the importance of the development of
trust between the alliance partners in ensuring the effective functioning of
alliances in the face of the many avenues of conflict arousal (Boersma et al.,
2003). As Parkhe (2004, 219) has observed, 'trust can lubricate alliances
and make alliances more efficient (inter)organizational modes'. Trust is a
dynamic concept, with multiple elements, including performance according to agreed guidelines and behavioural satisfaction (such as goodwill),
that are developed and assessed as a relationship evolves. Boersma et al.
(2003) found that trust was both an output and an input in alliance
progression from pre-agreement to the alliance functioning stage. The
pre-agreement negotiation phase can be important in building trust, and
research shows pre-existing contacts, market-based relationships and previous alliance experience between the same partners are potential contributors to the development of trust as a basis for new alliances (Gulati, 1995;
Inkpen, 1998; Scott-Kemmis et al., 1990). In one case within an investigation of the alliance–acquisition decision encompassing a number of
European countries, the interviewee commented: 'We prefer cooperation
with partners that we already know and with whom we have built up a trust
relationship. Each new partner not only increases the complexity of our
alliance portfolio, it also initially requires special effort to build up a good
inter-personal work relationship' (Hoffmann and Schaper-Rinkel, 2001,
148). Building trust takes time, particularly with large and complex
alliances, even when pre-existing connections have been developed, as in the
Volvo–Renault case, and these were insufficiently strong to save the alliance
from the breakdown that occurred at the interfaces between the two companies in alliance implementation (Bruner and Spekman, 1998).

Pre-alliance development of trust is more difficult in situations where, for
example, a JV is created through one party acquiring an interest in an existing foreign entity. Boersma et al. (2003) point to the importance of the 'execution stage' of alliance progression in the development of trust, when the
parties are called upon to fulfil their parts of what has been agreed to in the
lead-up to the start of alliance operations in the foreign market. Social relationships between individuals and inter-personal dynamics are a critical
part of the evolution and strength of trust. On the basis of a study of disparate alliances, in different industries and across many countries, Kanter
(1994, 97) concluded: 'they cannot be "controlled" by formal systems but
require a dense web of interpersonal connections and internal infrastruc-
tures that enhance learning'. These are also the interconnections through
which a critical part of trust develops. Furthermore an investigation of 129
US-based international JVs found that, over time, trust and social controls

'become key elements in the successful long-term management of IJVs' (Fryxell et al., 2002, 883). The authors speculate that trust enhances alliance flexibility in the face of changes in the environment and partner needs that may require substantive changes in alliance strategy and activities.

Alliance Performance

Performance evaluation is an important part of the functioning of an alliance, affecting the likelihood of continuance, although it can be a difficult issue because of the different ways of measuring performance, and the different perspectives on performance that the alliance partners have. Parkhe (2004, 219) argues that poor financial performance may be quite acceptable if an alliance is not simply a profit centre but rather a source of learning. There could be other benefits such as cost reduction or product enhancement that are picked up elsewhere in a multinational's global operations. Of course, if these benefits accrue to only one of the parents, such as when the alliance brings together a large multinational and a much smaller local firm, with the multinational seen to be the main beneficiary of the alliance operation, this is bound to have a destabilizing effect. The multinational is much better placed to use transfer pricing and other techniques to magnify benefits elsewhere in its network rather than in the alliance venture. This is one of the reasons it is argued that alliance partners need to agree in advance on what criteria are appropriate in evaluating alliance performance (Buchel et al., 1998). The criteria might include variables such as profitability, growth, market share, competitive position, productivity, cost efficiency and quality. The difficulty is to agree on satisfactory levels for the chosen criteria.

Various studies have found that the majority of international alliances examined do not achieve the financial expectations of their partners (Yeheskal et al., 2004), and some alliances are downright value-destroying projects for the shareholders of their parent companies (Merchant, 2004). Behavioural considerations (such as good relationships) also come into play in performance evaluation, although indicators of performance are difficult to identify formally in advance and measure as alliance operations unfold. However, companies can clearly identify when positive or negative inter-firm relationships have developed, and widespread research has shown the quality of these relationships to be important in whether an alliance has a future: whether formally or not, they are evaluated and it does matter. As shown in Figure 9.12, alliance outcomes are evaluated by the partners and, depending on their goals and strategy, affect their perception of alliance performance, influencing their preparedness to commit themselves to the alliance operation. In general, continued perceived poor

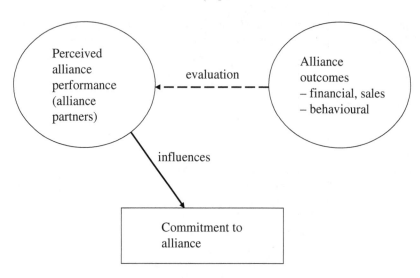

Figure 9.12   Alliance performance and commitment

performance, however it is measured, sooner or later tends to ensure the demise of an alliance.

Alliance performance, the nature of outcomes and the time frame to dissolution are connected issues. For example, it has been argued that alliances are 'inherently unstable, so may serve a perfectly useful function but only for a limited period of time' (Gant, 1995, 73). In other words, it should be expected that the inconsistencies in alliances eventually create an untenable situation and termination. Nevertheless, positive benefits can be created in the alliance situation for the period of its operation, to the extent that dissolution is an acceptable outcome, particularly when it is anticipated and prepared for. Termination of an alliance is not necessarily a sign of its failure to achieve the objectives sought by the participating partners (Hennart et al., 1998). Recent research has stressed the potential learning benefits of alliances, particularly when companies are conscious of this potential, and actively seek to access and transfer the array of unique knowledge and skills that an alliance partner possesses (Inkpen, 1998). To the extent that this is successful, it might be viewed as a positive outcome of alliance activity and thereby supportive of the continuation of an alliance. However, this outcome also could be destabilizing: the foreign firm has extracted all that it needs from the local firm and can therefore operate more readily on its own – perhaps via full takeover of the partner, as often occurs (Hennart et al., 1998; Reuer, 1998; Parkhe, 2004). While companies may be hesitant about operating in a new and culturally distant market by themselves initially, as in the case of the Norwegian companies entering the Indian market noted above, as experience in, understanding of, and network connections within the market develop, entrant firms are likely to be more prepared to contemplate the prospect of operating via non-alliance modes entailing greater direct involvement. As Kanter (1994, 97) has argued, alliances 'must yield benefits for the partners, but they are more than just the deal. They are living systems that evolve progressively in their possibilities. Beyond the immediate reasons for entering into a relationship, the connection offers the parties an option on the future'.

Disbandment

Given the inherent management, control and conflict issues noted above, it is not surprising that many studies find a low survival rate for alliances (not the same as failure), particularly in the form of joint ventures, the more readily measured form. The management consultants, Bain & Co, concluded that, of the ten alliances (out of 100) that make it past the negotiation stage, 'five fail to meet the partners' expectations for the venture. And of the five that produce acceptable results, only two survive for more than four years' (Gant, 1995, 73). As part of a group that 'followed hundreds of alliances from inception to their fifth birthdays', Osborn (2003, 38) found 'of the announced and operative alliances . . . about 60% have either failed to start or have faded away in five years'. However, there was considerable variation amongst different categories – some with an 80 per cent death rate, others having an 80 per cent survival rate. A key factor in many of the alliances examined was the extent of change in the external environment. 'Joint ventures failed miserably under highly volatile demand or rapid changes in product technology' (Osborn, 2003, 41). With relatively stable demand and technology, the survival rate for JVs improved dramatically, to about 75 per cent after five years.

Using a large, longitudinal study of the JVs of Japanese companies in a wide range of countries over the period 1986–99, Delios and Beamish (2004) concluded that JV performance and survival rates overall were similar to those for the companies' wholly owned subsidiaries. There was a difference, though, between majority-owned JVs (51–95 per cent Japanese equity) as a group, and 50:50 and minority-owned JVs (5–49 per cent Japanese equity) as a group: the former group had a roughly 50 per cent higher survival rate than the latter. Overall, the drop-out rate for JVs appears to have been accentuated by the broad move from JVs to wholly-owned operations, particularly in China as the government gradually liberalized the foreign direct investment regulations, allowing the establishment of, or shift to, wholly-owned operations by foreign companies in a widening range of industries

(Deng, 2001; Desai et al., 2004). While the general picture is of a low survival rate for alliances, in various studies and across a wide range of countries, with a positive association between poor performance and JV exit rates, there are also many examples of alliances persisting for some time after it becomes clear they are generating poor results. The variables identified as contributing to this seemingly perverse situation in a study by Delios et al. (2004) were high alliance termination costs, high sunk costs and high alliance visibility, generating significant negative publicity and lost goodwill and reputation effects in some countries when alliances were disbanded and the business closed. In addition, varied research indicates that companies do learn from preceding JV experiences in a way that tends to enhance JV management capacity and performance (Glaister et al., 2003).

It is clear that many companies do recognize the limited time span involved in most alliances, and take considerations of the 'after life' into any arrangement. This is why more and more companies are including flexible options in alliance agreements, particularly JVs, permitting exit on pre-agreed terms, or a shift to alternative arrangements, including full takeover of the JV partner (Petersen et al., 2000). For example, in 1989, Philips wanted to get out of the domestic appliance manufacturing business and so entered into a JV with Whirlpool. The equity breakdown was Whirlpool 53 per cent and Philips 47 per cent. As part of the JV agreement Whirlpool was given an option to buy the JV outright within three years. This it did, being able to assess more reliably the value and potential of the business from its perspective from the inside of the JV before making a full takeover commitment. Whirlpool quickly revitalized the business with a variety of changes in operations and marketing, transferring technology to the JV and integrating it into Whirlpool's broader systems and network (Nanda and Williamson, 1995). Despite the short life of this JV, it satisfied the objectives of both parties, illustrating the weakness of using JV survival rates as a sole measure of outcomes.

Alliance exit clauses have become more common in alliance agreements, adding to the demands of the initial negotiation stage: they are akin to a pre-nuptial agreement, settling the terms of a possible divorce before marriage is entered into and, seemingly, run counter to the idea of establishing a positive relationship between the parties through the pre-agreement interaction process. To the extent that exit clauses become a relatively common part of alliance agreements, there is likely to be less stigma associated with raising the issue in negotiations – it may well become a normal and expected part of the process. However, the insertion of exit clauses into alliance agreements is part of the broader concern for companies of how to build options into their mode strategies in a way that facilitates mode alterations as mode and partner experience evolve, and market outcomes and contexts change (Petersen et al., 2000). This issue will be covered in detail in the strategy part of the book.

The Philips–Whirlpool case indicates that what comes after the alliance may be as, or more, important than the alliance itself for a company seeking internationalization, even though the alliance may be a critical stepping stone. Even in alliances that end in a blaze of acrimonious dispute, there may well have been significant learning through the alliance experience – about the market, the culture and how to operate (and how not to) within it, including how to manage alliances, along with the development of useful networks, and even exposing alternative candidates for different mode arrangements. In Whirlpool's case the learning process was very deliberate, with a clear objective, as in alliance examples where the principal aim is technology acquisition. In other alliances learning processes are likely to be less controlled and formalized, with market penetration as the overriding driving force, and much of the learning unseen as a result of individual activity and informal personal interactions, but this can be important and potentially useful nonetheless. Much depends on whether management recognizes the knowledge assets developed through the alliance experience, and where and how staff connected to the alliance are used after its breakdown.

As shown in Figure 9.10, following disbandment, various outcomes are feasible, such as complete market withdrawal by the entrant firm(s); the creation of a new alliance, perhaps as a result of the entrant firm(s) linking with a different local firm but essentially carrying out the same business activity; or a shift to a different mode. The ability to continue to operate in the same market after an alliance is terminated depends on the entrant firm's retention of ownership and control of key assets such as intellectual property (trademarks, technology) and staff after the alliance folds. Acquisition of the local partner's share is one way the entrant firm can ensure that its key assets are retained, and even extended. Procter & Gamble went into a highly publicized 51 per cent-owned JV with the Indian company Godrej Soaps to exploit Indian market prospects in late 1992. It took only four years to end in divorce, as a result of market erosion rather than success, and arguments about each other's responsibility for the outcome. In the end, P&G acquired Godrej's share of the JV, and ensured that it retained what were considered the JV's crown jewels for continuing operations, its grassroots marketing network and salesforce, courtesy of Godrej: what might be considered a satisfactory outcome from the JV exercise from P&G's perspective (Ramaswamy et al., 1998). In a study of international alliances over the period 1985–95, Reuer (1998) found that, on termination, in almost 84 per cent of cases, one party acquired or sold to the other. Further, buyout of the JV was more likely when one party maintained 'significant control' over the

JV operation during its lifetime (Reuer, 2002). In only about 7 per cent of cases did either JV partner sell out to a third party. Of course, with some alliances, particularly informal ones, the cooperation may simply fade as circumstances change, with little recognition of the end or activity in response to it.

SUCCESS FACTORS

One of the more difficult questions to ask about alliances is, what drives or determines success? As already noted in the discussion above, it is difficult enough trying to clarify what is meant by success – or, in general, how performance is evaluated. Much depends on the goals of the alliance partners and how the alliance is used to achieve those goals. The fact that an alliance may be seen as a pathway to another form of operations, as in Whirlpool's interest in eventual takeover of its JV partner Philips, changes both the measures of success and the notion of what are contributors to alliance success. Likewise, the type of alliance influences the measures of success and its determinants. In addition, there is the issue of what time frame is appropriate for considering success and how this is built: long-term market penetration and eventual profitability may be preceded by short-term losses caused by a range of critical up-front commitments to the alliance operation. Given the failure of financial and survival measures to reflect adequately alliance success as viewed by the internationalizing firm using the alliance mode, Glaister and Buckley (1999) used perceptual measures of performance in their study of UK firms' international alliances: specifically, level of satisfaction with the alliance's overall performance and subjective evaluation of the alliance's cost–benefit. Important success factors to emerge in their study were (a) depth of analysis prior to alliance formation, (b) an ongoing and extended set of long-term relationships between the partners, (c) the behaviour and performance of the partner firm, and (d) cultural distance was not found to be a significant factor.

The first factor identifies the importance of getting to know a possible alliance partner well enough to be able to assess more effectively the fit of the parties and relationship and business potential. The second factor is in line with other research in this area emphasizing the importance of the relationship between the alliance partners, and that this is enhanced by any preceding connections, by the initial negotiation process and by any other connections, including other alliances with the same partner, beyond the focal alliance. An Australian study of the most successful alliances concluded that they were characterized by shared interests and complementary capabilities, good communication at the different levels, compatible firm cultures and trust: all aspects of positive relationship development (Scott-Kemmis et al., 1990). A strong relationship provides a more effective basis for dealing with the inevitable problems that arise over alliance management and operations, particularly as changes in the environment put stress on the performance of the alliance. Embedded in the relationship factor are aspects such as information, knowledge and technology sharing, and the development of positive inter-personal links at the various levels.

In assessing the reasons for failure of the Volvo–Renault alliance, Bruner and Spekman (1998, 149) concluded: 'one is struck by how much of it is explained *at the interfaces* of human behaviour: nations, cultures, allies, owners vs managers, and senior managers vs operating managers'. While the unimportance of cultural distance may seem surprising, other research points to the likely indirect effect of cultural factors on other relationship elements such as inter-personal interaction and trust (Reus and Ritchie, 2004). For example, without a common language it is difficult for the interacting partners to build strong interpersonal relationships. The behaviour and performance of the partner firm as a success factor is something of a 'catch-all', and could be expanded to the nature, extent and quality of commitment of both parties on a continuing basis to the alliance (including resources and managerial commitment). In a recent selective review of research on international JVs, similar factors to those mentioned emerged, but additional factors were noted under the general heading of environment-related influences, such as speed of change in markets and technology, environmental turbulence, competition and host-country political and economic conditions (Osborn, 2003; Reus and Ritchie, 2004). Overall, it is apparent there is no simple magic wand to wave and ensure alliance success, however defined. At the least, alliances demand patience and commitment by the alliance partners, and time for key underlying, supportive processes, such as cooperative relationships, to evolve.

CONCLUSION

Analysis of alliances as a foreign operation mode has shown that they offer a wide range of possibilities in solving the problem of how to penetrate foreign markets effectively. The diversity of alliance types, and the overlap with other forms of operation, make it difficult to generalize about their nature and impacts. However, this can be seen as one of their key strengths: the variety in forms of alliances means that there is an alliance to suit virtually every foreign market situation confronted by internationalizing companies. It is not surprising, therefore, to find a high level of global interest

among companies in using alliances, and among governments in supporting some forms to promote internationalization. Alliances offer the possibility of linking with and accessing a partner firm's resources – such as
knowledge, contacts, credibility, finance and technology – in foreign market
operations. These elements have the potential to assist market penetration,
accelerate the process and bolster the prospects of a successful outcome.
Alliances can assist companies in overcoming many of the barriers and
demands that are normally faced in pursuing foreign market activity,
including language, culture, government laws and regulations, and local
business practices. Many examples in this chapter have shown that this
potential contribution of local partner firms is often highly valued by
foreign entrant firms. This is why so many firms are undoubtedly considering the alliance option as they currently contemplate whether and how to
establish operations in China and/or India. Alliance capacity as a foreign
operation mode can be further enhanced by links with other mode forms,
as noted elsewhere, for example by using licensing agreements to cover the
use of technology and other types of intellectual property. The nature and
implications of alliance mode combinations are dealt with in the strategy
part of the book.

   However, while alliances offer many attractive aspects that amount to a
strong argument for their use in foreign operations, they come with a range
of potential problems and costs, and have some basic characteristics, that
often generate dissatisfaction and a high drop-out rate. Despite their
promise, alliances are like the other modes considered so far; they are
no simple panacea. Inevitably, given the different parties involved, and
conflicting interests, and their cross-cultural character in the bulk of situations, they are difficult to manage. Relationships at many levels have to be
built between the partners, and between the partners and the alliance entity
as a foundation for cooperation and to achieve effective coordination of
activities and strategy. This is why a consistent message emerging from the
research is that any forms of pre-alliance relationships, for example in
market-based buyer–seller interactions, contribute to a higher probability
of alliance success. Nevertheless, the termination of an alliance is not necessarily a sign of failure of the alliance to achieve what was expected of it
by one or both partners (or more), and can be a useful testing ground for
full-scale takeover by one partner. In fact, whether deliberate or not, the
reality of alliances is that they tend to have a relatively short 'shelf life', and
companies are increasingly treating alliances as a preparatory step for
something else in operation terms, in part because of the type of advice
emerging from consultants. Of course, treating alliances in an instrumental, stepping-stone manner tends to ensure that they do not persist in the
long term.

REFERENCES

Auster, E.R. (1987), 'International corporate linkages: dynamic forms in changing environments', *Columbia Journal of World Business*, **12**(2), 3–6.

Australian (2006), 'Nortel–Huawei link', 7 February, 34.

Baughn, C.C., J.G. Danekamp, J.H. Stevens and R.N. Osborn (1997), 'Protecting intellectual capital in international alliances', *Journal of World Business*, **32**(2), 103–17.

Boateng, A. and K.W. Glaister (2003), 'Strategic motives for international joint venture formation in Ghana', *Management International Review*, **43**(2), 107–28.

Boersma, M.F., P.J. Buckley and P.N. Ghauri (2003), 'Trust in international joint venture relationships', *Journal of Business Research*, **56**, 1031–42.

Bruner, R. and R. Spekman (1998), 'The dark side of alliances: lessons from Volvo–Renault', *European Management Journal*, **16**(2), 136–50.

Buchel, B., C. Prange, G. Probst and C.-C. Ruling (1998), *International Joint Venture Management*, Singapore: John Wiley.

Buckley, P.J. (1992), 'Alliances, technology and markets: a cautionary tale', in P.J. Buckley, *Studies in International Business*, London: Macmillan.

Bureau of Industry Economics (1989), 'Selling packaged software overseas: the successful channels', Research Report 31, Canberra: Australian Government Publishing Service.

Business International (1990), *Making Alliances Work*, London.

Chen, M. (1995), 'Technological transfer to China: major rules and issues', *International Journal of Technology Management*, **10**(7/8), 747–56.

Chessell, J. (2004), 'BHP hits record on China optimism', *Sydney Morning Herald*, 3 March, 21.

Contractor, F.J. and P. Lorange (2002), 'The growth of alliances in the knowledge-based economy', *International Business Review*, **11**(4), 485–502.

Delios, A. and P.W. Beamish (2004), 'Joint venture performance revisited: Japanese foreign subsidiaries worldwide', *Management International Review*, **44**(1), 69–91.

Delios, A., A.C. Inkpen and J. Ross (2004), 'Escalation in international strategic alliances', *Management International Review*, **44**(4), 457–79.

Deng, P. (2001), 'WFOEs: the most popular entry mode into China', *Business Horizons*, **44**(4), 63–72.

Desai, M.A., C.F. Foley and J.R. Hines jr (2004), 'Venture out alone', *Harvard Business Review*, **84**(3), 22.

Doz, Y. (1996), 'The evolution of cooperation in strategic alliances: initial conditions or learning processes?', *Strategic Management Journal*, **17** (special issue, summer), 55–83.

Economist (1998), 'The science of alliance', 4 April, 73–4.

Economist (2000), 'Managing alliances – trust us', 26 August, 56–7.

Emmott, W. (1993), 'Multinationals: back in fashion', *Economist* (Survey), 27 March.

Ferris, W.D. et al. (1985), *Lifting Australia's Performance as an Exporter of Manufactures and Services*, Canberra: Australian Government Publishing Service.

Ford, D. (ed.) (1990), *Understanding Business Markets: Interaction, Relationships and Networks*, London: Academic Press.

Fryxell, G.E., R.S. Dooley and M. Vryza (2002), 'After the ink dries: the interaction of trust and control in US-based international joint ventures', *Journal of Management Studies*, **39**(6), 865–86.

Gant, J. (1995), 'The science of alliance', *EuroBusiness*, **3**(5), 70–73.

Glaister, K.W. and P.J. Buckley (1996), 'Strategic motives for international alliance formation', *Journal of Management Studies*, **33**(3), 301–32.

Glaister, K.W. and P.J. Buckley (1999), 'Performance relationships in UK international alliances', *Management International Review*, **39**(2), 123–47.

Glaister, K.W., R. Husan and P.J. Buckley (2003), 'Learning to manage international joint ventures', *International Business Review*, **12**(1), 83–108.

Grayson, I. (2002), 'HP, NEC e-merge to outsource', *Australian*, 13 December, 25.

Griggs, T. (2005), 'Vodafone rings Indian mobile firm', *Australian*, 31 October, 34.

Gulati, R. (1995), 'Does familiarity breed trust? The implications of repeated ties for contractual choice in alliances', *Academy of Management Journal*, **38**(1), 85–112.

Hall, E.T. (1977), *Beyond Culture*, Garden City, NY: Anchor Books.

Harrigan, K.R. (1986), *Managing for Joint Venture Success*, Lexington, MA: Lexington Books.

Hennart, J.-F. (1988), 'A transaction costs theory of equity joint ventures', *Strategic Management Journal*, **9**(4), 361–74.

Hennart, J.-F., D.J. Kim, and M. Zeng (1998), 'The impact of joint venture status on the longevity of Japanese stakes in US manufacturing affiliates', *Organization Science*, **9**(3), 382–95.

Hoffmann, W.H. and W. Schaper-Rinkel (2001), 'Acquire or ally? – a strategy framework for deciding between acquisition and cooperation', *Management International Review*, **41**(2), 131–59.

Hyman, C. (1998), 'Joint ventures – a triumph of hope over reality?', KPMG Transaction Services.

Inkpen, A. (1998), 'Learning, knowledge acquisition, and strategic alliances', *European Management Journal*, **16**(2), 223–9.

Kang, N.-H. and K. Sakai (2000), 'International strategic alliances: their role in industrial globalisation', STI Working Paper 2000/5, OECD.

Kanter, R.M. (1994), 'Collaborative advantage: the art of alliances', *Harvard Business Review*, **72**(4), 96–108.

Kogut, B. (1988), 'A study of the life cycle of joint ventures', *Management International Review*, **28** (special issue), 39–52.

Kone News & Views (2004), 'KONE and TELC increase cooperation', **2**, 4–6.

Kumar, B.N. (1995), 'Partner-selection criteria and success of technology transfer: a model based on learning theory applied to the cost of Indo-German technical collaborations', *Management International Review*, **35** (special issue 1), 65–78.

Lu, J.W. and P.W. Beamish (2004), 'Network development and firm performance: a field study of internationalizing Japanese firms', *Multinational Business Review*, **12**(3), 41–61.

Lyons, M. (1990), 'Laboratory tests the export waters', *Business Review Weekly*, 16 November, 60–61.

Macdonald, S. (1992), 'Formal collaboration and informal information flow', *International Journal of Technology Management*, **7**(1/2/3), 49–60.

Merchant, H. (2004), 'Revisiting shareholder value creation via international joint ventures: examining interactions among firm- and context-specific variables', *Canadian Journal of Administrative Sciences*, **21**(2), 129–45.

Mintzberg, H. and J.A. Waters (1985), 'Of strategies, deliberate and emergent', *Strategic Management Journal*, **6**(3), 257–72.

Mockler, R.J. (1999), *Multinational Strategic Alliances*, Chichester: John Wiley.

Nanda, A. and P.J. Williamson (1995), 'Use joint ventures to ease the pain of restructuring', *Harvard Business Review*, **73**(6), 119–28.

Narula, R. (2003), *Globalization & Technology: Interdependence, Innovation Systems and Industrial Policy*, Cambridge: Polity Press.

Ohmae, K. (1989), 'The global logic of strategic alliances', *Harvard Business Review*, **67**(2), 143–54.

O'Neill, M. (2004), 'Consumer markets: breaking through', *China International Business*, October, 21–9.

O'Reilly, A.J.F. (1988), 'Establishing successful joint ventures in developing nations: a CEO's perspective', *Columbia Journal of World Business*, **23**(1), 65–71.

Osborn, R.N. (2003), 'International alliances: going beyond the hype', *Mt Eliza Business Review*, **6**(1), 37–43.

Parise, S. and A. Casher (2003), 'Alliance portfolios: designing and managing your network of business–partner relationships', *Academy of Management Executive*, **17**(4), 25–39.

Parkhe, A. (2004), 'International alliances', in B.J. Punnett and O. Shenkar (eds), *Handbook for International Management Research*, 2nd edn, Ann Arbor: University of Michigan Press.

Petersen, B. and L.S. Welch (2002), 'Foreign operation mode combinations and internationalization', *Journal of Business Research*, **55**(2), 157–62.

Petersen, B. and L.S. Welch (2003), 'Foreign operation mode combination strategy', in EIBA Conference Proceedings (on CD-Rom), 11–13 December, Copenhagen, Denmark.

Petersen, B., D.E. Welch and L.S. Welch (2000), 'Creating meaningful switching options in international operations', *Long Range Planning*, **33**(5), 688–705.

Peterson, R.B. and H.F. Schwind (1977), 'A comparative study of personnel problems in international companies and joint ventures in Japan', *Journal of International Business Studies*, **8**(1), 45–55.

Ramaswamy, K., L. Gomes and R. Veliyath (1998), 'The performance correlates of ownership control: a study of U.S. and European MNE joint ventures in India', *International Business Review*, **7**(4), 423–41.

Reuer, J. (1998), 'The dynamics and effectiveness of international joint ventures', *European Management Journal*, **16**(2), 160–68.

Reuer, J.J. (2002), 'Incremental corporate reconfiguration through international joint venture buyouts and selloffs', *Management International Review*, **42**(3), 237–60.

Reus, T.H. and W.J. Ritchie (2004), 'Interpartner, parent, and environmental factors influencing the operation of international joint ventures: 15 years of research', *Management International Review*, **44**(4), 369–95.

Robson, M.J., N. Paparoidamis and D. Ginoglu (2003), 'Top management staffing in international strategic alliances: a conceptual explanation of decision perspective and objective formation', *International Business Review*, **12**(2), 173–91.

Scott-Kemmis, D., T. Darling, R. Johnston, F. Collyer and C. Cliff (1990), *Strategic Alliances in the Internationalisation of Australian Industry*, Canberra: Australian Government Publishing Service.

Tatoglu, E. and K.W. Glaister (2000), 'Strategic motives and partner selection criteria in international joint ventures in Turkey: perspectives of Western firms and Turkish firms', *Journal of Global Marketing*, **13**(3).

Tomassen, S., L.S. Welch and G.R.G. Benito (1998), 'Norwegian companies in India: operation mode choice', *Asian Journal of Business and Information Systems*, **3**(1), 1–20.

Van de Ven, A.H. (1976), 'On the nature, formation and maintenance of relations among organizations', *Academy of Management Review*, **7**(4), 24–36.

Welch, D., L. Welch, I. Wilkinson and L. Young (2000), 'An export grouping scheme', *Journal of Euromarketing*, **9**(2), 59–84.

Welch, D.E., L.S. Welch, L.C. Young and I.F. Wilkinson (1998), 'The importance of networks in export promotion: policy issues', *Journal of International Marketing*, **6**(4), 66–82.

Welch, L.S. (1992), 'The use of alliances by small firms in achieving internationalization', *Scandinavian International Business Review*, **1**(2), 21–37.

Wong, P.L.-K. and P. Ellis (2002), 'Social ties and partner identification in Sino-Hong Kong international joint ventures', *Journal of International Business Studies*, **33**(2), 267–89.

Yeheskal, O., W. Newburry and Y. Zeira (2004), 'Significant differences in the pre- and post-incorporation stages of equity international joint ventures (IJVs) and international acquisitions (IAs), and their impacts on effectiveness', *International Business Review*, **13**(5), 613–36.

Yoshino, M.Y. and U.S. Rangan (1995), *Strategic Alliances: An Entrepreneurial Approach to Globalization*, Boston, MA: Harvard Business School Press.

10. Foreign direct investment

INTRODUCTION

The last major set of foreign operation methods is grouped under the general heading of foreign direct investment (FDI). The topic has been a preoccupation of international business thinking and research, and of countless articles and books, over the last five decades. FDI has been inextricably linked to the rise of multinational companies in global business activity and their far-reaching influence at all levels of the social, political and economic life of nations. While other modes are typically employed at different stages and in different locations in companies' international evolution and current operations, multinationals are in essence created and defined by FDI activity. The focus on multinationals has been a relatively recent phenomenon, although their evolution stretches back a considerable distance in history, with many examples arising in the 19th century in the wake of the burgeoning trade, migration and economic expansion of that period (Johanson and Wiedersheim-Paul, 1975; Wilkins, 1970). However, in line with the theme of this book, the focus is not on multinationals and their activities but on the use of FDI as a mode of foreign operations, in conjunction with, or as an alternative to, other modes such as those already examined, whatever the size and global reach of the company considering its use. Inevitably, though, any discussion of FDI in various ways brings multinationals into purview given that they are the major purveyors of FDI activity.

The widespread interest in, and concern about, FDI has been occasioned by its sheer size and resulting impact on global economic activity, overall and in diverse locations. The sales generated by companies' foreign subsidiaries constitute a major part of global gross domestic product (GDP), and far exceed the gross value of global exports of goods and services. Data from the 2006 World Investment Report (UNCTAD, 2006) indicate that global exports of goods and services in 2005 were only 57 per cent of the sales of the foreign affiliates (subsidiaries) of transnationals (multinationals). Overall, global inflows of FDI amounted to US$916 billion in 2005 (at current prices), a rise of 29 per cent over 2004, but still below the levels of 1999 and 2000 when totals exceeded US$1 trillion. The developed countries were the main recipients of FDI (59 per cent of total). Of the total FDI inflows for 2005, US$716 billion (78.2 per cent) were in the form of mergers and acquisitions (M&As). In order of importance, the main FDI recipient countries were the UK, the US, China and France. Japan stands out as a large, developed economy with a low level of inward FDI relative to other developed economies, particularly in the form of M&As. About 36 per cent of global inflows went to developing countries (predominantly China). In an UNCTAD (2005) survey of FDI prospects, India was listed as the third most attractive location (after China and the US), an indication of the likely increase in inflows to that country. FDI continues to be mainly in the services sector (about 63 per cent of M&As and 60 per cent of greenfield investment in 2004, with little change in 2005) so that the sector is now the repository of the bulk of global FDI stock. In 2005, there was a large increase in FDI in the primary sector, mainly in the oil industry. Equity capital is the largest source of FDI financing according to the UNCTAD (2005) data, representing about 67 per cent of inflows over the period 1995–2004. The rest was financed by intra-company loans (23 per cent) and reinvested earnings (12 per cent), although since 2001 there has been a sharp drop in the former and corresponding rise in the latter.

The developed countries are the source of the bulk of global FDI, con-tributing 83 per cent of total outflows in 2005 (UNCTAD, 2006). The two main sources over the period 2001–2005 were the EU and the US. While developing countries undertook a negligible level of outward FDI in the 1980s, there has been growing outward movement since then, reaching US$133 billion in 2005, 17 per cent of global outflows, and resulting in the accumulation of in excess of US$1 trillion of global FDI stock. While China is a major focus of inward FDI activity, it is illustrative of many developing countries in the way that its companies have quickly turned their attention beyond the home market, with early use of FDI in foreign company expan-sion. An example is Jinan Qingqi Motorcycle of China which set up joint venture assembly plants for its motorcycles in Pakistan and Lithuania in 1995, followed by similar facilities in Sri Lanka and Argentina (Saywell, 1999). While the level of outward FDI is low relative to inward flows, there is now substantial momentum in the outward movement of Chinese enter-prises. A survey indicated that about 75 per cent of Chinese manufacturing companies had foreign expansion plans (*Economist*, 2003, 59). The outward movement has received official encouragement by the Chinese government and various forms of tangible support (Saywell, 1999; Vatikiotis, 2004). Some Chinese companies have already become substantial international players, and show a readiness to use the acquisition path well travelled by large multinationals from developed countries. A case in point is the Chinese computer manufacturer, Lenovo, which acquired the personal computer business of IBM in early 2005 (*Economist*, 2005b). Likewise, successful

Indian companies in the IT software and business process outsourcing industry, such as Satyam, have been establishing extensive global networks of subsidiaries, and this process has spread to other sectors, with outbound takeover activity surpassing inbound flows in 2006 (Hayes and Mitchell, 2005; Leahy, 2006).

FDI tends to be seen as the most powerful method of foreign market incursion, the most substantial way in which a company can become involved in a foreign market, but normally requiring a heavy on-the-ground commitment of various types of resources: for example, finance, technology and people. It is typically regarded as being the means of a company extracting the highest gross returns from foreign market involvement, and of having the most direct and powerful influence on the way foreign operations are enacted and on controlling market outcomes. As a result, it tends to be viewed as something of an end point, or peak, in company internationalization, although earlier analysis of other modes like franchising has shown that there may be other mode steps after the move into FDI, while divestment and full market withdrawal appear to have become a more common feature of companies' global strategic landscape (Benito and Welch, 1997). The characteristics of FDI, though, mean that it is also viewed in recipient markets as the most confronting, threatening form of foreign activity, particularly when undertaken via full takeover of local companies, more especially when these are regarded as local icons. Examples abound of governments responding to public outcries about high-profile takeovers by intervening in various ways to ensure failure of the takeover attempts (*Economist*, 2006). For example, the media, telecommunications and electricity industries in South Korea are quarantined from takeover, and there are moves to widen the range of 'protected' industries in response to negative national sentiment toward hostile foreign takeovers (Fifield, 2006).

FDI has long been a focus of government attention in most countries, with various types of screening and approval mechanisms used to control its flow, although these often operate alongside encouragement schemes. In general, though, the trend over the last two decades has been towards increasingly liberal treatment of inward FDI, and growing competition among countries for this investment. UNCTAD (2003, 11) has reported that 'government policies [with regard to FDI] are becoming more open, involving more incentives and focused promotion policies . . . Facing diminished FDI flows, many governments accelerated the liberalization of FDI regimes'. UNCTAD (2005) data show that the overwhelming bulk of countries' regulatory changes affecting FDI since 1991 have been more favourable to its use. Recent steps by Chinese and Indian authorities to reduce the nature and extent of FDI restrictions are illustrative of the broad liberalization trend. For instance, foreign companies have been allowed to set up wholly owned subsidiaries in the retail sector in China since December 2004, whereas previously the limit was 65 per cent. Nevertheless, as noted above, even in seemingly FDI-liberal countries, governments are not immune from campaigns against the takeover of particular companies. A recent example was the attempted takeover of the US oil company Unocal by the state-owned China National Offshore Oil Corporation. The offer to buy was withdrawn after sustained political opposition in the US at the highest levels, based on concerns about the implications for the country's energy security (*Economist*, 2005a). Moreover, France has increased its range of defences against unwelcome foreign takeovers, supporting a more active interventionist government role, despite the opposition to its measures from other EU countries (Arnold and Minder, 2006).

FDI tends to be linked to the array of modes already examined in various ways, depending on the particular role assigned to the foreign enterprise which has been the outcome of the investment process, and the demands of the local context. Investment in the mining industry which is aimed at securing supplies of raw materials for industrial activities in another global location obviously generates exporting activities: that is the prime purpose of the enterprise. Likewise, FDI in manufacturing in a foreign location, the output of which is meant to be an input into a multinational's global production system, included with supplies of product and technology from the same multinational's network, inevitably sets up a complex global pattern of imports and exports, and perhaps also involving technology licensing. A wide variety of possible mode combinations may be built around the core FDI operation, a company which is partly or fully owned by the investing firm. Some of these combinations have been noted in the previous chapter on alliances: the Kone–Toshiba alliance referred to there, ultimately including an equity basis, is illustrative of the complexity of mode arrangements that may surround a core foreign invested enterprise, although in that case the investment was at the end of an alliance development process involving other modes. As noted in Chapter 4, mode use allied to the operation of a foreign invested enterprise may be about achieving objectives elsewhere in the multinational system, such as overall taxation and financial efficiency.

In Chapter 5, FDI was shown as a bundle of component parts, that may include technology, know-how, finance, equipment and people. As shown in Figure 10.1, the exact nature of the package and what is involved in the investment process are related to the foreign entity's designated role: for example, the establishment of a foreign sales subsidiary, which is often the first FDI move by internationalizing companies (Benito et al., 2003), is typically for the purpose of assisting export sales by the investing firm to the

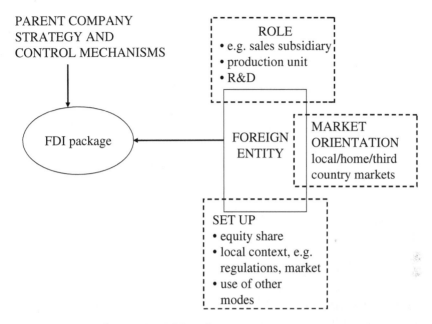

PARENT COMPANY STRATEGY AND CONTROL MECHANISMS

ROLE
• e.g. sales subsidiary
• production unit
• R&D

FDI package

FOREIGN ENTITY

MARKET ORIENTATION
local/home/third country markets

SET UP
• equity share
• local context, e.g. regulations, market
• use of other modes

Figure 10.1   Influences on FDI package

country in question, and may involve a very limited package initially, tied to the export support role (Luostarinen et al., 1994). In addition, research has shown that mode connections to FDI are related to the level of investment and equity in the foreign entity: for example, licensing is more likely to be used as a means of attempting to constrain technology leakage through a joint venture partner than in wholly-owned situations. Also, the pattern of associated mode use relates to the content of the package; for example, the way in which licensing is used can have an important impact on the technology component and its part in the FDI package. Licensing may be seen as contributing to the prevention of technology leakage through a joint venture partner, thereby making the investing firm more prepared to include up-to-date technology in its package. Perceived ineffectual local intellectual property protection, though, can have the reverse effect, leading to the inclusion of older technology in an FDI package, and in various other ways the local context of FDI influences package content (Tomassen et al., 1998).

FDI is typically preceded by other types of international operations, overall as well as in the individual countries of interest. As a result, it is appropriate to view FDI in the context of a company's general internationalization process, even though much of the FDI literature tends to

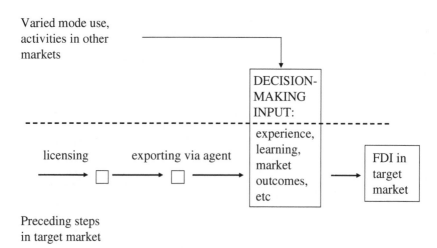

Figure 10.2 Antecedents of FDI

examine FDI disconnected from its antecedents (see Figure 10.2). The explanation of FDI, and its form and content, is related to the type of preceding experience and its outcomes, and the type of base that has been established. The Finnish multinational, Kone (lifts, escalators), is illustrative: a company that has grown to become a major global player in its field predominantly by the acquisition route. In 2004 alone, it acquired total or majority shareholdings in 32 companies in 17 countries. In all but one of these countries Kone already had a significant presence or representation. The exception was Korea, but the Asia-Pacific area director commented that 'our absence was not for lack of effort to establish operations . . . [we] worked long and hard to find a suitable way to enter Korea' (*Kone News and Views*, 2005, 28–9). The entry method ultimately used was a joint venture. We shall return to this issue later in the chapter, but it is important to note that companies seem to have become more adept at utilizing experience and learning from different countries and applying this to new markets in expansion via FDI.

DEFINITION/TYPES

For statistical purposes, authorities in different countries define FDI as occurring when the level of ownership via equity in a foreign enterprise reaches a certain level that is deemed to imply that the investing company acquires a significant influence, whether exercised or not, over the key policies of the foreign entity, through a long-term investment. A short time horizon is taken to mean portfolio investment rather than FDI; that is, investment for financial purposes. There is some variation in the trigger rate used by the authorities as a statistical indicator of FDI in different countries. Many have adopted 10 per cent as the indicative level, for example the US, France, Australia, Norway and Finland, and UNCTAD (2005) uses this level for data collection purposes, although others apply a higher rate of 20 per cent, for example Germany and the UK (for a discussion of the scope and limits of FDI data, see Stephan and Pfaffmann, 2001).

The above definition can clearly be applied to a wide range of foreign operations that include equity arrangements. Broad distinctions are usually made between investments that produce wholly owned (or nearly so) foreign subsidiaries and joint ventures with majority, 50:50 or minority (large to small) equity levels. As noted in the chapter on alliances, the differences tend to be viewed as important by investing firms, and a great deal of the research on FDI has focused on analysing the impact of these differences. In general, other things being equal, investing companies tend to prefer wholly owned operations as they facilitate greater control over the foreign entity (Gatignon and Anderson, 1988). Investment activity may be enacted via two main paths: acquisition of an equity stake, part or full, in an operating company within the target market; or establishment of a new company, with or without partners, and operations from scratch – a so-called 'greenfield' investment. An in-between form has been referred to as 'brownfield' investment, found mainly, but not only, in emerging markets, such as in East European markets in the wake of the collapse of their socialist economies in the late 1980s. In brownfield cases, a local enterprise and its assets in the target foreign market are acquired, but then the investing company undertakes wholesale restructuring of, and new investments in, the acquired entity to the point where it comes to resemble a greenfield operation. Meyer and Estrin (2001, 576–7) note the case of the acquisition of a majority share of the Hungarian enterprise, Budatej, an ice cream manufacturer, by the German company Schöller Lebensmittel. The German company 'reconstructed the factory, replacing all but one production line. The factory infrastructure was rebuilt . . . new freezers provided to the retail outlets'. Even Budatej's local brand was discontinued initially, to be replaced by Schöller's own brands.

In legal terms, an important distinction in FDI establishments is between branch and subsidiary arrangements. A branch establishment in a foreign country remains legally connected to and a liability of the parent firm. In contrast, a subsidiary is legally established within the foreign market and legally separate from the parent company, and legal responsibility within the local context is normally deemed to apply only to the operations and assets of the local subsidiary.

FDI DECISION MAKING: PROCESS AND SUB-CHOICES

As noted in Chapter 9, FDI, in JV or wholly owned form, can be viewed as a process rather than a single act. The FDI decision-making process unfolds over time, often a lengthy period, and the process itself may have a substantial impact on the ultimate form of the FDI chosen and implemented (Hood and Truijens, 1993). Indeed, the FDI step can be further placed in the longer and broader context of the firm's overall internationalization process (Welch and Luostarinen, 1988). In some cases the FDI activity is merely an extension of an existing FDI facility or operation in the foreign market; for example, when an assembly unit is upgraded to full manufacturing, or when a minority JV is moved up to a majority-owned basis, or in the takeover of a company's current distributor within the foreign market. Evaluation is a relatively straightforward exercise, given the existing base, experience and networks in the foreign market, allied with any equivalent, relevant experience from other foreign markets. Even from such a base, though, negotiation with a potential foreign partner or takeover prospect may be required, with all the potential vagaries of cross-cultural interaction and communication (such as language differences) that may be involved, as well as the commercial terms of any deal. As illustrated in Figure 10.3, the process of reaching a conclusion and a specific form

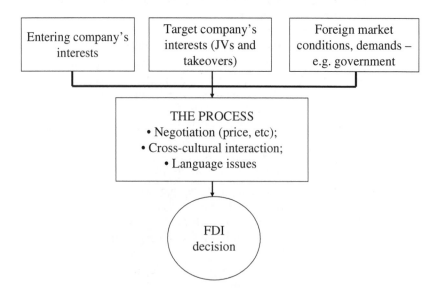

Figure 10.3   Process issues in FDI decision

of FDI affects the positions of the negotiating parties, and external factors and players can also affect the final outcome. The experiences of Norwegian companies entering the Indian market exemplify the type of adjustments that are sometimes made through the negotiation process preceding a final FDI commitment (Tomassen et al., 1998).

In fact, there is a wide range in the circumstances that might precede the FDI decision-making process. There are many examples of companies effectively being offered a going concern in a foreign market, as a result of opportunities emerging due to changes in government policy or foreign market conditions – in an unanticipated and unplanned way, but calling for a relatively rapid response, perhaps because of concern about the action of competitors. In these circumstances there may be considerable pressure to make a rapid decision, to truncate the normal decision-making process. An example is the takeover of the British motor vehicle manufacturer Rover by BMW in 1994. The head of corporate planning at BMW admitted that 'the speed of the deal limited BMW's ability to perform due diligence' (Davies, 1994, 19). In acquisition situations, Jemison and Sitkin (1986, 110) refer to 'powerful forces beyond managerial control that accelerate the speed of the transaction'. Canadian research has shown a surprisingly high proportion of mode change decisions (about a quarter) being made within 24 hours of the initial perceived impulse for change, illustrating the fact that it is difficult to depict a common FDI decision-making process and associated set of explanatory factors (Calof, 1993). The acquisition opportunity may come as a relatively complete package when the seller is seeking divestment of an existing business, minimizing the implementation end of the FDI process (Benito and Welch, 1997). Nevertheless, the decision-making process itself – how it unfolds – is important. Decision making is typically not a straightforward exercise. A seminal early study of the decision process found that 'the [FDI] decision results from a chain of events, incomplete information, activities of different persons (not necessarily connected with the particular project), and a combination of several motivating forces, some of them working in favour of such a decision, some against it' (Aharoni, 1966, 55; see also Larimo, 1995).

In greenfield situations, it is not only the decision-making process surrounding the FDI step that may be awkward and extended: the implementation end can also be demanding, involving construction of manufacturing facilities, offices, mines and the like, before the foreign entity can become an operational unit. A study of Japanese manufacturers establishing greenfield operations in Europe provides some indication of just how extended the overall FDI process might be, including implementation, as shown in Figure 10.4 (Hood and Truijens, 1993). The Japanese experience also illustrates how the FDI decision involves a number of sub-decisions, each of which

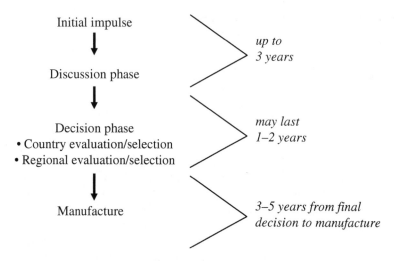

Initial impulse

Discussion phase

Decision phase
• Country evaluation/selection
• Regional evaluation/selection

Manufacture

*up to
3 years*

*may last
1–2 years*

*3–5 years from final
decision to manufacture*

Source: Adapted from Hood and Truijens (1993).

Figure 10.4   Japanese manufacturers in Europe: FDI decision and location

may be critical to the final go-ahead decision: for example, some companies are unprepared to engage in FDI unless they can be assured of full owner-ship of each foreign unit.

Some of the main FDI component decisions that have been shown to be important are the following:

- FDI vs/+ other operation modes,
- ownership level,
- acquisition v. greenfield,
- acquisition targets,
- FDI package content,
- location (country/region/city),
- scale and depth of operations (such as assembly v. full-scale manu-facturing),
- financing.

Finnish research indicates that companies tend not to consider fully the range of options in each sub-decision category of FDI. For example, the bulk of Finnish firms were found not to canvass different possibilities regard-ing countries, ownership shares, locations and target firms in their FDI choices (Larimo, 1987, 1995). Many of the companies in the study only con-sidered a very specific opportunity, in a specific country, rather than chasing alternatives (see also Calof, 1993). Often this is because of being approached to buy or buy into an existing foreign enterprise: thus the form of the emergent opportunity contains a ready-made answer in many of the sub-decision categories. Also, there is a tendency for companies to follow approaches to these questions that they have used successfully in the past. A study of the establishment and ownership practices of Japanese companies over the period 1969–1991 found that selections were based on past experiences with similar structures (Padmanabhan and Cho, 1999). Specific FDI opportunities in a foreign market sometimes arise through non-FDI operations such as exporting or licensing that expose opportunities or pressures for specific forms of deeper market commitment via FDI. In situations where the FDI represents full integration of an existing joint venture partner in an established operation, the main change and issue revolve around ownership level, and this may have been anticipated as part of the original JV negotiations in the form of an option-to-buy clause in the agreement (Petersen et al., 2000).

WHY FDI?

At the outset, in whatever form the FDI impulse arises, there is the basic question for the internationalizing company of whether FDI is the most appropriate way to operate, to respond to an emerging opportunity or threat in a foreign market – relative to other modes, even though alternative modes, as noted, are often not directly considered, evaluated and compared in the FDI decision context. The international hotel industry is perhaps one of the few examples where alternative modes of operating such as FDI, management contracts and franchising may be considered as direct alternatives. As stressed throughout this book, companies often use modes in combination, and FDI typically throws up a range of options in terms of the use of other modes to support the main FDI thrust, although these tend not to be critical to whether the FDI project goes ahead. Much depends on the context of the decision: how, and the form in which, the impulse arises; the company's relevant history; and the stage of the decision-making process, because information, evaluation and reasoning evolve through the overall process.

Some of the broad reasons found in research over a long period for companies to use FDI as the means of achieving international expansion are the following:

- powerful means of foreign market exploitation and expansion,
- proximity to customers,
- exploitation of unique assets such as technology, know-how, and brands,

- access to unique local assets,
- reducing costs (outsourcing),
- contribution to global network performance of multinationals,
- avoiding tariff and other barriers to trade – government-imposed and natural,
- following clients,
- responding to the action of competitors,
- bandwagon effect,
- import security,
- government incentives.

Market Exploitation

John Dunning suggests that the various motives for FDI can largely be grouped into four main categories: (1) market seeking, (2) resource seeking, (3) efficiency seeking, and (4) strategic asset seeking (Dunning, 1998). Given the goal of foreign market expansion, FDI almost inevitably comes into the choice mix because of a general perception that it is the most powerful and effective market penetration method on a sustainable long-term basis, albeit normally the most costly and risky. By setting up an operating company within the foreign market (JV or WOS), the investing firm establishes a vehicle through which it can bring to bear the full array of whatever market advantages it possesses – for example, brand name, or unique product, technology or market servicing techniques – and overcome the so-called 'disadvantages of foreignness'. The current heavy inflow of FDI to China reflects a strong market exploitation motive, and the perceived ability of FDI to deliver most effectively in this regard. The growth of the media and entertainment sector in India has already attracted substantial inward FDI as foreign companies position themselves to exploit expected future expansion: in the face of FDI restrictions that, for example, limit FDI in television distribution companies to 49 per cent and 26 per cent for providers of TV and print news content (*Australian*, 2006).

The drive to exploit foreign markets has often been referred to as an aggressive motive for FDI, whereas research shows that FDI is often driven by market defence motives (Hood and Truijens, 1993; Kim and Kim, 1993). As discussed earlier in the book, FDI is often a result of rivalistic behaviour among firms. This can apply in situations where a company has already established a strong foreign market position through exporting or other means but this position is under threat because of the actions of other foreign companies or local firms; or that the threat could be expected to emerge in the future. Multinational companies are acutely aware of their rivals' market incursion actions and likely moves in a global context and have shown a preparedness not to allow rivals to build strong, unchallenged positions in important foreign markets. By operating from inside the market, companies may attain competitive benefits such as not having to cope with various importing barriers, accessing unique local assets (for example intellectual or raw materials), deriving local government establishment and tax incentives or by co-locating with important customers.

Lower Costs

The search for lower-cost production locations and for cheaper sources of inputs has long been a factor in a part of the general growth of FDI. This has been accentuated in the global outsourcing boom of the last two decades, as noted in Chapter 6. The outsourcing phenomenon has been driven by the difference in costs, particularly labour, between countries. Starting with the manufacturing sector it has spread into the services sector – in software development, form processing, call centres, business processes, and the like – facilitated by a range of information technology (IT) developments including the Internet. The growth of outsourcing has always been linked to FDI. Many of the companies seeking lower-cost locations have preferred to operate via owned facilities rather than through contracts with independent suppliers, particularly when there are concerns about quality and the protection of technology. In other cases, companies have started with simple outsourcing to foreign suppliers, but have switched to FDI when it became clear that larger considerations were involved, as in China, and more particularly in India. Many of the large multinational IT companies have moved from contractually based outsourcing to FDI commitments in India. GE now has large investments in India that include a major R&D facility, production of a wide range of equipment and software, and outsourcing services for Indian and global markets (Slater, 2003). In some industries, for example textiles, clothing and footwear, the FDI in low-cost locations has been undertaken by specialists in contract manufacturing that are supplying an endproduct to marketing specialists like Nike, and major retailers such as Wal-Mart and Carrefour.

Some FDI has a focus that is aimed primarily at what it will do for the company as a whole rather than what it might contribute in terms of market penetration in the foreign market in question. This is most obvious in cases of establishment of stand-alone R&D facilities in foreign markets, many examples of which have been emerging in China and India, as noted with GE. UNCTAD (2005, 24) undertook a survey of the world's largest R&D spenders in 2004–5 and found that 'more than half . . . already have an R&D presence in China, India and Singapore'. Firms in the survey expressed a strong intention to increase the extent of foreign R&D. The setting up of call centres in other countries to handle firms' global customer response needs is another example of investment to serve a global, rather than local, company role. The local assets of cheap, readily available and suitably qualified workers are major reasons for the FDI, but the focus is on the role of the FDI in the multinationals' global network performance rather than on local market penetration. In explaining Nestlé's approach to global operations, Nestlé's CEO has commented that 'Nestlé's headquarters decides if a foreign operation should contract or expand based on its profitability for the overall enterprise' (Demos, 2006, 48).

Client Following

Companies that are supplying products or services to clients that are operating in global markets face pressure to follow the foreign market expansion moves of their clients, whether specifically enjoined to do so or not. Japanese manufacturers tend to put pressure on their component suppliers to follow them into foreign markets as a way of ensuring the quality and reliability of supplies in new markets. Not to follow the client in its global moves is potentially to put at risk the relationship in general, and associated international market growth possibilities. A large study of US firms in the services sector found that 'client following' was an important motive for foreign market entry (of which a large part was FDI) in general, although varying considerably across industries. It was strongest in advertising, accounting and banking but non-existent in consumer services (Erramilli, 1990). In a study of foreign business service companies that had entered the Finnish market via FDI, it was found that the internationalization of clients had a strongly positive influence on the entry decision for 51 per cent of entrant firms, and a slightly positive influence for another 24 per cent of firms (Paukkuri, 1987).

Competitors

The actions of competitors, actual and anticipated, have been shown to be an important general factor driving the FDI moves of multinationals, often in a direct, almost confronting way. If a close global competitor makes a large direct investment in a particular market which has been a limited focus of interest previously, but with substantial future potential (India is perhaps a current example), it is difficult to ignore. However, it is not just the action of competitors that can influence FDI moves: it is also the general trade and FDI activity of other business actors, including service providers, suppliers and customers, as well as the attention of media commentators and the like at a broader level, that can create general FDI momentum, and a focus on particular markets and regions, which has been described as the bandwagon effect or simply fashion effect (Knickerbocker, 1973; Vernon et al., 1996). The race into China and, more recently, India is indicative of this factor at work. It is difficult for managers to take a stand not to become involved in a market like China in the current climate of 'China fever'.

Import Security

Among the explanations of FDI, the issue of import security seems to be given attention in line with the pattern of commodity cycles: the current jump in the world price of oil, and rise in price of many other commodities associated with the needs of China's booming economy, creating demand for a wide range of raw materials for industry and infrastructure development, and energy supplies in general, has raised concerns in China, India, the US and many other countries about access to, and the reliability of, future critical imports of key commodities. As a result there have been almost frenzied attempts to lock in long-term lines of supply. In this respect FDI tends to be viewed as an important means of ensuring secure future raw material supplies. For example, Chinese companies, with the backing and active involvement of the Chinese government, have been scouring the globe for investment opportunities. China already has a number of investments in Australia's resources sector, in natural gas, iron ore and alumina, and, after signing a deal for the supply of uranium, has expressed a strong interest in undertaking future investments across the board in resources extraction in Australia (Wilson and Taylor, 2006).

Government Incentives

Many governments provide an array of incentives and actively promote inward FDI, often through inward FDI agencies (such as the UK investment attraction board). In some countries there is even internal state or regional government competition for inward FDI via the offer of financial incentives, land availability and the like. The US and Australia are countries where this occurs. Others have gone further by offering tax holidays for lengthy periods, while the establishment of free trade zones and their equivalent is usually associated with purpose-built infrastructure and removal of import duties when associated with export-oriented activity by investors (see the treatment in Chapter 6). Promotion and incentives generally apply to greenfield investments which lead to new business development and the creation of new employment for local workers. Research indicates that such incentives and information and support systems have little effect on whether an FDI will take place. Where they are more likely to have an effect is on the location of the FDI: for example, the country and region to site a new facility within Europe that is to serve the European market (Hood and Truijens, 1993).

OWNERSHIP LEVEL

Among the sub-decisions noted above, a key issue is the level of ownership. In many cases it is the principal consideration in determining whether a company is prepared to go ahead with the FDI or not. Examples in Chapter 9 illustrated the importance that many companies attach to attaining a greater than 50 per cent level of ownership in the foreign enterprise. In general, companies tend to show a preference for wholly owned sub-sidiaries (WOS) rather the joint venture (JV) form. Evidence indicates that the bulk of FDI by US transnationals is through fully owned subsidiaries (Desai et al., 2004; Gatignon and Anderson, 1988). Japanese companies' FDI similarly reveals a bias in favour of wholly owned operations (Osland et al., 2001; Jaussaud et al., 2001). Perhaps more telling is the way in which FDI in China has switched from mainly using joint ventures to fully owned operations once the FDI rules made this possible (Deng, 2001). Factors involved in this switch are summarized in Figure 10.5.

Equity JV Problems	Advantages of WOSs
• Shared control	• Highest level of control
• Divergent goals	• Strategic & operational
• Problematic partners	flexibility
• Leakage of proprietary	• Low dissemination risk
technology	(technology, know-how)

Changed external environment for WOSs
• Reduced government restriction on WOSs
• More open business environment & deregulated industries
• Decreased country risk

Source: Adapted from Deng (2001, p. 69).

Figure 10.5   Factors in the move to WOS in China

Why Preference for WOSs?

The preference for WOSs over JVs is not surprising: in essence it is about delivering the ability to be in charge of what happens in the foreign subsidiary, without having to take account of the interests of a partner firm. A WOS tends to be viewed as ensuring control over decision making by the subsidiary, over its policies and strategy, and over what happens with key assets transferred to the subsidiary, such as technology and know-how. WOSs also mean avoidance of disputation with a JV partner and not having to refer decisions to a partner, or partners, thereby contributing to faster decision making and greater responsiveness to rapidly changing market circumstances, an issue raised in some of the research on JVs (Osborn, 2003). A study of Japanese companies found that one of the reasons for a preference for WOSs over JVs was the ability to respond more rapidly to the actions of competitors (Osland et al., 2001). At a broader level, 100 per cent ownership of subsidiaries facilitates the full incorporation of subsidiaries into a multinational's network of operations, making it easier, for example, to institute transfer pricing and other inter-unit policies within the multinational that generate greater profit for the multinational as a whole rather than maximizing profit at each subsidiary unit. Developing, transferring and applying resources, such as technology and staff, within the multinational's subsidiary network are more readily directed and handled by the parent when WOSs are involved. In addition, a WOS regime ensures that the parent achieves the full return on assets like technology that are transferred and employed throughout a multinational's network, rather than sharing the benefits with partner firms.

Why Preference for JVs?

Despite the general preference for the WOS route in FDI activity, JVs are often preferred, for a variety of reasons, as identified in Chapter 9. A local partner in the foreign market can often deliver an array of benefits including local knowledge and networks, such as with key government officials, and provide an existing marketing infrastructure. An entrant firm pursuing a WOS policy may have to build that which is readily available from a local partner from scratch, and this may take a considerable amount of time and cost, particularly in greenfield situations. If the FDI has been preceded by other forms of operations, though, the time and cost of WOS development will be somewhat alleviated. In acquisition situations, an existing, operating entity is in place, reducing the need to build from scratch, although not removing all need to do so, but this has to be factored into the purchase price, often at a premium in competitive takeover cases.

As well, retention of staff with key knowledge and networks becomes an issue: any significant leakage means building anew. In general, JVs tend to be more politically acceptable than WOSs in target countries – even more so in takeover situations involving iconic local companies, thereby inviting various forms of contrary political action at government and trade union levels, as well as negative publicity in the media.

Companies do not always take final, definitive decisions about ownership level at the point of foreign market entry, or at least change perspective as foreign operations unfold, and attempt to change ownership level over time. Sometimes deliberately, often not, a start may be made with a joint venture, giving time to assess the market and the partner, without a full commitment, while moving to full takeover at a later stage. In some cases, companies negotiate an option-to-buy clause at the entry point, which can be taken up at a later date (Petersen et al., 2000). When Wal-Mart bought a 6 per cent stake in the Japanese supermarket chain Seiyu in 2002, part of the agreement was an option to raise that share to 66.7 per cent by 2007. It exercised part of that option just nine months later, with an increase to 37 per cent (Fackler and Zimmerman, 2003). The creation of switching options in international operation decisions is taken up as an issue in the 'strategy' part of the book.

ACQUISITION V. GREENFIELD (OR BROWNFIELD)

While FDI in the 1960s and 1970s was predominantly in the form of greenfield developments, emanating from the US, this pattern changed dramatically by the 1980s, with mergers and acquisitions (M&As) becoming the dominant means of undertaking FDI globally, and since then this pattern has remained unchanged. While the US has remained a major global FDI player via M&As during this period, European and other countries also became major contributors to the global trend. Companies from smaller countries such as Australia, Finland and Norway emerged in the 1980s, and were able to achieve substantial global inroads in a relatively short time by taking the acquisition path (for example, Foster's beer from Australia), bypassing the much longer route of building up each foreign entity from scratch. For example, from 1980 to 1987, more than 80 per cent of Australian FDI in the US, the major target market of the time, was via acquisition (Hywood, 1988).

The stand-out developed country that has defied the strong, general trend toward M&As is Japan. Inward FDI flows to Japan have remained low, with acquisitions, particularly hostile ones, being difficult to accomplish in the Japanese business context. On the outward side, the bias against

M&As by Japanese companies is not as pronounced, but in general there has been a stronger preference for greenfield investments than has been evident for companies from other developed countries. As noted above, companies from the developing countries have also become part of this general pattern, following others in their use of acquisitions to facilitate penetration of global, particularly developed country, markets. The purchase of the well-known British tea company, Tetley, by the Indian firm Tata Tea in 2000 for more than $US400 million is reflective of this developing trend. The two companies had operated a JV in India since 1992. For companies (and countries) starting international expansion at a later stage than the already established multinational operators, the acquisition path is often seen as the only feasible way of making any progress against powerful, entrenched global competition.

The general rush towards the use of acquisition in FDI has been occurring against a background of increasing divestment, as companies have become more prepared to offload foreign subsidiaries, for various reasons – including poor performance, changed strategies, and government action (see, for example, Belderbos and Zou, 2006). A study of Norwegian companies' FDI revealed a high level of divestment (more than 50 per cent) within ten years of the original investments. Using acquisition as a means of making FDIs turned out to be the single most important explanatory variable in that study (Benito, 1997). Similarly, a Portuguese study reported an early exit rate of more than 10 per cent for a sample of foreign owned subsidiaries in Portugal, with a significantly higher frequency of sell-off for acquisitions than for greenfield investments (Mata and Portugal, 2000; UNCTAD, 2003). An outcome is a ready-made global market at any time of companies available for purchase, so that divestment may be quickly linked with acquisition: in a sense, the two sides of FDI have come to feed on each other.

WHY ACQUISITION?

'For the modern manager, only acquisition reproduces the thrill of the chase, the adventure of military strategy. There is the buzz that comes from the late-night meetings in merchant banks, the morning conference calls with advisers to plan strategy. Nothing else puts your picture on the front page, nothing else offers so easy a way to expand your empire and emphasise your role' (Kay, 1996, 12).

Given the sustained general preference for the acquisition route rather than greenfield FDI, over a period of almost three decades, in the face of many divestments and difficulties in achieving acceptable performance within acquired enterprises, internationalizing companies obviously see strong arguments in support of this choice. The arguments are not dissimilar to those surrounding the use of alliances, including JVs, in foreign markets (see Chapter 9). They include the following:

- Speed of market entry or expansion;
- In mining and other natural resource-based activities, existing facilities mean established risk;
- Perhaps low price if divestment;
- Complementarity, synergy of operations;
- Diversification;
- Rationalization and restructuring;
- Assets of acquiree, such as:
  - market share,
  - well-known brand name,
  - international operations,
  - technology and know-how,
  - local knowledge and networks,
  - distribution and service capability,
  - established government approvals for relevant business activity.

Speed

There is a wealth of evidence that the time factor is a major consideration weighing in favour of acquisition. Companies recognize, sometimes from bitter experience, just how long it can take to build a new, operational facility in a foreign market from scratch (as illustrated in Figure 10.4 above) including the demands of obtaining various types of government approvals for the new business and its operations. Getting to the starting line, though, is only part of the battle: from then on there are the demands of building a business, garnering market share, getting one's products and/or services known and accepted in the marketplace, and building customer loyalty and a positive reputation around a brand – and these are major long-term tasks. The alternative of acquiring an existing company and its facilities offers the prospect of short-circuiting many, if not all, of these steps and obtaining a range of valuable local assets. The process may be further accelerated when companies are approached to buy a foreign enterprise, often in divestment situations, removing the perceived need to find an acquisition target that is amenable to takeover. A further attraction in divestment situations is the prospect of picking up a foreign entity at a low price, although this can be an indication of deep-seated problems within the company on offer. The European biotechnology company,

Serono, indicated that it had received many offers to sell after it announced that it had embarked on the acquisition trail and was prepared to spend up to $US10 billion (Simonian, 2006). GE Capital was reported to have spent about $15 billion over 1998–9 in buying 'distressed assets' cheaply in the financial services sector in Asia in the wake of the 1997 financial crisis (Slater and Amaha, 1999).

In competitive situations, the ability to move quickly against other multinational entrants may be crucial. There are times when companies feel that acquisition is the only option because of time pressure, assuming that acquisition targets are available. The US chairman of the large Australian packaging and box manufacturer, Visy, put the company perspective on the choice in the following terms: 'when you [opt for] greenfield you must take a longer-term view than if you acquire. When you buy someone, you grow overnight. But "greenfielding" can be a slow, painful process, so you have to do the hard yards' (Ferguson and James, 2003, 44). Somewhat contrarily, in spite of this position, the company had followed the 'painful' path. Even in brownfield situations where there is additional investment beyond the takeover, speed of access to the relevant market through an established market position, compared to the greenfield alternative, remains a key driving force (Meyer and Estrin, 2001).

Risk Avoidance in Natural Resources Sector

An investigation of the global mining industry revealed that risk avoidance was a major factor in the surge of M&As. For mining companies, global expansion by acquisition not only has the advantage of greater speed when existing mines are involved, but there is also greater certainty about outcomes – the risk factors have been established on the basis of ongoing operations. This is in contrast to the potentially long and costly path of exploration and development, with the attendant risk of failure (Gooding, 1997). In addition, mining companies are increasingly facing more stringent requirements with respect to environmental standards and requisite safeguards when developing new mines, further extending the time and cost of the development process. Some of these influences were evident in the takeover of the Australian company, Western Mining, in 2005 by the world's largest mining company, BHP Billiton. Among Western Mining's assets was ownership of a large uranium deposit, with immediate access, avoiding the political and environmental problems of developing a new uranium mine, in a climate of the global rush to find and lock in energy assets that have become more valuable with the rising price of oil and other forms of energy, and a renewed interest in nuclear energy amid concerns about global warming (Marsh, 2005).

Complementarity, Diversification and Rationalization

European research on the motives for M&As within the EU has shown that complementarity of operations, diversification and rationalization are important factors (European Commission, 1988–92). Complementarity can apply at both vertical and horizontal levels. In seeking to initiate or extend market penetration in foreign markets, companies might prefer to move into a closely related area of business via takeover, rather than attempting to gain further market share in its main line of business at high cost, and in the process leaving the competitive balance relatively undisturbed. Acquisition is also a means of accomplishing diversification into an unrelated area of business: it may be feasible to build on an existing company strength – such as servicing a specific market niche, like the elderly or a sporting group (for example cross-country skiers) – and offering a broader range of products and/or services. Of course, such steps are always more difficult to accomplish in unfamiliar foreign markets. They are more likely to be contemplated when placed alongside existing foreign operations. Serono, one of Europe's largest biotechnology companies, has recently embarked on an acquisition campaign in order to stimulate growth and to fill out its product range (Simonian, 2006). The EU data show that acquisition has been used to facilitate rationalization and restructuring of operations by companies, increasingly on an EU-wide basis, in the search to exploit the possibilities of economies of scale in R&D, production, distribution and marketing.

Assets of Acquiree

The acquisition of a foreign firm inevitably means acquisition of all of the assets that make up the foreign entity, which may be primarily local, but might extend to the regional or even global level. For smaller firms, or those looking at a long process of international expansion in order to become firmly established as a global entity, acquisition of companies that already have significant international operations and assets is a way of achieving a major jump in international activity. The ability to make such jumps depends on access to financing vehicles that will cover the necessary expansion in debt. The Australian beer and wine company, Foster's, was able to achieve major inroads in global markets through supportive financing of a range of takeovers, as it grew from a relatively small Australian base to become a major global player in its industry. When the Chinese company, Lenovo, took over IBM's personal computer business, Lenovo's sales were only a third of IBM's (Smith and Rushe, 2004).

There are many sides to the assets of a foreign acquiree that may be of interest to the acquirer. At the forefront is the market share of the acquiree – locally and/or internationally. Not only is market share obtained instantly, but the acquirer may be able to remove a competitor in relevant markets. As well, the market position obtained may be further enhanced by the purchase of a strong brand name and distribution outlets. As part of the takeover deal between IBM and Lenovo, the Chinese firm acquired the rights to use the IBM brand name for five years, one of the most highly recognized and valuable brand names in the world, as well as ownership of the ThinkPad and ThinkCentre brands (Smith and Rushe, 2004). Further, the acquired firm may have unique technology, and design and other people skills, which are able to make an important contribution to the acquirer's global operations. At the least, the acquired firm is likely to have essential local knowledge and networks to support the move to local operations.

While restrictions on FDI in general have been diminishing, entrant firms still run the gauntlet in terms of the array of government approvals and planning permission for various activities, and in many areas these have become even more restrictive, for example with regard to environmental effects, in mining and elsewhere, and acceptable site use. As noted in the franchising chapter, this was a concern for McDonald's in its attempt to expand in Italy. By taking over the local chain, Burghy, and converting existing outlets, it avoided many of the planning approval problems, and time, associated with undertaking outlet development on its own part.

ACQUISITION PROBLEMS

In many ways, it is not surprising that acquisition has been viewed so positively by internationalizing firms as the ready-made solution to the big questions around how to expand. The advantages appear almost overwhelming when set against the demands of using other modes and working with and through other companies, and of going it alone with FDI via greenfield development. As with the other modes, though, the positives have to be balanced against a range of potential drawbacks:

- high failure rate,
- integration difficulties,
- pressure to move quickly on acquisition prospects,
- over-confidence and acquisition surprises,
- lack of preceding market experience,
- difficulties in retaining key staff,
- divestments that have basic problems – difficult to turn around,
- lack of appropriate firms to acquire,

- competitive pressure may increase price of acquisition,
- acquisitions as distractions.

Failure

While there is considerable argument about the exact extent of acquisition failure, there is a relatively general conclusion from studies in many global contexts that the failure rate is high, that most acquisitions 'fail'. An influential early study of failure examined UK and US companies using acquisitions (116 in total) to enter new markets. Success was measured by the firm's ability to earn back its cost of capital or better on the funds invested in M&As. It was found that only 23 per cent of the acquisitions succeeded, 63 per cent failed, while 16 per cent were indeterminate (Coley and Reinton, 1988). Other studies have focused on whether acquisitions enhance shareholder value. A study of international acquisitions by US firms over the period 1978–90 concluded that, on average, they do not create value for the acquiring firm's shareholders. Further, in cases of high cultural distance, the negative outcome was accentuated (Datta and Puia, 1995). Studies by KPMG covering the periods 1996–98 and 1997–99 revealed that only 17 per cent of cross-border M&A deals added value in the first period, but this rose in the second period to 30 per cent, for the first year after completion of the deal (KPMG Transaction Services, 2001). High rates of divestment of acquired entities provide further indication of the difficulties of turning M&As into strategically successful and profitable operations. Research on Norwegian companies indicated that divestment of acquired foreign entities (75 per cent) was almost double that for greenfield establishments (48 per cent) over a ten-year period (Benito, 1997).

Integration Difficulties

The high failure rate of acquisitions begs the question, why this outcome? Much of the research literature and business press focuses on the problems of integration of two previously separate organizations, assuming that there has not been a preceding relationship. It is not just a question of merging the two companies' systems; there are informal processes as well, and the acquiring company may have to deal with different types of customers and unfamiliar technology. M&As inevitably involve the meshing of two firms' cultures, and in cross-border situations this means both company and national cultures. The former CEO of General Electric, Jack Welch, when asked what was his worst mistake in his time at GE, commented: 'without question it was not really understanding what I was preaching – how important the meshing of cultures is in the acquisition process' (Gottliebsen, 2003, 24).

While companies routinely undertake financial due diligence on takeover targets, a consultant in the field points out that most 'do not carry out due diligence on their target's culture, structure, processes and networks' (*Economist*, 1997, 62). The attempted blending is frequently undertaken in a context of staff reductions in order to compensate for the market premium that is typically paid to ensure M&A deal acceptance. Cross-cultural interaction processes may further constrain the effectiveness of integration. For example, choice of language can become an issue in mergers that bring together more than one language. When Merita, a Finnish bank, merged with Nordbanken, a Swedish bank, in 1997, Swedish was chosen as the company language for the combined entity, which caused some consternation on the Finnish side and communication problems overall. The issue was transformed when a further merger took place in 2000 with a Danish bank and English was adopted as the company language for the new company, effectively throwing two additional languages into the communication mix, complicating an already demanding merger process with three previously separate organizations having to be integrated and operating as a cohesive total unit (Piekkari et al., 2005).

Pressure to Move Quickly

Acquisition opportunities do not always arise as a result of a careful search and evaluation process, as already noted, but often arise from divestment situations, sometimes in virtual 'fire sale' situations. The offer may not have been anticipated, and there could be considerable pressure to mount a rapid response, perhaps because of the perceived likelihood of interest from competitors. The BMW takeover of Rover, referred to above, illustrates how the conditions surrounding an emergent M&A opportunity can force an acquirer to act more rapidly than it would otherwise have done, making a poor choice with potentially negative consequences. Six years after the 1994 acquisition, BMW sold out of Rover after incurring overall losses that may have been as much as US$5 billion (*Economist*, 2000). Even with time and care in the selection of an acquisition target, the dynamics of deal negotiation and conditions surrounding a deal, and the nature of the individuals involved and personal reward prospects, can put pressure on the parties to push to closure (Jemison and Sitkin, 1986). The need to keep the negotiations secret, particularly from those likely to introduce spoiling market offers, can add a further twist to the pressure to close the deal quickly. As well, key management staff, including CEOs, may be tied up for various periods in attempting to settle on a deal format, at a cost to existing operations, so that there is an inevitable attempt to keep the 'missing management' time to a minimum.

The prelude to the merger of Daimler-Benz and Chrysler in 1998 illustrates many of these considerations. There was an elaborate and concerted campaign to keep the negotiations secret – the fear was that the deal could be destroyed if share market players learned about what was happening and bid up the price of Chrysler to the point where the deal became non-viable. Clandestine meetings of the two CEOs were held in different locations. Despite the complexity of the deal, and the last-minute hitch over what to call the new entity (which company's name should appear first?), it was consummated in about four months. The positive personal chemistry of the two CEOs, and its impact on the general atmosphere of the negotiations, was seen as a major factor in the processes working and achieving a mutually acceptable outcome (Simonian, 1998).

Over-Confidence and Acquisition Surprises

Despite the wealth of cautionary evidence, it is clear from the continued preference for M&As that this evidence, which is well publicized in the business press, dissuades few companies from going ahead with perceived attractive deals. As some researchers have pointed out, there are typically substantial personal rewards for those directly involved in completing M&As. Likewise, acquisition deals are a way for CEOs to make their mark, of gaining publicity and media coverage for their actions, and they tend to exhibit exaggerated self-confidence (Hayward and Hambrick, 1997; Jemison and Sitkin, 1986). As a result, it is argued that this creates a bias in favour of pushing ahead with M&A deals, and results in higher premiums being paid by acquirers. The over-optimism about M&A deals revealed in various studies also extends to the degree of confidence about the ability to turn around struggling companies that are available via divestment. In their study of brownfield investments in Central and Eastern Europe, Meyer and Estrin (2001, 581) found many instances of 'ex post surprises' after foreign acquisitions, because of incomplete information about the true state of their targets prior to takeover, leading to failures of the new enterprises. While the focus of this research was emerging economies, there are many cases of similar outcomes in diverse takeover situations and country contexts, as the true state of acquirees is revealed after the event, sometimes precipitating legal action for non-disclosure of relevant information to the share market.

Market and Relationship Experience

The type and extent of preceding market and relationship experience of the two parties has an impact on the ease with which pre- and post-merger processes are handled and whether any restructuring is accomplished successfully. There is research indicating that the likelihood of successful acquisition is increased when it is preceded by relevant experience in the foreign market (Barkema and Vermeulen, 1998). In a four-country study of firms with considerable recent cross-border acquisition experience, Very and Schweiger (2001) focused on the acquisition process as a learning experience. They concluded that the acquisition learning process applied with respect to the focal deal as well as to acquisition activity in general, and that both forms were affected by the type of preceding experience in the foreign market in question. This is in line with an earlier study of European cross-border M&As from which it was found that 'success in integrating acquisitions is, above all else, a matter of experience. Frequent acquirers were significantly more successful in integrating their acquisitions than non-frequent acquirers' (Hamill, 1993, 23). However, a more in-depth study of the integration learning process in a set of cross-border M&As leading to the creation of the Nordic financial services group, Nordea, concluded that the process was context-specific, and there was considerable ambiguity about what was actually learned in a way that could be readily applied in new situations (Björkman and Tienari, 2005). In some cases, the acquirer will leave the acquisition undisturbed for a period of time, particularly where it lacks any preceding operations in the foreign market concerned or contact with the acquiree. This allows for a deeper understanding of the acquiree's operations and relationships, ensuring that the acquirer has a better base to undertake any important changes at a later stage.

Human Resource Management

The handling of human resource aspects of M&As and the resulting integration process is a key factor in whether they succeed or not. Loss of key staff, caused by concern about job prospects amid staff reductions, or job poaching by competitors, can doom an acquisition to failure. When Deutsche Bank took over Bankers Trust in the US, it reportedly set aside US$400 million to ensure that key staff were retained – so-called 'golden handcuffs' (Corrigan, 1998). In discussing the reasons for failure of international M&As, the president of Dow Performance Chemicals in the US stressed integration problems and the neglect of staffing issues pre- and post-acquisition (Ferguson and James, 2003). This is why many analysts argue that there needs to be a 'personnel due diligence' process leading into an acquisition, and careful development of appropriate personnel policies for the immediate post-acquisition situation, including the design of performance and reward systems, and company career mapping, to provide positive signals to important staff.

Suitable Takeover Targets and Price?

Companies will often bemoan the fact that, when they are in a position
to make a move into a foreign market via acquisition, there are no suitable targets amenable to being bought out, and hostile takeover may
be difficult to engineer, or impossible in the case of many smaller, private companies without share market listing. In some cases there is a
readily available target, but the question is the price, which tends to be
taken upwards in the sharemarket if a bidding war erupts. For example,
Carrefour, the large French supermarket chain, in the process of selling
its South Korean stores, encouraged a competitive bidding process by the
various suitors. Tesco, the British supermarket chain, was one of the
bidders in the final round, in competition with three domestic companies.
Tesco is already the second largest chain in South Korea. The strong competition ensured a high final sale price, although bidders were reportedly
discouraged by some of the contract terms, including the retention of all
workers in the outlets acquired (Callan, 2006; Jung-a and Guerrera,
2006). A local fashion retailer, E.Land, was the successful bidder. In the
early 1990s, the Australian company Pacific Dunlop was interested in purchasing Asian food companies as part of a major push into Asia, but was
in competition with many other companies, resulting in bidding 'wars' in
various markets: 'Dozens of foreign food companies are scouring Asia for
potential acquisitions . . . The feeding frenzy is pushing prices up to
unsustainable levels . . . We have already walked away from three potential acquisitions because the asking prices were too high' (Shoebridge,
1993, 47).

It is not unusual for companies' efforts to enter certain foreign markets
via acquisition to be completely halted for some time because of target
availability, suitability and price issues. In a study of 136 foreign consumer
products firms operating in China, 41 per cent indicated that they were
opposed to the use of acquisition as a means of expansion. Reasons
advanced for this position were 'few companies with strong enough brands
and products to acquire . . . failure of the due diligence process . . . and
the problem of cultural compatibility' (O'Neill, 2004, 28). A Norwegian
electrical cable company decided to switch from using a distributor in the
German market to having its own operation through acquisition. After an
extensive search process, six possibilities emerged. The three most interesting prospects were not able to be bought because the owners would not
sell, and they took another six months to negotiate the purchase of
company number four on the list. This case illustrates the fact that acquisitions, not unlike greenfield investments, can sometimes take considerable
time, in the search, negotiation and execution phases.

Distraction

It was noted above that major acquisitions can tie up key managerial staff for extended periods. Inevitably, this can have a distracting effect on the demands of current operations. For example, the chief executive of the French multinational insurance company, Axa, admitted that involvement in a major takeover of another French insurance firm distracted it from the poor market performance at the time of its Australian subsidiary and the need to take corrective action (Boreham, 2000). Other research indicates that aggressive acquisition strategies may have more basic distraction effects: tying up resources, creating high debt levels, and reducing the focus on marketing and innovation activity (Hitt et al., 1996).

The foregoing analysis demonstrates clearly that, despite its apparent attractiveness, acquisition is not a simple panacea for the problems of foreign operation mode choice and implementation. In many ways it indicates that companies ought to approach the use of acquisition in a far more cautious way, to look at a wider range of mode options, and to look into potential takeover prospects more thoroughly than is often the case, taking into account not just systems and technology, but also 'soft' areas such as managerial style, culture and human resources, in a more substantial manner.

WHY GREENFIELD?

The acquisition problems noted provide many of the basic arguments for the use of a greenfield approach to FDI. Despite the lower proportion of overall FDI undertaken in greenfield form, it represents a key alternative for companies. It has been used more extensively by Japanese companies, particularly in the European manufacturing sector, and more generally in particular market contexts, for example in developing countries (Somlev and Hoshino, 2005). From an overall perspective, an attraction is the investor's ability to build a company from the ground up in the foreign market – implanting its systems, culture and the like without having to take account of, and try to change, an existing, entrenched pattern in an acquired company. Apparently, this has been a major consideration for many Japanese companies (Bownas, 1991). It may be particularly important when complex technology transfer to the foreign subsidiary is required, or significant product and service adaptation is involved, and high control over the process is deemed critical. From UNCTAD (2005, Ch. 1, 9) research, it has been argued that 'greenfield investment is more likely to be used as a mode of entry in industries in which technological skills and production technology are key'.

In many cases, the lack of available or suitable acquisition targets forces investing firms to consider the greenfield path. Companies may feel it is essential to become involved in promising emerging markets, and are prepared to go against a predisposition in favour of acquisitions because of the limited development of relevant local businesses, as noted by some foreign firms in China (O'Neill, 2004). In certain less developed countries, from the investor's perspective there may seem to be no alternative to greenfield investment because of the unavailability of companies to acquire, but this could entail far more than construction of the company's facilities, perhaps extending to parts of relevant infrastructure, and basic employee education and training. Globally, in 2004, 'developing and transition economies attracted a larger number of greenfield investments than developed countries . . . [reflecting] the tendency for developing countries to receive more FDI through greenfield projects than through M&As' (UNCTAD, 2005, Ch. 1, 10).

LOCATION

It has been noted in preceding analysis that, in many situations, the question of location is not a stand-alone issue, but comes as part of the package when an offer to sell a particular company arises in the international arena. It is very specific. Consideration of the offer is bound to include the location as part of the evaluation process, but is less likely to extend to an attempt to unearth other prospects in different locations. Of course, many companies undertake ongoing search for, and evaluation of, potential acquisition prospects in various foreign markets, in advance of any market entry moves, and clearly location is an important aspect of this process. At the same time, research indicates that companies do not undertake a broad search of location options when undertaking FDI. The 'bandwagon' effect in overall FDI decision making referred to above applies particularly to the location question, with action and market location precipitated by the moves of competitors. Likewise, the 'following a client' factor in FDI activity effectively removes the location issue from consideration. Preceding operations in the relevant foreign market, that have created a valuable market position to defend, or a base from which to launch expansion, can also make the location decision somewhat superfluous, or strongly biased, although the comparative context of the company's international expansion strategy may bring the location question more to the forefront in the sense that expansion via FDI in the relevant country may have to compete against options available in other locations. The experience and knowledge gained through preceding operations in a given market are likely to have a substantial effect on the way the market and its prospects are perceived by a potential investor, including the sense of risk, as revealed in a study of Australian firms that had undertaken FDI in manufacturing in Indonesia (Zarkada-Fraser and Fraser, 2001). Taken together, these examples demonstrate that choice of location may not be a difficult or critical issue in diverse FDI cases, and almost pre-determined by the context and characteristics of the FDI stimulus.

However, location is an important issue in some FDI decisions, at times leading activity. This is seen most clearly in so-called 'footloose' industries and companies, such as in the textiles, clothing and footwear industries. Companies in these industries show a high level of preparedness to move locations in response to changing relative costs, especially of labour. Different locations tend to be comparatively assessed as to their ability to deliver lower costs of production, as well as satisfying quality and logistics criteria. Governments typically seek to influence such decisions through the offer of various incentives, including infrastructure development and the setting up of free trade zones (see Chapter 6). From a general perspective, given that a company has identified clear choices about where to locate prospective FDI, some of the key factors in decision making shown in extensive research over a wide range of countries and industries are the following:

- costs of production,
- market prospects,
- political, economic and business climate,
- network (e.g. supplier) linkages,
- cultural factors (e.g. language),
- distance to market/s,
- extent of corruption,
- legal framework,
- relevant government policy,
- availability of natural resources,
- availability of appropriately skilled workforce,
- infrastructure quality.

Market Factors and Investment Climate

In the broad range of studies of the determinants of FDI location, apart from differences in costs of production, two main general considerations stand out: market factors and investment climate. Market factors include overall market size, growth and prospects at the macro level, as well as the likely market prospects for a specific company's products and/or services.

In some foreign markets, companies are focused on anticipated future prospects rather than the current reality. However positive they might be, though, they have to be set against the challenges of operating in what might be an alien business context. Investment climate includes aspects such as political stability, economic and business conditions, and ways of doing business. The position, role and activities of governments are also an important part of this general picture. The rules governing FDI, and how they are administered by local authorities, are an important aspect of the local government's role: seemingly capricious intervention tends be viewed in a highly negative light by foreign investors (Fifield, 2006). How these various elements of investment climate are assessed feed into company evaluations of investment risk in the market concerned.

Network Linkages

Client following has been noted already as a significant factor in numerous FDI moves, but there is also the broad impact of the availability of a range of supplier and other useful network linkages, often nationally and/or culturally based, that make a particular location more attractive. Varied research has shown that the presence of other Japanese manufacturers in foreign locations is a major factor in Japanese manufacturing firms' FDI location decisions (Hood and Truijens, 1993; Lu and Beamish, 2004). A study by Chen and Chen (1998) indicates that network linkages in a broad sense, including local Chinese communities, have been influential in FDI location decisions by Taiwanese firms.

Culture

Long-standing research has shown the impact of cultural factors on FDI location choices, including the interaction of culture and colonial history. For example, these elements appear to have been important in Spanish FDI in Latin America. 'Over the past few years, Spain has become the largest European investor in [Latin America] . . . Spanish executives say this bias is explained by language and cultural ties, close knowledge of the countries involved and a confidence in Latin America's future (White, 1997, 13). Language is an important element of cultural influence, and can have an impact on the sequencing of FDI locations. Research has shown that the choice of the UK for many early greenfield investments in Europe by Japanese firms was strongly influenced by their use of English. 'Since most of the companies [already] had production facilities in the US, the presence of production engineers with international experience and English language ability was regarded as critical' (Hood and Truijens, 1993, 54; see also

Welch et al., 2001). An additional aspect of cultural influence on location is reverse investment by nationals of one country who have moved to another country, set up operations there, and then return to their home country, although the return of the diaspora may well come in subsequent generations (Gillespie et al., 1999). There is often a sense of attachment to and interest in the homeland, and there are also market entry advantages associated with cultural understanding, retained networks and language competence, which could be particularly significant for locations entailing large distance between the relevant mainstream cultures. There are increasing examples of FDI in China and India by their returning, globally dispersed diaspora.

Physical Proximity

The attractiveness of foreign markets on cultural grounds tends to be reinforced when this is associated with physical proximity as well. There are many examples of this connection in Europe (for example, Norway and Sweden), and in cases such as Canada and the US, and Australia and New Zealand. Apart from anything else, physical proximity aids inter-personal, face-to-face communication, facilitating the lowering of uncertainty. Nevertheless, physical proximity may be overridden by large cultural distance and historical factors, as in the case of the US and Cuba. The 'tyranny of distance' is a term often used in the Australian context, in spite of the impact of the Internet and other advances in information and communication technology, and distance to foreign markets is often advanced as a constraining factor on the foreign expansion of Australian firms (Ferguson and James, 2003).

Corruption

While corruption is a continuing reality of international business, its extent is substantially varied across countries, and forms an important part of the business climate. Not surprisingly, it has an effect on FDI location decisions. A study of 40 countries over the period 1991–97 concluded that 'the presence of high corruption and low transparency significantly hindered the inflow of FDI to host countries' (Zhao et al., 2003, 41). Other research has stressed the uncertainty-creating effects of corruption on potential foreign investors, effectively increasing the tax rate on multinationals, substantially in the case of high-corruption countries (Wei, 1997). The nature of a country's legal system and how it operates in dealing with corruption issues is an important aspect of this issue, and of course these are connected to the political context (see Chapter 7 on this issue).

Government Policy

The activity of governments in attempting to influence the location decisions of foreign investors has already been noted above (Hood and Truijens,
1993). There are instances where companies have been able effectively to
place potential locations in competition for a proposed investment, and
bidding up the incentives offered. Government policies in this regard have
been aptly referred to as something of a zero sum game in that the use of
particular government incentives and other policy instruments by one
country tends to be matched by others, ensuring that they cancel each other
out. In a study of FDI location choice by Japanese multinationals with a
focus on Singapore and countries in the surrounding region, it was concluded that '[government] policy factors were not important in the location
decision process . . . Japanese multinationals did not see the use of investment incentives by Singapore as different from the incentives offered by all
other countries in the region. The economic fundamentals (growth and the
size of the market) and political stability dominated the investment location calculations' (Nicholas et al., 2001, 147). Overall, it would appear that
governments' attempts to influence FDI location decision making have very
limited impact, if at all, and are more about parity of incentives relative to
competing locations.

Of course, government policy on tariffs and other import restraints can
impose significant restrictions on exporting, and force companies to consider other market-servicing strategies, including FDI, if the market is considered too important not to enter or maintain. For instance, when the
European Commission imposed a large extra duty on imports of spreadable butter into the UK from New Zealand, the New Zealand Dairy Board
was forced to quickly line up a European plant as an alternative line of
supply to avoid the duty. The UK market for spreadable butter had been
built up over a five-year period through a sustained promotional campaign, at considerable cost, so there was a substantial commitment to
defend it (Hall, 1996). For a number of Norwegian companies entering the
Indian market, the market prospects were viewed as being highly positive,
but import restrictions effectively ruled out exporting for many, leading to
the primary use of joint ventures and licensing (Tomassen et al., 1998).
Despite particular high-profile cases in most countries of ad hoc protection measures, and of retained high protection in certain industries such
as agriculture, the general trend over a long period has been of reducing
levels of protection, and of reduced independence of policy activity by
governments that are members of the World Trade Organization (WTO),
as illustrated by the changes forced on China prior and subsequent to its
entry in 2001.

Unique Resources

A final group of FDI location factors centres around the unique resources that may be available in particular counties. The availability, accessibility and quality of natural resources are an obvious example, and explain much of the global FDI in mining and energy. However, other resources are also important, such as an appropriately educated and skilled workforce, and the quality and density of the country's social infrastructure. It is often argued that the ready availability of workers with high education levels and English competence, apart from wage levels, explains much of the attraction of India as a destination for FDI in call centres, business process offshoring and software development. For example, the US call centre operator, Convergys, has been substantially expanding its Indian commitment in recent times. Nevertheless, it has also developed a centre in Hungary where labour costs are 25 per cent higher than in India, because staff in Hungary have multilingual skills which are important in servicing clients in a language-diverse European context, in spite of the relatively high level of use of English (Dolan, 2006).

FINANCING

The ability to finance FDI activities is, of course, a major factor in whether they are undertaken, and their ultimate form. However, it is not the intention here to examine this factor in detail as it is more appropriately dealt with in international finance textbooks. The cursory comments are not a reflection of the importance of financing questions in international operations, and the answers companies develop do have mode choice implications. The difficulties of small firms in financing the development of international activities have long been stressed as a significant constraint on their outward push, and on the foreign operation modes they are able to employ. Typically they are not able to use high commitment modes such as FDI during the early stages of internationalization because of an inability to finance this step, or there is an unpreparedness to take on the debt and risk that this would involve even if a source could be found. A study of four 'born global' Internet-based Norwegian companies that were established in the mid-to-late 1990s revealed some interesting reactions to mode choice options in the context of the dot.com boom of the time which delivered high cash reserves to undertake expansion choices not normally available to companies in such an early stage of development. Despite their heavy use of the Internet to access potential customers and deliver their products and services, there was a high level of early use of FDI in the form of sales subsidiaries. One company had set up sales subsidiaries in every country it entered. Another followed a similar pattern, setting up sales subsidiaries within a few months of starting export sales. When the boom turned to crash, and the inflow of cash dried up, the companies began a rapid withdrawal process from their subsidiary commitments, reverting to the use of direct exporting and sales agents. While the cases are few, they do illustrate how even small, newly internationalizing firms might more quickly move to the use of FDI, given ready access to low-cost finance (Borsheim and Solberg, 2002).

The cost, risk and debt implications of financing options are of concern to large companies as well, and likewise impose various constraints on mode choices, for example when companies opt for JVs rather than WOSs because of the reduced financing demands and associated lower risk perception (see the Norsk Hydro in India example in Chapter 9). On the positive side, companies in a strong financial position may be emboldened to become more aggressive in FDI activity. For example, the Australian company, Ramsay Health Care, the country's largest private hospital operator, was reported to be seeking acquisitions in Asia to add to its existing investments after an 80 per cent rise in profits. This improvement occurred at a time of strong cash flow and falling debt (Jiminez, 2006).

FDI financing possibilities may be enhanced or restricted by movements in exchange rates. The cost of a capital flow from country A to country B will be reduced by a fall in B's exchange rate relative to A's, thereby reducing the cost of financing FDI in country B for a company in country A from sources in A. The rise in the euro against the dollar of about one-third over the period 2002–2005 was apparently an important encouragement for many European firms to undertake investment in the US, producing a substantial reduction in financing needs when based on European sources (Weisman, 2005). Substantial exchange rate movements that are positive from a company's perspective at the least are likely to accelerate any plans for FDI, or support higher bid prices in acquisition situations. This is provided the changes are expected to last through the relevant time frame – an environment of exchange rate volatility may constrain FDI decision making. Financing costs may be further lowered through the incentives provided by local governments in greenfield situations. The incentives might include low-priced property, specialized infrastructure provision, loans and grants, all reducing the amount of finance that has to be raised to undertake an investment. Of course, exchange rate effects can act in reverse, promoting divestment. A case in point is the US multinational, Seagate, which closed its disc drive assembly plant in Ireland at the end of 1997, just a year after it had opened, moving the activity to Malaysia because of the large fall in the Malaysian ringgit. Not even the need to

Table 10.1   Sources of FDI finance

	Internal	External
Home/third countries	Intra-company loans*(3)	Equity capital*(1) Bank loans
Host country	Reinvested earnings*(2)	Equity capital (when local share market listing), bank loans

Notes: *( ) Most important sources in 2004 (UNCTAD, 2005).

repay $16 million in grants that it had received from the Irish government to set up in Ireland was enough to stop this relocation (Brown, 1997).

Taxation and interest rate differentials between countries are important factors in financing decisions by multinationals, particularly as to the source and location of finance, although with limited impact on the mode form decision (UNCTAD, 2005). Nonetheless, there are examples, as mentioned in Chapter 4, where inter-subsidiary licensing within a multinational is part of an FDI mode package as a way of lowering the taxation burden in one country (high tax) and ensuring that income appears in the licensor's country (low tax), as part of the financial management and taxation minimization processes of the multinational as a whole.

Basic FDI financing options are summarized in Table 10.1. As a way of lowering the financial demands of FDI, in some cases companies are able to finance their investments in JVs through intangible and real asset transfers, such as intellectual property, and machinery and equipment. However, the UNCTAD (2005) data presented in the introductory section of this chapter show that, in 2004, in global terms, equity capital was the main source of finance for FDI, followed by reinvested earnings and intra-company loans. A recent example of the raising of equity capital to finance FDI is that by Australian childcare centre company, ABC Learning Centres, reputedly the world's largest share market-listed firm in this business area, which recently raised about $AU600 million in a share offering. About 190 million or more was reported to be going into a 'war chest' to fund further acquisitions of childcare centres in the US (Webb, 2006). Banks and other financial institutions are also important sources of external finance for FDI in the form of loans, and multinational companies have a wide range of options to access in this regard, not just in their home countries. For example, the Australian share market-listed independent company, Domino's Pizza Australia New Zealand, is to buy 153 Domino's Pizza outlets in France, Belgium and the Netherlands based on funding from the Australian bank, Westpac (Andrusiak, 2006). Debt expansion, of course, is a limiting factor on the use of this avenue.

The re-invested earnings of companies' subsidiaries in foreign countries are a prominent part of FDI financing, although with substantial variability in their use across countries, and overall stronger use in developing than developed nations (UNCTAD, 2005). The funds available from this source could be used for expansion of existing operations, or for the construction of new facilities, aimed at a new area of business in the same foreign market. Of course, this option depends on previous FDI having been undertaken, and having functioned successfully for a long enough period for the requisite surplus funds to be generated. The variability of use of reinvested earnings across countries appears to be related to multinationals' taxation minimization policies: 'the distribution of large dividend payments by foreign affiliates in Germany reduces their retained profits, which can help reduce the taxes they pay in Germany' (UNCTAD, 2005, Ch. 1, 11). Again, such policies have limited impact on the specific mode choice decisions of companies, except in the general sense of generating additional funds to finance more costly expansion via FDI, and creating some location bias in favour of countries where it is deemed appropriate to use retained profits for investment purposes.

Cross-border intra-company loans are a further important source of finance for multinationals and, like reinvested earnings, are used extensively but variably across countries. Research indicates that differentials in taxation and interest rates have a significant impact on the pattern of use of this financing form (UNCTAD, 2005). For example, there is an incentive, other things being equal (exchange rate movements, changes in relative inflation rates and so on), for companies to borrow needed funds in locations where interest rates are low and internally transfer these for use in countries where interest rates are high, with mode choice decisions somewhat peripheral to such processes.

CONCLUSION

FDI dominates international business activity. It is *the* powerful foreign operation mode that has been at the forefront of the creation of the very large and influential multinationals we see today. The well-trodden path that has seen FDI flow primarily out of the large developed economies, principally the US and Europe, is being followed at a developing rapid pace from diverse developing and transition economies, such as China, India and Russia. It seems to be taken as almost a given that this is the appropriate path to global business influence and to ensuring benefit from global business involvement.

Much of the global FDI push, from both new and old sources, continues to be effected via M&As, in spite of their many, well-publicized flaws, as noted in this chapter. The problems and failures of numerous M&As have created a large, changing global pool of companies available for, or amenable to, purchase, leading to strong global growth in divestment activity. Overall, there is no evidence that this picture will change in the foreseeable future, including the 'churning' of ownership via divestment and M&As as new global entities arise from the different emergent economies.

However, the dominant overall role of FDI at the global level should not cloud consideration of its role as just one method in the box of mode tools available to companies in penetrating and servicing foreign markets. Powerful it may be, but it is normally a high-commitment and relatively high-cost mode for internationalizing companies, and with that it tends to be seen as a high-risk path, especially for smaller and newly internationalizing firms. The analysis of FDI in this chapter has shown that the concerns about FDI use are not misplaced, particularly in its M&A form, with high potential costs of failure. Managing a takeover, and integrating organizations and cultures, are demanding tasks. While FDI that leads to a WOS is the preferred outcome for most companies, it does not necessarily deliver the extent of control over the foreign operation that might be anticipated, even though this is a major driving force behind the WOS preference. This is most pronounced in situations where a company lacks experience in the relevant market and close knowledge of the takeover target. The control concern has been accentuated in an environment in which knowledge assets have come to be seen as critical to a company's long-term success in the international arena: JVs are viewed by many as a potential leakage point and therefore to be avoided if possible. However, as noted in the alliances and mode strategy chapters, many companies have been able build defences around a core JV through the development of comprehensive mode packages and intellectual property protection. It is interesting to note that, in a recent global survey of CEOs and the entry actions or plans for the emerging markets of Brazil, China, India and Russia, forming alliances with partners was the leading mode choice for their companies (PricewaterhouseCoopers, 2006). In market contexts that involve perceived high risk, for whatever reason, companies are still loath to engage in high-commitment FDI. Like all modes, FDI is not a simple panacea in all situations for the mode choice question.

REFERENCES

Aharoni, Y. (1966), *The Foreign Investment Decision Process*, Boston: Harvard University Press.

Andrusiak, K. (2006), 'Big shot', *Australian*, 2 May, 20.

Arnold, M. and R. Minder (2006), 'France bolsters takeover defences', *Australian*, 3 March, 23.

Australian (2006), 'Foreign investors flocking to India', 26 March, 38.

Barkema, H.G. and F. Vermeulen (1998), 'International expansion through start-up or acquisition: a learning perspective', *Academy of Management Journal*, **41**(1), 7–26.

Belderbos, R. and J. Zou (2006), 'Foreign investment, divestment and relocation by Japanese electronic firms in east Asia', *Asian Economic Journal*, **20**(1), 1–27.

Benito, G.R.G. (1997), 'Divestment of foreign production operations', *Applied Economics*, **29**(10), 1365–77.

Benito, G.R.G. and L.S. Welch (1997), 'De-internationalization', *Management International Review*, **37**(special issue 2), 7–25.

Benito, G.R.G., B. Grøgaard and R. Narula (2003), 'Environmental influences on MNE subsidiary roles: economic integration and the Nordic countries', *Journal of International Business Studies*, **34**(5), 443–56.

Björkman, I. and J. Tienari (2005), 'A learning perspective on sociocultural integration in cross-national mergers', in G.K. Stahl and M.E. Mendenhall (eds), *Mergers and Acquisitions*, Stanford: Stanford University Press, pp. 155–79.

Boreham, T. (2000), 'Axa's global "distractions" led to neglect of NatMut', *Australian*, 14 July, 25.

Borsheim, J.H. and C.A. Solberg (2002), 'The internationalization of born global Internet firms', *Cahiers de Recherche*, Bordeaux Ecole de Management, Talence, France.

Bownas, G. (1991), *Japan and the New Europe: Industrial Strategies and Options for the 1990s*, London: Economist Intelligence Unit.

Brown, J.M. (1997), 'Asian turmoil hits Irish plant', *Financial Times*, 13/14 December, 2.

Callan, E. (2006), 'Tesco a leading contender for Carrefour's Seoul stores', *Weekend Australian*, 15–16 April, 36.

Calof, J.L. (1993), 'The mode choice and change decision and its impact on international performance', *International Business Review*, **2**(1), 97–120.

Chen, H. and T.-J. Chen (1998), 'Network linkage and location choice in foreign direct investment', *Journal of International Business Studies*, **29**(3), 445–68.

Coley, S.C. and S.E. Reinton (1988), 'The hunt for value', *McKinsey Quarterly*, **2**(Spring), 29–34.

Corrigan, T. (1998), '$400m set aside for gold handcuffs', *Financial Times*, 1 December, 24.

Datta, D.K. and G. Puia (1995), 'Cross border acquisitions: an examination of the influence of relatedness and cultural fit on shareholder value creation in U.S. acquiring firms', *Management International Review*, **35**(4), 337–59.

Davies, S. (1994), 'BAe flies away from Rover with a sack-full of cash', *Financial Times*, 1 February, 19.

Demos, T. (2006), 'Going global – the most admired companies are more focused on managing from the center than on local initiatives', *Fortune (Europe)*, 6 March, 48–9.

Deng, P. (2001), 'WOFEs: the most popular entry mode into China', *Business Horizons*, **44**(4), 63–72.

Desai, M.A., C.F. Foley and J.R. Hines jr (2004), 'Venture out alone', *Harvard Business Review*, **84**(3), 22.

Dolan, K. (2006), 'Offshorers go offshore', *Business Review Weekly*, 27 April–3 May, 30–31.
Dunning, J.H. (1998), 'Location and the multinational enterprise: a neglected factor?', *Journal of International Business Studies*, **29**(1), 45–66.
Economist (1997), 'Why too many mergers miss the mark', 4 January, 61–2.
Economist (2000), 'Walking away from Longbridge', 18 March, 61–2.
Economist (2003), 'Chinese firms abroad – spreading their wings', 6 September, 59.
Economist (2005a), 'China bashing – giving China a bloody nose', 6 August, 49–50.
Economist (2005b), 'The struggle of the champions', 8 January, 57–9.
Economist (2006), 'European takeovers – to the barricades', 4 March, 55–6.
Erramilli, M.K. (1990), 'Entry mode choice in service industries', *International Marketing Review*, **7**(5), 50–62.
European Commission (various issues, 1988–92), *Report on Competition Policy*, Brussels.
Fackler, M. and A. Zimmerman (2003), 'Store wars: Wal-Mart takes on Japan', *Far Eastern Economic Review*, 25 September, 38–41.
Ferguson, A. and D. James (2003), 'Secrets and traps of overseas expansion', *Business Review Weekly*, 5 June, 40–46.
Fifield, A. (2006), 'S Korea tries to reassure foreign investors', *Financial Times*, 7 April, 2.
Gatignon, H. and E. Anderson (1988), 'The multinational corporation's degree of control over foreign subsidiaries: an empirical test of a transaction cost explanation', *Journal of Law, Economics and Organization*, **4**(2), 305–36.
Gillespie, K., L. Riddle, E. Sayre and D. Sturges (1999), 'Diaspora interest in homeland investment', *Journal of International Business Studies*, **30**(3), 623–34.
Gooding, K. (1997), 'Mining groups prefer M&A to exploration', *Financial Times*, 4 June, 24.
Gottliebsen, R. (2003), 'World's greatest boss says it's no time for wallflowers', *Australian*, 18 June, 21/24.
Hall, T. (1996), 'NZ to sidestep EU spreadable butter duty', *Financial Times*, 13 November, 6.
Hamill, J. (1993), 'Managing crossborder mergers and acquisitions in Europe', in M.J. Baker (ed.), *Perspectives on Marketing Management*, vol. 3, New York: John Wiley, pp. 3–26.
Hayes, S. and S. Mitchell (2005), 'Satyam set to expand locally', *Australian*, 1 November, 40.
Hayward, M.L.A. and D.C. Hambrick (1997), 'Explaining the premiums paid for large acquisitions: evidence of CEO hubris', *Administrative Science Quarterly*, **42**(1), 103–27.
Hitt, M.A., R.E. Hoskisson, R.A. Johnson and D.D. Moesel (1996), 'The market for corporate control and firm innovation', *Academy of Management Journal*, **39**(5), 1084–119.
Hood, N. and T. Truijens (1993), 'European locational decisions of Japanese manufacturers: survey evidence on the case of the UK', *International Business Review*, **2**(1), 39–64.
Hywood, G. (1988), 'Australian business turns to US', *Australian Financial Review*, 11 July, 3.
Jaussaud, J., J. Schaaper and Y. Zhang (2001), 'The control of international equity joint ventures: distribution of capital and expatriation policies', *Journal of the Asia Pacific Economy*, **6**(2), 212–31.

Jemison, D.B. and S.B. Sitkin (1986), 'Acquisitions: the process can be the problem', *Harvard Business Review*, **64**(2), 107–16.

Jiminez, K. (2006), 'Ramsay eyes Asia after lift', *Australian*, 28 February, 22.

Johanson, J. and F. Wiedersheim-Paul (1975), 'The internationalization of the firm: four Swedish cases', *Journal of Management Studies*, **12**(3), 305–22.

Jung-a, S. and F. Guerrera (2006), 'Carrefour sells its Korean stores to E.Land', *Financial Times (Asia)*, 29/30 April, 9.

Kay, J. (1996), 'Poor odds on the takeover lottery', *Financial Times*, 26 January, 12.

Kim, S.H. and S. Kim (1993), 'Motives for Japanese direct investment in the United States', *Multinational Business Review*, **1**(1), 66–72.

Knickerbocker, F.T. (1973), *Oligopolistic Reaction and Multinational Enterprise*, Boston, MA: Harvard Business School.

Kone News and Views (2005), 'Gearing up for Korea', **1**, 28–31.

KPMG Transaction Services (2001), *World Class Transactions: Insights Into Creating Shareholder Value Through Mergers and Acquisitions*, London: KPMG.

Larimo, J. (1987), *The Foreign Direct Investment Decision Process*, Vaasa: Vaasan Korkeakoulun Julkaisuja, Tutkimuksia No. 124.

Larimo, J. (1995), 'The foreign direct investment decision process: case studies of different types of decision processes in Finnish firms', *Journal of Business Research*, **33**(1), 25–55.

Leahy, J. (2006), 'Indian M&As growing apace', *Financial Times (Asia)*, 18 October, 16.

Lu, J.W. and P.W. Beamish (2004), 'Network development and firm performance: a field of internationalizing Japanese firms', *Multinational Business Review*, **12**(3), 4–61.

Luostarinen, R., H. Korhonen, J. Jokinen and T. Peltonen (1994), *Globalisation and SME*, Ministry of Trade and Industry, Finland, Studies and Reports 59/1994.

Marsh, V. (2005), 'BHP Billiton digs in to win over sceptics, *Financial Times*, 9 March, 28.

Mata, J. and P. Portugal (2000), 'Closure and divestiture by foreign entrants: the impact of entry and post-entry strategies', *Strategic Management Journal*, **21**(5), 549–62.

Meyer, K.E. and S. Estrin (2001), 'Brownfield entry in emerging markets', *Journal of International Business Studies*, **32**(3), 575–84.

Nicholas, S., S.J. Gray and W.R. Purcell (2001), 'Do incentives attract Japanese FDI to Singapore and the region?', in S. Gray, S.L. McGaughey and W.R. Purcell (eds), *Asia–Pacific Issues in International Business*, Cheltenham, UK and Northampton, MA, USA: Edward Elgar, pp. 129–50.

O'Neill, M. (2004), 'Consumer markets: breaking through', *China International Business*, October, 21–9.

Osborn, R.N. (2003), 'International alliances: going beyond the hype', *Mt Eliza Business Review*, **6**(1), 37–43.

Osland, G.E., C.R. Taylor and S. Zou (2001), 'Selecting international modes of entry and expansion', *Marketing Intelligence & Planning*, **19**(3), 153–61.

Padmanabhan, P. and K.R. Cho (1999), 'Decision-specific experience in foreign ownership and establishment strategies: evidence from Japanese firms', *Journal of International Business Studies*, **30**(1), 25–44.

Paukkuri, M. (1987), 'Foreign business service companies' direct investments in Finland', Master's thesis, Helsinki School of Economics, Finland.

Petersen, B., D.E. Welch and L.S. Welch (2000), 'Creating meaningful switching options in international operations', *Long Range Planning*, **33**(5), 688–705.

Piekkari, R., E. Vaara, J. Tienari and R. Säntti (2005), 'Integration or disintegration? Human resource implications of the common corporate language decision in a cross-border merger', *International Journal of Human Resource Management*, **16**(3), 333–47.

PricewaterhouseCoopers (2006), *9th Annual Global CEO Survey: Globalisation and Complexity*, downloaded from company website, accessed 29.4.06.

Saywell, T. (1999), 'Outside chance – China encourages manufacturers to invest overseas', *Far Eastern Economic Review*, 15 April, 82.

Shoebridge, N. (1993), 'Pacific Dunlop rethinks its Asia push', *Business Review Weekly*, 27 August, 44–7.

Simonian, H. (1998), 'Four months of fortune that favoured the brave', *Financial Times*, 14 May, 19.

Simonian, H. (2006), 'Serono looks at acquisition offers', *Financial Times (Asia)*, 21 April, 16.

Slater, J. (2003), 'GE reinvents itself in India', *Far Eastern Economic Review*, 27 March, 42–5.

Slater, J. and E. Amaha (1999), 'King of the crisis', *Far Eastern Economic Review*, 6 May, 10–13.

Smith, D. and D. Rushe (2004), 'Out of Big Blue, Chinese business takes a giant', *Australian*, 13 December, 11–15.

Somlev, I.P. and Y. Hoshino (2005), 'Influence of location factors on establishment and ownership of foreign investments: the case of Japanese manufacturing firms in Europe', *International Business Review*, **14**(5), 577–98.

Stephan, M. and E. Pfaffmann (2001), 'Detecting the pitfalls of data on foreign direct investment: scope and limits of FDI data', *Management International Review*, **41**(2), 189–218.

Tomassen, S., L.S. Welch and G.R.G. Benito (1998), 'Norwegian companies in India: operation mode choice', *Asian Journal of Business and Information Systems*, **3**(1), 1–20.

UNCTAD (2003/5/6), *World Investment Report 2003/5/6*, New York and Geneva: United Nations.

Vatikiotis, M. (2004), 'Outward bound', *Far Eastern Economic Review*, 5 February, 24–7.

Vernon, R., L.T. Wells Jr and S. Rangan (1996), *The Manager in the International Economy*, 7th edn, Upper Saddle River, NJ: Prentice-Hall.

Very, P. and D.M. Schweiger (2001), 'The acquisition process as a learning process: evidence from a study of critical problems and solutions in domestic and cross-border deals', *Journal of World Business*, **36**(1), 11–31.

Webb, C. (2006), '$600m for ABC Learning', *Age*, 27 April, Business 2.

Wei, S.J. (1997), 'Why is corruption so much more taxing than tax? Arbitrariness kills', *NBER Working Paper*, no. 6255, Cambridge, MA: National Bureau of Economic Research.

Weisman, R. (2005), 'Weak dollar lets foreigners grab U.S. firms', *International Herald Tribune (European Edition)*, 15 February, 14.

Welch, L.S. and R. Luostarinen (1988), 'Internationalization: evolution of a concept', *Journal of General Management*, **14**(2), 34–5.

Welch, D.E., L.S. Welch and R. Marschan-Piekkari (2001), 'The persistent impact of language on global operations', *Prometheus*, **19**(3), 193–209.

White, D. (1997), 'Return of the conqueror', *Financial Times*, 5 March, 13.

Wilkins, M. (1970), *The Emergence of Multinational Enterprise: American Business Abroad from the Colonial Era to 1914*, Cambridge, MA: Harvard University Press.

Wilson, N. and P. Taylor (2006), 'Wen signals more local investment', *Australian*, 3 April, 4.

Zarkada-Fraser, A. and C. Fraser (2001), 'Australian manufacturers' perceptions of Indonesia as a host for direct investment', in S. Gray, S.L. McGaughey and W.R. Purcell (eds), *Asia-Pacific Issues in International Business*, Cheltenham, UK and Northampton, MA, USA: Edward Elgar, pp. 151–68.

Zhao, J.H., S.H. Kim and J. Du (2003), 'The impact of corruption and transparency on foreign direct investment: an empirical analysis', *Management International Review*, **43**(1), 41–62.

PART III

Strategies

11. Mode switching and stretching strategies

INTRODUCTION

Most companies with international operations will eventually experience switches of foreign operation methods (FOM), and some companies may even develop standard routines for such undertakings. Mode switching allows more intensive operations to be developed in the markets concerned, supporting a strategy of deeper market penetration. Alternatively, mode switching might be used to recover a problem situation in a foreign market associated with existing mode use. It is, therefore, important that company managers are aware of the potential pitfalls pertaining to mode switches and take measures to avoid them. The avoidance of potentially excessive switching costs will usually require managers to prepare the mode switch well ahead of the actual event; in other words, formulate and follow a mode switch *strategy*. When companies incur high switching costs it is often a consequence of a misguided collaboration with the local operator – in the sense that the conditions for a possible future disengagement (or switch) have not been settled in the agreement, and therefore no exit options have been assured. In the absence of such options, an entrant firm may at some point in time find itself locked in with the local operator. The problems of the Danish company, Nilfisk, illustrate such a lock-in situation: see Box 11.1.

When mentioning mode switches, internalization is a common outcome, that is, a transition from serving the foreign market through an outside agent to an in-house operation in that market, most often in the form of an FDI. Examples of internalization processes are switches from independent distributors to sales subsidiaries, from licensing arrangements to production subsidiaries, and from franchised to company-owned outlets. The ideal internalization process stands out as being smooth and frictionless, a process in which the independent operator accepts the end of cooperation arrangements or agrees to the conditions for dual distribution collaboration or other forms of mode combination (see next chapter). However, dysfunctional internalization processes are not unusual and can be dramatic: sometimes the parties break up, resort to the courtroom and subsequently fight each other vigorously in the foreign market. Here, the entrant firm is

BOX 11.1   LOCKED IN WITH THE LOCAL DISTRIBUTOR:
            NILFISK IN SPAIN

In the beginning of the 1990s the Danish producer of household and industrial vacuum cleaners NILFISK A/S (Ltd.) found itself in a locked-in position
with the local distributor in Spain, *Nilfisk Aspiradoras SA*. The servicing of
the Spanish market by an independent intermediary was the sole exception
to this Danish company's general and explicit rule about foreign market servicing: namely that all the major export markets – to which Spain definitely
belonged – should be served by own sales subsidiaries. In the 1970s and
1980s, the Spanish distributor, domiciled in Barcelona and with affiliates in
Madrid, Bilbao and Valencia, had carried out an impressive marketing effort
in the Spanish business market, the result of which was a 50 per cent share
of the total Spanish sales of industrial vacuum cleaners. However, the head
of the family-owned distributor company, Sr. Borrás, and since the late eighties his successor and oldest son, Joaquin Borrás, resisted the repeated
attempts by the Danish producer to take over the control of their company.
The Danish producer was only allowed a minority share (originally only 10
per cent) in *Nilfisk Aspiradoras SA*. As an effect of the persistent takeover
attempts and refusals, the relationship deteriorated from being a very
friendly one in the early eighties to, ten years later, being one of outright confrontation. During the 1990s Sr. Borrás Jr. even took on the role of harsh
spokesman for the foreign distributors of NILFISK, defending their independence *vis-à-vis* the Danish producer. Since the after-sales service was
essential to the industrial customers and probably the key to the success of
the Nilfisk product, the Spanish distributor was able to keep the local customers hostage and use this situation in negotiations with Nilfisk. In effect,
the local customers would identify the Nilfisk vacuum cleaner with the local
service organisation rather than with the foreign producer. With loyalty resid-
ing at the local distributor, a clear-cut termination of the relationship would
consequently impose a considerable loss of Nilfisk customers in Spain.
Equipped with a product substitute, the local distributor would still be in business, whereas NILFISK could be expected to take some time and incur considerable costs in building a Spanish customer base. With these prospects
in mind, the Spanish could forcefully insist on 'business as usual'.

Sources: Press release (28.3.1990) and personal communication; reprinted
from Petersen, Welch and Welch (2000) with permission from Elsevier.

likely to incur significant 'take down costs' in the form of lawsuit expenses
and compensation (severance payment) to the local operator. The more
serious financial losses incurred by an entrant firm are those of forsaken
sales revenue in the foreign market – both before and after termination of
cooperation with the local operator: first, the sheer risk of being terminated
may have deterred the independent, local operator from developing the
local market, and second, the same operator may be able to maintain the
loyalty of the local customers after the break-up.

Mode switches in the form of externalization are perhaps less obvious, but nevertheless not uncommon. Examples are conversions of company-owned shops into franchised shops, and outsourcing of foreign subsidiary production to local contract manufacturers. Some FOMs are more or less destined or pre-designed for externalization: for example, turnkey operations and Build–Operate–Transfer arrangements (see Chapter 7) which have the characteristics that the entrant firm, at a certain point in time, transfers control of the assets to a local operator – often a private or semi-governmental party. International equity joint venture arrangements may, depending on the circumstances, imply externalization as well as internalization. Externalization takes place when the entrant firm (being one of the parents of the equity joint venture) sells off its share to the other parent(s), but continues collaboration on a contractual basis. Conversely, internalization occurs when the entrant firm buys out the assets and share(s) of the other parent(s) of the joint venture and turns it into a sole venture.

Both internalization and externalization processes in the foreign markets are so-called 'inter-mode switches', that is, switches that imply a change of organizational form ('mode'). In contrast to inter-mode switches entrant firms also make intra-mode switches. In the case of intra-mode switches the entrant firm maintains the organizational form (or FOM) but a new local operator is appointed. As an example, an entrant firm may cancel the contract with a local sales agency and subsequently appoint a new sales agent. In this chapter, we examine inter-mode switches only, and delimit ourselves from discussing circumstances in relation to change of foreign partners. For a study of intra-mode switches (replacement of foreign intermediaries), see, for example, Petersen et al. (2000).

WHY MODE SWITCH?

Firms switch FOMs for two basic reasons: either as a correction of managerial misjudgments or as an adaptation to new circumstances as foreign operations evolve. In the following, we will examine these reasons, starting with correction of managerial misjudgments.

Mode Switch as Correction of Managerial Misjudgments

For various reasons, managers may find that the initial mode of foreign operations was founded on false premises, and a mode shift thus seems compelling. Managers quite often rush into mode decisions that generate negative outcomes (Calof, 1993). Sometimes managers (or their successors) recognize their FOM misjudgments and take steps to correct them. For example, an entrant firm establishes a production subsidiary based on estimates of local supply and demand conditions that later on are recognized as being too optimistic. Realizing that the true unit costs are considerably higher than expected, the entrant firm divests and subsequently serves the foreign market through exports (Benito and Welch, 1997). Furthermore, there might be factors which, from the outset, affect the entry mode in a negative way. For example, difficulties in evaluating an outside agent, such as a local, independent distributor, exist from the first day of entry, and such difficulties are likely to persist. As pointed out by Hennart (1991), employees are less inclined to 'cheat' than outside agents. Whereas employees are paid for following instructions, the income of outside agents depends on their output, that is, the sales they achieve in their market.

Agents are therefore likely to concentrate on marketing activities that have an immediate impact on their revenues, rather than spending time and effort on activities with a less distinct link to actual sales, such as providing customer service (Anderson and Oliver, 1987). In general, the performance of agents with regard to such activities is hard to measure, and requires information beyond that given by sales figures alone. The exporting company may therefore need to monitor the behaviour of foreign agents, obviously at a cost. The monitoring problems associated with relying on outside agents therefore provide a permanent incentive to internalize the foreign business activities.

Mode Switch as Adaptation to New Circumstances

Another, and perhaps more important, reason for mode shifts is that internal as well as external factors may change considerably after the initial foreign market entry, sometimes in rather unforeseen ways, rendering the entry mode less suitable. If the benefits of putting in place a new FOM more than offset the anticipated costs of switching, rational managers will undertake a mode shift. The change factors triggering mode shifts are numerous and of very different character (see Calof and Beamish, 1995; Pedersen et al., 2002; Benito et al., 2005, for overviews of change factors). However, in most cases the changes relate to (i) the local market, (ii) the local operator, or (iii) the entrant firm itself. Using this categorization we shall briefly outline some commonly seen adaptive factors causing mode change.

Dissatisfaction with local operators is a major reason for *intra*-mode shifts, but less so for *inter*-mode changes (Anderson and Narus, 1990; Shamdasani and Sheth, 1995; Coughlan et al., 2006). Since the dissatisfaction is with the operator rather than the operation mode as such, entrant firms in many cases will remedy the dissatisfaction by replacing the operator (for example, appointing a new licensee or a new distributor). Sometimes, however, suitable alternative operators may not be available, forcing the entrant firm to take over (internalize) the local operations. Furthermore, dissatisfaction is an important triggering – rather than underlying – change factor (Calof and Beamish, 1995). The dissatisfaction with the local operator often prompts a critical appraisal of the existing operation mode: 'If changes are to be made anyhow, perhaps we should change the operation mode as well?' Decision theory demonstrates that managers often take actions (for example, make mode shifts) as reactive, ad hoc responses to emerging problems (such as poor performance of local operators), in contrast to proactive follow-up on recurrent appraisals of existing business practices. In practice, mode shifts tend to appear as problem-solving devices rather than as systematic streamlining of the entrant firm's organizational structure. The important exceptions to this are mode shifts in connection to changes of management in the entrant firm. A new management team is more inclined to enforce changes and unlikely to indulge with business-as-usual expectations of the organization. New management teams may very well consider existing FOMs as obvious targets for scrutiny and change (Benito and Welch, 1997).

Growth aversion within local operators may lead to increasing dissatis-faction within the entrant firm. Paradoxically, this dissatisfaction grows out of business success, namely the increasing sales in the local market which at a certain point strain the management resources of the local operator. In a rational world the local operator would just expand the management team and increase the delegation of managerial tasks. However, local oper-ators may be closely-held firms in which the founders take pride in main-taining the daily control of all business functions. The founder may resist management delegation and, effectively, expansion of the firm beyond a certain, controllable firm size of, say, 20 to 50 employees. The growth aver-sion of founders/entrepreneurs and family firms in general seems to be a universal phenomenon that many governments – aiming for more jobs and higher economic growth – are struggling with (see, for example, Gallo, 1994).

Sometimes change is triggered by new ownership or management of a local operator. In principle, the entrant firm can just accept the new own-ership/management or appoint another local operator (that is, make an intra-mode shift), but only in principle. In practice, the suitability of an entry mode tends to be closely related to the identity of the operator. In a management decision context, the two issues – FOM and identity of the local operator – are not always separable. For example, a licence arrange-ment may be regarded as a superior FOM because of the manufacturing skills and market position of the particular licensee. In the case of the local operator's exit, licensing may not constitute an optimal FOM to the entrant firm, because an equivalent local operator may not be available or willing to become a licensee. Furthermore, replacing a local operator often evokes increased communication and bonding costs in relation to a new partner. It may take years to obtain the level of informality and confidentiality that characterized the previous relationship. In other words, the entrant firm must foresee higher communication costs and more uncertainty during the first years of collaboration with a new operator, and these additional costs may tip the balance in favour of internalizing the local market activities.

Local market growth is probably the most decisive factor for both re-localization and internalization of international operations. At a certain point in time, local market growth may justify local production instead of serving the market from home, that is via exporting (Horst, 1974). As pointed out in Chapter 2, in their discussion of the optimal timing of foreign direct investments (FDIs), Buckley and Casson (1981) use a micro-economic line of reasoning to show that, in terms of total cost minimization, it is favourable to export to a foreign market first and switch to working through a production subsidiary later. Sometimes it will be preferable to include licensing as an intermediate stage. The change factor in their model is the growth of sales in the local market. Assuming that the production unit – a manufacturing plant – has a certain minimum efficient technical scale, below which unit production costs rise rapidly, at a certain point sales in the foreign market will reach a volume that allows for throughput (and thereby scale economies) sufficient for running a local production unit cost-efficiently.

Whereas local market growth may induce local production, market integration and lowering of transport costs pull in the opposite direction. Hence, the European market integration ('The Single Market') of the 1990s prompted many multinational companies to restructure and consolidate their European subsidiaries. As an example, the Quaker Oats Company closed down its cereals production facility in Denmark in 1992 and has since then served the Scandinavian market via imports from other production sites in Europe. Similarly, more efficient transport technologies (such as container transport systems with intermodal terminals) have expanded the export territory that a production plant can serve economically. Furthermore, sales growth in the foreign market may induce not only shift of location, but also change of ownership of the operation mode. Klein et al. (1990) found sales volume to be an important discriminating factor in the choice between independent, local operators (foreign distributors and sales agents) and in-house arrangements (sales subsidiaries and home-based sales forces) where large sales volumes favour employee sales arrangements.

As a multinational company achieves increasing market acceptance of its brand and business format, opportunities for externalization through franchising also increase. The development of international franchisors frequently occurs via market entry with a small number of company-owned outlets followed by numerous franchised outlets: see Chapter 3 (Gallini and Lutz, 1992). The company-owned 'flagship' outlets are needed for demonstrating the viability and profitability of the business format in a local market context.

Finally, market liberalization (change of local government policy on foreign ownership) is a potentially important external factor. More often than not, governments in emerging markets have imposed restrictions on foreign ownership of companies in certain, strategic industries, thereby impelling entrant firms to form joint ventures with local companies. As these restrictions are lifted, as has been the case in, for example, China and India over the past five to ten years, entrant firms tend to switch to fully-owned subsidiaries. Change of local government policy on foreign ownership has been for many years a major cause of conversions from international joint ventures to wholly-owned subsidiaries (see, for example, Gomes-Casseres, 1987, 1990).

Change factors may also relate to the entrant firm itself. First, the growth of the entrant firm can be important. When a foreign market entry is to be undertaken, the entrant firm may be constrained in terms of capital and management resources (Ali and Camp, 1993; Welch and Luostarinen, 1988). As a consequence, the firm excludes any method of operation that involves substantial requirements of capital and/or management resources, choosing instead some low-commitment mode (that is, low in terms of capital and management resources), such as independent distributors (Albaum et al., 2004), licensing (Contractor, 1981) or franchising agreements (Oxenfeldt and Kelly, 1969). Over time, however, the entrant firm may accumulate capital and generate excess management resources, as a result of realized managerial scope economies (Lafontaine and Kaufmann, 1994; Penrose, 1956, 1959). In this new situation of abundant capital resources and underutilized management capacity, it would seem appropriate to replace the low-commitment method of foreign operations with in-house arrangements, such as sales subsidiaries and company-owned outlets. Furthermore, the entrant firm may, over a period of time, expand its product range and thereby achieve economies of scope in various business functions, including marketing and sales. During the 1990s, the Danish company Coloplast, a worldwide provider of high-quality and innovative healthcare products and services, systematically expanded its product range through a number of acquisitions in order to facilitate the establishment of viable sales subsidiaries. The management of Coloplast considered the servicing of its local markets via independent distributors as temporary, second-best solutions which should be replaced by sales subsidiaries to the extent this would be economically feasible (source: personal communication).

Second, the entrant firm may become less risk-averse as a result of business diversification: growing bigger, the entrant firm may become less risk-averse and therefore more inclined to take over operations in foreign markets (Benito et al., 1999). In the first phase of international expansion firms usually pursue rather limited geographical diversification. As novices in international marketing, they are inclined to be averse to risk, thus tending to avoid high-commitment modes such as having their own subsidiaries and relying on external agents instead. Their foreign partners (a foreign sales agency or a licensee) often have no geographical diversification either, but they usually spread their business risk over product lines (or, in the case of a sales agency, over several exporters). Accordingly, they tend to be risk-neutral. After some years, however, the risk profiles are likely to change. While the entrant firm often increases the number of foreign markets in which it operates, the local sales agent and the licensee may find a growing proportion of their total turnover is concentrated in the product line(s) of the entrant firm. Consequently, the entrant firm moves towards becoming less risk-averse (eventually becoming risk-neutral), whereas the foreign sales agent and licensee move in the opposite direction, or keep their risk preferences unchanged. As a result, at a certain point the entrant firm may find it economically beneficial to take over the business risk by integrating the overseas operations. Hence, as suggested by agency theory, by switching from an outcome-based to a behaviour-based or fixed remuneration, the entrant firm saves the relatively high-risk premium otherwise commanded by the risk-averse local operators (Jensen and Meckling, 1976).

Last, but not least, learning about the local market and go-alone FOMs may evoke mode changes. According to Johanson and Vahlne (1977), decision makers tend to perceive market risk as being high whenever they lack knowledge about a foreign market. The uncertainty regarding market conditions tends to restrict their choice of entry mode to low-commitment arrangements such as independent distributors and licensees (Welch and Luostarinen, 1988). Over time, entrant firms gradually accumulate market knowledge: partly because information flows increase as a result of their interaction with local operators, but also by more actively seeking information through visits to the local markets. Even though the accumulation of market knowledge may occur at a decreasing rate, as entrant firms become more knowledgeable about a foreign market, the attraction of high-commitment operation methods increases (Barkema et al., 1996). Often, the main motive for entrant firms to form joint ventures with local companies is to benefit from the local market knowledge of the latter, knowledge that is difficult to buy on an arm's-length basis (Hennart, 1988). As an entrant firm manages to tap into this knowledge, the benefits of sustaining the joint venture diminish accordingly. At a certain point in time the entrant firm may find that it is better off operating the local business on its own (Gomes-Casseres, 1987; Nakamura et al., 1996).

The outline presented above suggests that initial FOMs quite often will come under pressure for shifts either owing to realized managerial mistakes or, presumably more frequently, as a consequence of changes in the environment or in the entrant firm itself. In the next section we will look at some factors that potentially impede such corrections or adaptations of current operation methods; that is, barriers to mode switches.

BARRIERS TO MODE SWITCH

There are many barriers which may hamper companies' switch of foreign operation mode. Some switching barriers are very distinct and tangible, such as indemnification costs associated with termination of distributors, whereas others are more subtle, as with uncertainty about the true costs of acquiring a local distributor, including estimation of post-acquisition costs. In many cases, the switching barriers are not so much about expected *costs*, but more about the opportunity costs of sales *revenue* that may be sacrificed as a consequence of dismissing an outside agent who maintains strong bonds with local customers. Hence switching barriers refer to outlays and expenses incurred as well as potential loss of revenues. For example, a shift from a foreign sales agency to a sales subsidiary may entail switching costs in the form of severance payment to the former sales agent, that is, a sum of money paid to the agency to compensate for the premature cancellation of its contract. Another example could be the legal expenses paid by an entrant firm when a dispute regarding the conditions of terminating a local operator's contract is settled by litigation. Similarly, if customers in a particular market are more loyal to the local distributor than to the entrant firm, then taking over the marketing activities in that market could lead to a direct loss in sales, either permanently or for a time.

The Nilfisk case referred to earlier (Box 11.1) is an example of an entrant firm confronted with significant switching barriers in terms of sales revenue losses. Cancelling a contract with a local distributor could also result, albeit more indirectly, in revenue losses elsewhere, by affecting the reputation of the entrant firm adversely with distributors in other markets. As an illustration, an exporter's termination of a distributor in one of its foreign markets gives rise to uncertainty among distributors in other markets about the exporter's general commitment to long-term collaboration. The other distributors may take precautions in response to this uncertainty. Either the distributors will ask for economic guarantees in the form of credible commitment to continued collaboration (for example by insisting on long-term, irrevocable contracts) or the distributors will adjust their investments and activities accordingly, reasoning that operations which entail exposures to hold-up risk should not be undertaken (Williamson, 1983). Hence the loss of reputation as regards enduring relations may entail (indirect) switching costs in the entrant firm's markets as a whole (Benito et al., 1999).

While not making any distinction between outlays and revenue losses, Weiss and Anderson (1992) call the above costs 'take-down' costs (or barriers). In addition, mode shifts also entail various expenses and revenue losses connected with setting up a new mode: the set-up costs. Most obviously, by dropping an outside agent the entrant firm must undertake what are often quite substantial investments in hiring and training people in order to establish its own marketing or production apparatus in the foreign market (Luostarinen and Welch, 1990). Also, as is commonly noted in the internationalization literature, firms that are expanding into new markets, and/or serving markets in new ways, cannot usually rely entirely on their existing stock of knowledge (or consequently their routines). Much of the knowledge needed is of an experiential kind, which can only be gained through a process of learning-by-doing (see, for example, Johanson and Vahlne, 1977; Welch and Luostarinen, 1988). Typically, adjusting and fine-tuning business activities in order to become fully competitive in a new market context will take a while, during which time efficiency is likely to suffer. Likewise, since novice firms are more prone to making mistakes resulting in lost sales, revenues may also suffer. Hence, to the extent that firms are unfamiliar with the markets and/or the operation methods in question, the anticipated learning costs (and the loss of revenue) may act as an impediment to setting up new operations.

Sometimes, the entrant firm switches mode by taking over (parts of) the local operator instead of breaking up and starting from scratch with a new organization. However, acquisitions may – just as with taking down operations – be constrained by switching costs, although of a different nature. First of all, the acquirer may incur 'bundling costs'; that is the costs of acquiring assets of little value, but nevertheless imposed as part of a greater deal. As an example, an entrant firm may acquire a local distributor in order to get access to a valuable distribution network, but as part of the acquisition package inherit a number of distributorships of producers with which the entrant firm has only vague, or no, relations. These distributorships represent assets of little or no value to the entrant firm, and any price paid for these useless assets effectively constitutes a 'switching cost'. Similarly, post-acquisition integration costs may be considered as set-up switching costs that in some cases are very substantial indeed (Birkinshaw et al., 2000).

Theoretically at least, the barriers that are associated with the cost and loss of revenue noted above can be quantified and taken into account in a decision-making framework that sees firms as rational decision-making entities. For instance, set-up switching costs can be treated as an additional cost of a particular FOM, which should be taken into consideration when deciding what FOM to select. The inclusion of switching costs (SC) can be done in a straightforward manner, for example in an extension of Buckley and Casson's (1981) simple model of the choice between exporting, contracting or performing an activity in a subsidiary (FDI). Setting up a foreign subsidiary typically entails extra costs due to the training of necessary personnel and having to learn how to manage the foreign subsidiary. Just to illustrate and assuming, for simplicity, that switching costs are scale-invariant (that is, that their level is independent of the size/volume of the operation), such costs add to the fixed costs of using a subsidiary as the mode of operation, thereby increasing the total costs of that mode. In Figure 11.1, this is shown as the upward shift from the original cost curve C_{FDI} to $C_{FDI} + SC$. As a result, the switch point moves from a market size of Q^{**} to Q^{***}. Put differently: positive set-up costs lead to a postponement of the FDI option, or even prevent its use altogether if the market size stays below the switch point Q^{***}. Similarly, an increase in the switching costs of the contract option could lead to leapfrogging, for

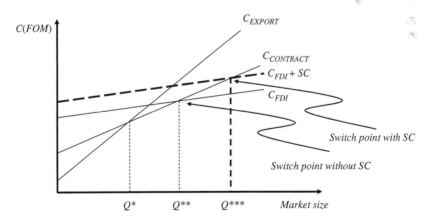

Source: Adapted from Buckley and Casson (1981).

*Figure 11.1   The impact of switching costs (*SC*) on change of FOM*

example going directly from exports to operating in a foreign market by means of a subsidiary.

Another conceptually different type of switching cost concerns barriers of a more qualitative kind, such as the way decision makers perceive risk and uncertainty, their relations with other people, or even an apparent attachment on their part to specific courses of action – which in turn may of course reflect a vested interest in maintaining the status quo. An important type of perceptual switching cost is the increase in assumed *risk* that decision makers perceive when they consider replacing a well-known, low-commitment method with an unfamiliar, high-commitment FOM. Case research suggests that changes in the mode of foreign operation are sometimes delayed for a considerable time, or are not carried out at all, even though they might seem appropriate in an economic or strategic perspective, as often occurs when the growth of sales justifies a switch from an intermediary to a sales subsidiary, but the performance of, and relationship with, the intermediary restrain the move (see Chapter 8). One critical factor appears to be the perceptions and opinions entertained by managers and entrepreneurs (Andersson, 2000). Because the managers of an exporting company may be reluctant to accept anything but a small incremental increase in the commitment of resources and the attendant market risk, a switch from a sales agent to a wholly owned sales subsidiary may very well be impeded by the higher market risk involved in setting up a subsidiary (Johanson and Vahlne, 1977).

As well as constituting set-up barriers, perceptual switching costs may also be in operation when it comes to discarding current business practices; that is, they may act as a take-down barrier, perhaps because personal ties have been developed with a foreign agent over a long period (Ellis, 2000). Also, since changing current operation methods can be interpreted as an admission of earlier mistakes in the choice of entry mode, decision makers may regard a change as carrying a personal risk: loss of prestige, or even a possible career setback. Consequently, rather than exposing themselves to such risks, they retain their established practices (Benito and Welch, 1997). The various types of switching barriers are summarized in Table 11.1.

MODE SWITCH STRATEGIES: HOW TO PLAN AND IMPLEMENT MODE SWITCHES

The ideal mode switch strategy aims for more than eliminating switching costs: it also ensures that the switch – or rather the anticipation of a switch – in no way makes the local operator disinclined to exploit the

Table 11.1   Types of switching barriers

Categories of switching barriers	Take-down barriers	Set-up barriers
Costs	• Termination compensation (severance payment) • Lawsuit expenses	• Hiring/recruiting and training costs • Foreign operation learning costs • Costs of acquiring local operator assets of little or no value to the entrant firm
Revenue losses	• Reputation effects among local operators in other markets • Loss of customers owing to their loyalty to current agent	• Loss of customers owing to failures in initial phase of own operation • Costs of integrating the acquired local operator
Perceived barriers	• Personal bonds to individuals in existing foreign operations • Loss of prestige for managers responsible for initial mode decision • Risk of career setbacks	• Risk associated with 'new' foreign operation method perceived as being unacceptably high

Source: Adapted from Benito et al. (1999).

opportunities in the market. In other words, the entrant firm should see to it that its local operators consider a mode switch as a natural and acceptable – or even a welcome – part of the collaboration, and, as such, an event which is discussed and negotiated openly between the business parties. The Nilfisk case (Box 11.1) illustrates how an entrant firm, fearing a substantial loss of sales revenue, was effectively prevented from taking over the operations in the foreign (Spanish) market. Another Danish company, Coloplast, followed a strategy of forward integration, despite considerable revenue losses in its foreign markets (see Box 11.2).

The loss of customers resulting from dismissing the local distributors usually precipitated a sales curve taking the shape of a hockey stick: a short, but steep downward slope followed by a long and steadily growing sales curve. Moreover, the switching strategy of Coloplast was costly to the extent that the distributors (presumably deliberately) restrained their sales effort in anticipation of forward integration by Coloplast. The latter

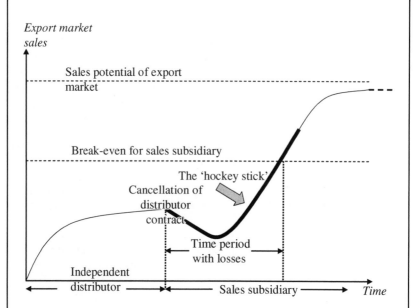

BOX 11.2   COLOPLAST AND THE 'HOCKEY STICK EFFECT'

In the beginning of the 1990s, the Danish producer of wound care products, Coloplast, faced a sales pattern as depicted in the above diagram. Poor sales results of its foreign distributors impelled Coloplast to cancel the contracts and internalize the sales activities. However, as a consequence of the cancellation, Coloplast lost customers and, for a two to four-year period incurred penalty costs of operating sales subsidiaries at sales volumes below break-even. Eventually, having experienced considerable set-up switching costs, Coloplast reached break-even and profitability from its export markets.

Source: Personal communication.

consequence may be even more detrimental to the profitability of the entrant firm inasmuch as it is compelled to integrate prematurely, thereby entailing high penalty costs of operating a subsidiary on the basis of uneconomic sales volume. The poor effort of the local distributor can be explained by the so-called 'termination dilemma'.

The Termination Dilemma

As mentioned earlier in this chapter, some degree of dissatisfaction with the intermediary is usually a common triggering factor in termination. Poor performance of the local distributor, as perceived by the entrant firm, increases the likelihood that the collaboration will come to an end. Alternatively, the entrant firm may replace the local distributor with its own sales organization operating from the home country or located in the export market. In this case, it is less obvious that dissatisfaction with the local distributor is the only decisive motivator for the termination. The entrant firm's decision to integrate the sales and marketing responsibilities may be triggered by large sales in the local market, which could in fact mainly be a result of the effort made by the local distributor (Nicholas, 1986; Klein et al., 1990). To the extent that ending the local distributor relationship can be ascribed to the successful sales effort of the same local distributor, this is an unfortunate and somewhat paradoxical consequence seen though the lens of the distributor.

There are strong reasons to believe that local operators are generally aware of the termination risk they are facing. In order to keep the assignment (the sales agency, distributorship, licence or franchise) local operators may therefore aim for mid-level performance. However, local operators cannot know exactly what the entrant firm considers to be the basis for termination. Put differently, there are limits to how well local operators know the utility functions of their foreign business partners (the entrant firms). Furthermore, exogenous factors may affect the foreign market performance in an unforeseeable positive or negative direction. The sales revenue achieved in the foreign market, being only partially controlled by the local operator, may turn out to be less than acceptable to the entrant firm, but also more than sufficient for establishing a subsidiary. In both cases, a likely result is termination.

Hence, both low and high performance will put the foreign distributor at risk of being terminated. If performing poorly, the entrant firm may lose patience, terminate the relationship, and then appoint another local distributor in the foreign market (Beeth, 1990; Petersen et al., 2000); if the local distributor is doing well and boosting the sales in the foreign market the entrant firm may find it lucrative to terminate the distributor contract and take over the sales and marketing responsibilities (Benito et al., 2005; Ellis, 2005; Petersen et al., 2006). Caught in this termination dilemma the foreign operator is better off providing a mediocre effort, that is, generating a certain level of local sales, but not reaching a volume that economically justifies the entrant firm's establishment of a subsidiary in the local market.

Needless to say, it is vital for entrant firms to release their foreign partners from the termination dilemma. If not, the entrant firm may lose out in several ways: first, in the absence of goal congruence between the two parties, the entrant firm risks sacrificing potential sales revenue in foreign markets, and/or incurring the otherwise avoidable costs of prematurely establishing a subsidiary in a given market. The business press regularly refers to cases of exporters experiencing losses during the first years of operation of subsidiaries, occasionally leading to shutdowns of non-profitable foreign affiliates, supposedly as a result of over-ambitious entries into markets where the sales revenue generated did not support the considerable fixed costs of setting up and running a subsidiary. These issues are general in the sense that they are relevant for entries into any market. The importance of adequate incentive structures for foreign partners is particularly crucial in relation to entering emerging markets, such as China, India and Vietnam (Estrin and Meyer, 2004). Entrant firms from Western countries may 'miss the boat' completely in these emerging markets because competitors accrue important first mover advantages in terms of pre-emption of sales channels, sales outlets and shelf space, or in terms of erecting other barriers to entry (Peng, 2000). In the next section we will look at different strategies for tackling the termination dilemma and switching operations in general.

Termination or Integration – Reveal or Conceal?

Given the tendency of entrant firms to seek greater control through alternative operation modes over time, it would seem important that entrant firms put in place the means to facilitate switching modes in a way that minimizes the associated difficulties and costs. In the following we shall outline a framework for managing such processes (see Petersen, Welch and Welch, 2000).

Table 11.2 presents some of the alternative approaches that the entrant company can take, at the outset, to planning for later operation mode switch. The switch options have been compressed into two main categories, termination and integration, and form the columns in Table 11.2. Termination involves the formal ending of the relationship with the local operator (such as a sales agent or a licensee) and the establishment of a new, unrelated entity. Integration implies that the existing foreign operation is absorbed in some form into the entrant firm's concern, such as a switch from exporting via a sales agent to the use of a sales subsidiary; or a switch from a licensing arrangement to a wholly-owned production subsidiary; by means of taking over, or merging the existing agent's or licensee's operation. While it is difficult for the entrant company to fully anticipate its

Table 11.2   Basic strategic alternatives for future switch of operation mode

Approach to switching issue during initial negotiations:	Operation mode switch via:	
	Termination	*Integration*
Conceal	CONCEAL–TERMINATE (e.g. Norfall[a], Hospeq[a])	CONCEAL– INTEGRATE (e.g. Nilfisk, LEGO[b])
Reveal	REVEAL–TERMINATE (e.g. Amcor, GM/Toyota)	REVEAL–INTEGRATE (e.g. Scanbech, LEGO[c])

Notes:
[a]   Company name disguised.
[b]   Applies to LEGO's business operations in Taiwan, Indonesia and the Philippines.
[c]   Applies to LEGO's business operations in Thailand, Malaysia and the People's Republic of China.

Source: Reprinted with permission from Elsevier, Figure 1 'Basic Strategic Alternatives for Future Switching of Operation Mode', in B. Petersen, D.E. Welch and L.S. Welch (2000), 'Creating meaningful switching options in international operations', *Long Range Planning* **33**(5), 688–705.

future steps in the foreign market, consideration of termination or integration options at the outset is an important starting point in the quest for strategic flexibility.

Linked with this is a more fundamental question: should the entrant firm *conceal* or *reveal* its possible future intentions to the other party during the initial negotiations? For example, the entrant firm needs to decide whether it should discuss, during negotiations with a potential licensee, the option of future takeover, and seek to have this option written into the formal licensing agreement, thereby revealing its possible future intentions. These two approaches to the switching issue during initial negotiations form the rows in Table 11.2. Generally, an entrant firm will conceal its intentions as to when or if termination or integration may apply: to conceal may be regarded as the default option. Thus, during the initial negotiations, most international firms will address the issue of termination in terms of stipulating the notice of termination, property rights subsequent to termination and, occasionally, compensation (severance payment). Furthermore, the agreement will usually stipulate that termination can take place in the case of breach of contract by one of the contract parties, sometimes specifying what events may qualify as contract violation. However, firms in general seldom address the question of when termination or integration is likely to take place as part of the entrant firm's overall strategy for the market in question. As an example, the entrant firm may have the intention of substituting a sales subsidiary for the local intermediary as soon as sales in the foreign market have reached a level that justifies the higher fixed costs of a subsidiary.

Table 11.2 shows four basic strategic alternatives open to a company when considering operation mode switches that may be deemed necessary, or appropriate, in the future. These are now outlined and discussed with reference to company cases.

Conceal–Termination

In this situation, the entrant firm conceals its ultimate intention to terminate the initial operation mode arrangement. The company may already have a firm idea of the form of operation it wants to switch to at a later stage, or may want to keep its options open as to the replacement operation mode upon termination. In either case, the initial form is viewed as a 'stepping stone' to something else. As part of this strategy, during the negotiation process the entrant firm may be concerned that to reveal its possible or firm intention to terminate will be viewed as a sign of mistrust and thus jeopardize the deal. Available data on the form and extent of concealment of intention in pre-foreign entry negotiations are rather limited: firms are naturally loath to disclose what could be judged as deceptive behaviour. Danish research on distributor agreements indicates that, in some cases, Danish companies prefer to enter into informal agreements with their distributors, particularly in common law countries, such as the US and the UK, because such agreements can be more easily terminated. The ultimate intention to terminate is concealed in these cases (Slipsager, 1975). Of course, as noted above, in many foreign operation mode negotiation situations, contractual terms relating to termination arrangements are normally raised as part of the process. Agreeing to terms, however, does not automatically reveal intention to terminate. The ability to maintain a 'conceal–terminate' approach, and to have real options at a later stage, will also depend on how the initial operation form and the relationship with the local operator are handled in the implementation phase.

In a study of Danish companies operating in South-East Asia (Petersen et al., 2001), the large manufacturing company 'Norfall' (name disguised) revealed the way in which it applied a conceal–termination strategy with regard to its intermediaries. The company indicated that it approached foreign markets with termination in mind in case a market proved to be profitable enough to justify their own operation. However, this intention was concealed during entry negotiations with a prospective intermediary.

When seeking to terminate, Norfall had two approaches: to facilitate as quick a termination as possible, the company merely reducing its sales support, or increased transfer pricing. However, in situations where the company required a longer lead time, it provided sufficient support to its intermediary to maintain Norfall's market position. The difficulty, according to the company informant, was to enable the intermediary to function without gaining leverage through sales growth when the time for termination arrived.

Another approach was taken by the Danish medical supplies company, 'Hospeq' (name disguised). In interviews, the company informant explained that, provided the market developed sufficiently to justify its own subsidiary establishment, termination was intended from the outset, though this was concealed from the intermediary. Instead of taking a 'phasing out' approach in the Australian market, it took rapid action ('lightning strike') in order not to lose the market and engaged lawyers to minimize any severance payment resulting from this action (details of the study can be found in Pedersen and Petersen, 1998).

Conceal–Integration

Here the entrant firm intends to integrate the local operation at some future point but, for various reasons, will conceal this purpose from the prospective local operator during initial negotiations. Ultimately, it may be able to integrate with the consent of the local operator, but it will not necessarily require this; that is, the company may be prepared to go as far as a hostile takeover, if it is feasible in the relevant market. Alternatively, the company can effectively integrate the local operation through strategic hiring of key local staff, such as specifically targeting personnel from research and development or sales departments as a means of obtaining critical know-how and networks. Of course, in some cases, a company may not have a clear intention to integrate but, unless it puts in place the means to do so, effectively the company ends up in a conceal–integrate situation.

The case of Nilfisk (see Box 11.1 earlier in this chapter) is an example of a conceal–integration strategy that failed in one of the company's foreign markets. During the 1970s, Nilfisk managed to integrate a number of foreign intermediaries without having prepared for these switches initially. In Spain, Nilfisk's intention to integrate was unsuccessful and jeopardized the relationship with the intermediary. LEGO's approach to its operations in East Asia (see Box 11.3) is another example. In Indonesia, Taiwan and the Philippines, LEGO preferred to follow a conceal–integration strategy.

BOX 11.3   INTEGRATION AND CONCEAL–REVEAL
CONSIDERATIONS: LEGO IN EAST ASIA

LEGO has practised both reveal and conceal policies when negotiating
distributor agreements in East Asia – a geographical region where the
company saw a large sales potential for its LEGO, DUPLO and TECH-
NICS toys systems. LEGO, with 9000 employees, HQ in Denmark and an
annual turnover of about one billion $US in the late 1990s, sold through
24 wholly-owned sales subsidiaries throughout the world. In East Asia,
LEGO operated sales subsidiaries in Hong Kong and Singapore (the
latter also functioning as a regional HQ). The country markets were
served through local, independent distributors. In Taiwan, Indonesia
and the Philippines, LEGO followed a conceal–integration strategy. In
Thailand, Malaysia and China, the distributor was the East Asiatic
Company (EAC), a Danish-owned international trading company with its
headquarters in Singapore and the bulk of its trading activities in East
Asia. Each of the distributor-served countries held a potential for operating wholly-owned LEGO sales subsidiaries (such as the one in
Singapore), and the issue of a later integration of the local distributor –
mainly in the form of taking over key sales personnel – was discussed
openly with the EAC during negotiations about distributorship in the
region. As the consistent cooperation with EAC took the form of
'repeated games', a policy of concealing intentions became somewhat
illusory. However, with the Taiwanese distributor, the possibility of a
future integration was discussed. LEGO had not applied a consistent
conceal–reveal policy towards their distributors. Rather, the conceal–
reveal decision was taken on an individual basis, where the actual policy
was contingent upon situation-specific circumstances, such as local
customs and knowledge about the prospective distributor. In the 1990s,
the integration process of the independent distributors followed a certain
pattern, where the sequence of integrated activities was (1) marketing
(2) sales (3) logistics. LEGO does not necessarily accomplish a complete
takeover of the marketing function. It may very well be that logistics is left
to the local distributor on a permanent basis.

Source: Annual reports and personal communication. Reprinted from Petersen,
Welch and Welch (2000) with permission from Elsevier.

Research on terminated international joint ventures provides an indication of firms entering such ventures with the intention of subsequently
acquiring the other partner (Hamel, 1991; Reuer, 1991). For example, of 83
US–Japanese joint ventures studied, Reuer (1991) found that 62.7 per cent
had been taken over by the Japanese partner. While it is not clear what proportion of these takeovers was revealed up-front, one could speculate that
many partners would have concealed their true intention during the initial
negotiations.

Reveal–Termination

Here, the conditions under which the relationship is to be terminated at the completion of the arrangement (or even before contract completion) are negotiated and spelt out clearly beforehand. The formal agreement is likely to contain specific clauses relating to matters such as the obligations of both parties at the end of the contract, severance payment, extension option, buy-backs, intellectual property rights and so on.

Some companies have taken the reveal approach a stage further and sought to include comprehensive terms and conditions for termination of the contractual arrangement, particularly in the case of joint ventures. In such instances, the terms of the 'divorce' settlement are negotiated in advance (in the nature of a 'pre-nuptial' agreement) including such aspects as asset transfer prices. For example, the Australian paper and packaging company, Amcor, entered both the United States and New Zealand via equity joint venture arrangements. The arrangements included options that allowed Amcor to pursue full ownership or withdraw altogether at pre-agreed prices, depending on performance of the business in each market (Welch and Welch, 1996). Based on a survey of British companies' foreign joint ventures, KPMG went so far as to include 'establish exit mechanism' as one of its Ten Golden Rules of Joint Venturing (Hyman, 1998). Likewise, the European director of Arthur D. Little argues that 'It is vital that exit provisions and let-out clauses are negotiated up-front [in alliances]' (Gant, 1995). However, Serapio and Cascio conclude, from an analysis of a number of US-based alliances, that 'Planned divorces, such as the case of NUMMI [General Motors–Toyota joint venture], are the exception rather than the rule' (Serapio and Cascio, 1996). This approach of revealing termination plans, though, may be difficult to apply in cultures where the notion of discussing 'divorce' before the parties have even embarked upon a relationship is difficult to comprehend.

Reveal–Integration

This involves a company signalling in advance to a future foreign intermediary or contractual partner (in whatever form), its intention eventually to integrate the foreign operation. Various forms and degrees of integration are feasible, including a takeover, a strategic alliance or joint venture, a share swap, or the transfer of capital assets and/or market information banks. Placing the option of future integration on the table in the initial negotiations does reveal the entrant firm's possible future intentions, but, if the prospective local operator agrees to the integration proposal, the entrant firm has created a switching option for the future. As previously noted, if a prospective licensee agrees to the inclusion of an option-to-buy clause in the licensing agreement, the licensor has created a clear, legal option of future takeover.

An example of the inclusion of a takeover mechanism in the negotiated agreement is the way Scanbech, a Danish producer of packaging materials for personal care and pharmaceuticals, handled its German operations (see Box 11.4).

BOX 11.4   REVEAL–INTEGRATION CONSIDERATIONS:
SCANBECH IN GERMANY

In the restructuring of its German network of intermediaries in 1999 SCANBECH, a Danish producer of packaging materials for personal care and pharmaceuticals, for the first time practised a reveal–integration policy in negotiations with new sales agents. Until then, the export managers of SCANBECH had never discussed openly issues of termination with their distributors and sales agents. As a medium-sized firm (250 employees and an annual sales in 1998 of approximately UK £20 million), with exports spread thinly over countries in all world regions, SCANBECH is very dependent on its distribution network of local sales agents and distributors. SCANBECH has affiliates in five countries (UK, Poland, Russia, Ghana and France), but four of these are production sites. The sales office in France is the exception to SCANBECH's general rule of serving export markets via independent intermediaries. Together with Austria and the Benelux countries, Germany was pinpointed as a potential growth market for SCANBECH's products. Based on experiences in the French market, the German customer base was expected to justify a wholly owned sales affiliate within 3–5 years. The sales performance of the former intermediaries in Germany was poor, with market shares way below those achieved in other primary export markets. Based on this background, it was decided to appoint four new sales agents in Germany (responsible for different regions) as a temporary arrangement that eventually might lead to the establishment of a sales subsidiary for Germany as a whole. According to the Export Area Manager, Christian Daugbjerg, the German counterparts were somewhat astonished by SCANBECH's openness about its subsidiary plans. However, the parties have managed to negotiate agreements about future buy-out options and dual distribution arrangements in relation to 'key customers' in the German market. Subsequently, the 'atmosphere' of the cooperation has been very positive with frequent and smooth exchanges of market and product information.

Source: Personal communication with Export Area Manager Christian Daugbjerg. Reprinted from Petersen, Welch and Welch (2000) with permission from Elsevier.

A similar case is that of Diesel (the Italy-based multinational clothing company) in the establishment of its Danish sales agency in 1984 – its third outside Italy at the time. The company founder and managing director knew the Danish sales agent from previous meetings at fashion fairs in Europe. The agreement between Diesel and the Danish agency includes an option for Diesel (on a recurrent five-year term) to buy out the Danish agent should it want to establish a sales subsidiary. In effect, the goodwill value of the sales agency has been fixed within the agreement (personal communication). The Scanbech and Diesel cases exemplify country-specific arrangements that include a contractual option for future buy-out.

As can be seen from Box 11.3, in its operations in East Asia, LEGO did not adopt a consistent reveal–conceal strategy across countries. Instead, LEGO handled each market on an individual basis, although it was more consistent with its use of a reveal–integration strategy with the East Asiatic Company (EAC) due to EAC's distributor role in Thailand, Malaysia and China (see Table 11.2). There was also variation in the level of integration LEGO sought in different markets.

REVEAL–CONCEAL OPTIONS

Without any preceding relationship between the entrant firm and the local operator, there would seem to be a strong argument for not revealing future intentions at the initial negotiation stage. There is an inevitable tendency for the entrant firm to seek to evaluate the performance of the local operator before reaching a firm decision regarding its future options, and this will reinforce a conceal preference. Further, the entrant firm may believe that it is better to negotiate terms and conditions when the actual decision to terminate or integrate has been made, although clearly this may be an unacceptable position for the local operator. Of course, the entrant firm's hand may be forced during the negotiations should the local operator raise the issue of termination.

Whether termination or integration is intended, a reveal approach carries considerable risk. It has the potential to colour the negotiations and any future relationship. For example, if the entrant firm selects reveal–integration, and the local operator is resistant to any contractual arrangement regarding future integration, the choice for the entrant firm then is whether to look for another operator, or make overt concessions, thus allowing a possible shift to a conceal strategy with the original intention maintained. Once the 'future intentions' card is placed on the negotiation table, though, it is difficult to erase the impression generated by its revelation. From the potential local operator's perspective, the mere outline of a possible future switch may evoke an examination of the future in a way that it had not previously done. Reveal–conceal options may also be considered by the local operator, thereby opening up a range of strategic alternatives for the entrant firm not dissimilar to those presented in the matrix in Table 11.2. Despite these risks, the cases of Scanbech, Diesel and LEGO show that it is possible to implement a reveal strategy to build in future switch options.

If the entrant firm reveals its intention to terminate, there is a risk that the local operator will only invest at a minimal level in the business, so that the full market potential is not realized, particularly if success of the local operations is dependent on a high level of initial investment, such as warehousing, distribution network development, and the like. Likewise, even though the intention to terminate is concealed, settling termination arrangements in contract negotiations may have an adverse effect on the commitment of the local operator. To avoid such a low investment and poor performance situation, the entrant firm may need to safeguard the position of the local operator. In a reveal strategy, the parties can negotiate the required investments and associated safeguards. The safeguards may consist of a long-term contract that will allow the local operator to write off the investments, or to have 'adequate' indemnification in case of termination, or a combination of these.

Other things being equal, the greater the investment the entrant firm requires of the local operator, the higher the indemnification that would be expected in the case of premature termination. The obvious alternative to excessive costs of indemnification is integration of the local operator. Indemnification recognizes that investments undertaken by the local operator that cannot be readily used in other ways or relationships nevertheless have value for the entrant firm. Whereas indemnification represents a *loss* in the form of exit costs, a partial or full integration of the local operator may add to the value of the entrant firm. For the local operator, selling off part of its organization on attractive financial terms can be just as valuable as receiving a severance payment. Hence integration rather than termination may appear to be the obvious option in prospective high-commitment relationships.

It should be noted, though, that non-economic/non-financial considerations might have a bearing on how the company handles the reveal/conceal issue. Concealment of true intentions tends to have a negative connotation in some cultures. As Frankenstein and Worm (2000, 274–5) point out:

> In the guilt-focused religions and universalistic cultures of the West, deception is considered immoral. In particularistic cultures, honesty is only a norm that concerns the in-group or people with whom one has established personalized relations . . . In China, deception is considered a neutral term and it is acceptable if it embraces the 'greater good', ie the well-being of the family or the network.

The cultural context may restrict the range of effective switching options available. In Japan, for example, hostile takeovers tend to be frowned upon, so that they represent a small proportion of total acquisitions within Japan. This may imply that a company will have to play a relationship or networking-oriented 'game' rather than following market-based contractual solutions, as a way of building strategic flexibility in operation mode use.

PROCESS ISSUES IN REVEAL–CONCEAL STRATEGIES

The matrix presented in Table 11.2 concerns strategic alternatives as viewed by the entrant firm when initially establishing foreign operations in a given market. Whatever the approach adopted, the ability subsequently to switch operation mode will be affected by the way the entry process and ongoing market activity are handled. To illustrate how process factors may enhance or diminish a firm's switching options two factors – the role of market information and relationship development – are discussed briefly below.

The Role of Market Information

Information and knowledge about the foreign market are an important element of the ability to plan and undertake appropriate changes in operation mode. As noted earlier, for the entrant firm, the lack of foreign market knowledge is often a factor in the initial selection of an operation mode that entails low commitment and control, while increased foreign market knowledge plays a role in the preparedness to shift to a higher-control mode (Johanson and Vahlne, 1977). For the local operator, market knowledge (about local business conditions, customers and so on), and networks are critical assets that justify its position. Over time, though, some of this knowledge advantage will inevitably be lost as the entrant firm acquires its own market knowledge – from the local operator, and through its own contacts with the market. This is always a fine balancing act for the local operator: too ready access to information by the entrant firm may diminish the incentive to integrate, and hasten termination.

Clearly, for the switch option to have value, the entrant firm needs access to new market information in order to assess if and when the time is right for a switch to a higher-control mode. As pointed out earlier, local sales volume is the decisive variable for many entrant firms. Usually, information about *actual* sales in the local market is at hand, but this may be considerably less than the local sales *potential*. Local sales potential may have grown beyond what is deemed necessary for a switch to a higher control mode (for example, agent to sales subsidiary). Often this is difficult for the entrant firm to determine. It can ask the local operator to provide market analyses but this information tends to be biased inasmuch as the local operator has an overt interest in underestimating the sales prospects (Bergen et al., 1992). This is because good sales prospects are often not seen as an outcome of the local operator's contribution to the realization of the sales potential. Instead, an estimation of large sales potential tends to increase the risk of termination and mode switch.

In the case of concealed intentions about future termination or integration, the entrant firm is exposed to the risk of new information being subject to 'tactical' manipulation by the local operator. Alternative or supplementary information channels are required to overcome this problem. Of course, some of this alternative information will be forthcoming as a result of normal visits to the market, dealing with customer problems that cannot be handled by the local operator, and the like. However, a more proactive approach to the development of alternative channels may be necessary, although there are additional costs in adopting this. For example, the entrant firm may put in place a 'dual distribution system' (see next chapter) where some selected foreign market customers are served directly, enabling the entrant firm to obtain a better grasp of market opportunities through these foreign 'house accounts'. Dutta et al. (1995) recognize, though, that a dual distribution system may signal 'credibility of termination'; that is, a credible threat of taking over the business which runs counter to the aim of concealing intentions. A strict conceal strategy would require that the use of alternative information channels be unknown to the local operator.

Relationship Development

Whether terminating or integrating, the nature of the relationship that is built between the entrant firm and the local operator can be a critical factor in undertaking an operation mode switch. For instance, if the company desires to integrate the foreign operation, and it has not been able to include this option in the formal contract (or has adopted a conceal strategy) a good relationship with the foreign operator may enable the integration to proceed more readily. The literature indicates that strategic alliances tend to perform better when the parties have evolved into the alliance state from preceding interactions that resulted in extended connections between the two organizations, particularly as key individuals play an important role in facilitating cooperation between organizations (Lorange and Roos, 1992; Scott-Kemmis et al., 1990 – see Chapter 9). Likewise, research relating to takeovers indicates that the merging of cultures is important in the ability of two previously independent companies to integrate successfully (Nahavandi and Malekzadeh, 1988). Even when the takeover option has been built into the initial contract, the ability to do so has to be facilitated through the conduct of the relationship with the local operator: only then does it become a real option in strategic terms (Svensson, 1986). The letter of the contract may be effectively nullified by a negative relationship. The termination process is also affected by the type of relationship that develops between the parties involved, including situations where the entrant firm has adopted a reveal–termination strategy. Where there has been a high level of interaction, and a positive relationship has evolved, the entrant firm's ability to operate independently is likely to have been enhanced through a better understanding of the foreign market situation, as a result of improved information flow and contact, and links to key local networks. There may even be situations where the relationship between the two parties becomes so strong and effective, and the local operator is performing so well, that protection of the relationship is given a higher priority than implementation of the intended termination strategy.

MODE SWITCH AS AN INCREMENTAL PROCESS: STRETCHING STRATEGIES

The above presentation of mode switching strategies has been based on the implicit and – as will be demonstrated in the next chapter – somewhat simplified assumption that FOMs are mutually exclusive. In other words, we have until now assumed that a switch implies one operation mode being replaced by another. Furthermore, we have assumed FOMs to be distinguishable organizational forms in relation to which switches constitute clear-cut changes. Several of our examples have referred to mode switch as one-off internalization operations of the foreign market activities. In these examples, the switch from, for example, a local outside agent to a fully integrated in-house operation is very distinct. In practice, mode switches may be a great deal subtler. Mode switches sometimes emerge as incremental processes in which one operation mode virtually 'grows' into another. First of all, the operation methods that an entrant firm uses in a specific market over a period of time are not necessarily sequential, that is, mutually exclusive; it is not uncommon for entrant firms to add new operation methods to existing ones, thereby practising mode combination. The strategic implications of mode combination will be the topic of the next chapter, and will not be pursued here. Secondly, mode switches may be incremental in the sense that within-mode changes precede as well as follow a formal shift of ownership and organizational form.

In general, there is a variety of ways of easing the path of mode switches which are not obvious in the overall form of operation mode. It is not uncommon for companies to hire staff from their former, or current, agent to facilitate the transition to use of a sales subsidiary. Cooperative forms of association with the agent may be used even after the sales subsidiary set-up, representing a type of organic extension of the existing arrangement, as a way of easing the demands and risks associated with the mode switch. Sales subsidiaries can also be set up in a form that minimizes the degree of commitment by the company. A study of Danish companies' mode switches in south-east Asia revealed a highly minimalist approach to the establishment of sales offices in Singapore (Petersen et al., 2001). In some cases the Danish company employee sent to staff the office was effectively working out of his apartment. Finnish research has indicated a wide range in types and uses of the sales subsidiaries of Finnish companies (Hentola, 1994). Thus, in assessing the significance of a mode switch from an internationalization perspective, whatever the overt pattern, much depends on the changes that have taken place prior to the formal switch, and also on the form of the 'new' mode. The essence of change is not simply captured by the existence of a mode switch.

It is even conceivable that a mode change which would normally have been viewed as an escalation in international commitment might in fact amount to de-escalation. For example, a situation in which a company has invested heavily in its agency operation as a base for exporting, then switches to a sales subsidiary in the foreign market, but is poorly supported, staffed on a part-time basis only and provides a very limited service to customers in that foreign market, could be described as a de-escalation of commitment.

There is potentially a wide variation in the extent of a company's commitment to its foreign intermediaries, as reflected in aspects such as visits, support and internal company adjustments for the foreign market servicing operation. These can be generalized as within-mode changes along three main scales: activities, resources and organizational changes. The resources dimension is a very broad indicator of the extent of involvement with a foreign intermediary, but it tells us little about the nature of that involvement. It is the activities and organizational change dimensions that provide better indicators of whether there has been significant change in the use of a particular foreign operation mode through time, including aspects such as the extent and form of communication, staffing, training and other forms of support. Extension of the range of activities may be part of a process of extension of control over foreign market penetration, leading to the ultimate step of takeover or replacement by a company-owned sales operation. The activity dimension can also be linked to likely changes in experiential knowledge, although there may well be substantial differences in the knowledge effects of different types of activities: for example, as between formal communication and personal visits.

Along with activity extension it might also be deemed necessary to make organizational changes to organize these within mode developments. An export department could be established at the home base of the entrant firm, or other changes made in its structure. Extension of activities will normally require that staff be used in different ways, which may also require a variety of organizational changes regarding foreign market visits, additional staff deployment, training programmes, and the like.

This framework could of course be applied to other foreign operation modes: the changing set of activities, organizational adjustments and resource commitments through time is indicative in any mode form of the extent and type of within-mode change, providing a basis for understanding the nature and significance of mode switch and ultimately the character of internationalization.

REFERENCES

Albaum, G., J. Strandskov and E. Duerr (2004), *International Marketing and ExportManagement*, 5th edn, London: Pearson Higher Education.

Ali, A.J. and R.C. Camp (1993), 'The relevance of firm size and international business experience to market entry strategies', *Journal of Global Marketing*, **6**(4), 91–108.

Anderson, E. and R.L. Oliver (1987), 'Perspectives on behavior-based versus outcome-based salesforce control systems', *Journal of Marketing*, **51**(4), 76–88.

Anderson, J.C. and J.A. Narus (1990), 'A model of distributor firm and manufacturing firm working partnerships', *Journal of Marketing*, **54**(1), 42–58.

Andersson, S. (2000), 'Internationalization of the firm from an entrepreneurial perspective', *International Studies of Management & Organization*, **30**(1), 65–94.

Barkema, H., J.H. Bell and J.M. Pennings (1996), 'Foreign entry, cultural barriers, and learning', *Strategic Management Journal*, **17**(2), 151–66.

Beeth, G. (1990), 'Distributors: finding and keeping the good ones', in H.B. Thorelli and S.T. Cavusgil (eds), *International Marketing Strategy*, 3rd edn, Oxford: Pergamon, pp. 487–93.

Benito, G.R.G. and L.S. Welch (1997), 'De-internationalization', *Management International Review*, **37**(2), 7–25.

Benito, G.R.G., T. Pedersen and B. Petersen (1999), 'Foreign operation methods and switching costs: conceptual issues and possible effects', *Scandinavian Journal of Management*, **15**(2), 213–29.

Benito, G.R.G., T. Pedersen and B. Petersen (2005), 'Export channel dynamics: an empirical analysis', *Managerial and Decision Economics*, **26**(3), 159–73.

Bergen, M., S. Dutta and O.C. Walker (1992), 'Agency relationships in marketing: a review of the implications and applications of agency and related theories', *Journal of Marketing*, **56**(3), 1–24.

390 Strategies

Birkinshaw, J., H. Bresman and L. Håkanson (2000), 'Managing the post-acquisition integration process: how the human integration and task integration processes interact to foster value creation', *Journal of Management Studies*, **37**(3), 395–425.

Buckley, P.J. and M.C. Casson (1981), 'The optimal timing of a foreign direct investment', *Economic Journal*, **91**(1), 75–87.

Calof, J.L. (1993), 'The mode choice and change decision process and its impact on international performance', *International Business Review*, **2**(1), 97–120.

Calof, J.L. and P.W. Beamish (1995), 'Adapting to foreign markets: explaining internationalization', *International Business Review*, **4**(2), 115–31.

Contractor, F.J. (1981), 'The role of licensing in international strategy', *Columbia Journal of World Business*, **16**(4), 73–83.

Coughlan, A.T., E. Anderson, L.W. Stern and A.I. El-Ansary (2006), *Marketing Channels*, (7th edn), Upper Saddle River, N.J: Pearson/Prentice-Hall.

Dutta, S., M. Bergen, J.B. Heide and G. John (1995), 'Understanding dual distribution: the case of reps and house accounts', *Journal of Law, Economics & Organization*, **11**(1), 189–204.

Ellis, P.D. (2000), 'Social ties and foreign market entry', *Journal of International Business Studies*, **31**(3), 443–69.

Ellis, P.D. (2005), 'The traders' dilemma: the adverse consequences of superior performance in mediated exchanges', *International Business Review*, **14**(4), 375–96.

Estrin, S. and K. Meyer (eds) (2004), *Investment Strategies in Emerging Markets*, Cheltenham, UK and Northampton, MA, USA: Edward Elgar.

Frankenstein, J. and V. Worm (2000), 'The dilemma of managerial cooperation in Sino–Western business operations', *Thunderbird International Business Review*, **42**(3), 261–85.

Gallini, N.T. and N. Lutz (1992), 'Dual distribution and royalty fees in franchising', *Journal of Law, Economics & Organization*, **8**(3), 471–501.

Gallo, M.A. (1994), *Global Perspectives on Family Businesses*, Chicago: Loyola University, Family Business Center.

Gant, J. (1995), 'The science of alliance', *Eurobusiness*, **3**(5), 70–72.

Gomes-Casseres, B. (1987), 'Joint venture instability: is it a problem?', *Columbia Journal of World Business*, **22**(2), 97–102.

Gomes-Casseres, B. (1990), 'Firm ownership preferences and host government restrictions: an integrated approach', *Journal of International Business Studies*, **21**(1), 1–22.

Hamel, G. (1991), 'Competition for competence and inter-partner learning within international strategic alliances', *Strategic Management Journal*, **12**(4), 83–103.

Hennart, J.-F. (1988), 'A transaction cost theory of equity joint ventures', *Strategic Management Journal*, **9**(4), 361–74.

Hennart, J.-F. (1991), 'The transaction cost theory of multinational enterprise', in C. Pitelis and R. Sugden (eds), *The Nature of the Transnational Firm*, London and New York: Routledge, pp. 81–116.

Hentola, H. (1994), *Foreign sales subsidiaries and their role within the internationalization process of a company: A study of the Finnish manufacturing firms* (doctoral thesis), Helsinki School of Economics and Business Administration, HeSE print, Helsinki.

Horst, T. (1974), 'The theory of the firm', in J. Dunning (ed.), *Economic Analysis and the Multinational Enterprise*, London: George Allen & Unwin.

Hyman, C. (1998), *Joint Ventures – A Triumph of Hope Over Reality?*, London: KPMG Transaction Services.

Jensen, M.C. and W.H. Meckling (1976), 'Theory of the firm: managerial behaviour, agency costs and ownership structure', *The Journal of Financial Economics*, **3**(4), 305–60.

Johanson, J. and J.-E. Vahlne (1977), 'The internationalisation process of the firm: a model of knowledge development and increasing foreign market commitment', *Journal of International Business Studies*, **8**(1), 23–32.

Klein, S., G.L. Frazier and V.J. Roth (1990), 'A transaction cost analysis model of channel integration in international markets', *Journal of Marketing Research*, **27**(2), 196–208.

Lafontaine, F. and P.J. Kaufmann (1994), 'The evolution of ownership patterns in franchise systems', *Journal of Retailing*, **70**(2), 97–113.

Lee, M. and E.G. Rogoff (1996), 'Comparisons of small business with family participation versus small business without family participation: an investigation of goals, attitudes, and family/business conflicts', *Family Business Review*, **9**(4), 423–37.

Lorange, P. and J. Roos (1992), *Strategic Alliances: Formation, Implementation and Evolution*, Oxford: Basil Blackwell.

Luostarinen, R. and L.S. Welch (1990), *International Business Operations*, Helsinki: Export Consulting KY.

Nahavandi, A. and A.R. Malekzadeh (1988), 'Acculturation in mergers and acquisitions', *Academy of Management Review*, **13**(1), 79–90.

Nakamura, M., J.M. Shaver and B. Yeung (1996), 'An empirical investigation of joint venture dynamics: evidence from U.S.–Japan joint ventures', *International Journal of Industrial Organization*, **14**(4), 521–41.

Nicholas, S. (1986), 'The theory of multinationals as a transactional mode', in P. Hertner and G. Jones (eds), *Multinationals: Theory and History*, Aldershot: Gower.

Oxenfeldt, A. and A. Kelly (1969), 'Will successful franchise systems ultimately become wholly-owned chains?' *Journal of Retailing*, **44**(4), 69–83.

Pedersen, T. and B. Petersen (1998), 'Explaining gradually increasing resource commitment to a foreign market', *International Business Review*, **7**(3), 483–501.

Pedersen, T., B. Petersen and G.R.G. Benito (2002), 'Change of foreign operation methods: impetus and switching costs', *International Business Review*, **11**(3), 325–45.

Peng, M.W. (2000), *Business Strategies in Transition Economies*, Thousand Oaks: Sage.

Penrose, E.T. (1956), 'Foreign investment and the growth of the firm', *Economic Journal*, **66**(262), 220–35.

Penrose, E.T. (1959), *The Theory of the Growth of the Firm*, New York: John Wiley.

Petersen, B., G.R.G. Benito and T. Pedersen (2000), 'Replacing the foreign intermediary: motivators and deterrents', *International Studies of Management and Organization*, **30**(1), 45–62.

Petersen, B., T. Pedersen and G.R.G. Benito (2006), 'The termination dilemma of foreign intermediaries: performance, anti-shirking measures and hold-up safeguards', *Advances in International Marketing*, **16**, 317–39.

Petersen, B., L.S. Welch and K.V. Nielsen (2001), 'Resource commitment to foreign markets: the establishment patterns of Danish firms in South East Asian markets', in S.J. Gray, S.L. McGaughey and W.R. Purcell (eds), *Asia-Pacific*

Issues in International Business, Cheltenham, UK and Northampton, MA, USA: Edward Elgar Publishing Company, pp. 7–27.

Petersen, B., D.E. Welch and L.S. Welch (2000), 'Creating meaningful switching options in international operations', *Long Range Planning*, **33**(5), 688–705.

Reuer, J. (1991), 'The dynamics and effectiveness of international joint ventures', *European Management Journal*, **16**(2), 160–68.

Scott-Kemmis, D., T. Darling, R. Johnston, F. Collyer and C. Cliff (1990), *Strategic Alliances in the Internationalization of Australian Industry*, Canberra: Australian Government Publishing Service.

Serapio, Jr., M.G. and W. Cascio (1996), 'End-games in international alliances', *Academy of Management Executive*, **10**(1), 62–73.

Shamdasani, P.N. and J. Sheth (1995), 'An experimental approach to investigating satisfaction and continuity in marketing alliances', *European Journal of Marketing*, **29**(4), 6–23.

Slipsager, F. (1975), *Salgsagentens rolle i international afsætning* [The sales agent's role in international distribution], Copenhagen: Nyt Nordisk Forlag.

Svensson, B. (1986), 'Acquisition of technology through licensing in small firms', *R&D Management*, **17**(1), 75–6.

Weiss, A.M. and E. Anderson (1992), 'Converting from independent to employee sales force: the role of perceived switching costs', *Journal of Marketing Research*, **29**(1), 101–15.

Welch, D.E. and L.S. Welch (1996), 'The internationalization process and networks: a strategic management perspective', *Journal of International Marketing*, **4**(3), 11–28.

Welch, L.S. and R. Luostarinen (1988), 'Internationalization: evolution of a concept', *Journal of General Management*, **14**(2), 36–64.

Williamson, O.E. (1983), 'Credible commitments: using hostages to support exchange', *American Economic Review*, **73**(4), 519–40.

12. Mode combination strategies

INTRODUCTION

In this chapter, we will address the questions of why and how firms *combine* foreign operation methods (FOMs), and the implications for companies and theory. Key questions considered are the following:

- Why do companies, such as the two Israeli firms, Gilat Satellite Networks and Fundtech (see Box 12.1) use multiple modes in a foreign country, sometimes even for the same value chain activity (R&D, manufacturing, marketing and so on)?
- How do managers combine foreign operation methods?
- What benefits do mode combinations offer?
- What are the barriers and pitfalls that managers should seek to overcome and avoid?

As demonstrated in the previous chapter, the switch from one foreign operation method (FOM) to another is a natural part of doing international business. We have presented mode switch as a replacement of one FOM by another in a given foreign market (for example, a sales agent being replaced by a sales subsidiary). This is in accordance with the notion of the 'establishment chain' (Johanson and Wiedersheim-Paul, 1975), a sequence of FOMs representing successively higher degrees of resource commitment (see also Chapter 1). The generalized establishment chain sequence is:[1] *Unsystematic export* → *sales agent* → *sales subsidiary* → *production subsidiary.*

However, instead of replacing one FOM with another, firms may add an FOM to an existing one. The appropriate term to use for this phenomenon would be 'mode addition' rather than 'mode switch'. The addition of one – or several – modes to an existing one may be a very temporary arrangement where two FOMs overlap in a short, transitional period. In other cases, however, the mode addition may take on the characteristics of a long-term, or even permanent, arrangement. The possibility of combining different FOMs raises a number of interesting management issues, including the coordination challenge. We will use a value chain approach to tackle the management issues surrounding mode combination (see Box 12.2). But

BOX 12.1   MODE COMBINATION AS PRACTISED BY ISRAELI FIRMS IN US

In 1999, Gilat Satellite Networks, an Israel-based provider of end-to-end telecommunications and data networking solutions via satellite, operated five different modes in the United States. Gilat's R&D and production operations in the United States were both conducted via greenfield as well as acquired wholly-owned subsidiaries. Marketing and customer support to the American market, on the other hand, were simultaneously provided through distributors, a sales office, a strategic alliance and an equity joint venture.

Likewise, Fundtech, an Israel-based provider of software solutions that facilitate payments, settlement and cash management between businesses and their banks, had at the same time its American R&D activities conducted simultaneously via a joint venture, a greenfield subsidiary and an acquired subsidiary. In parallel, Fundtech's marketing and customer support services to the American market were conducted through distributors, a joint venture, a greenfield sales office and an acquired subsidiary.

Source: Database (of 76 Israeli multinational companies) compiled by Tamar Almor (Graduate School of Business – Tel Aviv University), Niron Hashai (Jerusalem School of Business Administration – The Hebrew University), and professor emeritus Zeev Hirsch. The use of the company examples is by courtesy of the three professors.

BOX 12.2   WHAT IS A 'VALUE CHAIN'?

The value chain is an activity template which is used to deconstruct the firm into the individual activities it undertakes to create value for the customers. The value chain concept was introduced in 1985 by Michael Porter as a benchmarking tool for companies: do the activities performed by a focal company generate more value or incur less cost than those of its rivals? To answer that question, Porter identified nine basic activities through which a company potentially achieves above-normal margins. The figure indicates the nine value chain activities. Five activities (in columns) were distinguished as primary and the remaining four as supporting activities or back-office activities (in rows).

The activities contained by a value chain are by definition governed by a focal firm. Production inputs, such as intermediate goods and back office services that are purchased on an arm's-length basis, are not part of the value chain of the focal firm. To the extent that strategic suppliers are included, the value chain goes beyond the boundaries of the focal firm. On the other hand, a diversified firm with multiple divisions or strategic business units may comprise more than one value chain and, in Porter's terminology, constitute a *value system*.

Firm Infrastructure					Margin
Human Resource Management					
Technology Development					
Procurement					
Inbound Logistics	Operations	Outbound Logistics	Marketing & Sales	Service	Margin

Although Porter introduced the value chain as a *generic* activity template, which in theory should be an analytical tool applicable to companies across different industries and business sectors, it essentially pertains to traditional, manufacturing firms, characterized by upstream and downstream flows of physical goods. The value chain is less applicable to service firms. In relation to service firms, such as trading companies, banks, consulting firms and telecommunication firms, it is difficult to identify distinct production sequences. For these firms the value creation is more a result of iterative and cyclical production flows. Among others, Stabell and Fjeldstad (1998) have pointed out the sector or industry specificity of 'value creation logics'. Being fundamentally different from 'value chains', Stabell and Fjeldstad suggest 'value shops' and 'value networks' as value creation logics applicable, for example, to consulting firms and banks, respectively.

first, we will address the question of *why* firms – like Gilat Satellite Networks and Fundtech – combine modes.

WHY MODE COMBINATION?

A firm may combine modes to enter or develop a given foreign market for various reasons. More specifically, we can identify five, basically different, reasons. The analytical framework presented in Figure 12.1 makes it possible to establish the underlying reasons for an observed mode combination in a foreign market. However, managers may also use the framework proactively (as a decision tree) to identify needs and opportunities for combining operation modes in a foreign country. In the following we explain and exemplify with practical cases each of the five rationales for mode combination.

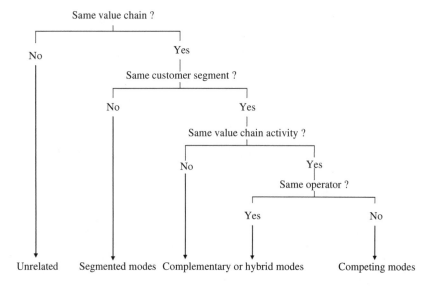

Same value chain ?

No   Yes

Same customer segment ?

No   Yes

Same value chain activity ?

No   Yes

Same operator ?

Yes   No

Unrelated   Segmented modes Complementary or hybrid modes   Competing modes

Source: Adapted from Petersen and Welch, 2002.

Figure 12.1   Different types of multiple mode operations

Unrelated Business Units (Different Value Chains)

A company may use more than one operation method in a foreign market
where there is no connection between their uses within that market. This
may reflect the operations of a firm that conducts business across different
industries or product markets. Thus the operations of large, diversified
multinationals in a foreign country are likely to be handled by different
strategic business units of the same firm. Or, in the terms of Porter (1985),
a firm may operate several value chains (or, value creation logics: cf. Box
12.2) in a foreign market which altogether make up a value system in which
different FOMs pertain to different value chains. The Norwegian multinational Norsk Hydro's operations in India in the 1990s provide an example
of unrelated modes. Five of its product divisions, using different FOMs –
including licensing and production subsidiaries – operated relatively independently (Tomassen et al., 1998). The Danish multinational, Coloplast, a
provider of wound care products and services (see also Box 11.2 in preceding chapter) is another example of mode combination explained by different
value chains. In Hungary, Coloplast is operating through a sales representative, a sales subsidiary (of another product division) and, since 2002, also

has a production subsidiary: a global supply factory (source: personal communication with Production Manager in Coloplast, Allan Rasmussen).

Serving Different Customer Segments

A firm may combine modes in relation to the same product category or value chain to serve different customer segments. Valla (1986, 33) suggested segmentation as one explanation of the mode combinations observed in his study of French exporters: 'In some cases, [the incidence of mode combination] means that separate segments of the customer portfolio are handled differently. For instance, the largest customers may be handled directly, while others are handled through distributors or sales subsidiaries.'

Market segmentation based on firm size, to which Valla referred, is indeed very common. Many international firms have opted for servicing large, multinational customers directly (thereby becoming 'key accounts'), because these customers are important and require a standardized service delivery across countries (Coughlan et al., 2006). Handing over the servicing of these multinational customers to local distributors could easily result in varying and inconsistent product and service offerings, and thereby create confusion and dissatisfaction among these key accounts. On the other hand, the servicing of small and local customers is usually better off in the hands of local, independent distributors because of their fine-grained sales network and local customer knowledge.

In addition to size and multinationality of customers, other forms of segmentation may be used, including geographical regions, households versus business organizations and infrequent buyers versus repeat buyers. As an example of the last-mentioned segmentation criterion, a multinational fast-food restaurant chain may decide to use firm-owned outlets at locations where customers tend to be infrequent buyers (such as outlets close to freeways) and franchised outlets where customers are mainly frequent buyers (Brickley and Dark, 1987). By this mode differentiation, the fast-food restaurant chain curbs the risk of franchisees free-riding on its trademark. Segmentation on the basis of geography is another, perhaps more obvious, segmentation criterion. Large countries (in terms of both area and population), such as the US and the People's Republic of China, do not always lend themselves to servicing by a single business unit. Two or more units are often needed to cover separate geographical regions, and these units may represent different FOMs. Although they are related through a shared product concept, foreign operations for different segments can exist independently of each other. A production subsidiary in North Carolina may operate independently of a licensee in Oregon producing for, and marketing to, the east and west of the US, respectively.

Value Activity Specialization (Division of Labour)

Here, multiple modes are used in a combined, mutually supportive way to achieve the firm's objectives. The entrant firm is using different FOMs for different value chain activities. '[T]he objective of such combined approaches is clearly to increase efficiency, without being based on any specific segmentation. An example is a firm-employed person based permanently in the country in order to back up an agent' (Valla, 1986, 33). The combined modes focus on the same segment but are concerned with different activities in the value chain. The separation of manufacturing and marketing in foreign operations is seen most strongly in the global activities of sports shoe and clothing firms such as Nike and Reebok.

However, the division of labour may be more subtle and take place within one of the general business functions, such as sales and marketing. As an example, a sales subsidiary and local franchisees could both be subordinate to the same principal (for example, a multinational franchisor) and cater to the same customer segment, but the franchisees act as retailers, whereas the sales subsidiary takes care of wholesaling activities. This kind of vertical division of responsibilities exists among Danish clothing firms (Petersen and Welch, 2000). At the beginning of the 1990s, Lotus Development's servicing of the European market had a similar vertical division of tasks between subsidiaries and independent dealers. The European subsidiaries undertook local market research, customization of the base spreadsheet programme, training of the dealers' sales staff, advertising and dealer support. The independent dealers were responsible for retail sales, product demonstrations, and user training and support (Williamson, 1992). In their study of sales channels in the European PC industry, Gabrielsson et al. (2002, 78) found an increasing number of so-called 'hybrid' sales channels where 'the marketing functions are shared by the producer and the channel intermediary; the former usually handles promotion and customer generation activities, whereas the intermediary is in charge of sales and distribution . . . The hybrid channel strategy is based . . . on cooperation and partnership'.

A division of labour might exist because economies of specialization relate to particular activities and processes rather than to production and marketing activities as a whole (Dixon and Wilkinson, 1986). Take as an example a home-based, large-scale production plant and a foreign-based, small-scale production subsidiary, both plants producing the same product line. Some processes are more sensitive to scale economies and are undertaken in the domestic plant. Other processes can be run cost-effectively at a low scale and are labour-intensive. Because of the availability of cheap labour and in order to minimize value-added tariff payments, these processes are undertaken by the local production subsidiary. In this case the firm exports and produces abroad simultaneously for the same line of products and the same foreign country. The two operation modes, exporting and the production subsidiary, complement each other. Almost by definition, any assembly plant operation in a foreign country will involve export to that country (Cavusgil et al., 1993), but sourcing from the country-of-origin is a common occurrence among 'fully-fledged' production subsidiaries as well (Moxon, 1982). For example, component sourcing from the parent is a frequently used strategy for European and Japanese manufacturing subsidiaries in the People's Republic of China (Schroath et al., 1993). In all these cases the division of labour necessitates close coordination among the different modes: they operate in a complementary way. Hence multiple modes are a package that cannot be easily unbundled. Modes are working together in an integrated, cohesive manner in order to achieve foreign market objectives. We will come back to this 'mode packaging' later in the chapter.

Perhaps somewhat counter-intuitively, entrant firms may also combine modes in relation to one specific value activity in the foreign market. They may do this in two very different ways: either the specific value activity is carried out by a local outside agent in tandem with the entrant firm itself (for example, dual distribution), in which case head-on competition prevails; or the entrant firm conducts the value activity single-handedly, but uses two combined governance forms, namely, contracting and partial ownership. As we shall demonstrate below, the reasons behind the two different kinds of mode combination in relation to one specific value activity are indeed very different.

Bolstering Commitment and Control

As has been pointed out by many corporate governance scholars (for example, Berle and Means, 1932; Jensen and Meckling, 1976; Grossman and Hart, 1986) the separation of management and ownership may cause agency problems; although supposed to care for the interests of the owner, the hired manager may take advantage of information asymmetries and act in a self-opportunistic way that does not maximize the wealth of his principal. In order to safeguard his interests and suppress moral hazard, the owner (and principal) may insist on sharing ownership (residual rights) with his agent(s). In this way goal congruence between the principal and agent is promoted: in the case where the agent (the hired manager and co-owner) mismanages the business he will impose a loss on himself to the extent that his minority share loses market value. The widespread use of stock options as part of managers' remuneration provides evidence of the seriousness with which owners (shareholders) look at this agency problem. One may say that the agency problem arises from moral hazard in combination with the difficulties of writing and enforcing perfect contracts, that is, contracts that regulate any possible aspect of the agent's responsibilities and take into consideration all future contingencies ('contingent claim contracts'). Usually, principals remedy these contractual inadequacies by monitoring the agents' behaviour closely, but less so in international business. Because of the considerable physical and cultural distances in international business, monitoring is a costly and sometimes unreliable control instrument. Another remedy for contractual insufficiencies – joint ownership (or co-ownership) – may therefore be brought into use.

The hotel industry provides good examples of the use of contractual modes in combination with joint ownership. Management contracts (see Chapter 5) are frequently used in the hotel industry as a foreign operation method. Here, the management contractor is a company with extensive knowledge about hotel management, sometimes acquired through operating a hotel chain on a worldwide scale. Hence, in the 1990s, the US Hilton Hotel chain entered management contracts with Russian hotel owners. In some cases, minority ownership is linked to a management contract. Of course, one may see Hilton's minority investment as a purely voluntary financial transaction in a promising emerging market. However, the alternative (or supplementary) explanation is that the Russian hotel owners (and in this case principals to the Hilton management group) wanted to combat potential agency problems by insisting on an equity joint venture. In this perspective, the minority share imposed on the Hilton organization by the Russian hotel owners should be seen as a kind of collateral that effectively prevents opportunistic behaviour by the foreign contractor.

In franchising, bolstering of commitment is primarily in response to an agent's need rather than that of a principal. The profitability of the franchisee's business operations very much hinges on a continuous flow of new, saleable products and marketing support by the franchisor. The franchisee usually owns the physical assets of the local business operation, but in some cases the franchisor takes ownership of part of the assets, presumably as a token of commitment and good faith in the financial prospects of the local franchise operation. As an example, in their domestic and international operations in the fast-food restaurant industry McDonald's will insist on franchisee ownership of the restaurant stock and fixtures (including kitchen equipment and restaurant furniture) but will accept ownership of the property (the site and building). Again, this may be interpreted as a purely financial investment (portfolio investment), but makes more sense as a commitment bolstering the local franchise venture.

Often, licensing agreements and joint ownership go hand in hand in international business (see Chapter 4). As with franchising, joint ownership in licensing can be explained by a bolstering of the principal's (the licensor's) commitment. The licensee is often uncertain about the market value of the licensed technology and the extent to which the licensor is committed to provide services associated with the technology and to update the technology on a continuous basis. On the other hand, the licensor may also see joint ownership as an opportunity for closer control (monitoring) of the licensee. It is the persistent concern of licensors that their licensees sell licensed products outside the agreed-upon territory or misuse the licensed technology in other ways, or eventually become competitors. The licensor's co-ownership opens the door to the boardroom of the licensee's organization, thereby enabling supervision of the licensee's managers. Sometimes the technology transfer goes both ways and the joint ownership secures commitment from both sides (see Chapters 4 and 9). In this case, the co-ownership may be in the form of an equity joint venture or as an exchange of shares (a cross-equity arrangement) – or both.

It is not always clear whether the co-ownership supports the contract or vice versa. In some countries, such as China and Malaysia, foreign direct investment was for many years only allowed as joint ventures with local partners holding at least 50 per cent equity. In these joint ventures many foreign companies felt a need to bolster control through contractual arrangements. Licensing, as an example, plays a primary role in ensuring contractual control over the way the firm's technology is used and that the technology is not disseminated elsewhere by the joint venture partner. The licensing agreement also has the potential to deliver a degree of control over marketing, management and other aspects of the joint venture's operations. This was found to be an important part of the use of licensing by some Australian firms in their Malaysian joint venture operations, when they were restricted to equity levels below 50 per cent (Welch, 1985).

In some cases, management contracts are used to bolster control in minority joint ventures. The case of FedEx in China, (see Box 12.3), shows how a management contract enabled the US company to exercise control of the daily operations of the joint venture. The management contract provided the degree of control that FedEx felt was lacking in its previous Chinese operations.

Benchmarking Local Operators

In this case a firm uses multiple operation modes that compete head-on with each other in the foreign market. The operation modes target the same customer segment(s)[2] and perform the same business activities, but are

---

BOX 12.3   FedEx IN CHINA

The Chinese operations of FedEx, the US-based express delivery firm, are illustrative of some of the influences and responses noted above; for example, until recently foreign freight forwarding and express delivery firms have faced government restrictions on taking a majority interest in local Chinese joint ventures (Wozniak, 2003).

When FedEx first entered China in 1984, it used a representative office in Beijing and agents in various parts of China, eventually teaming up with a local logistics company (EAS), which acted as its sole agent in many cities. FedEx was conscious of the risk involved on entry and its lack of experience in the area and so opted for a low-commitment, low-risk form of operations, but also with a low profit margin. Because of what they found to be high operating costs, intense competition in the Chinese market and problems in achieving effective control, FedEx began to look for an alternative operation form in the early 1990s, focusing on joint venture possibilities. It took a considerable period of time before it found a suitable partner: the 50:50 joint venture it formed eventually with the Chinese company DTW, a local logistics company, began operations toward the end of 1999.

Of particular note with this joint venture was what went with it – a management contract which ensured FedEx management control of the daily operations of the joint venture. Through the joint venture, FedEx has achieved better connections with the Chinese government and the local market, while the management contract has provided the degree of control that FedEx felt was lacking in previous operations. Clearly, the move to a mode combination form enabled FedEx to deal more effectively with the specific issues it faced in what was perceived to be a difficult and constrained market environment.

Source: Chen et al. (2003).

---

under different ownership: the entrant firm has its own operations parallel with those of the local operators. The concept of 'dual distribution' found in the marketing channel literature (for example, Coughlan et al., 2006; Dutta et al., 1995) may apply in the choice of international distribution channels. 'Dual distribution' enables the manufacturer to benchmark independent dealers by keeping house accounts served by their own sales people in the dealers' sales districts. Furthermore, the manufacturer establishes a credible threat of taking over the dealer's district inasmuch as take-down and set-up switching costs (cf. previous chapter) are likely to be moderate. The permanent termination threat may prevent the local operator from shirking (Dutta et al., 1995; Petersen et al., 2006). In addition to suppressing shirking, the in-house sales channel may have another purpose, namely to demonstrate new and more effective sales and marketing techniques. The concept of 'flagship stores' is well known from franchising where the franchisor is anxious to show the full sales potential of its franchising format. However, as pointed out by Coughlan et al. (2006, p. 144), dual channels ('make *and* buy') are challenging and fraught with the risk of dysfunctional conflict between the manufacturer and the local distributors: the two channels tend to view each other with a great deal of suspicion and treat each other as rivals. Moreover, B2B customers are quick to play in-house and outside channels against each other.

Over the last ten years, many MNCs have added direct, online sales channels to their existing sales network of foreign intermediaries. The addition of an extra online sales channel may be seen as an attempt to expand market reach by catering to new customer segments. However, from the perspective of the local intermediaries, the new sales channel can easily appear to be cannibalizing existing export sales channels. By introducing direct, online sales channels entrant firms may very well evoke uncertainty and dissatisfaction among existing distributors – if not open channel conflicts. This was the experience of the Danish company Chr. Hansen A/S when online sales were introduced in the US market. Chr. Hansen is a producer of natural ingredient solutions to the food, pharmaceutical and agricultural industries. In the US, Chr. Hansen sells its products via a regional HQ in Milwaukee. In addition to the production subsidiary in Milwaukee, Chr. Hansen operates six other factories in the US. In order to sell its products to the wine industry, the company has appointed an intermediary, GusmerCellulo, in California. Hence Chr. Hansen is practising mode combination in order to maximize coverage of the US market. In 2003, it introduced a so-called 'Customer Web Centre', where customers can order direct through the Internet. At the time of introduction the intermediary did not have the possibility of offering online sales, and an issue was how to handle customers who want to be able to order online without ending up in channel conflict (source: personal communication with Product Manager in Chr. Hansen A/S, Sarita Bairoliya).

Competing modes may occur when a firm attempts a hostile take-over of an export market. The existing local distributor might be able to resist giving up the market, depending on the nature of existing contractual obligations, but the exporter nevertheless establishes a wholly-owned, local sales organization. A study of Danish firms indicated that 27 per cent of them retained their independent intermediaries after a subsidiary had been established (Pedersen and Petersen, 1998).

In some situations, the distinction between the five above-mentioned rationales for mode combination becomes blurred because of changes in the foreign market and in a firm's strategy and organization; for example,

Strategies

when separate distribution operations in a market are coordinated by a new subsidiary, thereby creating a more integrated system. The degree of integration or coordination of complementary modes can vary across different foreign markets even for the same firm. Even though unrelated and segmented modes do not directly support each other, indirect support might be provided in a more general way, such as common staff training programmes, staff transfers, sharing of some overheads, sharing of market information and contacts, and the like.

HOW TO COMBINE MODES? ('MODE PACKAGING')

As demonstrated above, mode combinations may appear in a variety of forms in foreign market operations. In this section we explore the deliberate use of mode combinations in achieving foreign market outcomes. Particular modes can be used in different ways to achieve various objectives, such as providing more customized services or exercising better control over a licensee. A starting point for preparing a mode combination strategy may very well be to consider if any of the outlined five reasons for mode combination apply to the needs of the individual company. Often the mode combination strategy has to be formulated in relation to a foreign market in which the company already operates. If, for example, we assume that a company in the current situation serves a foreign market through a licensing agreement, this operation method may, as a point of departure, be considered as a primary mode. However, the company may consider associate modes to better accommodate the fulfilment of the market objectives defined for the particular foreign market. Table 12.1 presents various mode combinations pertaining to different objectives of the foreign market operation (see rows A–E). In the table, the foreign operation method of licensing is indicated as the primary mode which may, or may not, be combined with other FOMs, including exporting and joint ventures, plus marketing and production subsidiaries (the columns of the table). The primary mode ensures fulfilment of the main objective(s) of the foreign operation, for example revenue generation or technology control.

To the extent that the combination of modes is carried out as a deliberate and concerted action, it is reasonable to talk about mode packaging (Luostarinen and Welch, 1990; Benito and Welch, 1994; Petersen and Welch, 2002). The operations of each FOM of a mode package are coordinated with the other FOMs, in this way making up an integrated system. The mode package may fulfil a single objective, such as serving different customer segments by using more specialized FOMs, but the term 'package' particularly makes sense where several objectives are in

Table 12.1 Examples of mode combinations with different rationales

Mode combination rationale	Operation modes			
	Primary mode	Associate operation modes		
	Licensing	Exporting	JV	Marketing subsidiary	Production subsidiary
A. Different customer segments	X	X			
B. Commitment and control	X		X		
C. Different value activities	X			X	
D. Different value chains	X				X
E. Benchmarking local operators	X	X		X	

play. A comprehensive mode package may, as an example, aim for the fulfilment of the objectives indicated in the first three rows in Table 12.1 (A–C). Here, the three associate modes (export, JV and marketing subsidiary) fulfil the needs for market segmentation, more commitment and management control, as well as allowing specialization (in marketing). This comprehensive mode package is illustrated in Figure 12.2. In the stylized triangle the three associate operation modes surround the primary mode of licensing. The licence agreement fulfils the important objectives of (1) revenue generation in the form of royalty payments, (2) technology control, that is, contractually regulated use of the licensed technology, and (3) local manufacturing and sales (with marketing being the responsibility of the licensor).

The term 'mode package' makes less sense in relation to the last two rows (D and E) in Table 12.1 since the degree of coordination between the operation modes may be very modest or completely absent. Accordingly, the objective of benchmarking the local operator (the licensee) does not apply in Table 12.1, and for the same reason the licensor has no production subsidiary located in the licensee's territory (country).

It may well be the exception that mode packages are as comprehensible as indicated in Figure 12.2. However, the real-world mode package examples of Lundbeck (in China) and Kone (in Japan) – see Boxes 12.4 and 12.5 respectively – not only include several operation modes, but, apparently, also fulfil multiple objectives. Until recently, Lundbeck's mode package in China revolved around licence and distributor agreements with two local operators. The associated mode of a representative office fulfilled the need for supporting (marketing specialization) and

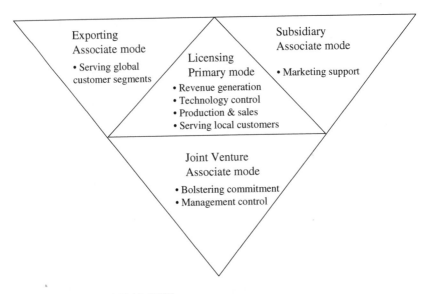

Source: Petersen and Welch (2002).

Figure 12.2 Stylized example of 'mode packaging'

monitoring the operations of the local partners. However, in 2006, Lundbeck expanded its in-house sales and marketing activities dramatically, and the sales subsidiary emerged as the company's new, primary operation mode in China.

In the case of Kone's mode package in Japan, it is more difficult to identify a primary mode, although a licensing agreement seems to play a key role in the company's mode package. The cross-equity/joint venture arrangement established in 2001 was added to the existing licence agreement, presumably in order to bolster commitment of both parties as a kind of 'exchange of hostages' (Williamson, 1985).

The two mode package cases of Lundbeck and Kone give evidence of the dynamism of mode packages. Mode use is a dynamic process subject to transitions and modifications such as mode additions or deletions over time. Clearly, the driving forces regarding mode packages and the roles of its component parts are bound to differ as a result of variation in external factors such as government regulations, market pressures (such as the type and level of competition), the availability of suitable partners, as well as internal factors, including control, resource availability and previous international experience, including mode experience (Luostarinen and Welch, 1990). Given the complexity of mode packages, it is difficult to identify

BOX 12.4   LUNDBECK'S MODE PACKAGING IN CHINA

Lundbeck is a fully integrated international pharmaceutical company which researches in, develops, produces and markets pharmaceuticals for diseases in the central nervous system (CNS). Lundbeck's blockbuster drug is the antidepressant, Cipramil. Lundbeck is operating in more than 80 countries, 50 with local subsidiaries. In the mid-1990s, Lundbeck entered the Chinese market via Hong Kong, signing a licence and distributor agreement (1998) with Shenzhen Kangzhe Pharmaceutical Co. Ltd. (SKP) covering a full package of Lundbeck's products. The licence arrangement did not include local production of Lundbeck medicine, only downstream activities. However, SKP is formally a licensee, paying a royalty fee based on sales generated in the region.

In 2000, Lundbeck established a representative office in Beijing with three purposes: (1) to seek intelligence about the Chinese market; (2) to support the partner in terms of educating the local sales people about the products and sharing its latest research findings; (3) to monitor the marketing and sales efforts of the Chinese partner. Since SKP was performing well on only one product (Deanxit), Lundbeck in 2002 entered another licence and distributor agreement, this time with Xian-Janssen Pharmaceutical, on Cipramil and its successor Lexapro.

As of 2006, Lundbeck was in the process of revising its mode package entailing an arrangement between Lundbeck and Xian-Janssen for co-promoting Lexapro. The co-promotion involves Lundbeck and Xian-Janssen distributing the same product (under the same name, in contrast to Lundbeck's co-marketing where the same product is distributed under different names), but targeting different customer segments. Hence Lundbeck is using different operation modes – a sales subsidiary and an independent distributor – based on different customer segments in China, and not dual distribution. Still, co-promotion requires a good understanding with the local partner in order to obtain an effective segmentation of the market.

Furthermore, Lundbeck was turning its representative office into a fully-fledged sales and marketing subsidiary prepared for launching the company's two new product lines in China, Ebixa and Serdolect – drugs for the treatment of Alzheimer's disease and schizophrenia.

In the new mode package set-up, Lundbeck's sales subsidiary serves as the primary operation mode in ensuring the objectives for the Chinese market are met. SKP and Xian-Janssen serve as supporting modes; while SKP's main function is to generate revenue in order to sustain Lundbeck's expanded activities, Xian-Janssen's role is twofold: besides generating revenue, Xian-Janssen also has an important function in building up the market position for Lundbeck's two strategically important products, Cipramil and Lexapro.

Sources: Annual reports and press releases of Lundbeck.

BOX 12.5   KONE'S MODE PACKAGING IN JAPAN

Kone (Finland) and Toshiba (Japan) are major players in the global supply
and service of elevators and escalators, with Toshiba heavily focused on
the Japanese market whereas Kone is an important supplier in a wide
array of global markets.

While there had been informal interactions and discussions between
the two companies from 1982 onwards, the first major step by the two
parties was in 1995, when Kone began exporting 'hydraulic passenger
elevators' to the elevator systems division of Toshiba. In order to ensure
that the product fitted Toshiba's requirements, technical cooperation
formed an important part of the ongoing relationship between the two
organizations. In 1997, Kone won a contract to supply 57 elevators for
Tokyo Metro's new subway line, in competition with Toshiba. However, the
two companies agreed to cooperate on installation and maintenance in
fulfilment of the contract. In 1998, the relationship was extended further
through the signing of a licensing agreement covering the transfer of new
technology (elevators and hoisting machines) that had been developed by
Kone. The licensing agreement gave Toshiba exclusive marketing rights to
use the new technology in the Japanese market, and non-exclusive rights
to China, Hong Kong, Singapore, Malaysia, Taiwan and Indonesia. The
companies also agreed to extend technical cooperation into new product
development.

In 2001, the alliance was further extended: Toshiba established a subsidiary, Toshiba Elevator and Building Systems Corporation, in which
Kone took a 20 per cent share, while this same company purchased 5 per
cent of Kone's shares. This was the culmination of a gradually extending
alliance which, at the same time, demonstrated the way that market penetration might be enhanced through mode package development. From a
start via exporting with some cooperation on product modification, the
alliance extended to a mode package that included exporting, widespread
technical, market (for example, in China) and systems (for example, component sourcing) cooperation, as well as licensing and a cross-equity
arrangement. In the end, it is difficult to say what Kone's primary mode of
operation in the Japanese market is: all modes in the package play essential roles in the overall activity that could be loosely termed a strategic
alliance.

Sources: Annual reports and personal communication.

clearly the nature and significance of mode changes and mode use over
time. A switch in roles for a given mode within a combination might
amount to the equivalent of an overall mode change, such as when a firm
decides to change from exporting to licensing as the primary market penetration vehicle within an existing mode package. The firm may have been

using the foreign licensee to assemble exported parts and distribute the final product. Sometimes a firm is unprepared to invest in its own production facility within the foreign market, even though the licensing arrangement has resulted in inadequate servicing of customers. In this situation the firm might see the alternative as more fully involving the licensee in production and service provision, along with a reduced exporting role for itself. The main structure of the package remains unchanged but there is a significant change in the roles played by different modes.

Adding and eliminating roles within an existing package adds a further complication. An example reported in the literature is when a foreign sales subsidiary established to undertake marketing activity in the foreign market is called upon to assist in purchasing. Research on US firms indicates that their foreign subsidiaries are the most frequently used resource when foreign sources of supply are being sought (Giunipero and Monczka, 1990). In a Finnish study, some use of foreign-based sales subsidiaries for assistance with foreign purchasing was found but it was not a common occurrence (Korhonen, 1999). Such changes in roles could contribute eventually to expansion into production in foreign markets, further deepening the firm's international operations.

The foregoing discussion of the way operation modes may be used within packages indicates the potential diversity of roles involved in foreign market entry and development. Supporting or associate modes may play an important part in achieving particular outcomes that are of concern to the firm, in addition to, or in support of, those sought through the primary mode. We have described cases where added revenue, foreign market penetration and other objectives can be achieved through more extensive and appropriate mode packaging. The analysis demonstrates that adding a mode to an existing operation, or changing the roles of modes within an unchanged overall package, may be a more effective way of responding to a change in market circumstances than undergoing the disruption and dislocation of a complete mode switch. It also assists in maintaining knowledge, staff and network assets developed through a pre-existing mode arrangement.

BARRIERS TO MODE COMBINATION

With its obvious advantages, one might expect mode combination, including mode packaging, to be a standard strategy ingredient of any international firm. However, from what we know of firms' internationalization behaviour, this seems not to be the case, and one might speculate about which barriers to mode combination would explain the seemingly moderate use of mode combination, including mode packages, shown in empirical studies of mode use. In the previous chapter we showed how switching costs in many cases make up an effective barrier to otherwise desirable FOM changes. In relation to mode combination, we can identify three further barriers to desirable mode arrangements.

Insufficient Scale of Foreign Market Value Activities

Managers make mode decisions for all value chain activities – not only for one or a few. This is obvious in relation to the formulation of outsourcing strategies of firms, but should be equally evident in relation to foreign market entry strategies (Reve, 1990; Quinn and Hilmer, 1994). In a similar vein, we would expect managers to make operation mode decisions in relation to each identifiable value activity of the firm. In other words, managers may take the individual value activity as the level of analysis in relation to the organization of their international activities. Thereby, we implicitly assume that decision makers are able to distinguish different value activities in terms of the optimal FOM and mode package. Although the individual value activity is taken as the unit of analysis, this by no means implies that all decision makers consider the same range or number of value activities in terms of optimal FOM. The differentiation of value activities by FOM only makes economic sense if two preconditions are fulfilled: first, the individual value activity has to exceed a certain minimum economic scale in order to make it identifiable and independently amenable for benchmarking against market providers. Hence decision makers of small firms may only know the economics of a few value activities whereas large MNC decision makers may know the economics of many more. Second, the value activities should differ substantially in terms of the optimal FOM, in line with Porter's definition of value chain activities as business activities involving significantly different economics (Porter, 1985).

Hence the number of separable value activities in a foreign market that decision makers can discern as to the optimal mode of operation is to a large extent contingent on the scale of the individual value activities. As an echo of Adam Smith's theorem that 'the division of labour is limited by the extent of the market', we would expect the number of different FOMs used by (entrant) firms to be limited by the scale of the individual value activities. If a decision maker is unable to differentiate the value activities in terms of scale and scope economies, asset specificity and other economic characteristics, there is no cost-effective basis for introducing mode combination, either.

Fixed Costs of Setting up Multiple Modes

The introduction of separate FOMs in a foreign market has to be economically justified by the cost savings or revenue gains of the value activities that
result from allotting them governance forms of their own – after deduction
of fixed costs associated with adding new modes. When Lundbeck established a representative office in China to support and monitor the local distributor (see Box 12.4), one must assume that the fixed costs incurred by this
mode addition (finding suitable premises, recruiting personnel and so on)
were justified by the extra revenue gained in the Chinese market as a result
of this mode combination. Likewise, the fixed costs of establishing a licence
arrangement (costs of writing, negotiating and enforcing the licence contract) in addition to an existing joint venture should be justified by the
reduced risk of technology leakage (which would result in diminished
revenue gains). Again, scale matters because the set-up costs tend to be fixed:
the 'ink costs' of a licence contract are approximately the same irrespective
of the market value of the licensed technology. Accordingly, we would
expect mode combination to be less common for small firms operating in
small foreign markets. As an example, all the activities of a small, Danish
dot.com firm, serving customers in a small country like Liechtenstein may
be exercised as in-house activities (sole ventures) from its home country.
Conversely, mode combination may very well be observed in a large Swedish
multinational company serving its US customers through sole ventures
in the US and Sweden as well as via local joint ventures and licensing
operations.

Cognitive Limitations ('Mode Myopia')

There is a danger that firms become too narrow and fixed in the range of
FOMs they employ. Companies tend not to consider the full array of operation mode possibilities when approaching foreign market entry (Larimo,
1987; Calof, 1993) and there is a risk of becoming locked into a particular
foreign operation mode. An operation mode that may have been used at first
by 'chance' becomes the mode best understood, or one bad experience
means that a particular operation mode is locked out. Hence, when international companies suffer from 'mode myopia', they find it difficult to introduce a previously unused mode into an existing package. There is comfort in
continuing to employ those modes that the company has become knowledgeable about, and adept in using, in different foreign markets. A somewhat
extreme example is the British firm Pilkington, which extensively internationalized its float glass business over a very long period pre-eminently via
the licensing of manufacturers in other markets (Taylor, 1994).

In general, therefore, a major task for the internationalizing firm is to ensure a high level of awareness and knowledge among key staff of the full range of operation forms and their potential to be packaged and used in ways that strengthen the process of foreign market penetration.

A MODE COMBINATION STRATEGY FRAMEWORK

Analysis of foreign operation mode combination strategies used by companies gives an indication of the extent to which they are employed already by internationalizing companies in a wide variety of situations, utilizing diverse and sometimes complex mode packages, as in the case of Kone in Japan (see Box 12.5). At the same time, it is evident that considerable potential exists to extend this role, to raise consciousness about this issue in strategic thinking about international operations. For companies, there are significant practical demands in developing a more powerful mode use strategy in international markets, with an upgrading of the role of mode packages. There may be the need for learning about many ways of operating that have not been used before. A company will only develop the potential strategic flexibility provided by mode packages if staff are equipped and prepared to use them – in response, at times, to situations where rapid reaction is required.

Thus companies need to embark on a deliberate programme to develop mode combination strategies for different foreign markets, which might include the following steps:

1. investigation of the current state of knowledge of, and practice in, mode package use within the company;
2. identification of weaknesses relative to the broader scope which is regarded as appropriate for a more effective mode combination strategy;
3. undertaking an exercise in which different mode packages are assessed in terms of the achievement of strategic outcomes in various foreign markets;
4. selection of a preferred mode package for each market, including the delineation of the different roles or contributions of different parts of each package to objectives;
5. training in a wider range of modes where appropriate; implementation of the new approaches to mode package use; and
6. development of a contingency plan for adjustments of the mode package in response to possible internal and external changes.

NOTES

1. Other establishment chains including other FOMs than the four (e.g. joint ventures and licensing) are indeed conceivable; see, e.g., Petersen and Pedersen (1997).
2. And hence, in theory – but presumably less so in practice – differ fundamentally from the earlier mentioned mode combination based on market segmentation.

REFERENCES

Benito, G.R.G. and L.S. Welch (1994), 'Foreign market servicing: beyond choice of entry mode', *Journal of International Marketing*, **2**(2), 7–27.
Berle, A.A. and G.C. Means (1932), *The Modern Corporation and Private Property*, New York: Commerce Clearing House.
Brickley, J.A. and F.H. Dark (1987), 'The choice of organizational form: the case of franchising', *Journal of Financial Economics*, **18**, 401–20.
Calof, J.L. (1993), 'The mode choice and change decision process and its impact on international performance', *International Business Review*, **2**(1), 97–120.
Cavusgil, S.T., A. Yaprak and P.L. Yeoh (1993), 'A decision-making framework for global sourcing', *International Business Review*, **2**(2), 143–56.
Chen, J., S. Cheng and J. Zhang (2003), 'FedEx in China', MBA Project, Mt Eliza Business School, Beijing, China.
Coughlan, A.T., E. Anderson, L.W. Stern and A.I. El-Ansary (2006), *Marketing Channels* (7th edn), Upper Saddle River, N.J: Pearson/Prentice-Hall.
Dixon, D.F. and I.F. Wilkinson (1986), 'Toward a theory of channel structure', in L.P. Bucklin and J. Carmen (eds), *Research in Marketing Volume 8: Distribution Channels and Institution*, Greenwich, Conn.: JAI Press, pp. 27–70.
Dutta, S., M. Bergen, J.B. Heide and G. John (1995), 'Understanding dual distribution: the case of reps and house accounts', *Journal of Law, Economics, & Organization*, **11**(1), 189–204.
Gabrielsson, M., V.H.M. Kirpalani and R. Luostarinen (2002), 'Multiple channel strategies in the European personal computer industry', *Journal of International Marketing*, **10**(3), 73–95.
Giunipero, L.C. and R.M. Monczka (1990), 'Organizational approaches to managing international sourcing', *International Journal of Physical Distribution and Logistics Management*, **20**, 3–12.
Grossman, S.J. and O.D. Hart (1986), 'The costs and benefits of ownership: a theory of vertical and lateral integration', *Journal of Political Economy*, **94**, 691–719.
Jensen, M.C. and W.H. Meckling (1976), 'Theory of the firm: managerial behaviour, agency costs and ownership structure', *The Journal of Financial Economics*, **3**(4), 305–60.
Johanson, J. and F. Wiedersheim-Paul (1975), 'The internationalization of the firm – four Swedish cases', *Journal of Management Studies*, **12**(3), 305–22.
Korhonen, H. (1999), *Inward–Outward Internationalization of Small and Medium Enterprises* (doctoral thesis), Helsinki: Helsinki School of Economics and Business Administration, HeSE print.
Larimo, J. (1987), 'The foreign direct investment decision process', *Research Paper*, No. 124, Proceedings of the University of Vaasa, Finland.

Luostarinen, R. and L.S. Welch (1990), *International Business Operations*, Helsinki: Export Consulting KY.

Moxon, R.W. (1982), 'Offshore sourcing, subcontracting, and manufacturing', in I. Walter (ed.), *Handbook of International Business*, New York: John Wiley and Sons, 38.3–38.19.

Pedersen, T. and B. Petersen (1998), 'Explaining gradually increasing resource commitment to a foreign market', *International Business Review*, 7(3), 483–501.

Petersen, B. and T. Pedersen (1997), 'Twenty years after – support and critique of the Uppsala internationalisation model', in I. Björkman and M. Forsgren (eds), *The Nature of the International Firm*, Copenhagen: Copenhagen Business School Press, pp. 117–34.

Petersen, B. and L.S. Welch (2000), 'International retailing operations: downstream entry and expansion via franchising', *International Business Review*, 9(4), 479–96.

Petersen, B. and L.S. Welch (2002), 'Foreign operation mode combinations and internationalization', *Journal of Business Research*, 55(2), 157–62.

Petersen, B., T. Pedersen and G.R.G. Benito (2006), 'The termination dilemma of foreign intermediaries: performance, anti-shirking measures and hold-up safeguards', *Advances in International Marketing*, 16, 317–39.

Porter, M.E. (1985), *Competitive Advantage. Creating and Sustaining Superior Performance*, New York: Free Press.

Quinn, J.B. and F.G. Hilmer (1994), 'Strategic outsourcing', *Sloan Management Review*, 35(4), 43–55.

Reve, T. (1990), 'The firm as a nexus of internal and external contracts', in M. Aoki, B. Gustafsson and O.E. Williamson (eds), *The Firm as a Nexus of Treaties*, London: Sage Publications.

Schroath, F.W., M.Y. Hu and H.Y. Chen (1993), 'Country-of-origin effects of foreign investments in the People's Republic of China', *Journal of International Business Studies*, 24(2), 278–90.

Stabell, C.B. and O.D. Fjeldstad (1998), 'Configuring value for competitive advantage: on chains, shops, and networks', *Strategic Management Journal*, 19, 413–37.

Taylor, A. (1994), 'Pilkington emerges with advantages', *Financial Times*, 27 May, 6.

Tomassen, S., L.S. Welch and G.R.G. Benito (1998), 'Norwegian firms in India: operation mode choice', *Asian Journal of Business and Information Systems*, 3(1), 1–20.

Valla, J.P. (1986), 'The French approach to Europe', in P.W. Turnbull and J.P. Valla (eds), *Strategies for International Industrial Marketing*, London: Croom Helm, pp. 11–41.

Welch, L.S. (1985), 'The international marketing of technology: an interaction perspective', *International Marketing Review*, 2(1), 41–53.

Williamson, O.E. (1985), *The Economic Institutions of Capitalism. Firms, Markets, Relational Contracting*, New York: Free Press.

Williamson, P.J. (1992), 'Europe's single market: the toughest test yet for sales and distribution', *The Economist Intelligence Unit: Multinational Business* (Summer), 57–76.

Wozniak, L. (2003), 'DHL and FedEx race to integrate China', *For Eastern Economic Review*, 27 February, 42–4.

13. Internationalization, international strategies and FOMs

INTRODUCTION

In this chapter, we examine the choice, switch and combination of foreign operation methods (FOMs) in relation to firms' varying degrees of internationalization and different international strategies. The focus is on optimization of FOM choice, switch and combination on a global scale by an entrant firm, or a relevant, specific strategic business unit (SBU)[1] of the entrant firm, sometimes contrary to the interests of local operations. In such a global corporate perspective, FOM decisions may be subordinated to the need for retaliation against global competitors, global sourcing strategies or other corporate requirements that may be in conflict with the interest of local stakeholders, including the local management. In particular we contrast two basic international strategies – a multi-domestic strategy vis-à-vis a global strategy (Porter, 1986; Prahalad and Hamel, 1990; Bartlett and Ghoshal, 1989; Yip, 1992; see also Chapter 1) – and discuss the implications for mode choice, switch and combination.

In addition to firms' international strategy, their stage of internationalization makes up a second dimension that potentially determines the choice, switch and combination of FOMs. The optimal choice, switch and combination of entrant firms are likely to depend, in part, on where they are in the internationalization process. Quite a few classifications of internationalization stages can be found in the literature (for an overview, see Andersen, 1993). For reasons of simplification, however, we will only distinguish between infant and mature multinationals. The infant MNC is characterized by having a distinct home country in which the management is concentrated. Foreign value added activities – upstream or downstream – may be significant, but are subject to central coordination. In contrast, the mature MNC is characterized by a lateral corporate structure in which the individual country units may operate quite independently or be assigned specialized responsibilities on which the corporation as a whole is dependent.[2]

Furthermore, among the infant MNCs we identify two groups of firms performing opposite value chain configurations: one group consists of firms that primarily have internationalized their upstream activities (including procurement and manufacturing); the other group includes MNCs in which foreign activities are mainly downstream (sales and marketing, customer servicing). We label the two types of infant MNCs the Export Sales Firm and the International Sourcing Firm, respectively.

The mature MNCs are split into two groups as well: those that are following a strategy of local responsiveness, labelled Multi-domestic Corporations, and MNCs that are subscribing to a global integration strategy, labelled Global Corporations. The distinction follows the integration-responsiveness framework outlined in Chapter 1 and Michael Porter's (1986) distinction between dispersed and concentrated global value chain configurations. In the latter case, firms configure their value chain in such a way that the individual activity is carried out in only one location. In the extreme case, all value chain activities of a firm are carried out in different countries, taking full advantage of factor endowment differentials. The local subsidiary is the sole supplier of specific activities in the firm's value chain and, as such, it is assigned a corporate world mandate. In other words, a global division of labour takes place within the value chain of the corporation. Of course, such a well-developed international division of labour creates a strong need for coordination among the various units of the MNC. In contrast, a company may configure its international activities in a very dispersed way, where value chain activities are replicated from country to country. In some countries, only a few activities, such as sales and marketing, are replicated, whereas in other countries the corporation may replicate the full range of activities of the value chain, in this way forming a 'mini-replica'.

The four identified groups of MNCs constitute extremes, or archetypes, of international firms. In the real world, many infant MNCs are internationalizing upstream and downstream activities simultaneously, and most mature MNCs will combine strategies of integration and responsiveness in their pursuit of transnational solutions (Bartlett and Ghoshal, 1989). Nevertheless, the four archetypes fence in the platform on which international firms operate and in the balance of the chapter we will discuss choice, switch and combination of FOMs in relation to these four archetypes.

THE EXPORT SALES FIRM

The first archetype, the Export Sales Firm, is characterized by mainly contractual downstream activities – sales, customer servicing and sometimes marketing – in multiple countries and (internalized) sourcing only in its home country; see Figure 13.1.

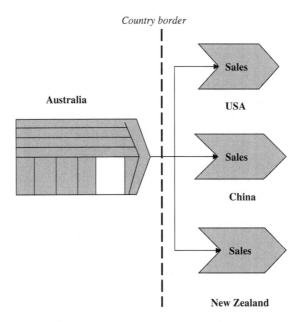

*Figure 13.1   Example of value chain configuration of an Export Sales
Firm*

Various examples of companies similar to the Export Sales Firm have
already been presented in previous chapters (Chapter 8 in particular, but
also the Scanbech and Lundbeck cases in Chapters 11 and 12, respectively).

Mode Choice Strategies

The Export Sales Firm wants to gain sales volume quickly to accrue scale
economies in its activities (R&D, production, marketing, administration)
at home. The quick fix is the appointment of foreign intermediaries (distributors, sales agents) or franchisees (see Chapters 8 and 3, respectively).
Since these outside agents may only require a limited commitment of
resources by the entrant firm, numerous foreign markets can be entered
within a short time. However, because of hold-up risks and growth aversion
(see Chapter 11), exploitation of the full export market potential may not
be achievable through the use of outside agents. Therefore, the outside
agents are often seen as temporary, second-best mode choices. Besides
achieving basic sales in the export market the pragmatic objective of using
outside agents is to get an idea of the market potential, acquire some basic
knowledge about the market and, if possible, to develop the market to the

breakeven point for an economically justifiable internalization of the local sales apparatus.

Mode Switching Strategies

A major FOM challenge for the Export Sales Firm is to plan and execute as smoothly as possible the switch from external sales intermediaries to internal sales subsidiaries (representative sales offices), as noted in the case of the Danish producer of packaging materials for personal care and pharmaceuticals, Scanbech (see Box 11.4).

Mode Combination Strategies

To the Export Sales Firm combination strategies pertain to the design of its foreign sales channels. As a first step towards internalizing its export sales channels, the firm may insist on serving certain key accounts (or 'global accounts') directly. The segmentation of the market into local and global customers may be combined with the division of marketing responsibilities between the foreign intermediaries and the entrant firm itself. These two forms of mode combination have elements of both cooperation and confrontation, where a dual distribution arrangement would represent an outright confrontation strategy and a hybrid contract–equity mode would represent a collaborative strategy (see also Chapter 12). Through dual distribution the entrant firm makes a short-cut to gauging the export sales potential and, moreover, obtains valuable hands-on market experience; but both benefits come at a risk of an open channel conflict. The hybrid of combining contractual and equity modes is a way of bolstering commitment on both sides of the dyad, which in turn makes it more likely that the foreign intermediary will develop the export sales up to, and even beyond, the break-even point of internalization.

THE INTERNATIONAL SOURCING FIRM

The International Sourcing Firm is characterized by contractual upstream activities, such as manufacturing, procurement and business process outsourcing, in multiple countries but with (internalized) sales only in its home country; see Figure 13.2.

This type of firm may not be as common as the Exporting Sales Firm, but several examples are found in the textile and apparel industry in some industrialized countries where price competition from Asian producers has led to substantial offshoring of labour-intensive upstream activities.

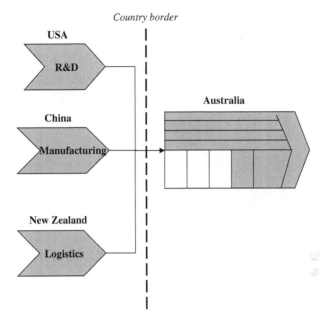

Figure 13.2   Example of value chain configuration of an International Sourcing Firm

Mode Choice Strategies

The International Sourcing Firm typically contracts out – or outsources – upstream activities to foreign operators in order to benefit from their large-scale operation facilities and to gain access to cheap labour. As an example, the International Sourcing Firm might use contract manufacturing in low-cost developing countries, such as China and Vietnam. Sometimes, these low-cost suppliers are operating as Original Equipment Manufacturers (see Chapter 6). The Danish textile and apparel industry has for many years accommodated firms with traits of the International Sourcing Firm. The internationalization of these firms has taken off on the sourcing side through offshoring of labour-intensive value chain activities to low-cost countries. In the 1960s, 1970s and 1980s, the Danish textile and apparel firms targeted South European countries as offshoring destinations. Later, in the 1990s and 2000s, they relocated to East European countries, the CIS countries and to South and South East Asian countries. During these 40–50 years, different offshoring business models, with increasingly more value chain activities being relocated, have been developed in the industry; see Figure 13.3.

Design Logistics Procurement Processing Cutting Sewing Packaging Quality Distribution
control

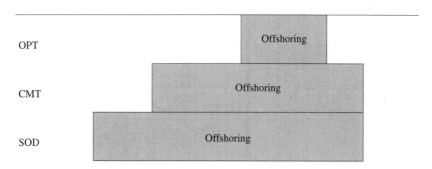

Notes: OPT = O(utward) P(rocessing) T(raffic); CMT = C(ut), M(ake), T(rim); SOD = S(ourcing), from O(wn) D(esign).

Source: Development of Danish textile and apparel industry, 1989–99.

Figure 13.3   Concepts of offshore production in textiles

In the 1980s, the so-called OPT (Outward Processing Traffic) offshoring business model was dominant, as shown in Figure13.3. During the 1990s, the CMT (Cut, Make and Trim) model took over, and, recently, this model was replaced by the SOD (Sourcing from Own Design) offshoring business model (The Danish Textile Industry Association, 2003).

Over the years, contractual arrangements have been preferred for standardized blue-collar activities such as cutting, sewing and packaging. These activities are typically carried out as large-scale operations that are difficult to internalize for entrant firms with scarce resources and sales outlets limited to the home market. However, as the offshored activities move up the value chain – including procurement, quality control and even design – the need for internalization becomes more pressing. Where the internalization of the Export Sales Firm is driven by a call for combating motivational problems among outside agents, the International Sourcing Firm tends to internalize as the strategic importance of the offshore activities increases. Hence a fashion house's sourcing of pattern designs in a foreign country is very likely to take place as an in-house operation, that is, via a wholly-owned subsidiary. To organize pattern designs as an outsourcing operation would not only involve an extant risk of leakage of strategic, sensitive know-how, but also could result in an erosion of core competencies (Prahalad and Hamel, 1990; Quinn and Hilmer, 1994).

Mode Switching Strategies

The International Sourcing Firm may source along a markets–hierarchies spectrum ranging from pure arm's-length procurement (one-off import transactions) to captive offshoring (wholly-owned subsidiary); see Harland et al. (2001) and Gereffi et al. (2005). Most of the sourcing, however, will be organized as contractual arrangements, that is, as hybrid governance forms somewhere between markets and hierarchies. As a general rule, the development is in the direction from markets to hierarchies: the International Sourcing Firm usually commences its internationalization by importing standardized goods and services, which, over a period of time, gradually evolves into more customized, build-to-order procurement. The customization implies relationship-specific investments by the contractee that in turn prompt the parties to negotiate contracts that vary in length, depending on the depreciation period of the specific investments. The development from short-term vendor contracts to long-term outsourcing contracts reflects a stretching of one particular FOM (subcontracting) rather than a mode switch as such. Since the move to a long-term outsourcing contract may have far-reaching, strategic consequences for the International Sourcing Firm, it is only to be expected that the finish of the contract is normally preceded by smaller and less idiosyncratic transactions with the contractee. As an extra precaution, the first outsourcing contract may be limited to a well-specified, encapsulated project. In that way, the International Sourcing Firm obtains a first-hand assessment of the supplier's qualification without putting too much at stake. Other stretching strategies are indeed conceivable, the purpose of which is to generate high-commitment subcontracting alliances.

A switch from a contractual to a wholly-owned FOM is rarely an imperative for the International Sourcing Firm. As mentioned, subsidiaries are prevented from reaching a minimum efficient scale by their limited home markets. As a halfway internalization, the International Sourcing Firm may form equity joint ventures with the local provider or with a similar entrant firm. The Danish Steel Cluster Pvt Ltd in the KIADB industrial area of Bangalore, India, is an example of the latter. The parents of the equity joint venture are three small steel manufacturing firms from South-East Jutland in Denmark that have offshored the production of certain labour-intensive processes to India to cut costs (source: www.dscplindia.com).

Mode Combination Strategies

Mode combination may be used by the International Sourcing Firm to bolster commitment in the dyad: the contractual pledges of the entrant firm are strengthened by minority equity shareholding – and vice versa. However, it is indeed more likely that the local vendor/contractee is the party who signals commitment through acquiring shares in the International Sourcing Firm. Hence a large outsourcing contract may be pre-conditioned by an equity investment in the outsourcing project (segregated as a joint venture) or in the International Sourcing Firm as a whole.

THE MULTI-DOMESTIC CORPORATION

The Multi-domestic Corporation is characterized by replication of down-stream activities in multiple countries, as was the case with the Export Sales Firm; but the Multi-domestic Corporation also replicates upstream and back-office/supporting activities in large and/or distant markets, such as the US and China, in relation to an entrant firm from Australia, for example, as exemplified in Figure 13.4.

In other words, the Multi-domestic Corporation practises a dispersed global value chain configuration, meaning that the individual value chain activity is replicated from country to country (Porter, 1986). For examples of companies illustrating the Multi-domestic Corporation archetype, see Box 13.1.

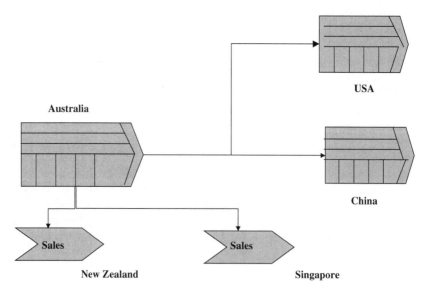

*Figure 13.4	Example of value chain configuration of a Multi-domestic Corporation*

BOX 13.1   EXAMPLES OF MULTI-DOMESTIC CORPORATIONS

For most companies, a completely concentrated value chain configuration is neither attainable nor desirable, for example, for supply security reasons. For other companies a concentrated value chain is disadvantageous because of high transportation costs. This is the case for companies with high-volume/weight–low-value products, such as breweries and insulation material companies. These companies will maintain local production sites and replicate breweries and insulation plants from country to country. In other words, the Multi-domestic Corporations will dominate in certain manufacturing industries and the services sector in general. As an example, the international facility service provider, ISS (employing 350 000 people in cleaning, office support, catering and property services), replicates its world-wide service activities from country to country (see www.issworld.com).

Still, the lowering of transportation and communication costs in combination with the integration of markets is in general forcing mature international firms into a transition in the direction of more concentrated value chain configurations.

Danfoss, one of the largest industrial groups in Denmark, is an example of a Danish company whose value chain configuration is in the process of transition. Danfoss traditionally located the bulk of production in European markets and operated a 'one product, one plant' philosophy, implying that, for every new product invented, a corresponding new production facility was built. Plants operated independently with a high degree of product specialization, practically with the entire value chain for each product localized in one plant. With the vision of becoming a global player, today Danfoss is slowly moving away from its original philosophy towards a more concentrated value chain configuration, as a more global production network is considered necessary for global sales. In an effort to optimize the geographical location of production, production is increasingly becoming more interlinked and located in order to obtain cost advantages. In 2003, Danfoss established three international purchasing offices in China with the purpose of sourcing low-cost supplies for Danfoss factories around the world. However, cost considerations are not the only driving factors for location. Proximity to its main markets, including a presence in the main regions (Europe, Asia and the US) and limiting the number of products produced in each plant, are also still key considerations. Thus the transition towards a more concentrated value chain configuration is a slow process, and is still in its initial phase. As explained by regional director, Leif Fløjgaard: 'It is only now that we are linking and synchronizing all the elements of the process of moving abroad, from logistics to product development and R&D.'

Source (Danfoss):   Pyndt and Pedersen (2006, 105–28).

Mode Choice Strategies

A Multi-domestic Corporation is likely to use a broad range of FOMs: exporting, contractual as well as equity investment modes. The latter forms of FOMs are predominantly used in large markets that allow sufficient scale in the various upstream and downstream value chain activities (see also Buckley and Casson, 1981).

Mode Switching Strategies

In markets with great sales and sourcing potential (such as China and the US; cf. Figure 13.4), the Multi-domestic Corporation at some point in time is likely to internalize its upstream as well as downstream activities, for example switches from a licence arrangement to a wholly-owned production subsidiary, or from a distributor to a sales subsidiary. In addition to scale, global competition and the mitigation of parallel importing may induce internalization. Hence, in certain foreign markets, the Multi-domestic Corporation may want to lower its prices below total costs in order to hurt competitors (Knickerbocker, 1973; Graham, 1978). In other markets, the threat of parallel importing may necessitate the sacrifice of price differentiation opportunities (Simon and Kucher, 1995). As pointed out by Hill et al. (1990), these oligopolistic rivalry strategies are difficult to implement using outside agents in foreign markets. For example, one would expect a foreign distributor to object fiercely to dramatic price cuts for global rivalry reasons.

However, the Multi-domestic Corporation also engages in switches from in-house to externalized value chain activities: upstream from own manufacturing to contract manufacturing for example, and downstream from company-owned to franchised outlets, for example. The externalization (or outsourcing) of local activities is typically caused by a need for specialization that would be uneconomical if organized as a small-scale in-house operation.

Mode Combination Strategies

It is likely that the Multi-domestic Corporation will put in place mode packages in large markets, such as the US market, where mini-replicas are often established; cf. the examples of Gilat Satellite Networks and Fundtech (Box 12.1). The mini-replica hosts a range of value chain activities, some of which may be susceptible to outsourcing and others kept captive. The occurrence of complementary mode combination depends, among other things, upon a trade-off between the economies of FOM specialization and the fixed costs of setting up different FOMs (see also discussion in Chapter 12). Hence, a major FOM challenge to the Multi-domestic Corporation is how to practise various types of mode combination when individual value-added activities are to be performed in countries where size only allows a limited scale.

THE GLOBAL CORPORATION

The Global Corporation is characterized by replication of downstream activities in foreign markets,[3] but a global division of labour in relation to upstream activities (R&D, manufacturing, logistics) with specialized units – mainly internalized – in multiple countries; see Figure 13.5.

Hence the Global Corporation employs a *concentrated* global value chain configuration, meaning that the individual value chain activity is performed in only one or a few locations (Porter, 1986). For examples of companies emulating the Global Corporation archetype, see Box 13.2. To these companies the prime FOM challenge is to coordinate very interdependent foreign activities on a global scale.

Mode Choice Strategies

The Global Corporation has concentrated upstream and back-office activities and geographically dispersed downstream activities. The strong interdependence between the concentrated activities implies that these are overwhelmingly internalized, that is, organized as equity investment modes. The incompatibility between interdependence and use of outside agents (contractual modes) is explained by several factors. First, the interdependence creates vulnerability in terms of supply security, and this vulnerability may be exploited by an outside agent. Second, the concentration of value chain activities is associated with strong specialization. The foreign units acquire world mandate responsibility and appear as centres of excellences (Frost et al., 2002). In other words, the specialized units in the global corporation assume strategic importance, and as such, they are deemed to be inappropriate for outsourcing. Third, the global division of labour is associated with intense internal transfer of intermediate goods, services, property rights and knowledge (also in the form of patents). In the Global Corporation the internal exchanges tend to be traded off via transfer pricing rather than through arm's-length pricing; and transfer pricing is difficult, if not impossible, to practise unless the involved units are internalized, that is, being parts of the same legal unit (Eccles, 1985).

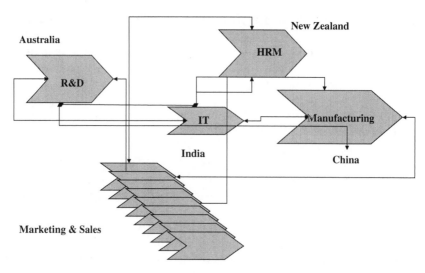

*Figure 13.5   Example of a value chain configuration of a Global
Corporation*

BOX 13.2   EXAMPLES OF GLOBAL CORPORATIONS

The multinational hearing device producer GN Resound is an example of a Danish firm[1] that during the past few years has transformed its value chain configuration from a dispersed to a more concentrated one. As an outcome of a series of amalgamations and acquisitions up to the year 2000, GN Resound came to consist of five former independent producers: Danavox, Resound, Viennatone, Beltone and Philips. As a consequence of this, GN Resound operated a highly dispersed value chain, with plants in Praestoe (Denmark), Taastrup (Denmark), Cork (Ireland), Vienna (Austria), Eindhoven (Netherlands), Xiamen (China) and Chicago (US), undertaking many of the same activities. Assembly, for instance, took place in five different locations. Another result was a very large product portfolio with more than 400 product families. Operating with a low earnings margin of 5 per cent compared to 20 per cent for industry leaders caused GN Resound to initiate a process of integrating the organization on a global scale, with the aim of achieving synergy/cost benefits as a result of a more globally oriented structure. As expressed by Jesper Mailand, CEO and President of GN Resound: 'We need fewer production units, fewer brands, fewer products and fewer systems. . . .' Key areas of concern were a consolidation of production sites to attain the benefits of a global scale production, restructuring R&D departments into fewer integrated units and a streamlined product portfolio. The outcome of this process of integration has meant a far more concentrated value chain configuration for GN Resound. Today, production generally takes place in an integrated production network, assembly is centralized in one main plant in Xiamen, with a small back-up assembly plant in Cork, R&D units have been integrated into two centres of excellence in Denmark and the US, and the product portfolio has been reduced.

The computer mouse producer, Logitech, is an example of a company that relatively early (in the 1980s) took on the characteristics of a Global Corporation. Several value chain activities were concentrated in a single country. Hence finance and hardware development (mouse) were located in Switzerland; software development (PCs) and hardware development (scanner) were located in the US; and manufacturing, procurement and mechanical development were located in Taiwan (with some manufacturing in Ireland as well). Sales were replicated on an individual country level with regional marketing centres in the three countries.

Source (GN Resound):   Pyndt and Pedersen (2006, 57–84).
1.   GN Resound was acquired by Swiss Phonak in September 2006.

Mode Switching Strategies

As the individual (upstream and back-office) value chain activities become more and more concentrated, the Global Corporation tends to switch the FOMs to in-house arrangements (equity investment modes). As regards the downstream activities, internalization for the above-mentioned reasons is less likely, to the extent that sales and customer servicing are maintained as geographically dispersed activities.

Mode Combination Strategies

On the upstream side, the units in the Global Corporation typically conduct activities on a large scale, simply because these activities are for global/corporate use rather than local use. Hence the scale would indicate combinations of FOMs since economies of specialization justify the transaction costs of putting in place, and operating, different operation modes. Conversely, if the value chain activities conducted in an individual country are few (in the extreme case, only one), there is little room for mode combinations based on a division of labour. In other words, there is little room for complementarities between the local value chain activities. The pressing need for internalization for the above-mentioned reasons also delimits the scope for mode combination. However, the scope for mode combination in relation to downstream activities is somewhat wider: here, mode combination explained by market segmentation may be feasible.

FOMs AND FIRMS' TRANSITION TOWARDS GLOBALIZATION

Until now, our discussion of mode strategies has been related to individual archetypes of international firms. Hence our analysis has not included the internationalization process as such, that is, the phenomenon of firms transcending from infant to mature stages of internationalization. Firms may follow different paths towards a more mature stage of internationalization. Internationalization processes of firms can be very idiosyncratic and there are hardly two firms that are identical in terms of their internationalization pattern. As a consequence, we only look at the FOM implications of some very stylized and general paths of internationalization, namely, the transformation of our two infant archetypes – the Export Sales Firm and the International Sourcing Firm – into either a Multi-domestic or Global Corporation. In order to simplify the analysis even further, we exclude the FOM analysis of certain potential paths and explore only three paths that we consider to be predominant: (a) the transformation of the Export Sales Firm into a Multi-domestic Corporation, (b) the conversion of the International Sourcing Firm into a Global Corporation, and (c) the development of the Multi-domestic Corporation into a Global Corporation; see Figure 13.6.

The three predominant paths are indicated with bold arrows (A, B and C). As mentioned, other internationalization paths are indeed conceivable (including those that are indicated by broken arrows in the figure). As an example, some firms may be transformed from Global to Multi-domestic Corporations. Such a 'de-globalization' of firms may have varying explanations: one could be that the management of an international corporation becomes more risk-averse and, as a consequence, avoids a global value chain strategy where a sudden discontinuation of a sole, world mandate supplier may be fatal. Another explanation of such a transformation could be changes in the global production and trade environment, including factor cost convergence across countries, growing import barriers, or increasing transportation costs – all change factors that favour a multi-domestic strategy.

However, through several consecutive decades, the general trend of the international business environment has been one of value chains becoming persistently more global. The trend is partly driven by the market liberalization of a number of important economies (including China, India and the CIS) combined with the spectacular advances of information and communication technologies. In tandem, these two 'mega-drivers' have enticed more and more international firms to emulate the Global Corporation archetype. As a result, our challenge is to examine the FOM implications of firms' quest for globalization, going from infant to mature forms of internationalization, as well as replacing multi-domestic strategies with

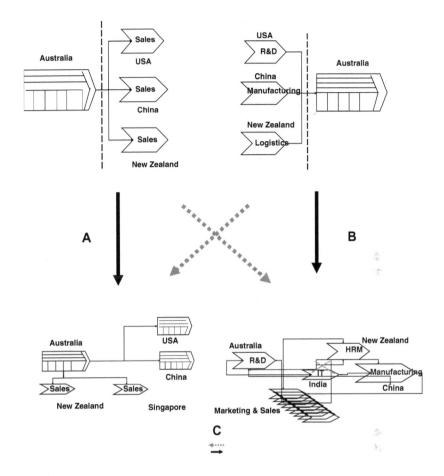

Figure 13.6   Different paths towards a global value chain configuration

global ones. Table 13.1 summarizes the most important FOM implications of firms' globalization on two levels: the firm/corporate level and the level of the individual affiliate/country.

It is noticeable that the transformation of firms towards ultimate globalization has two major FOM implications. One is the internalization of foreign operations, that is, a shift from contractual to equity investment modes. The other important implication is the narrowing range of FOMs used in individual foreign markets, effectively limiting the scope for mode combination.

However, these implications pertain to a very 'advanced' degree of internationalization, namely that of global specialization. Less advanced

Table 13.1 *Major FOM implications of various internationalization sequences*

	Internationalization Sequence		
	Transformation from an Export Sales Firm to a Multi-domestic Corporation	*Transformation from an International Sourcing Firm to a Global Corporation*	*Transformation from a Multi-domestic to a Global Corporation*
Major FOM implications on the firm/corporate level	As upstream value chain activities are introduced to foreign markets, the firm's range of FOMs expands significantly	As downstream value chain activities are introduced to foreign markets, the firm's range of FOMs expands somewhat	As upstream activities in foreign markets are internalized, the firm's range of FOMs shrinks
Major FOM implications on the affiliate/country level	Mode combination is likely to occur in those (predominantly large and distant) markets where upstream value chain activities are introduced	Owing to global interdependencies, upstream value chain activities are internalized. Mode combination is likely to occur in markets where both upstream and downstream value chain activities are carried out	Upstream value chain activities are internalized or exited (that is, consolidated into fewer locations), thereby narrowing the scope for mode combination

stages of globalization, for example, as represented by the Multi-domestic Corporation, are likely to imply opposite FOM effects: a broadening scope of FOMs and the introduction of mode packages in individual markets. Hence the internationalization path of the Export Sales Firm may very well include an intermediate stage (or sometimes a permanent stage) of emulating the Multi-domestic Corporation. Accordingly, the further internationalization of the Export Sales Firm may initially widen its FOM range considerably, and then – later on – narrow it again.

CONCLUSION

This chapter provides evidence of the importance of firm characteristics to mode strategies. FOM choices, switches and combinations are contingent on where in the internationalization process the firms are and what international strategy they are pursuing. It was demonstrated how strategies of mode choice, switch and combination are heavily influenced by these two dimensions. This, in turn, points to the dynamism of the FOM decisions and the context-specificity of mode strategizing.

The complexity of international strategies and internationalization processes required several simplifications in the chapter, such as introducing four archetypes of international firms and identifying three predominant internationalization paths. The critical reader should indeed note these simplifications and consider if FOM choices can be presented in a less deterministic way. Strategies are basically about discrete managerial choices, and the FOM choices are a lot more discrete than our presentation suggests, as noted in the mode analysis part of this book. Two firms, examined through the lens of an outside observer, may seem identical in terms of internationalization, but practise significantly different mode choices, switches and combinations, simply because important contextual factors (such as managers' risk preferences and cognitive limitations) are at play, and such factors also should be included in the analysis of mode strategies.

NOTES

1. A Strategic Business Unit or SBU is understood as a business unit within the overall corporate identity which is distinguishable from other business because it serves a defined external market where management can conduct strategic planning in relation to products and markets. When companies become really large, they are best thought of as being composed of a number of businesses (or SBUs). A Strategic Business Unit can encompass an entire company, or can simply be a smaller part of a company set up to perform a specific task. The SBU has its own business strategy, objectives and competitors and these will often be different from those of the parent company. Source: *Wikipedia – The*

Free Encyclopedia (http://en.wikipedia.org/wiki/Strategic_business_unit). Here, we analogize an SBU with a value chain (cf. Box 11.2). For expository reasons we will assume entrant firms encompass only one SBU and use the terms 'entrant firm' and 'corporation' analogous with SBU and value chain.
2. Our infant-versus-mature MNCs framework is inspired by Hedlund's (1986) distinction between hierarchies and heterarchies and Forsgren et al.'s (1992) differentiation between internationalization of the first and second degree.
3. In some industries, characterized by very few and large potential customers, and for dot.com firms in general, it is indeed conceivable that the downstream activities as well are concentrated in only one geographical location. However, these industries and firms are exceptions to the general rule that sales and customer services are organized as dispersed activities.

REFERENCES

Andersen, O. (1993), 'On the internationalization process of firms: a critical analysis', *Journal of International Business Studies*, **24**(2), 209–31.
Bartlett, C.A. and S. Ghoshal (1989), *Managing Across Borders: The Transnational Solution*, Boston, MA: Harvard Business School Press.
Buckley, P.J. and M.C. Casson (1981), 'The optimal timing of a foreign direct investment', *Economic Journal*, **91**(361), 75–87.
Danish Textile Association (2003), 'Udviklingen i den danske tekstil- og beklædningsindustri 1987–1999' [The development of the Danish textile and apparel industry 1987–1999], www.textile.dk.
Eccles, R.G. (1985), *The Transfer Pricing Problem: A Theory for Practice*, London: Lexington Books.
Forsgren M., U. Holm and J. Johanson (1992), 'Internationalization of the second degree: the emergence of European-based centres in Swedish firms', in S. Young and J. Hamill (eds), *Europe and the Multinationals*, Aldershot, UK and Brookfield, US: Edward Elgar, pp. 235–53.
Frost, T.S., J.M. Birkinshaw and P.C. Ensign (2002), 'Centers of excellence in multinational corporations', *Strategic Management Journal*, **23**(11), 997–1018.
Gereffi, G., J. Humphrey and T. Sturgeon (2005), 'The governance of global value chains', *Review of International Political Economy*, **12**(1), 78–104.
Graham, E.M. (1978), 'Transatlantic investment by multinational firms: a rivalistic phenomenon?', *Journal of Post Keynesian Economics*, **1**(1), 82–9.
Harland, C.M., R.C. Lamming, J. Zheng and T.E. Johnsen (2001), 'A taxonomy of supply networks', *The Journal of Supply Chain Management*, **37**(4), 21–7.
Hedlund, G. (1986), 'The hypermodern MNC: a heterarchy?', *Human Resources Management*, **25**(1), 9–36.
Hill, C.W.L., P. Hwang and W.C. Kim (1990), 'An eclectic theory of the choice of international entry mode', *Strategic Management Journal*, **11**(2), 117–28.
Knickerbocker, F.T. (1973), *Oligopolistic Reaction and Multinational Enterprise*, Cambridge, MA: Harvard University Press.
Porter, M.E. (1986), 'Competition in global industries: a conceptual framework', in M.E. Porter (ed.), *Competition in Global Industries*, Cambridge, MA: Harvard Business School Press, pp. 15–60.
Prahalad, C.K. and Y. Doz (1987), *The Multinational Mission: Balancing Local Demands and Global Vision*, New York: Free Press.

Prahalad, C.K. and G. Hamel (1990), 'The core competence of the corporation', *Harvard Business Review*, **68**(3), 79–91.

Pyndt, J. and T. Pedersen (2006), *Managing the Global Value Chain – A Case Approach*, Copenhagen: CBS Press.

Quinn, J.B. and F.G. Hilmer (1994), 'Strategic outsourcing', *Sloan Management Review*, **35**(4), 43–55.

Simon, H. and E. Kucher (1995), 'Pricing in the new Europe – a time bomb?', *Pricing Strategy & Practice*, **3**(1), 4–13.

Yip, G.S. (1992), *Total Global Strategy*, Englewood Cliffs, NJ: Prentice-Hall.

PART IV

Conclusion

14. Conclusion

INTRODUCTION

In preceding chapters, foreign operation modes have been analysed in their own right, as well as in combination, from various angles: their characteristics and implementation issues, and from theoretical and strategic perspectives. It is clear that mode choice, in both foreign market entry and mode change situations, is not a simple issue for companies, or for those conducting research and developing theory on the subject. There is no neat formula for companies that can be simply applied to the decision about which mode, or modes in combination, is most appropriate in given circumstances. Much depends on what the company is trying to achieve through a given strategic international move, the resources it can access to undertake the activity, the preceding international experience of the company and key staff, the type of product, service or system it sells, the particular set of circumstances faced by a company, including aspects such as the availability of suitable partners or takeover targets in the foreign market in question, relevant government policies, the actions of competitors and the level of risk and uncertainty in the mode decision that these various aspects are seen to generate. Some of these factors are shown in Figure 14.1, which draws together key influences on mode decision making.

While analysis of the various modes in this book provides an overall picture of when and how companies have used them, comparative evaluation in decision-making situations is difficult, and it is not surprising that companies frequently resort to simplified decision rules to deal with the fraught demands of mode choice. There is a wide range of mode options in any given situation, and the choice is often complicated by the link to other key choices, such as which foreign market to enter or expand in, and the product/service mix. It is little wonder research shows that companies tend to look seriously at only a limited range of options. A given mode may be preferred, even before a particular foreign market has been chosen, without much analysis or consideration of alternatives. Prior decisions often create a certain degree of path-dependence and a mode may be favoured simply because success has been achieved with that mode in other countries, and expertise has been developed within the company with its use. In some cases, for alternatives to be seriously considered, there has to

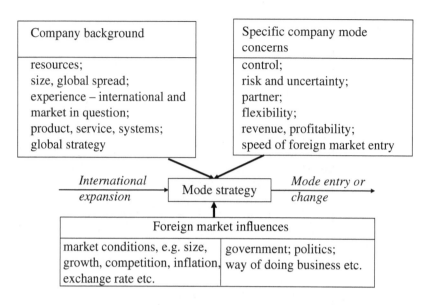

Figure 14.1   Influences on foreign operation mode decision making

be pressure from the external environment in such a way that a different mode from the preferred one is contemplated.

An important complication in mode evaluation stressed in this book is the fact that companies frequently deal with mode combinations rather than singular modes in their international activities. There is a bewildering array of mode options when combinations are considered, as noted in the strategy section, and it is beyond the scope of decision makers to examine and evaluate the full range of combination options. From a theoretical perspective, the introduction of mode combinations is even more troubling: it is not surprising that there have been few studies including mode combinations as decision options. In general, international business theory remains closeted behind the idea of simple, singular mode change, whereas companies deal with the reality of mode combinations in the normal course of international operations. A basic question that mode combinations raise is, what does the concept of 'foreign operation mode' mean? We would argue it typically means mode combination rather than use of a single mode.

An even more difficult question is, what does 'mode change' mean in a world of mode combinations? For example, if a company adds a mode to an existing set of modes used in a foreign market, does that constitute mode change? This might be carried out via the addition of licensing to an existing foreign joint venture operation. Mode deletion from an existing package could likewise be undertaken without change in the mainstream operation. In other words, there is another range of mode options for a company around adjustments in a mode package without wholesale change. This is an important consideration for companies in that, rather than the potential disruption and partner problems associated with whole-sale mode change, it may be possible to stretch existing mode use through judicious mode additions and deletions to achieve the same result. In the face of the plethora of mode strategies that can be used in a multitude of foreign market penetration situations, companies nevertheless have to make decisions, seeking to develop the optimal set of modes in the light of the information at hand. Companies frequently refer to the many mistakes that are made on this front – mistakes that become obvious, sometimes painfully so, as operations unfold. Some of the mistakes are irrecoverable and cause companies to withdraw from the markets where these have arisen. In other cases, companies have had to accept and live with the mistake, such as a poor choice of foreign partner, because the market is deemed to be too important, and have sought other ways of improving mode performance. The treatment of mode switching in this book demon-strates that many firms have sought to deal with the difficulties of achiev-ing optimality in mode and partner choice, of predicting future outcomes on the basis of limited information and experience, by building switching options into the initial mode arrangements, despite the additional negotia-tion difficulties this may entail. In a sense, this is an admission that design-ing the optimal mode arrangement for an unknowable future is an impossible dream. The mode switching chapter (Chapter 11) also high-lights the fact that foreign operation mode choice in companies' inter-nationalization processes is about far more than the entry mode decision, the preoccupation of much of the mode research literature.

At the least, though, coverage of mode types and mode issues in this book has proceeded on the basis that much can be learned about foreign operation modes which can assist in assessing what different sets of modes are capable of contributing to the objective of foreign market penetration. In this concluding chapter, we will consider some of the approaches that can be taken to assessing mode options in decision making situations, although within the context of the limitations we have noted. Coverage of the various mode forms in this book can be seen as a process of assembling a box of tools, one or more of which may be applied in achieving foreign market penetration in a variety of circumstances, as an entry or change strategy. The toolbox is the same for SMEs and MNCs, for initial entrants and experienced international operators, although the knowledge of, and ability and means to use, the full range of tools varies substantially. The aim of this book has been to enhance understanding of foreign operation modes as a basis for the development of strategies and their deployment. Ultimately, though, no matter how thoroughly modes are evaluated and how appropriate the decisions taken, it is how well mode strategies are implemented that will determine the success or otherwise of the strategies adopted. For example, poor partner relations can readily kill licensing, exporting via intermediaries and joint venture arrangements, however appropriate the original mode choice might have been.

MODE CHOICE AS A PROCESS

The Nera case (see Box 14.1) demonstrates that foreign operation mode selection is more appropriately viewed as a process in the bulk of foreign market situations rather than a singular act. As well, it is a process over which an entering or expanding firm is not in full control, and at the end of the process the resultant mode may look very different from the form intended at the start of the process. Nera's experience was common amongst other firms in a study of mode choice by Norwegian companies entering India (Tomassen et al., 1998). The sales manager of another Norwegian company, Autronica, a producer of fire alarm systems, described his personal involvement in the negotiation process surrounding an attempt to start operations in India in the following terms: 'And the negotiations take time. For two years I traveled to India four or five times a year. It's like before an eventual marriage. "Do I like this person, can I join his company for a long period of time? Is he trustful and faithful? Can I talk to him, man to man?" Questions like these seem to be more important than business' (Tomassen, 1996, 90). Apart from these interactions, the Indian government became involved and made a number of demands that added a further level of complication. While exporting/importing and direct investment options were considered and quickly rejected because of, respectively, high trade barriers and risk concerns, a licensing agreement and buy-back package was eventually agreed upon. Figure 14.2 summarizes influences on mode choice, although filtered through the various elements of an interaction and information generation process that precedes, and impacts upon, eventual mode choice, called the mode determination process.

The stimulus to mode use may arise in various forms – exposed foreign market opportunities or threats – and through various avenues, such as external approaches, or as a result of internal evaluation of ongoing foreign operations. There may not be a strong, specific mode stimulus, particularly in mode change situations. Calof (1993) found that the approach to mode change for many companies in his study was embedded in the management

---

BOX 14.1   MAKING A FOM DECISION: NERA IN INDIA

The experience of the Norwegian company Nera, a producer of low and medium capacity microwave radio link systems, in penetrating the Indian market is illustrative of the disparate range of influences that may operate in a company's foreign operation mode choice, and that company preferences have to be placed within the context of the foreign market situation and negotiation process which ensues when foreign partners are involved in some form, ensuring a final outcome that is a compromise at different levels. The sales manager commented in an interview that the final operation method accepted by the company was 'in essence, a compromise between our ideal wishes and the Indian reality' (Tomassen et al., 1998, 11). This process was played out over a period of four years, before entry was finally achieved. In this case the starting point was the choice of market rather than mode – India was viewed as a market with significant market potential for the company, so that it was keen to engineer entry: 'India is an auspicious market . . . We had to be in the India market before the "big flood" was a reality' (11). The company was conscious at the outset that competitors would also eventually respond to the growth potential of the Indian market.

The difficult question then was what mode to use. The company's approach to this question was outlined by the sales manager in the following terms, from an overall perspective of viewing establishment in India as part of a long-term penetration strategy:

- 'Export into India was out of the question – it was impossible to compete with Indian firms, or foreign firms established in India, owing to extremely high tariff barriers.
- A wholly-owned operation would have been too risky – we didn't know the market and we had no serious business in the country beforehand.
- The Indian market is difficult and complex. It is good to have a partner who knows the business and the bureaucracy, a partner who has the right connections.
- The technology into India is second to last – we are not so afraid of technology larceny thanks to the fact that our most up-to-date technology is back in Norway' (10–11).

These comments illustrate something of the thinking and issues raised in mode choice, that have to be enacted in a dynamic (drawn out for Nera) process of information gathering, negotiation and interaction across cultural boundaries, in the Nera case involving substantially different cultures. The outcome is by no means a given. The final form adopted was a joint venture arrangement with an Indian partner, established in 1992, in which Nera held a 30 per cent equity position. This was extended in 1994 to a 45 per cent holding. Today (2006), Nera's subsidiary in India is a 100 per cent owned daughter company.

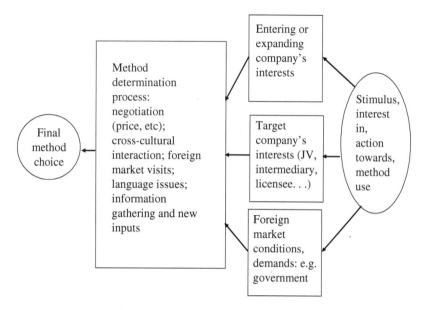

Figure 14.2   Foreign operation method choice

demands of preceding activities and sales outcomes in foreign markets, and the mode learning process that these generated. In a sense, for many the mode solution had already been established and was levered into place as management perceived that foreign market changes warranted change. The mode determination process is then about investigating the practicalities, the form of the preferred mode, which can still throw up discomforting issues and even force changes in the original mode concept: for example, because of difficulties in acquiring a distributor in the foreign market.

However, treatment of the various mode options in preceding chapters provides many examples of new inputs to mode decision making that may be unearthed in activities preceding a final decision. These include aspects beyond the obviously important negotiations about a mode form or package, for example, the content of a licensing agreement, an alliance arrangement or an acquisition deal. The nature, characteristics and impact of the foreign direct investment decision process in determining whether an investment goes ahead and its final form were identified early in Aharoni's (1966) seminal study. As noted in the Autronica case, personal interaction is a critical part of the process, involving cross-cultural exchanges and often language issues that are important to outcomes, affecting judgments about risk and uncertainty, and the preparedness to commit. As well, there will be a range of new information inputs in the pre-decision phase, whether deliberately sought or not, that could change thinking about the form of foreign market commitment.

The Autronica case also illustrates the potential impact of external forces, such as the host government (at different levels), that may constrain mode choice, and introduce external players into the negotiation process. Companies undertaking foreign direct investments typically have to work their way through a plethora of planning approvals, particularly for greenfield establishments that raise contentious environmental issues. Research indicates that governments in companies' home countries may also have an impact on mode decision making through various incentives and support schemes, which often contain mode bias. Export promotion schemes have been a traditional focus of such programmes. A UK study of internationalizing small high-technology firms found that assistance for exporting was perceived as being quite extensive, whereas that for other operation modes was relatively poor. For example, the manager in one company commented: '[government advisors] were OK for export inquiries but we were interested in licensing . . . they . . . haven't a clue about other things like licensing, joint ventures and setting up (a subsidiary) overseas' (Crick and Jones, 2000, 77). Despite the importance of the mode determination process, theoretical treatments of mode choice have struggled to include this aspect in meaningful ways, typically avoiding any reference to its influence. The neglect of political factors is perhaps due to their seeming non-economic basis, which is often considered to lie beyond the scope of models of business behaviour. Process-oriented frameworks have been extended to take into account the role of external networks (see, for example, Johanson and Vahlne, 1990), but the emphasis remains on the business side with little consideration given to political and regulatory issues. Economics and strategic approaches to mode choice view such decisions as essentially a question of finding the appropriate (or, as sometimes argued, the 'optimal') foreign operation method, typically in the sense of what degree of control is needed to conduct a set of activities abroad efficiently and on a sustainable basis. Political and regulatory issues may thus be seen as constraints that could lead to the adoption of second-best solutions, but including them in the analysis would be done in an ad hoc manner, that is, to the extent that they would be regarded as relevant in a given situation.

From a managerial perspective, there is a clear message about the need to be flexible in foreign operation mode choice situations: as a process there are likely to be diverse demands to react and adapt initially developed mode strategy for certain foreign markets. The final mode format may be markedly different from the preferred arrangement, and require some degree of mode learning before implementation. Some of the adjustments may be anticipated, if not in scope, but others will evolve in the course of negotiations in an unanticipated way. Some companies enter the mode determination process with very fixed ideas about the appropriate mode, and will view negotiations and other demands as issues to be dealt with in implementation of the chosen mode strategy. However, the many examples of ultimate mode choice throughout the book demonstrate that international operators are not masters of their mode destiny; for example, negotiations with a potential partner about alliance arrangements frequently expose relationship problems and lead to withdrawal from the intended alliance before consummation, and alternative partners may not be readily available or appropriate. Even large multinationals are required to adapt their mode strategies as they attempt to penetrate some markets. A notable example was the range of adjustments McDonald's made in its initial foray into the former Soviet Union, through a negotiation process extending over more than a decade (Vikhanski and Puffer, 1993). Inevitably, in the context of such mode determination process issues and sometimes unexpected developments, 'optimal' mode choice becomes a very blurred concept, and perhaps in reality companies are, and should be, seeking effectiveness rather than optimality, whatever that means, in mode selection.

A RANGE OF MODE OPTIONS

Preceding chapters have exposed a smorgasbord of mode options and strategies, individually and in combination, that are available for companies to use in international expansion. At one level the options are so numerous as to be almost overpowering. At another level, though, they offer considerable scope for companies to fine-tune the way they operate in foreign markets so as to become more effective internationalizers. The chapters on mode strategy provide many examples of the way in which companies are, for example, using mode combination and stretching strategies to enhance their international operations, in quite creative ways. Research on Danish companies in South-East Asia illustrates the extent of mode addition over time rather than simple mode replacement, which was important in enhancing penetration in the markets concerned (Petersen et al., 2001). Such approaches to mode strategy receive little coverage in the international business literature so it is difficult to know just how extensive this pattern is. At the least, one could speculate that it is far more extensive than existing research has revealed, simply because mode studies have not pursued the issue and researchers have not asked the questions that might have exposed mode diversity through time and in change processes. These are important questions, for theory and practice pertaining to foreign operation mode adoption and use.

The way in which, within mode and overall mode package, adjustments are made over time in foreign market penetration may provide powerful empirical confirmation of the extent of 'gradualism' in internationalization – far greater than has hitherto been shown in broad mode studies. While many in international business research have come to regard mode issues as a relatively settled domain, we argue that there is still considerable uncharted territory that needs to be explored. In part, this could be a problem of research methodology, given the dominance of large cross-sectional studies that lack mode nuance and a longitudinal perspective. In contrast, in-depth, qualitative research that focuses on longer-term process issues, and has the potential to better expose the more complex reality of mode choice and change, struggles for credibility and acceptance in international business research and publications (Marschan-Piekkari and Welch, 2004). One of the objectives of the book has been to highlight the wide array of options available in mode choice situations through the various stages of internationalization, in a diversity of foreign market penetration circumstances, so as to increase awareness of the mode strategy possibilities that companies can productively exploit. Not surprisingly, as companies develop expertise in using particular modes, this tends to bias judgment in decision making about which modes are the most appropriate to employ as operations are expanded in new foreign markets or as conditions warrant change in existing foreign markets.

FACTORS INFLUENCING FOM CHOICES

What determines the choice of a given mode or mode package? Figures 14.1 and 14.2, above, provide an outline of specific factors that appear to be important, such as international experience, as well as pointing to the process of interaction, feedback and new inputs preceding a final choice that impacts on the final choice (mode determination process), and within which the various influences are played out, many of which arise within the process (for example, cross-cultural personal interaction) and are to varying degrees unanticipated and unprepared for. Companies have to chart a path through the various influences and exposed options in reaching a final mode decision, at times when they are under considerable pressure to make a rapid response. In a Canadian study, almost a quarter of the companies making mode change decisions did so within 24 hours of the stimulus for change being exposed (Calof, 1993). Most companies took more than a month, but the study confirmed the reality that mode choice decisions are sometimes made in response to a very mode-specific external approach, such as when a foreign company is offered for sale. In other situations, a threat to an existing foreign operation may emerge that calls for a response that may entail advancing a mode change move. For example, a threatened takeover of an important foreign distributor could force an early attempt to integrate the distributor through a counter-takeover offer. In such cases, the form in which the stimulus arises – for example an opportunity or threat – creates a strong, sometimes overwhelming, mode choice bias.

The general pattern for internationalizing companies is that the range of modes and the sophistication in their use tends to increase over time, as learning develops and foreign market diversity and pressures create the need for broader and deeper mode strategies. In some cases, though, companies either do not recognize or consider even a reasonable range of mode options available in a given choice situation, driven by past experience or simply ignorance. A coping strategy for many companies, in the face of the complexity and range of mode options, is to follow simple decision rules that remove many of the options from serious consideration, as in the Nera case noted above, and for many of the Norwegian companies seeking to enter the Indian market (Tomassen et al., 1998). Such decisions are often treated in a sequential way as part of the simplification process, with perhaps the market, or the mode, or the 'partner' as the starting point. The problem with such an approach is that more appropriate mode solutions may not get into the consideration set, and therefore will not be adopted, unless strong external pressure for an alternative arises and forces a rethink. One of the lessons arising from the analysis of modes in this book is that even small, resource-stretched companies can use a diverse range of modes and combinations to better assist internationalization, but there needs to be an adequate understanding of modes to allow more nuanced mode paths to be laid. The exporting to FDI path is not necessarily the most appropriate for all internationalizing companies.

INTERNAL/EXTERNAL FACTORS

The mix of influences on mode choice can be divided into two broad groups, either internal or external to the firm, irrespective of the timing and strength of their impact. In Figure 14.1, the internal factors are further divided into company background and specific company mode concerns. A company's background as an influence on mode choice is reflected in aspects such as its resource base: financial, technological, knowledge, networks, skills and managerial; its size and the extent of global activities and commitments; the type and extent of experience relevant to international operations; the products, services and systems that a company offers in the marketplace; and its global strategy which includes the nature and extent of its international ambitions.

Company Background

The resources that a company can readily access are obviously important in driving the type of modes that it will be prepared to countenance using. Widespread research on SMEs shows that their resource limitations, in broad terms, particularly in the earlier stages of internationalization, bias them toward low-commitment, less resource-demanding modes, and away from forms like foreign direct investment. Financial resources consistently show up in studies as a significant influence, but human resources are sometimes critical at certain points in deciding mode type and its deployment. There are cases of companies being prepared to set up in unfamiliar markets because they have an employee from that country, with the relevant language, who can be used to head the operation. The size of a company and its existing international platform are important in opening up mode options, including the likelihood of approaches about new market prospects, and as a link to its resource base, in areas such as cross-cultural human resources and foreign market networks. The type and extent of international mode experience has been noted already as a factor in creating mode biases, because of the managerial focus and expertise, even core competence, generated, as it feeds into different parts of the company's resource base. The type of product, service and/or system that a company produces may influence mode choice, and this is seen most strongly for certain forms of services, such as education, health and law, that are difficult to offer from a distance, and force companies to look at modes that will deliver a direct, on-the-ground presence in the foreign market, resulting in an interest in alliances or FDI forms even in early internationalization. Companies that offer industrial systems with critical expertise, service and after-sales maintenance components often stress the need to set up or buy existing facilities as a critical part of foreign market penetration: customers look for far more than the product itself. On the other hand, companies offering digital products may be able to avoid setting up any facilities in foreign markets while extensively internationalizing. A company's objectives for its international operations, as part of its overall international strategy, impact on mode choice at a broad level. With limited international goals, companies are less likely to adopt high-commitment modes.

Specific Mode Concerns

While various aspects of a company's background may predispose it towards the use of particular modes, there are also certain specific, key concerns about modes and what they are seen to deliver that have an impact on the choice process. The concern about control has been stressed as a key factor in mode choice throughout the book, not just in the initial mode choice, but as a potent driving force in many mode change situations. In Chapter 9, the case of Heinz's establishment of a JV in Zimbabwe is noted. While the JV partner's contribution was seen as important in terms of local familiarity and the provision of production facilities, 51 per cent equity was seen as crucial to the investment because it meant control (O'Reilly, 1988). More recently, control concerns have been important in the shift from JVs to wholly owned subsidiaries in China: for example, 'foreign financial firms would love to get into China – without Chinese partners . . . The sticking point in all these ventures . . . is control. Asset managers hate joint ventures . . . Many . . . rule them out on principle' (*Economist*, 2003, 67). However, one of the points stressed in Chapter 12 is that equity is only one means of assuring control, and many companies have been able to assemble packages around a core JV, including licensing and management contracts, as a way of enhancing control.

Risk and uncertainty have also been featured as mode influences throughout the book. There are many sides to these concerns and the way they are perceived in relation to mode decisions. The risk and uncertainty attached to a foreign operation may be perceived in various aspects of the foreign market – economic, political, business and technological – and tend to be accentuated in situations where companies have limited experience of the foreign market in question. In the cases of Nera and Autronica noted above, lack of knowledge of, and experience in, the Indian market, combined with a lack of cultural affinity, created a strong sense of external (or environmental) risk that affected the approach to mode selection. Perception of high external risk and uncertainty associated with operations in a foreign market tends to constrain a company's preparedness to undertake a high commitment mode such as a wholly-owned FDI. From another perspective, companies are able to negate a given level of risk perception through the choice of mode. High risk perception in a foreign market can be countered through a low commitment mode, but, at the other extreme, low risk perception, other things being equal, supports a high commitment mode.

Risks associated with the company's relationship to its partners, especially those that are local, may have a different impact on choice of mode. The risk of loss of technology is a concern that many companies factor into the decision process. Reducing one's control over foreign operations does not attenuate such risks. Instead, when companies recognize that there may be some uncertainty regarding the trustworthiness of a foreign partner, precautions will often be taken, either by not sharing the newest and most valuable technology – as Nera did in its entry into India – or by organizing activities in such a way that they retain control over the way the technology is used, with wholly owned operations on occasion being the evident solution. There is, hence, sometimes a trade-off between the different types of risk companies may face: whereas high environmental risk may call for a low commitment mode, high partner risk calls for more control and thereby commitment to be taken.

Foreign partners, in whatever form (such as licensees, intermediaries and alliance participants), are an important consideration in mode decision making with issues connected to their availability, price in purchase situations, business viability and perceived compatibility. For example, in the longer term, relationship breakdowns are a common reason for companies to consider mode change. In addition, there are many cases of entrant firms having to delay or reconsider their initial mode choice because of the inability to find a suitable partner. Research indicates that many companies are not aware at the outset as to how important foreign partner issues can be in foreign market performance, and as problems unfold their reaction is against the mode form chosen rather than partner choice and relationship management. As a result, they want mode change, in some licensing examples vowing never to use licensing again in any markets.

Flexibility in mode arrangements appears to be a growing pattern, and concern, for example with the inclusion of exit clauses in JV deals, increasingly encouraged by external consultants. In part, this seems to reflect a growing recognition on the part of internationalizing companies that mode change may well be called for at some point, because of the inevitable change in market conditions and outcomes in diverse foreign markets. The anticipated revenue and profitability of the different mode forms in a company's consideration set, to the extent that reliable estimates can be developed, are obviously important in mode choice. Even in relatively clear-cut situations such as licensing, where the shape of revenue flows and costs is well known in advance through the terms of the contract, success still depends on the ability and commitment of the licensee to pursue market development. Notwithstanding such commitment, bringing a product or process to a new market is always an uncertain exercise, and it is difficult to judge the extent of market success in advance, particularly when different cultural and market environments are involved. Ultimately, any estimates of revenue and profit have to be judged alongside other factors. Higher estimated profitability for one mode may have to be put alongside higher risk, and the latter consideration may drive the choice of another mode that entails lower profit. Speed of foreign market entry may be a factor in some mode decisions, particularly when choosing between acquisitions or greenfield FDIs. Contractual modes inevitably involve partner selection and contract negotiation processes that can take considerable time, compared to exporting, which may be accomplished relatively rapidly in new foreign markets, perhaps without the use of foreign intermediaries.

External Factors

In the FDI chapter it was noted that interesting acquisition targets may not be amenable to takeover, or only at what are deemed to be unreasonably high prices, so that alternatives have to be considered if foreign market entry or expansion is a strong goal, including a switch to different forms of operation. Similarly, exporters may locate an agent in a foreign market who seems to be suitable to represent the firm, but the agent may not be prepared to take on the exporter. Some licensors approach the attempt to sell licensing arrangements in new foreign markets with a list of potential licensees in the expectation that they will not necessarily be able to sign up their preferred choices. In some foreign markets, though, the pool of interesting potential licensees, intermediaries or acquirees may be very limited. These examples illustrate the fact that, whatever the mode predisposition of a company, and its attempts to institute a given mode strategy, the situation in the foreign market may constrain or prevent execution, and this applies to far more than partner availability and price, potentially forcing the company to consider alternative mode arrangements.

Government policy and action, in various forms, as noted in the Nera case above, and through determinations in diverse areas such as import restrictions, FDI rules and media ownership laws, often cause companies to rethink their preferred way of operating in some foreign markets. For example, despite the many overall moves to liberalize the conditions of entry and operation for foreign firms in China, the Chinese government still exercises a high level of control, often in opaque forms, and not just at the central level of government. The Australian cotton producer, Colly Farms, found it difficult to compete against highly subsidized US cotton producers and eventually established a JV within the US. Through this means, it was able to obtain US subsidies and compete on a similar basis. The actions of competitors in a foreign market, both local firms and other foreign operators, and the extent to which they are entrenched in the market (including that via government support) and the way they operate may lead to changes in mode strategy by an entrant firm, perhaps seeking an alliance with a strong local company as a way of utilizing that company's local strength, rather than pursuing direct confrontation through a fully-owned FDI.

Foreign market conditions are always factored into mode calculations, including aspects such as the projected size of the local market – a small market often leads to the use of a low commitment mode; high inflation and political instability similarly weaken companies' preparedness to undertake large-scale commitments; and large cross-cultural differences, as in the experience of Norwegian companies entering the Indian market, had a broad impact of increasing perceived uncertainty, leading to the search for Indian partners, rather than going it alone, as a way around the lack of cultural confidence regarding Indian involvement. As joint operations unfold, though, lack of cultural compatibility may hamper relations between JV partners, to the extent that it can become a factor in foreign firms wanting to move to wholly owned operations without a partner, once they become sufficiently confident at operating in the market in question in their own right, as has emerged in the Chinese market for many foreign firms (O'Neill, 2004).

EVALUATING MODES: A MANAGERIAL PERSPECTIVE

Mode choice is a difficult domain for companies. The preceding analysis makes that abundantly clear. The more a company engages in systematic investigation as a prelude to mode choice, the greater the number of mode options that are likely to be exposed, with increased complexity of potential combinations, and the more that unresolvable, conflicting objectives in the choice process may be unearthed. On conflicting objectives, take the case of a high-technology SME that is concerned to minimize dissemination risk and the risk of training future competitors, and therefore is opposed to licensing as a way of operating internationally. However, because of limited resources, it wants to use a mode that involves minimal financial commitment, thereby favouring the use of licensing. To complicate evaluation and choice, whatever the company's perspective, the foreign market context imposes its own set of constraints on the choice process, and a decision may have to be made under considerable time pressure.

In the end, each individual company determines the importance or weighting of different objectives that form the basis of a mode evaluation process, rather than any pre-determined formula. A simple assessment of mode characteristics against these objectives or specific mode concerns provides a starting point to the evaluation activity, as shown in Figure 14.3. There are no weightings of the mode concerns, a necessary accompaniment to complete the exercise from a decision-making perspective. This evaluation is undertaken against individual modes, and the next stage is to consider in what ways these constructions could be altered, and enhanced, in terms of the fulfilment of objectives, through judicious mode packaging. The analysis of licensing, management contracts and franchising in the relevant chapters revealed evidence that a high proportion of use of these modes in international business activity is as part of broader mode packages. For example, licensing is frequently used as a supportive mode to mainstream FDI operations, and in JV situations sometimes as a means of restricting the possibility of technology leakage through the partner firm.

Specific company concerns					
Operation methods:	*Risks*	*Control*	*Revenue/ profits*	*Financial commitment*	*Speed of entry* →
Licensing *Franchising* *Management* *contract* ↓					

Source: Adapted from Luostarinen and Welch (1990, p. 246).

Figure 14.3   Mode evaluation

As a result, mode evaluation is not simply an exercise of setting each mode off against others, but of exploring the possibilities of developing a far stronger mode penetration regime through mode packages: Figure 14.3 should be seen as merely the first step in the process.

As pointed out in Chapter 12, a way around the deficiencies identified in a single mode may be provided through a mode package in which other modes cancel out the identified deficiencies of the mode in question. Inevitably, though, adding a stage of mode package exploration in the evaluation process complicates and extends the range of mode choices, and makes the ideal of an optimal mode set difficult, if not impossible, to identify. In this context, the creation of mode switching or exit options within the initial mode arrangements in the event of problems in implementation outcomes is particularly important. Empirical research shows that companies frequently experience a wide range of problems in mode use, resulting in mode switches (Benito et al., 2005; Calof, 1993). The concept of an optimal mode set is virtually meaningless given that so much of the success in mode use is determined by the way in which the foreign operation is handled: mode failure may not be in the initial choice, but in the management process, and it is difficult to disentangle these when assessing mode performance at a later date, after implementation.

Of course, mode choice by a company for a given foreign market, whether in entry or change situations, is undertaken in the context of the totality of operations in all markets, and is influenced by that overall context, in aspects such as mode learning, and the transferability of experiences and personnel, and the competing claims on limited resources. Company strategy may mean that certain markets are given greater prominence, and high commitment modes are employed, whereas other markets are deemed to be of lesser importance, even experimental, so that there is a bias towards low commitment modes. An exporter might use distributors in designated core markets, but operate through a trading company in non-core experimental or smaller markets. In this sense, the concept of a mode package applies not just within countries but also across countries.

REFERENCES

Aharoni, Y. (1966), *The Foreign Investment Decision Process*, Boston: Harvard University Press.

Benito, G.R.G., T. Pedersen and B. Petersen (2005), 'Export channel dynamics: an empirical analysis', *Managerial and Decision Economics*, **26**, 159–73.

Calof, J.L. (1993), 'The mode choice and change decision process and its impact on international performance', *International Business Review*, **2**(1), 97–120.

Crick, D. and M.V. Jones (2000), 'Small high-technology firms and international high-technology markets', *Journal of International Marketing*, **8**(2), 63–85.

Economist (2003), 'Banking in China – strings attached', 8 March, 67–8.

Johanson, J. and J.-E. Vahlne (1990), 'The mechanism of internationalization', *International Marketing Review*, **7**(4), 11–24.

Luostarinen, R.K. and L.S. Welch (1990), *International Business Operations*, Helsinki: Export Consulting KY.

Marschan-Piekkari, R. and C.L. Welch (eds) (2004), *Handbook of Qualitative Research in International Business*, Cheltenham, UK and Northampton, MA, USA: Edward Elgar.

O'Neill, M. (2004), 'Consumer markets: breaking through', *China International Business*, October, 21–9.

O'Reilly, A.J.F. (1988), 'Establishing successful joint ventures in developing nations: a CEO's perspective', *Columbia Journal of World Business*, **23**(1), 65–71.

Petersen, B., L.S. Welch and K.V. Nielsen (2001), 'Resource commitment to foreign markets: the establishment patterns of Danish firms in South-East Asian markets', in S. Gray, S.L. McGaughey and W.R. Purcell (eds), *Asia-Pacific Issues in International Business*, Cheltenham, UK and Northampton, MA, USA: Edward Elgar, pp. 7–27.

Tomassen, S. (1996), 'An empirical investigation of foreign operation methods into a developing country', Master of Science thesis, Norwegian School of Management BI, Sandvika.

Tomassen, S., L.S. Welch and G.R.G. Benito (1998), 'Norwegian companies in India: operation mode choice', *Asian Journal of Business and Information Systems*, **3**(1), 1–20.

Vikhanski, O. and S. Puffer (1993), 'Management education and employee training at Moscow McDonald's', *European Management Journal*, **11**(1), 102–7.

Index

acquisition 6, 13–14, 26–7, 73–9,
117, 136–7, 255, 259, 272–81, 298,
302, 307, 312, 314, 316, 321–4,
331–44, 350–51, 354–7, 367,
369–71, 385, 390–92, 426, 442,
449–50
adaptation 7, 59, 69, 77, 82, 84–5,
132–3, 175, 253, 267, 343, 363–4,
369
Africa 154, 199
African 177
agency theory 27, 368
agent 4–9, 27, 36, 82, 107, 150, 186,
206, 216, 222, 231, 240, 243–4,
250, 253–6, 259, 266–9, 295, 320,
350, 361–73, 376, 382–3, 386–8,
392–3, 398–402, 417, 420, 424–5,
450
Argentina 316
Asia 82–4, 91–3, 96, 136, 159–60, 188,
212, 218, 225–8, 235, 254, 262,
269, 294, 335, 342, 350, 354–7,
378–80, 383, 388, 423, 444
Asian 17, 68, 71, 82, 137, 146,
188, 191, 210, 215, 225–8, 242,
253, 258–9, 266, 271, 275, 313,
342, 354–7, 391, 414, 418–19,
453
Asia–Pacific 17, 59, 72, 197, 271, 320,
355–8, 391, 453
asset 23–7, 30–31, 42, 97, 107–8, 141,
200–202, 281, 289, 298, 307, 321,
325–8, 331, 334–6, 351–3, 363,
370–73, 381, 385, 400, 409–10,
448
non-marketable assets 27
asset specificity 24, 410
Australia 37, 54–5, 58, 62, 68–9, 73–7,
82–7, 91, 103–9, 116–17, 121, 136,
141, 152, 161, 169, 212, 254,
270–72, 281, 321, 329, 332, 347,
351, 417–22, 426, 429

Australian 11, 17, 40, 54, 57–65,
69–88, 91–3, 101–7, 112–36,
141–3, 149–52, 161, 182,
209–13, 216, 221–2, 229–32,
239–40, 244–5, 250–57, 264–7,
269–71, 281, 284–6, 289, 292,
308, 311–13, 332, 335–6, 342–7,
350–55, 358, 379–81, 392, 401,
450
Austria 382, 426

Bangladesh 96
barrier 33, 41, 115, 119, 127, 156, 183,
192, 237, 291, 294, 310, 326–7,
369–73, 376, 389, 393, 409–10,
428, 440–41
see also switching barrier
Belgium 351
Belgian 73
Born Global 36–9, 43–6, 349, 354
Brazil 32, 83, 169, 223, 353
Brazilian 83
Britain 269
British 45, 54, 130, 265, 271–2, 298,
323, 333, 342, 381, 411

Cambodia 70
Canada 45, 55, 68–9, 82, 86, 104–6,
175–6, 188, 191, 194, 244, 280, 347
Canadian 93, 110, 242–4, 260–62,
267–9, 280, 312, 323, 445
capability 23, 28, 44, 191, 206, 334
China
Chinese 71, 88, 99–100, 137, 151,
172, 189–90, 199, 213–14, 222,
226–7, 236, 245, 252, 271, 281,
284, 293, 316–17, 329, 336–7,
346, 255–7, 401–2, 407, 411,
448–51
Colombia 251, 270
commercial 86, 94, 97, 104–8, 118, 123,
154, 171, 225, 256, 266, 322

462 *Index*